Books by Roderick Cameron

THE GOLDEN HAZE

VICEROYALTIES OF THE WEST

Viceroyalties of the West

THE SPANISH EMPIRE IN LATIN AMERICA

Roderick Cameron

VICEROYALTIES OF THE WEST

The Spanish Empire in Latin America

WITH ILLUSTRATIONS

LITTLE, BROWN AND COMPANY
Boston   Toronto

PRINTED IN THE UNITED STATES OF AMERICA

To
Mona Baring, Henry McIlhenney and William Whitticker who
shared in different parts of my travels, and Margarite McBay who
assisted with a protracted loan of a hasselblad

Contents

List of Illustrations

List of Illustrations

List of Illustrations

List of Illustrations

following page 174

following page 198

List of Illustrations

following page 206

following page 230

List of Illustrations

Maps

*Maps drawn by **Surrey Art Designs***

Acknowledgments

The author and publishers are grateful to all of the copyright owners mentioned above for permission to reproduce their pictures.

Illustrations Nos. 10, 19, 51 and 65 were photographed by Robert Schalkwijk; Nos. 22, 58 and 91 by John R. Freeman & Co.; Nos. 108, 128, 129 and 131 by Hernan Díaz; Nos. 122 and 124 by Jorge Neumann; and No. 47 by Hugo P. Rudinger. All other photographs were taken by the author.

The author would like to express his gratitude to Señora Josefa F de H de Martínez del Río and Signor Manuel Romero de Terreros for allowing him to reproduce the portraits from their private collections.

Viceroyalties of the West

THE SPANISH EMPIRE IN LATIN AMERICA

1

The Shape of an Hour-Glass

I have been travelling now for some twenty years, and have covered a considerable portion of the globe – most of Europe and the Middle East, much of Africa, large tracts of Asia and the Antipodes, and, more recently, the South-Pacific islands. My own country, though I was not brought up in the United States, I know quite well; but, until I began to write this book, I had never set foot in Latin America. I decided therefore that my next venture should deal with the vast empire that Spain staked out for herself across the New World; and that I would attempt to interpret Mexico, Central America and its great southern appendage in much the same way as I had already described the so-called 'South Seas'. Much of my material would be drawn from the past – the past seen through the eyes of the present day. I intended not to produce a history, but to record my personal impressions of the countries I had visited, and to supplement my narrative, wherever I could, with stories told by previous travellers. My aim was to build up a composite picture – a mosaic of today and yesterday.

The area involved runs roughly from 40° south latitude to 38° north latitude, a territory more than six thousand miles in length with a far greater expanse than present day Russia, that reaches into both temperate zones and includes torrid, hurricane-swept coasts, vast tablelands, snow-fields, trackless forests, swamps and even sandy deserts.

This ambitious programme needed careful preparation, and months were spent in preliminary research. What an impressive amount of material our predecessors have left us to draw on! The conquistadors and their historians describe the early years, while subsequent travellers fill in the more modern details. Although foreigners were forbidden entry to the Spanish possessions, a great many of our informants came from countries overseas – Henry Hawks, for example, and John Chilton, and, following them, Thomas Gage, another Englishman. Gage produced one of the liveliest accounts of life in the Spanish colonies during the seventeenth century. Although Catholic-born, he took a stern line with the abuses of the Roman Church, dubbed the priests 'imps in lace and silk', and accused the friars of 'looseness of living'. The erudite young Baron von Humboldt, the product of a more enlightened age, struck quite another note. His inquisitive mind delved into statistics, and he tabulated for our benefit the production of the silver mines. We learn from Humboldt about the frequency of earthquakes, and about the dire effects of the dreaded black vomit. Further afield, in Peru, the son of a missionary from Honolulu discovered the lost city of Machu Picchu. Among comparatively modern historians, William Prescott, in his *Conquest of Peru*, evoked the splendours of the Inca, a majestic figure encased in gold, with a cloak of bat's wings.

In my own travels I had some strange experiences – as when I was driving from La Paz, in Bolivia, to the pilgrim church of Copacabana, which is situated on a promontory on the southern shores of Lake Titicaca. Here the mountains fall sheer to the lake, and the road winds around their rugged contours. Suddenly, we confronted a wild-looking personage who straddled the road armed with an enormous rock held above his head at arm's length. Our driver slowed down, somehow giving us the idea that this menacing apparition was not wholly unexpected. The wild man advanced, demanding money, at which the driver merely got out and, going to the back of the car, reappeared with a length of rubber hosing with which he proceeded to make a counter-demonstration. The effect was immediate: our assailant dropped his rock and burst into a flood of tears. Our driver subsequently explained that he was a well-known character in the district, and was regarded by his fellow Indians as an elemental, but that superstition prevented them from having him committed to a madhouse.

There is so much that is both beautiful and dramatic in the lesser-known regions of South America. My drive from Lima to Cuzco, for instance, took me over the empty grasslands of high Peru where, day after day, the only living creatures I saw beside the road were herds of woolly-coated llamas, their haughty profiles silhouetted on the skyline against lowering banks of rain-cloud, and the Indian shepherdesses who usually accompanied them, muffled in heavy layers of skirt and coiffed with a primitive form of bowler hat. I remember, too, Mexico's sixteenth-century monasteries, Renaissance churches, approached by avenues of organ-pipe cacti, and some grandiose private houses. In a surprisingly brief period, the Spanish colonists raised a prodigious number of splendid buildings. Handsome twin-towered cathedrals dominate the plazas of almost every fair-sized town.

Just as remarkable are lesser works of art – religious paintings inlaid with plaques of mother-of-pearl, and feather-pictures made by nuns, their bird-bright colours applied like enamel in cloisonné, a technique

VICEROYALTY OF
NEW SPAIN

ATLANTIC OCEAN

Mississippi

Tropic of Cancer

20°N

CAPTAINCY GENERAL
OF CUBA

Cuba

Hispaniola

Jamaica

Porto
Rico

Caribbean Sea

NEW GRANADA

CAPTAINCY
GENERAL OF
GUATEMALA

VICEROYALTY OF NEW GRANADA

CAPTAINCY
GENERAL OF
VENEZUELA

GUIANA

Equator

VICEROYALTY

BRAZIL
(Portuguese)

20°S

Tropic of Capricorn

PACIFIC

OCEAN

OF

PERU

CAPTAINCY GENERAL OF CHILE

VICEROYALTY OF LA PLATA

ATLANTIC

OCEAN

Spanish possessions

0   1000
MILES

The Spanish Empire

that the Spaniards inherited directly from the Aztec. Equally fascinating is the work of the mestizo and Indian artists. The two famous sculptors who flourished at Quito were both of Indian descent. Cuzco, another city built on the foundations of a pre-Columbian capital, produced a highly individualist school of painters.

In time, as in space, I have had to set myself some definite limits. The Viceregal Age, a period of some three hundred years, beginning with the first quarter of the sixteenth century, is the era on which I decided to concentrate. I have by-passed the Revolutionary Wars, which form a completely separate theme, but I have included allusions to the Archduke Maximilian and his wife Charlotte – or Carlota, as she was later to sign herself, in a pathetic attempt to appease her Creole subjects. I have also consulted the correspondence of Madame Calderón de la Barca, the wife of Spain's first envoy to Mexico after the Revolution, whose letters, written early in the century, throw an extraordinarily vivid light on the Central-American scene. My book is to be shaped like an hour-glass. Mexico and Peru were the principal centres of Spanish government during the Colonial Period; and thus they will be treated here. Brazil, as a one-time Portuguese possession, I have thought it better to leave undescribed.

The New World was discovered by mistake, for it was to Asia, not to the west, that the first navigators imagined they were sailing. Ferdinand and Isabella had sent Columbus across western waters to map out a short sea route to Asia – source of the rich spice trade, which, until that time, had been largely monopolized by Moslem merchants. Columbus set out from Palos on 3 August 1492, heading due west. With him he carried a copy of Marco Polo's remarkable *Voyages* and two men who spoke Arabic. As an additional precaution, he took letters of introduction addressed 'to the Exalted Potentates of the Orient'. Blank spaces headed each document, to be filled in by the Admiral when he learned their names.

There were many anxious moments on the voyage, as when the three vessels ran into the Sargasso Sea, immense plains of pelagic weed which occupied a space in the Atlantic almost equal to seven times the extent of France. The sight of this brown algae terrified the sailors, who thought that they might be coming upon submerged rocks. They had been over three months at sea before they made a landfall – at the small island known as Guanahani, or Island of Iguanas, which Columbus named San Salvador.[1]

Columbus was to return three times to the Caribbean, and on each occasion his objective was the discovery of the legendary westward passage to the Indies and Cathay. On the first voyage, having explored

[1] Now known as Watling Island, in the Bahamas group.

the coast of Cuba, he landed on Haiti, known then as Hispaniola, or Little Spain; next year he returned to establish a colony, the first of a number of settlements that afterwards grew up on the islands. During his third voyage, he explored Guiana and Venezuela, and in 1502, on his last expedition, he landed in Central America, on the northern shores of Honduras.

The exploration of America, known always to the Spaniards as *las Indias*, the Indies, was now pushed ahead with great speed. Diego Velázquez conquered Venezuela in 1499, and Cuba in 1511. The famous conquest of Mexico by Hernán Cortés took place between 1517 and 1524. Settlements were also founded in Paraguay and Colombia, while Balboa's discovery of the Pacific in 1513 led to the eventual conquest of Andean South America, and the use of the Isthmus of Panama as a route for the transportation of goods from Peru and Argentina. The Philippines, discovered in 1521, were formally occupied in 1565 during the reign of Philip II, after whom they were named. But, skirting the islands, let us make straight for Mexico, the most important of the viceroyalties and, as it were, the upper globe of our hour-glass.

2

La Ciudad de los Muertos

The east coast of Mexico is singularly monotonous, curving gently southward in a succession of swampy lagoons, sand bars and submerged reefs. There are no natural harbours and thus Vera Cruz, sheltered behind its island fortress of San Juan de Ulúa, was until recent times the chief point of entry to New Spain. The port had a monopoly on the Atlantic trade with Mexico and here all immigration into the colony was controlled.

Along with these privileges, however, it enjoyed the reputation of being the most unhealthy spot in the world. *La Ciudad de los muertos*, the Spaniards called it, and this was no exaggeration. For five months of the year, from May to October, Vera Cruz was prey to yellow fever, the dreadful *vómito*, or black vomit. A good fifth of the inhabitants perished from it annually. Some years the toll was even higher. In June 1820, for instance, people were dying at the rate of one hundred a week. 'The stranger,' Bullock wrote, 'shudders every hour he remains within its walls,'[1] and those who could afford it had litters waiting for them as they landed at the mole, ready to carry them inland to higher country out of harm's way. The roads were too rough for carriages so litters, slung on poles between two mules, were the usual mode of travel. As can be imagined, riding in these *litera* was something of an ordeal, especially during the rains, but anything was preferable to staying in the city.

After one particularly severe epidemic it was suggested that the city should be razed and another port built elsewhere – obviously not a very practical solution. More reasonable was the projected shutting of the port during the summer months, thus limiting the entry of vessels to winter, when Europeans ran no risk of contracting the yellow fever. But this, too, had its drawbacks, for the winter months were the season of the winds, the fierce *norte* which blew from October to April. Reading the different reports one realizes that these winds were, indeed, as

[1] W. Bullock, *Six Months Residence and Travels in Mexico*, Murray, London, 1824.

6

1 Vera Cruz. 'Some of the houses have preserved their old watch towers' (page 18)

2 *View of Vera Cruz by Daniel Egerton. The fort of San Juan de Ulúa can be seen on the left and in the foreground one of the litters in which new arrivals escaped to higher country* (*page 6*)

3 Vera Cruz. The convent of San Francisco now a public library (page 18)

dangerous, in their way, as the fever. Friar Thomas Gage, writing in the seventeenth century, testified to their violence when he described them as blowing with such force one night 'that we thought it would blow us out of our beds'. The slight boarded houses tottered and shook and 'we expected hourly that they should fall upon our heads'.[1] A *norte* likewise attended Gage's landing and he recalled the confusion it caused on board. 'Hallowed wax candles were lighted by the friars, knees bowed to Mary, litanies and other hymns and prayers sung aloud unto her till towards the dawning of the day, when behold the north wind ceased to blow . . . "*Milagro, Milagro, Milagro*, a miracle, a miracle, a miracle," they cried.' Although Gage scorned his companions' 'superstitious howling', he was nevertheless relieved when boats came out to pilot them 'between those rocks which make the port as dangerous as any I have discovered'. Prior to the building of a sea wall the only safe anchorage at Vera Cruz was the roadstead to the leeward of the fort. Ships would attach themselves to massive brass rings sunk into the fort's walls and thus ride out the storm. Those of the ships not fortunate enough to find a mooring were obliged to put to sea.

The approach of a norther is generally preceded by a lurid, saffron-tinted sunset along with the clustering of sea birds, shoulders hunched, the length of the shore. Sir Henry Ward commented on the violence of the *norte*, 'nothing can be more melancholy than the appearance of Vera Cruz during the winds. The air is filled with sand and the sky darkened with clouds, while the waves are driven with such impetuosity upon the beach that the whole line of coast is one sheet of foam.'[2] Madame Calderón, Scottish wife of a Spanish diplomat in the nineteenth century, dashed the waves even farther, in her description, making them tumble over the quay into the town itself, 'covering the customs house with spray and the houses in the back streets with incrustations of salt'.[3] Ships were frequently driven ashore.

There was little to choose from, then, between the dangers of navigation and mortal disease. Quite obviously Vera Cruz was a place to be avoided, and all the merchants rich enough to afford it had country houses some fifty miles inland at Jalapa, up in the mountains away from the suffocating heat, the winds and the mosquitoes. Only the most pressing business brought them down to their offices in the *tierra caliente*, and that only during the season of the *norte*.

There exists a quantity of material on the subject of the black vomit and most of it makes fascinating, if somewhat lurid reading. Totally

---

[1] *Thomas Gage. The English American. A New Survey of the West Indies 1648*, edited with an introduction by A. P. Newton, George Routledge, London, 1928.
[2] H. G. Ward, *Mexico in 1827*, Henry Colburn, London, 1828.
[3] Madame Calderón de la Barca, *Life in Mexico*, Chapman and Hall, London, 1843.

unaware that the disease was transmitted by mosquitoes (a discovery made towards the end of the nineteenth century), the Spaniards were at a complete loss to know how the fatal ague was contracted. Various fanciful theories were put forward. In Vera Cruz contamination was attributed to the miasmic exhalations rising from the mud and the stagnant puddles which pockmarked its streets. John Chilton, an English merchant resident in Cadiz and travelling to Vera Cruz in 1568, told how its citizens were in the habit of driving some two thousand head of cattle through the town every morning 'to take away the ill vapours'.[1]

Following this came more permanent sanitary measures in the form of paving stones. This, of course, had the effect of exterminating the mosquito larvae in the immediate vicinity of the city, and, indeed, the *vómito* disappeared altogether for several years. It was, however, a temporary respite. The vicious, blood sucking *Aedes aegypti*, the yellow fever mosquito, retreated to some adjacent marshes where they multiplied without interruption. Dusk and dawn were the dangerous hours for these creatures when they would appear regularly over the city in veil-like clouds of infernal buzzing. Within a matter of weeks the town was in the grip of a new epidemic; forty to fifty deaths a day were reported.

To aggravate what must already have been an alarming situation, the citizens of Vera Cruz believed the fever to be contagious, and always ignorant of its cause, they experimented with different theories, hoping to find a deterrent for the disease. It was noticed that the mortality rate was especially high among the muleteers and the soldiers recruited in Mexico City to garrison Vera Cruz. 'Every imaginable care,' wrote Baron von Humboldt, 'has been bestowed on these unfortunate young men.'[2] They were first posted to Jalapa with the idea that the gradual descent would acclimatize them better to the tropics. For the final stage of the journey they were mounted on horses and ridden through the night 'that they might not be exposed to the sun in crossing the arid coastal plains'. Arriving at the fort they were lodged in lofty, well-aired apartments, and, of course, they succumbed to the fever as rapidly and as violently as the soldiers for whom no precautions had been taken.

The new arrivals by sea were quite understandably terrified when they heard of the high mortality rate. They landed sniffing pomanders and clutching kerchiefs impregnated with aloes; all, of course, totally ineffectual. Panic seized them when even those who got straight into their litters from the ship were struck down before reaching Mexico City. Frequently the passengers were stung by the mosquitoes while still on board, and as the incubation period after a bite from the *Aedes*

[1] *Halkuyt's Voyages*, London, 1927.
[2] Alexander von Humboldt, *Political Essay on the Kingdom of New Spain*, London, 1814.

is from three to five days, it was a common occurrence for a traveller to fall sick *en route*.

A pain in the lumbar region, headaches, fever and congestion of the face are the first symptoms. Jaundice, haemorrhages and the vomiting of black blood follow in the later stages. The black matter, Humboldt wrote, resembles coffee grounds 'and I have sometimes seen that it left indelible stains on linen, or on the wall'.

The drive to Jalapa was at the most a question of two days and could, if necessary, be accomplished in half that time so that the traveller, if affected, seldom betrayed definite symptoms so early on in the journey. Be that as it may, the Jalapans pretended to an extra-sensory perception as far as the fever was concerned and prided themselves on being able to detect the malady merely by the expression on a traveller's face. One young man arrived at Jalapa feeling perfectly fit but on going to an Indian barber for a shave was told that he would be struck down that same evening. 'The soap dries as soon as I put it on your face. A never failing sign', commented the barber ominously. Indeed, the barber appears to have been peculiarly insensitive, for he further informed the victim that during the twenty years he had practised his trade, three gentlemen out of every five he had shaved had died before reaching Mexico City. One wonders what effect this 'sentence of death' had on the young man. He was, in fact, struck down within a few hours, on his way to Perote, and was obliged to return to Jalapa. History does not relate the end of the story.

It is more than probable the young man died, for the *vómito* is a virulent disease acting on the liver, kidneys and heart. Recovery really depended on the patient's stamina and on careful nursing. Medicine as practised in those days was not always of a nature to help the victim; most Europeans arriving in the Spanish colonies were automatically bled 'while in the enjoyment of perfect health'. But apart from this blood letting, which was prescribed for any disease until the end of the eighteenth century, the doctors in Mexico seem on the whole to have handled their patients rather sensibly. One reads that 'a good habit of body is important before reaching the coast' and that 'too great an exposure to the sun should also be avoided'. The cures in fact were very similar to those in practice today: baths along with abstinence from food and a great deal of liquid. The Spaniards considered sherbets an important palliative, and a special *posta de nieve*, or snow post, was established. Snow from the extinct volcano of Orizaba, its crystal peak borne on high, invisible in the clouds, some hundred miles away, was packed in dried herbs and ashes and loaded on relays of mules that were led at a smart trot. Speed was obviously imperative because of the heat.

Reading such reports, we find it difficult to understand how Vera Cruz survived its reputation. Indeed, the early settlement had been moved, but by 1599 it had been returned to the original site chosen by Cortés. Here, surrounded by arid plains and shifting sands piled high by the winds, grew New Spain's first settlement, *La Villa Rica de la Vera Cruz* – The Rich City of the True Cross – gateway to the Mexican capital through which, as Frederick Ober put it, 'poured those tides of wealth that have filled the coffers of Spain'.[1]

There exists a variety of references to Vera Cruz since it was founded, and by choosing amongst them we can form a fairly comprehensive picture of the city throughout its history. Bernal Díaz del Castillo, one of the soldiers with Cortés, described the settlement when it consisted simply of mud and wattle huts. It would appear that Cortés himself actually lent a hand in their building, but this was, no doubt, nothing more than a ritual hauling of the first basket of stones and sand. It was at this time also, in some swamps to the south of the encampment, that the Spaniards saw their first alligator, 'a creature like unto a serpent, and having no wings'. It is interesting to note that not one of the conquistadors mentions the *vómito*. Colonel Ashburn, who made a special study of the disease, suggests that yellow fever was absent altogether during the first years of the Spanish settlement.[2] According to him it was indigenous to the west coast of Africa and, like malaria, was brought over in the first slave ships.

All writers are in agreement about the tropical nature of the city. At every period one reads of its stagnant lagoons and oppressive climate. The reverberation of the sun striking the dunes added to the suffocating heat of the air. At one time a wall surrounded the town, completely closing it in, thus contributing to the general discomfiture by cutting off any circulation of air. There are, however, occasional pleasant glimpses of tropical vegetation and of dark, star-hung nights brilliant with the dancing of fire-flies.

Both Humboldt and Bullock writing at the beginning of the nineteenth century described the city as being built entirely of coral, 'the stoney habitation', as Humboldt put it, 'of madrepores drawn from the bottom of the ocean'. Bullock added that the coral became very hard and eventually polished like marble from constant friction. This pleasant finish the twentieth century has seen fit to cover over with coatings of whitewash. Bullock's piazzas, arched over the pavements, are still there, 'a great accommodation to passengers, protecting them

---

[1] Frederick Ober, *Travels in Mexico*, Warne & Company, London, 1887.
[2] Colonel P. M. Ashburn, *The Ranks of Death. A Medical History of the Conquest of America*, Coward McCann, New York, 1947.

from the sultry heat of the sun and the heavy rains which descend in torrents in the wet season'.[1]

The streets are set at right angles in a gridiron plan, a common method of town-planning in Mexico and indeed throughout the vice-royalties, and one that was inspired certainly by the pre-Columbian cities where rectangular blocks were intersected at right angles with streets or canals. Countess Kollonitz landing with Empress Carlota was struck by the city's layout, though, to her, haunted no doubt by thoughts of the *vómito*, 'the roofless white houses in straight rows in the broad uniform streets give the impression of a cemetery'. She complained also that 'the nearer they approach the town the more noxious become the odours'.[2] One reads of cobbled streets with open sewers running down the centre and full of 'bluish, bubbling sludge'. But Ober assured us it was such a clean city that 'if any refuse escapes the eye of the sanitary authorities those other members of the Board of Health, the vultures, are sure to snatch it up and bear it away, or devour it on the spot'. These valued birds are still seen by the hundreds, perched on every rooftop, and waddling through all the streets. The Mexicans call them *zopilotes* and the Aztec considered them sacred, but not so Mr Terry who dubbed them 'an unfragrant lot, rich in vermin'.[3] He assured us that their flight was accompanied by 'malodorous waves', but he exaggerated for I have never noticed anything and I have often watched them wheeling overhead, their gun-metal wings spread taut against the heat-paled sky. They are, in any case, now protected by the government, a fine of five *pesos* being imposed on anyone who maltreats them.

About the interiors in Vera Cruz little is known: only two histories deal with what might be called their 'furnishings'. Madame Calderón made a brief reference to her bed wreathed in mosquito netting and made up with lace-trimmed pillows and sheets – little did she appreciate her good fortune in having such netting. She gives us no further details. Were the walls whitewashed and the room pleasantly empty? It is more probable that the houses, like the people, were vastly overdressed. This certainly is the impression given by Gage who made the crossing with a newly appointed viceroy. 'As soon as we came to shore we found very solemn preparations for entertainment, all the town being resorted to the seaside.' He described the different religious orders 'all with their crosses before them, to guide the new Viceroy, in procession, to the cathedral'. Detaching himself, Gage repaired immediately to a Dominican cloister where the Prior received him 'very lovingly' with sweetmeats and chocolate. 'The Prior,' he explained, 'was no staid,

[1] *Six Months Residence and Travels in Mexico.*
[2] Countess Kollonitz, *The Court of Mexico*, Vienna, 1868.
[3] *Terry's Guide to Mexico*, Houghton Mifflin, New York.

ancient, grey-haired man, such as usually are made Superiors to govern young and wanton friars, but a gallant and amorous young spark, who (as we were there informed) had obtained from his Superior, the Provincial, the government of that convent with a bribe of a thousand ducats. After dinner,' Gage continued, 'he had some of us to his chamber.' They had expected a stately library, 'which might tell us of learning and love of study; but we found not above a dozen old books, standing in a corner covered with dust and cobwebs'. No library greeted them but a room 'richly dressed and carpeted, and hung with many pictures'. Silk covered the tables and the cupboards were crammed with rare porcelains. The young Prior's conversation 'was nothing but vain boasting of himself, of his birth and his parts, and his favour with the Provincial'. He further shocked his audience by giving details of the rich merchants' wives who were in love with him. Later he entertained his guests with some songs, accompanying himself on a lute. They were his own lyrics, 'verses to some lovely Amaryllis which he delivered in a clear and excellent voice'. During the performance acolytes handed round sweetmeats that 'smelt of musk and civet wherewith' their epicurean host 'had seasoned his conserves'.

'Thus,' wrote Gage, 'were we transported from Europe to America.' He dwelt on the marked contrast with the tedium the company had endured at sea when 'even the noise of mariners hoisting sails' had got on their nerves. This was indeed a very different world and hardly one they could have expected.

So much then for the town itself, but the real importance of Vera Cruz lay in its port, and consequently its life-blood pulsed, not so much in the streets, but in the wooden hulls that cast anchor off the shores, in the great silver fleets that sailed annually to Europe loaded down with prodigious hoards of bullion and exotic merchandise.

Trade with the New World had started out in a casual manner with single ships sailing at the convenience of their captains. The precious nature of the cargoes they carried, however, made it unlikely that such simple arrangements could endure. The very first shipment from Vera Cruz was in itself enough to assure future trouble. It consisted of the presents sent to Cortés by Montezuma and shipped by Cortés to his Emperor, then with his court at Brussels. The whole of Europe was agog at the display. Albrecht Dürer on a visit was allowed to view the treasure. 'All the days of my life,' he wrote, 'I have seen nothing that rejoices my heart so much as these objects, for among them are wonderful works of art.'[1] Benvenuto Cellini also mentioned them. Cortés in his first letter to Charles v dwelt on the extraordinary quality of their workmanship. 'These objects,' he wrote, 'were of the greatest beauty,

---

[1] *Literary Remains of Albrecht Dürer*, translated by Martin Conway, London, 1889.

and I doubt if any other prince of earth ever possessed anything similar to them.' He added that 'all which the earth and ocean produces, of which King Montezuma could have any knowledge, he had caused to be imitated in gold and silver, in precious stones, and feathers, and the whole in such great perfection that one could not help believing he saw the very objects represented'.

Aztec codices list the more usual treasures: bracelets of gems and golden bells, a gold sceptre studded with pearls, and a costume with a topaz mask supposed to have been worn by Quetzalcoatl. The most astonishing single object appears to have been 'the sun all of gold', nearly seven feet wide. Another great wheel in silver represented the moon. Dürer also mentioned two rooms full of armour: shields made of gold and mother-of-pearl, and jaguar-skin surcoats adorned with gems. There were gold mitres, jade disks, bracelets and anklets of gold, also an emerald necklace with a hundred and eighty-three emeralds. Díaz mentioned 'thirty gold ducks of splendid workmanship exactly resembling the living bird'.

Alas, little of all this survived. The stones were probably reset and the gold reduced to bullion; as for the rest of the objects, few regarded them as works of art. Specialists have been able to discover only about a score of these that have survived, mostly in museums. The Museo Preistorico in Rome has a shell and turquoise encrusted mask, and in the British Museum there is an extraordinary human skull with staring pyrite eyes rimmed round with bone. A band of turquoise mosaic runs a macabre mask across the eye sockets while another strip of blue frames the jaw, setting off the bared white teeth. The Völkerkunde Museum in Vienna has Montezuma's quetzal plumed head-dress. This circled the Emperor's head with disks and half-moons of gold, sweeping upwards to a central panel of iridescent feathers.

In 1522 Cortés sent a further shipment of treasures to Spain, but this time the two vessels bearing the objects were intercepted and captured by Verrazano, a Florentine pirate in the pay of the French. It was a spectacular haul, for it comprised the loot taken in the sack of Mexico. Amongst the jewels were pearls the size of hazel nuts. The pearls alone, Oviedo, the Spanish historian, tells us, weighed six hundred and eight pounds. There was also Montezuma's great pyramidal emerald, as large as the palm of the hand. This eventually became part of the French crown jewels but disappeared during the Revolution.[1]

Verrazano's exploit had immediate repercussions. François I, a rival of Charles V, far from decrying the deed, encouraged further escapades, and a variety of adventurers immediately gathered on the seas. Spain's shipping was mercilessly plundered, and by 1529 her losses had become

[1] S. K. Lothrop, *Treasures of Ancient America*, Albert Schira for Nelson, New York, 1964.

so serious that counter-measures had to be taken. Until this time trade with the New World had been allowed to pass through several Spanish ports; it was now confined to Seville. The overseas route was carefully prescribed and ships were obliged to sail in company. Later this rule was more rigorously enforced, when a regular convoy was ordered to the Canaries on the outward voyage and from the Azores on the return. The system was further developed when, by the end of the sixteenth century, two regular fleets had been organized: one destined for Vera Cruz and New Spain and the other for Cartagena and Puerto Belo, the ports of the Southern Continent, or *Tierra Firme*, as it was then called. These armed fleets sailed once a year and consisted, on an average, of fifteen to thirty ships. The fleet destined for Vera Cruz was known as *La Flota* and was accompanied by two warships; the other destined for *Tierra Firme* was called the Armada. Their course was always the same: first to the Canary Islands, then south-west across the Tropic of Cancer to one of the islands of the Lesser or Outer Antilles. The duration of the voyage depended on the weather and varied from five to seven weeks. A good passage in the sixteenth century lasted forty-one days.

The return voyage took a more northern course to Cuba and through the dangerous Bahama Channel and so north-eastward until a prevailing northerly wind was picked up. From there the ships sailed eastward to the Azores.

The fleets were rigidly disciplined and under the surveillance of a ship called the *Capitana*. The *Capitana* was the first to leave and enter the ports and always sailed at the head of the convoy. Roll call was kept by each ship's firing salvoes, twice a day, once in the morning and again in the evening. Fluttering bravely from the foremast of the admiral's galleon was the fleet's flag: three horizontal bands of red, white and yellow, the white central band bearing the double-headed eagle of the House of Austria surrounded by the Order of the Golden Fleece.

Gales frequently scattered these convoys, and the galleons then ran the risk of being mercilessly dashed to pieces on some rocky headland, or worse, becoming prey to the ever lurking privateer. Spanish ladies apparently never embarked on Caribbean travel without a poison capsule, but when the dreaded moment came, few of them had the courage to swallow it. Some regretted their cowardice, but there were those who grew reconciled and lived for years aboard pirate ships, wearing the silks of the Orient and the jewels of Inca queens.

In contrast to the gales were the dead calms that held the ships for days on end as if they were fastened by hooks to the sea. But even with the fairest of winds the journey in these great lumbering galleons must have seemed agonizingly slow. There were, however, diversions to break the monotony. Gage described the celebrations held on board the

Santa Gertrudis, one of the ships in his convoy, on which a party of Jesuits was travelling. It was the last day of July and the brothers were commemorating the founding of their order by St Ignatius. Masts and tacking were hung with paper lanterns while the thirty Jesuits paraded round the decks 'singing their superstitious hymns and anthems to their supposed saint, and all this seconded with roaring ordnance and the firing of squibs'. There later followed another saint's day, marked this time with a stately dinner of 'both fish and flesh'. Afterwards came a comedy by the famous Lope de Vega acted by soldiers, friars and passengers 'which I confess was as well acted and set forth in that narrow compass of our ship, as might have been upon the best stage in the Court of Madrid'. Other pastimes included cockfights, shark fishing and illuminations, these consisting again in the firing of squibs and the shooting of ordnance.

The excitement of arriving at Vera Cruz must have been somewhat diluted by the dangers of the approach; there were, however, well known landmarks to guide the pilot through the shallows to his anchorage. Once berthed, a tedious amount of paper work followed. The New World was not easy of access, especially if one wished to emigrate there. The fame of its wealth and the return of the first galleons laden with riches had attracted hoards of adventurers to its shores. Already by 1525, four years after the Conquest, Andrea Navagiero, the Venetian Ambassador to the Court of Spain, was commenting on the fevered exodus, 'Seville stripped of its male inhabitants has become a city left almost to the women.' It was to guard against this loss of population that an embargo was put on emigration. No one was allowed to leave Spain for the Americas without the King's licence, and the penalty for carrying unlicensed passengers was death. These permits were given sparingly and only to men of approved character. There were, of course, cases of unlicensed emigrants – a favour to the captain and they were smuggled on board – but this was rare.

Restrictions were also imposed on learning, Spain having very definite views concerning education in her colonies. She felt that her powers depended in great measure upon the low level of education maintained. 'By disseminating the blessings of education amongst her subjects,' wrote Ward, 'she would virtually have undermined her own authority and made them impatient of a yoke, which comparison would have rendered doubly galling.'[1]

The Inquisition established in New Spain in 1571 had special charge of guarding against what it considered seditious literature. Not only were vessels ransacked upon their arrival in port, but the captains were held personally responsible for the correctness of the list of books on

[1] *Mexico in 1827.*

board. Zeal was carried to ridiculous lengths, one man towards the end of the eighteenth century being arrested for having an undeclared volume of Rousseau in his possession.

Arbitrary in her dealings with the passengers, Spain was no less despotic about the regulations governing her trade. From the first, she reserved to herself the exclusive right to supply all the wants of her colonies, and they, in turn, were forbidden to manufacture or grow any article that the mother country could supply.

Gage listed some of the merchandise: skins of oil and of wine, figs, raisins, olives, cloth and linen for the shops, iron, and mercury for the extraction of silver in the mines. The merchants protected by the exclusion of foreign competition sold their goods at exorbitant prices, or rather exchanged them at favourable rates for the produce of the colonies – silver, cochineal, indigo, chocolate and hides. Added to these were the exotic wares of the East, the rich cargoes of the Manila galleons that docked at Acapulco with silks, tea and porcelain from China. The porcelain, Friar Navarrete informs us,[1] was packed either in pepper grains or cloves to keep it from breaking. Ivory and sandalwood from India would also have been included, along with curiously fashioned furniture based on European designs and assembled by Asian craftsmen. The goods were sold at the great annual fair held at Jalapa after the arrival of the fleet.

Of all the different wares, it must almost certainly have been the cocoa bean and the baskets of dried cochineal that most intrigued the visitor. It is from the cochineal that the Aztecs procured the beautiful carmines and crimson lakes used in dying their linens those shades of colouring that recall the famous Tyrian dyes of antiquity. In Tyre juices were extracted from a shell, while in Mexico the colouring comes from an insect, a dark brown, little creature about the size and shape of a dog-tick. Aniline dyes have largely replaced the cochineal in our times, but its culture still goes on in certain outlying districts where the nopal grows. The platter-like leaves of this cactus are the insect's favourite haunt and it is off their green flesh that it prefers to feed. Only the female cochineal produces the colouring matter, and the harvesting, accomplished with a flick of a feather, occurs once or twice a year after their breeding season. The processing involves boiling the insect just long enough to make it swell, after which it is dried in the sun. Eventually minute red crystals of colouring matter are extracted, but this last operation is carried out by the dyers at the factory. At the Jalapa fair the insects would have been found in the intermediary stage, looking like fluted grains, heaped into great piles.

[1] *The Travels and Controverses of Friar Domingo Navarrete 1660–86*, edited by J. S. Cummings, The Hakluyt Society, London, 1960.

As for the cocoa bean, it had served the Indians not merely as a beverage but as money too, and for some time after the Conquest it continued to be used as a ready medium of exchange. Considering the bean's double function, it must have been an extravagant habit to use it as a beverage. Among the Aztecs, who called it *chocolatl*, it was drunk only by the ruling classes, probably because only they could afford it. Bernal Díaz tells us that chocolate was always served cold, and from others we learn some of the details of its preparation. The beans were pounded in a mortar together with small, very hot green chillis, a vanilla pod and some aniseed. Maize flour was then added and the whole stirred into water and boiled. When cool it was beaten with a swizzle-stick and drunk while still foaming. The Spaniards only learned to appreciate chocolate after a little sugar was added to the recipe, but once they acquired the taste it became almost a vice. Gage drank four or five cups a day between meals. When travelling he had an Indian whose sole job was to carry his *petacalli*, or wicker hamper 'wherein was my chocolate and all the implements to make it'. Despite the enormous meals served to travellers at monasteries *en route*, Gage complained of always feeling hungry. He put it down to the altitude, 'our stomachs would be ready to faint so we were fain to support them either with a cup of chocolate, or some conserve or biscuit'. In Guatemala women could not endure mass unless fortified by a cup of hot chocolate brought to them by a servant. This caused 'so great a confusion, interrupting both mass and sermon', that the bishop was obliged to threaten his parishioners with excommunication if they persisted in the practice. One hears also of a convent of nuns in Oaxaca who excelled in preparing the drink a special way. The exact recipe is now lost, but some of the ingredients were cinnamon, cloves, almonds, hazel-nuts, orange-blossom water, musk and vanilla. Once compounded, the mixture was coloured with *achiote*, an orange-yellow dye from the *Bixa orellana*, or annatto tree.

Although so popular in the New World, the habit of drinking chocolate did not spread to Spain until the end of the sixteenth century. A regular import trade in cocoa beans then developed, but only after the very first shipment had been intercepted in the Caribbean by completely mystified buccaneers who threw it overboard thinking it sheep dung. However, they did not repeat their mistake, and by the time chocolate reached England it was known as a West Indian drink rather than a Spanish one. The first chocolate shop in London was opened by a Frenchman in 1657. By the end of the century it was drunk as we know it, with milk. Though appreciated in England, chocolate never attained the popularity it enjoyed in the Spanish colonies, probably because it was overshadowed by another newly acquired habit: drinking tea.

This then is a bird's eye view of Vera Cruz as it used to be, but what impression does it make on the traveller today? I remember my own reactions: it was the season of the winds, but mercifully the *norte* was not blowing. As for the dreaded *vomito*, inoculation and the systematic eradication of the *Aedes aegypti* have all but eliminated the fever; the people of Vera Cruz are no longer obliged to fly to the hills.

Little remains of Spain's City of the True Cross. It has the appearance of any tropical port: a crowded waterfront buzzing with flies and the singsong of the mulatto or zambo stevedores scantily clad in cottons bleached a blinding white by the sun. All is glare and hustle and noise, a composition of furled sails outlined against the rust-streaked sides of coastal freighters. In the markets are mottled, yellow-green fruit, blotched oranges and vividly coloured fish. The shops trade in tortoise-shell, lumps of coral and the distended, bladder-like corpses of dried parrot fish. Architecturally Vera Cruz is a disappointment. Little is left of its original aspect except an occasional doorway, a balcony or a glimpse into a courtyard. Nevertheless there are traces of the old town if one hunts carefully. Some of the houses have preserved their old watch towers where the family gathers in the cool of the evening and where, as an English naval officer wrote, 'the anxious merchant looks out upon the coming sail',[1] once an important event announced by the tolling of San Francisco's bell. Part of this same convent survives and is now a public library with great bookcases ranged haphazard along its leprous, peeling walls. Other religious buildings have been less fortunate, among them a charming little Baroque chapel which serves as the repair shop of a neighbouring garage.

La Paroquia, the parish church, is the only religious building to have come down to us unchanged. Never of any particular interest, it may be said to have even benefited from the years of political unrest, for in it now gleam four handsome crystal chandeliers. Made originally by Baccarat for Emperor Maximilian, they arrived, by an irony of fate, after his execution and were seized by the Mexican customs who sold them eventually to some pious donor.

The Fort of San Juan, or Castillo di San Juan de Ulúa, is the most rewarding place to visit. For nearly three hundred years this grim island fortress has defended the approaches to New Spain. Here also the last handful of Royalists held out against the Revolutionary forces.

It stands about half a mile from the shore on a shallow that at high tide is covered by three feet of water. One can almost drive out to the fort on a mole that now joins the flats to the mainland, but the last hundred yards have to be negotiated on foot across muddy, crab-

---

[1] Captain G. F. Lyon, R.N., *Journal of a Residence and Tour in the Republic of Mexico*, John Murray, London, 1828.

infested sands. The building has remained practically unchanged since 1771 when the fort was last altered. Watch-towers and turrets still command views out to sea, and from them the Gulf is seen as wedges of vivid blue, framed by the loopholes that pierce the carapace of masonry. To the leeward side, where the waters run deep, one can still find the great brass rings to which the galleons were tied; they hang heavily from the pitted walls.

San Juan had been a small, self-contained community with its dry dock and shipyard, hospital, chapel, and also dungeons, for at times the viceroys had used the fort as a penal settlement. Political prisoners had been immured in the thickness of its walls, in great chambers designated as 'limbo' or 'moras'. Lettering thus describing them is still visible on plaques by the side of each door. The cells were well named, for at high tide water seeps in over the rocky floors and damp drips mercilessly from the vaulted ceilings, long years of dripping having hung them with stalactites like some Caliban's cave.

3

El Camino Real

All the main arteries of travel in New Spain, whatever their condition, were designated *Caminos Reales*. Some of the King's roads were little better than trails through the mountains – not, however, the road between Vera Cruz and Mexico City. It was one of the few highways to really merit its name. Everyone arriving from Europe was obliged to pass this way. Up its precipitous inclines have wound long files of soldiers, merchants with their trains of mules, suites of the viceroy, governors in their litters, bishops and judges. Every so often the traveller would have found a porphyry column engraved with the mileage and the elevation. The altitude was a point of vital information for, as Humboldt explains, it announced the approach 'of that fortunate and elevated region, in which the scourge of yellow fever is no longer to be dreaded'.[1]

For us today this route, a distance of some two hundred miles, is merely a few hours' journey, but during the Spanish occupation it was a three- to four-day trip. We shall follow the road in its entirety, for it offers a prototype of travel in the colonies, a model as it were of all the roads.

From Vera Cruz the road climbs steadily until it reaches Jalapa, an altitude of nearly five thousand feet. At an even greater height comes the garrison town of Perote followed by monotonous miles of desert. Another climb follows, this time through pine forests, and then there is a sudden shock as one comes upon Mexico City. On several occasions I have viewed the city from these heights and each time I have experienced the same pleasurable sensation of shock, the same pent-up feeling of excitement.

The present road is not exactly the route followed by Cortés on his march inland; however it corresponds closely enough for there to be little or no topographical difference.

While it is not my intention here to retrace the first stages of the

[1] *Political Essay on the Kingdom of New Spain.*

Conquest, it is quite impossible, on the other hand, to completely ignore them. Again and again one's thoughts turn back to those first weeks after Cortés disembarked, a young man of thirty-six commanding five hundred soldiers, sixteen horses and fourteen pieces of artillery, a token force with which he proposed to subdue an empire six times the size of England and numbering some seven million inhabitants. He was never to guess the exact extent nor the potential power of the Aztec empire, but he cannot have been entirely unaware of the magnitude of his undertaking. Indeed, the Spaniards' first meetings with the Aztecs must have been far from reassuring. In the beginning royal emissaries came bearing Montezuma's extravagant gifts along with his polite but firm message that a visit to the capital was out of the question. An encounter followed with some of the Emperor's tax-collectors who arrived to extract the tribute due from the recently subjected Indians in the coastal area where Cortés was billeted. Díaz described the officials as sophisticated dandies who sauntered about their business dressed in richly worked mantles with their glossy hair combed upwards in tufts tied with gold rings. Attended by slaves to fan off flies, they carried elaborate staffs of office and small nosegays of sweet smelling flowers. Díaz called them roses, but this is not possible for no species of rose was indigenous to Mexico; they were only imported later. Díaz was thoroughly impressed, noting with surprise that 'they passed by our quarters; but behaved with such reserve and so haughtily, that they addressed none of us',[1] not even Cortés. As for the Indians with whom the Spaniards were staying 'the very mention of the Mexicans filled them with trembling, the caciques turning quite pale with fear'.

Purposely I have not gone into the details of Cortés' march on the capital for there exist many versions of this remarkable undertaking. Its success largely depended not so much on force and extraordinary luck as on politics. As Ralph Beale put it 'the conquest of Tenochtitlán was less a conquest than it was a revolt of dominated peoples'. Cortés playing on the subjected tribes' discontent managed to assemble a formidable army of Indian allies, and this, together with an unshakeable belief in his own destiny, had enabled him to carry the day. Nevertheless his initial decision to march on Mexico was an act of remarkable courage. From all that the Spaniards had seen and heard it must have been obvious that they were opposed by a civilized and highly organized state, and not by just a tribe of primitive Indians such as those occupying the Antilles. By the time Cortés had received a second injunction from the Emperor again refusing permission to enter his city, the Spaniards knew that somewhere between Vera Cruz and

---

[1] *The Memoirs of Conquistador Bernal Díaz del Castillo*, translated by John Ingram Lockhart, J. Hatchard & Son, London, 1844.

Tenochtitlán lay the Aztec army reputed to be over ten thousand strong. The invaders' courage and endurance were amazing. Day after day they faced exhausting marches, mostly through hostile country. Imagine them clad in their armour, long stockings and high leather boots; the dust and the heat must have been intolerable. There were moments when the men were so thirsty that they chewed thistle to make their tongues and lips bleed so at least their mouths would be moist. At other times 'the only way we could in some measure refresh our parched tongues was to hold the edge of our axes between our lips'.[1] Profuse bleeding from the nose and the mouth was yet another torment, 'occasioned', so Díaz tells us, 'by the weight of our arms, which we durst never lay aside'. Writing about his experiences in later years, Díaz claimed that he grew so accustomed to being armed that it took him quite some time to get used to undressing at night or to 'make use of a bed, sleeping better in soldier fashion than on the softest down'.

One reads further harrowing details. For instance it was a custom during the sixteenth century to bathe wounds with oil in order to prevent them from hardening. In Mexico, for want of oil, the soldiers dressed them 'with the fat of corpulent Indians killed in battle'. The Aztecs, I learnt subsequently, treated their cuts with finely ground obsidian. One wonders which side fared the better.

Supplies were another problem. At times the coarse mountain grasses were the men's only form of sustenance. Dogs, when they could catch them, were considered 'delicious joints', but so they were in Tahiti too, where Captain Cook frequently made a meal of them. The Tahitians raised a special breed which has since died out. Their Mexican canine cousins, however, still exist, although they are certainly rather rare. *Sholos* they are called, their correct name in Nahuatl, the Aztec language, being *Xoloitzcuintli*. They are lively, charcoal-coloured creatures, on the fat side and about the size of a terrier, with a broad head, pointed ears and snout, small eyes, a long wispy tail and not a trace of hair anywhere on their bodies. Touching them is like picking up a bag of soft, warm leather. N. P. Wright, an authority on *sholos*, remarks on their peculiarly high body temperature which is several degrees higher than that of an ordinary dog. 'Even today,' he writes, 'country women when they feel indisposed go to bed with a *sholo* to warm their stomachs.'[2]

Added to the soldiers' physical hardships were their fears of the 'barbarous' Indians. Actually the Totonacs, Cempoalans and the Tlaxalans were a highly civilized people, yet to the Spaniards, blinded

---

[1] *The Memoirs of Conquistador Bernal Díaz del Castillo.*

[2] N. Pelham Wright, F.Z.S., *A Guide to Mexican Animals*, Minutiae Mexicana, Mexico D.F., 1965.

4 Madame Calderón de la Barca (page 26)

5 The Puente Nacional, formerly
the Puente del Rey (page 27)

6 Perote. The fort of San Carlos (page 33)

7 'At the entrance to the prison I had noticed two
weather-worn stone sentinels' (page 33)

9 Painting of banditti who plagued the country from early on in its history (page 35)

10 The Valley of Mexico by José María Velasco (page 37)

by their religious fanaticism, they must have seemed positively satanic. How else could the Spaniards explain the atrocities they witnessed? There is no doubt that Cortés was deeply shocked and regarded the Indian manner of life as not only pagan but monstrous too. Díaz tells us that 'hardly a day passed that these people did not sacrifice from three to four and even five Indians'. Their hearts were torn from their bodies and their blood smeared on the temple walls. Their arms and legs 'were cut off and devoured, just in the same way as we would fetch meat from the butchers'. 'Indeed,' adds Díaz, 'I 'even believe that human flesh is exposed for sale in the markets.'

A great deal of material exists on the subject of human sacrifice, much of it written by actual eye-witnesses like Fray Aguilar, a companion-at-arms of Díaz, or another writer known as the Anonymous Conquistador, thought to be Francisco de Terrazus, Cortés' major domo. A third source is Fray Diego Durán's *Historia de las Indias*, compiled from notes made some thirty years after the Conquest. All concur on the general procedure of these sacrifices which were enacted in full view of the public. The sacrificial stone, in front of a dark sanctuary, was reached by a steep flight of steps up which the victim was led by four priests whose task it was to stretch their unfortunate ward upon the altar, keeping a firm hold of his limbs. The sacrifice itself was performed by a high priest, or, if it were a special occasion, by the Emperor himself. Seizing an obsidian or chalcedony knife the executioner plunged it into the breast and ripped out the heart. Judging from drawings in different codices, it would appear that the operation was accomplished by plunging straight into the rib case at a point near the heart, but from a purely anatomical viewpoint this is hardly likely. The gash more probably was made directly under the thorax and penetrated the muscles of the diaphragm. The priest could then thrust his hand into the cut and feel around for the heart. According to one witness the deed was accomplished 'in the time it would take one to make the sign of the cross'. The victim, according to Fray Aguilar, 'seldom uttered a sound'.[1]

The priests must have presented a really terrifying spectacle. They dressed only in black or dark green and had skulls embroidered on their cloaks. They wore their hair long and kept it permanently matted. 'It would have been impossible to put it in any shape or order without cutting it', and, adds Díaz, their blood-encrusted clothes were 'so completely clogged that it impeded their walk'. Their finger nails 'were uncommonly long' and their whole person 'stunk most offensively of sulphur and putrid flesh'. At one point during the march inland the

[1] *The Chronicle of Fray Francisco de Aguilar*, translated by Patricia de Fuentes, Cassell, London, 1964.

Spaniards came upon some priests who had been officiating at a sacrifice 'and blood still trickled down over their ears'. The priests were generally boys of good families and they were vowed to celibacy. 'But,' adds Díaz, they 'were wholly given to unnatural offences.' On various occasions he refers to sodomy, mentioning 'young men in female garments' who made a livelihood 'of their cursed lewdness'. 'Most of the Indians particularly those living on the coast and in the hotter climates were given to unnatural lusts.'

It can be imagined what effect all this must have had on the Spaniards, most of whom were young rustics from the provinces. They knew nothing as yet of the Aztec belief that the sun was a god of animal nature nourished by food and drink. Unless completely satiated the sun would not merely cease to yield warmth, but would perish altogether out of the heavens. Blood was a magic fluid indispensable to the conservation of the universe, and as Soustelle explains, human sacrifice was an alchemy by which life was made out of death, 'blood was spilled on the altars to keep the sun moving in its course, so that darkness should not overwhelm the world'.[1]

But all the soldiers had witnessed thus far was as nothing compared to what would greet them at Tenochtitlán, for sacrifices enacted in the temples of the great city were far more harrowing. In his description of the dedication rites of the main temple, Durán said that eighty thousand were killed in a slaughter that lasted four days without interruption. Streams of blood poured down the temple steps, clotting as it cooled. Durán writes that priests went about scooping blood up in large gourds, afterwards daubing it on the walls of the other temples. 'They also smeared the idols and the rooms, both inside and out,' and the stench was such 'that it became unbearable to the people of the city'.[2]

In the Mexican National Museum of Anthropology there is a small model of the Great Temple, a pyramid rising in terraces to two sanctuaries, one sheltering the image of the all powerful Huitzilopochtli, god of war and of the sun, and the second containing the image of Tlaloc, god of fecundity and rain. Cortés, when he eventually reached Mexico City, begged to see the gods. Díaz, who was with him, described Huitzilopochtli as 'a fat-looking figure with distorted and furious eyes, covered all over with jewels, gold and pearls which were stuck to him by means of a special paste'. Andreas de Tapia, a young captain also with Cortés, tells us the 'paste' was made from 'all kinds of seed which had been ground and kneaded with the blood of virgins and boys'. The paste, however, was not just an adhesive. The entire idol, 'a mass

---

[1] Jacques Soustelle, *Daily Life of the Aztecs*, Weidenfeld & Nicolson, London, 1961.
[2] Fray Diego Durán, *History of The Indies of New Spain*, translated by Doris Heyden and Fernando Horcasitas, and entitled *The Aztecs*, Cassell, London, 1964.

thicker than a man and as high', was moulded of it. In front of these monstrous images stood the sacrificial altars. Beside them was a great drum, stretched with serpent skin, which Díaz described as 'so vast that it could be heard eight or twelve miles away'.

There must also have been moments of great splendour amidst the horror. The temple's dedication rites described by Durán were enacted some twenty-two years before the Conquest when those officiating would have been Montezuma's father and Tlacaelel, a warrior of royal blood and a popular national hero.

One can evoke the mounting excitement as the auspicious hour for sacrifice approached. Smoke pours in scented clouds from numerous braziers. From the temple top comes the drum's constant thudding accompanied by the shrill, hellish music of shell trumpets and horns. A sudden hush announces the arrival of the great lords in their litters. Slowly, very slowly they begin the steep ascent, their long mantles of state trailing out behind them, dragging on the steps. Following the stately figures comes a cortège of priests 'painted all over with red ochre, even their loin cloths and tunics'. In contrast, the Emperor and Tlacaelel are dyed a shining black 'that catches the light'. Gold sheaths protect their arms and great nodding headdresses of plumes and gems sweep up from their glistening brows. On reaching the summit there follows a brief pause as the high priest hands over the slaughtering knives. The thudding of the drum increases . . .

It is difficult to leave so engrossing a subject, but the Aztec sacrificial rites are not our real concern. Rather we must return to the *Camino Real*. Many have described the journey from Vera Cruz to Mexico City, but none more vividly than the thirty-four-year-old Madame Calderón de la Barca. Let her, then, take us over the opening stages.

'There is much disturbance,' she wrote, 'as to the mode in which we are to travel to Mexico. Some propose a coach, others the *literas*, others advise us to take the diligence.' Madame Calderon tells us that the diligence took four days while the *literas* took anything up to nine or ten days. Both the English and French consuls strongly advised the *literas*. 'Monsieur de —— prophesies broken arms and dislodged teeth if we persist in our plan of taking the diligence', but Madame Calderón, with a mind of her own, chooses the diligence. At least 'the diligence has food and beds provided for it at the inns – the others nothing'.

The Calderóns planned to rise before daybreak, having arranged to breakfast *en route* with Antonio López de Santa Anna, the famous soldier-politician who rose to the presidency after the Revolution. He was a native of the *tierra caliente* and owned a great *hacienda* among bananas and bamboos in the hills behind Vera Cruz.

Before going any further, perhaps we should consider the lady with whom we are going to travel, because she will often be our guide. Madame Calderón's letters are those of an immensely likeable person. Certainly the august William Prescott, author of *The Conquest,* found her so, and it was thanks to his efforts that her 'instructive and amusing' letters were eventually published. Few subjects escaped Madame Calderón's sharp pen, but like so many sympathetic people she remains strangely silent when it comes to describing herself. Occasionally she provides a fleeting glimpse of herself as a good horsewoman and as a musical amateur who sometimes played the harp for special Masses in the cathedral. She never refers to her clothes except for one travelling costume, a dark calico gown, large panama hat, a *rebozo* tied on like a scarf and a thick green barège veil. Apart from her portrait we have only the vaguest impressions of her as a person, none of them particularly enlightening. 'I think her most remarkably agreeable and accomplished,' wrote an old English colonel. Somebody else described her as a 'little lady with a bird-like voice'.

Prescott, although a friend of Madame Calderón, tells us nothing of her life. Henry Baerlein, in the foreword to the *Everyman* edition of her letters did, however, sketch in a few details. Her maiden name was Inglis (pronounced Ingalls) and she was born in Edinburgh in 1804, being one of a family of four brothers and six sisters. While she was still a child, Fanny's father lost his money and for unexplained reasons moved the family to Normandy, where he died. Then followed a general exodus to the United States, to Boston where Mrs Inglis started a school for young ladies. From Boston the Inglises moved to Staten Island and next settled finally in Baltimore, where no doubt Fanny met Don Angel Calderón de la Barca, a Spanish diplomat in Washington. They were married in 1838 and in the following year Don Angel was named the first official Spanish envoy to Mexico since the 1825 Revolution. After his Mexican assignment Calderón was reappointed to Washington before ending his career as Minister of Foreign Affairs in Madrid. It was here that the widowed Fanny entered royal circles, first as governess and ultimately as lady-in-waiting to the Infanta Isabella, the Queen's eldest child. In recognition of her services she collected the title of Marquesa along the way. She was seventy-eight when she died, the result of a cold caught at a dinner party.

But the Marquesa's court life has little to do with the cheerful, lively Madame Calderón we read about in Mexico. We must go back to the oppressive heat of Vera Cruz, back through the years to moonlit streets and a merciful breeze that wafts in from the sea.

It is two o'clock in the morning and the Calderóns have dressed by candlelight. 'Two boxes, called carriages, drawn by mules, were at the door, to convey us to Magna de Clavo,' the Santa Anna *hacienda*. A paved causeway, *Calle de la preciosa Sangre de Christo*, leads them to the outskirts of the town and then, after plunging through several miles of sand they reach 'symptoms of vegetation'. A change of mules is made at a pretty Indian village of thatched bamboo huts. Indian women with long black hair and half-naked children watch from the doorways. 'We seem to have been transported, as if by enchantment, from a desert to a garden . . . the air so soft and balmy, the first fresh breath of morning,' dew glitters on the banana leaves 'and all around so silent, cool and still'.

The *hacienda*, when it finally appeared, was 'slight-looking' but pretty. 'We were received by an aide-de-camp in uniform and several officers,' who conducted the Calderóns 'to a large cool, agreeable apartment . . . into which shortly entered Señora de Santa Anna, tall, thin, and, at that early hour of the morning, dressed to receive us in clean white muslin, white satin shoes, and very splendid diamond ear-rings.' Madame Calderón was impressed with the General, finding him good looking, quietly dressed and rather melancholy with fine dark eyes which 'were soft and penetrating'. He suffered pains in a leg which no longer existed: he had lost it in an action against the French at Vera Cruz. 'Knowing nothing of his past history, one would have said a philosopher, living in dignified retirement.'

Breakfast, when announced, was 'very handsome', consisting of innumerable Spanish dishes, meat and vegetables, fish and fowl, fruits and sweetmeats 'all served in white and gold French porcelain, with coffee, wines, etc.'. The meal over, the Señora dispatched an officer for her cigar case, 'which was gold, with a diamond latch'. It was passed round but Madame Calderón declined.

Santa Anna must have been favourably impressed with his guests, for when preparing to depart the Calderóns found that their 'box of a carriage' had been transformed, Cinderella fashion, into 'a handsome new coach, made in the United States, drawn by ten good-looking mules, and driven by a smart Yankee coachman'. They had been warned about the roads which were unexaggeratedly infamous, a succession of holes, rocks and jolts so bad as 'to prevent us from being too much enraptured by the scenery, which increased in beauty as we advanced'. They arrived at the *Puente Nacional*, formerly the *Puente del Rey*. To judge from drawings, the bridge has hardly changed and is 'paved in the greatest nicety and set with handsome masonry'. The Calderóns walked to the bridge, pulled numbers of large white flowers, admired the river dashing over the rocks below and then drove on amongst their lumbering escort of Mexican soldiers. The escort was changed every twenty miles.

Today the *Camino Real* has an excellent surface and is expertly cambered, but the countryside can have altered but little. The same dense vegetation is smothered in vines. Gradually, twisting and turning, the climb begins. There is a subtle change in the air and within sixty miles an altitude of over four thousand feet has been attained. A further short climb and Jalapa is reached. Above rise great basaltic ridges fringed with pine in whose branches are caught ragged edges of mist. These are the remains of noble cloud-banks that sail in over the ocean, meet with the cold mountain air, condense, and release a gentle drizzle, euphonically named *chipi-chipi*. *Chipi-chipi*, alternating with dazzling sunshine, produces a delicious rainbow-hued atmosphere, a perpetual dampness that stains the roofs of the houses with moss. Below, from the windows of these same houses there are views over the surrounding hills, planted with coffee, tobacco and bananas. Orchids spangle the forests and on one *sierra* above the town the Indians still gather the tuberous root of a purplish-rose convolvulus, the once famous *Ipomoea Jalap*, or more correctly *Ipomoea purga*. Dried and grated, the tuber produces a grey-white powder that in days gone by was considered essential in the treatment of any dropsical condition. It was also very popular as a purgative and used to be much in demand among the Spaniards who claimed that the drinking of chocolate had a marked binding effect on the bowels.

The town itself I found depressing: progress has completely effaced the past. Gone are the attractive houses and cloistered gardens where once the rich merchants lived, and with them has died the legend of Jalapa's bewitching women. No sign either of the cobbled streets on which the nervous traveller from Vera Cruz once alighted, free at last to stretch and to 'take his first deep breath without fear of drawing in the germs of yellow fever and malaria disease'.[1] Nor can Jalapa be recommended for its lodgings. While suffering an indifferent hotel I thought back on descriptions I had read of some of the earlier inns, places where the water, kept in great earthen vessels, was so cold 'that it maketh the teeth to chatter'. It is not discomfort or even rustic simplicity one minds when travelling, but mediocrity, and ugliness, the soul-destroying powers of the second rate.

Gage on his way through Jalapa had spent the night with some Franciscan friars. As usual he was disapproving. He reminds us that the Franciscans are a mendicant order vowed to poverty: their habits should be of sackcloth, no stockings or shoes, or at the most, wooden clogs or hempen sandals. A friar should not own a horse and travelling ought to be accomplished, painfully, on foot. Any breach of these restrictions 'they acknowledge to be a deadly and mortal sin'. Having carefully described the utter abnegation in which a Franciscan should

[1] *Political Essay on the Kingdom of New Spain.*

live, Gage gleefully launched to the attack. 'It was to us a scandalous sight to see a friar of this cloister riding in with his lackey boy by his side.' The unfortunate man had been to the other side of the town to confess a dying Indian, but his unnecessarily elegant figure furnished a perfect victim for the malicious Gage. Mounted on a fine gelding the friar had hitched up his long habit and tucked it into his girdle, thus exposing a 'pair of orange silk stockings and a neat Cordoban shoe'. The finishing touch, though, seems to have been the man's drawers 'with lace three inches broad at the hem!' In a frenzy of indignation Gage subjected the entire monastery to his prying, critical eye. We are told of doublets quilted with silk and of holland shirts with lace at the wrist. 'After supper,' he writes, 'there was even talk of carding and dicing!'

Gage's *Travels* are full of acutely observed incidents, yet one wishes that he had not been so hopelessly biased. His attitude, however, is easily explained. Born of a strict Catholic family in England and educated by the Jesuits in Spain, he suddenly converted to Protestantism at the age of forty-five. As Professor Newton points out in his introduction to *The Travels*[1] 'a convert is usually more hostile to the faith he has left than an impartial observer'. Also the book was written some twenty years after Gage had left Mexico and was dedicated to Sir Thomas Fairfax, Captain-General of Cromwell's army. Quite obviously the author included material that an anti-Catholic audience would relish most.

Doubtless the prior at Vera Cruz and the Jalapan friars were exactly as described, but Gage completely ignored the positive accomplishments of early missionaries like Bartolomé de Las Casas, the Dominican monk who became Bishop of Chiapas and who spent a lifetime pleading the cause of the Indians. Las Casas died some seventy years before Gage reached Mexico but Gage must certainly have been familiar with his remarkable *History of the Indies* and with his even more remarkable but alarming *Destruction of the Indies*. Gage could not have read Díaz's memoirs, first printed only in 1632, but he probably was familiar with much of the material: the arrival, for example, in 1524 of the first important company of Franciscans. Landing at Vera Cruz they walked barefoot 'in the meanest garments' the whole way to Mexico City. Cortés with all his officers and men, accompanied by Cuauhtémoc, the last of the Aztec emperors, had ridden out to meet them, and 'as soon as we beheld these pious men', writes Díaz, 'we dismounted and walked up to them and fell down on our knees, kissing their hands'. The Viceroy Velasco, writing to Philip II in 1558, refers to the friars in their rough homespun and described their diet as being 'so frugal as hardly

---

[1] *Thomas Gage. The English American. A New Survey of the West Indies 1648*, edited with an introduction by A. P. Newton, George Routledge, London, 1928.

to support life'. This is not exactly the impression given us by Gage.

Following the Franciscans came the Dominicans and after them the Augustinians, succeeded eventually by the Jesuits. By the end of the sixteenth century these three religious orders between them had established over four hundred monasteries. While the ethics of the conquistadors may certainly be questioned, the good intentions of the Church are recorded in the strict injunctions the Pope sent to the religious missions across the Atlantic. Their instructions stressed that Spain and Portugal's claims to the Americas, their rights of tenure, would be supported by the Church only as long as and solely on the condition that the powers spread the Gospel as well as, in the words of Pope Alexander VI, 'their good government of the Indian nations'.

Again and again one comes across references to the extraordinary devotion of the early missionaries. No sooner had they arrived than they had to set about the arduous task of learning Nahuatl and the numerous different Indian dialects (there were sixty altogether) before they could begin to teach their wards what they believed to be the only true way to salvation. History, science and Latin were also included in the curriculum and apparently the Indians were receptive students. No doubt they were astonished at the generally amiable atmosphere of this new religion and most certainly must have compared its rites favourably, in fact with relief, to what Humboldt terms 'the ceremonies of their former sanguinary worship'.

Ironically enough the only people not well satisfied were the conquistadors themselves. To settle the new territories Cortés adopted the allotment system practised in the reconquered Moorish provinces of Spain. A man was granted a tract of land and with it the trusteeship of the Moors, or in this case, of the Indians inhabiting it. These allotments were called *encomiendas* from the verb *encomendar*, to entrust. The man owning the land was the *encomendero*. In theory the Indians were committed to his protection : he was responsible for their well-being and was supposed to concern himself also with spiritual matters. He was in fact not only an overlord but also a lay missionary. In return for these benefits the Indians were to pay their *encomenderos* tribute. On paper it was a benevolent system, in practice it too often resulted in the abject enslavement of many of the natives. It can readily be understood how the *encomendero*, unless a paragon of righteousness, would object to his slaves being prepared for racial equality. Nothing would suit the *encomendero* better than having his Indians kept in perpetual tutelage, but here were the friars teaching them all sorts of useless details, 'even', explodes a certain Díaz de Vargas, 'to the scandalous extreme of wearing gloves!'[1]

[1] François Chevalier, *Land and Society in Colonial Mexico*, University of California Press, 1963.

One realizes then that the friars were made of sterner stuff than Gage would lead one to suppose, and with this more complete picture one can afford to enjoy his expostulations over lace knickers.

Now what about Gage himself? Where Madame Calderón must have been charming, the same, I am afraid, cannot be said of Gage; entertaining, witty even, but somehow I feel one would not have liked him. He was of good yeoman stock and belonged to a family that had risen to prominence in the service of the Tudors, his great-grandfather having held an important post at the Court of Henry VIII. As stated already the family were ardent Catholics and while still in his teens Gage had been sent off to Spain to study for the priesthood with the Jesuits. That country was chosen because of the family's Spanish connections, traceable back to Philip II's residence in England. For various reasons, none of them very explicit, the young man conceived a deadly aversion for the Brotherhood and left the Jesuit college at Valladolid, 'passing over', as Professor Newton puts it, 'to the Dominicans'. His father, a great admirer of the Jesuits, took this change very badly, so badly in fact that he disinherited him. Cut off from home and finding himself without any money, the young Gage decided to embark for the Philippines as a missionary. It is evident from his own narrative that the lure of gold rather than religious zeal inspired him. But no matter, he was young, only twenty-five, and his adventuresome spirit is to be admired, particularly because his English nationality automatically disallowed him entry into Spanish colonies. Under the assumed name of Fray Tomás de Santa María he had himself smuggled on board ship in an empty biscuit barrel. Once arrived in New Spain, Gage decided against the Philippines; and the day before the missionaries were to sail, he and three other Dominicans gave their company the slip and set out instead for Chiapas, one of the Mexican states on the Guatemalan frontier. Twenty years elapsed before Gage returned to England, and it was in his maturity, at the age of forty-five, that the serious flaws of his character became apparent. Observing the trend of politics in England and realizing the hopelessness of the Stuart cause, he made a complete *volte-face*, swearing allegiance to the English Church. Appreciating that all converts were regarded as suspect by the Puritans, he got married to prove his sincerity, and went one step further, stooping so low as to give secret information against some of his former Jesuit friends. A near relative of his sister-in-law and Father Peter Wright, his brother's chaplain, were both hanged on his testimony. Publishing the account of his travels was another example of his cunning. Cromwell, at the time, had his eye on Spain's rich South American possessions so when *The English American* appeared in 1648, stressing the defencelessness of the Spanish colonies, it quite possibly was a deciding factor in launching the

Protector's 'Western Design'. Certainly it helped to procure Gage's appointment as chaplain to the expedition. While the expedition failed in its attempt on Hispaniola, it did procure for England the invaluable island of Jamaica, on which Gage died in 1656.

Several editions of the *Travels* exist and all are illustrated with engravings of the young friar; whether these are apocryphal or not it is impossible to know. In the first German edition Gage is tonsured and seated at a table receiving gifts from his parishioners, a heterogeneous collection presumably of Guatemalans, for a volcano explodes in the background. In the Dutch edition, dated 1700, he stands, Gospel in hand, gesticulating, as though conducting an orchestra, at a dark-skinned beplumed crowd that in return for the salvation of their souls offers him every conceivable remuneration. Neither representation is very convincing. These could be any pompous young man in a Dominican habit. One really does not know what Gage looked like, but an amusing experience he recounted when in Chiapas suggests that he was not without a certain lively spirit. 'The women of the city of San Cristóbal de las Casas,' he wrote, 'are somewhat light in their carriage and have learned from the Devil many enticing lessons and baits to draw poor souls to sin and damnation.' One gentlewoman of his acquaintance had a very poor reputation; unable to seduce the bishop, she is said to have given him poisoned chocolate. Gage was teaching her son Latin and found her 'very merry and of pleasant disposition'. Often she would send conserves and boxes of sweets, 'a kind of gratuity', Gage thought, 'for the pain that I took in tutoring her son'. One day a package arrived tied up in a handkerchief. Not without a certain pleasurable anticipation Gage loosened the knots thinking to find 'some rich token, or some pieces of eight'. Instead, buried in jasmine and roses he found a large plaintain (a form of banana). Wonderingly he explored further and perceived, cut into the skin of the fruit, a heart transfixed by an arrow. Gage was not amused and forthwith returned the offending object with a second inscription in short rhyme; '*fruta tan fria, amor no cria*'. Soon after this incident Gage departed for Guatemala, a wise precaution, no doubt, considering the bishop's chocolate.

But enough, now, about Gage. We return to Jalapa, for there still remains a long stretch of road to cover. Climbing above the town one drives through the charming little village of Banderilla, dating from Colonial times. Plastered, one-storeyed houses crowd along the length of a gently sloping hill. The roofs are tiled and dip out over the sidewalks, supported by rustic columns. The road winds higher and higher till eventually swirling mists are reached. It is the world of a Japanese screen: fir and cedar mount in subtle gradations of colour, their trunks varying from brown to grey, and then above them, glimpsed in occasional clearings, the darkness of wet greens. One climbs and dips and then, abruptly, the landscape flattens. The garrison town of Perote has been reached. I look at the altimeter and notice that it registers eight thousand feet. The mists have cleared, dispersed by the sun which shines with that hard brightness usual to high altitudes.

In the ascent from Vera Cruz, climates succeed one another so quickly that within a matter of hours the traveller passes every conceivable variety of vegetation. From the hothouse atmosphere of the *tierra caliente* one arrives suddenly to the *tierra templada*, the temperate region, and from the temperate region to the *tierra fría*. In no other country of the world can one pass so rapidly from zone to zone, from the shores of the tropics to the region of pines and lichen and perpetual cold.

Mexico City, strictly speaking, lies in a cold country, as indeed does Perote and most of the great Central Plateau, but it is cold only in comparison to the heat of the coast. The temperature never drops lower than thirty-five degrees fahrenheit. The climate is a battle between the latitude (Mexico's Central Plateau extends roughly from eighteen to twenty degrees latitude north of the Equator) and the altitude. The result is a brilliant pure atmosphere with a great scarcity of moisture. Vast plains follow each other in endless succession rimmed around with bare, distant hills. Perote lies on the edge of such a plain, and about half a mile out of the town is the old Fort of San Carlos whose frowning walls face out over bleak stretches of sandy desert. The fort dates from the second half of the eighteenth century and was built to accommodate troops patrolling the road. It is now used as a military prison and after some good-humoured badinage, much clanking of keys and the temporary confiscation of my camera, the authorities allowed me in. Arched barracks face inwards onto a glaring parade ground occupied by aimless groups of cotton-clad Mexicans. Amongst them stood a good-looking fellow in his late twenties who came forward to offer his services as guide. He spoke almost faultless English, but being at sea as to his status, guard or prisoner, I was hesitant to question him so what information I did gather was of a purely impersonal nature.

At the entrance to the prison I had noticed two weather-worn, stone sentinels presenting arms. I asked my friend about them. The statues represent two soldiers who had fallen in love with the same woman in Spain. Although garrisoned together, they had never met until mounting guard one night. The hour and the isolation encouraged confidences and during the course of the conversation it became apparent that they had lost their hearts to the same person. A duel ensued in which both were killed, transfixed by each other's bayonets. Normally this would have been the end of the incident had the commandant of the camp not been such a stern disciplinarian. As an example to the other soldiers he had the rival lovers court-martialled for dereliction of duty. As dead men could not be cashiered, the two were sentenced instead to stand eternal guard in effigy and were shipped to the New World where they were placed at the gates of San Carlos, then just recently completed.

From Perote we dip down into an area known as the *mal pais*. Empty, stripped of trees, the desiccated, calcine land is punctuated only with yuccas and funnels of whirling dust that twist frantically to their extinction in the heat-troubled haze. A gradual rise and we lose the grey-white clouds boiling up from under our wheels, traced in long straight lines across the plains. Grass lands replace the desert, but always in the distance are bare mountains, a constant jostling of ridges as we progress. It is a grandiose and lonely landscape; the only signs of human habitation are the crumbling remains of walled caravanserais along the way.

For years mule teams were Mexico's main form of transport and these caravanserais, or *posadas*, were their stopping places. The ordinary traveller would have stayed at an inn, or *venta*, while officials would have lodged at the nearest monastery. There were not many roads in the early days and both *posadas* and *ventas* must have been constantly crowded and very uncomfortable. Ward described the *ventas* as noisome places where 'the most agreeable smells to greet the traveller were the odours of garlic and dried beef'. The *posadas*, of course, were very primitive. On the other hand, those lucky enough to merit a monastery fared remarkably well, for a typical meal consisted of three or four dishes: mutton, veal or beef, kid and turkey or some other fowl. The actual travelling arrangements were fairly uniform throughout Mexico and rather elaborate. 'A mule,' Gage wrote, 'was prepared to carry my bedding.' Other mules were loaded with a variety of leather chests, and an Indian servant delegated to each mule. There was a rearguard 'and three more Indians to ride before me', these acting as guides. Quite a cortège for a simple friar.

As horses and mules were unknown in America before the Spaniards, the roads under the Aztecs must have presented a very different spectacle. Before the advent of pack-animals transport depended entirely on manpower. There was a special sect of porters called *tlamemes*. These men, travelling at a steady jog, were capable of averaging fifteen miles a day. The loads they shouldered weighed anything up to fifty pounds.

The only articulate foreigner to visit the New World within fifty years of the Conquest was Benzoni, an Italian, who gives us a general impression of what Mexico was like. Indians worked in and about the Spanish houses, some occupied in the new employment of tending cattle imported from Spain, others busy with their own plantations, husbanded (Benzoni says) in 'a rude and primitive way'. The Indians were also employed in building the new churches and monasteries and frequently hired themselves out as mercenaries. Across the traveller's path would have moved a small, fully armed body of Spaniards followed by hundreds of Indians, and everywhere, on all the tracks and by-paths, would have been seen the *tlamemes*, bent double under their loads. But here a harsher note creeps in, for amongst the struggling men there were many who did not belong to the official porter class. The Spaniards had adopted the practice of making all rebellious Indians their slaves. It was a dark, iron slavery, the missionaries tell us, compared to the servitude imposed by the Aztecs. Their former masters had apparently treated them as children, but not so the Spaniards who branded them like cattle, burning their names into their foreheads with hot irons. Fortunately the Madrid government on hearing about it reacted strongly and by 1528 branding had become a criminal offence.

After Perote the only place of any note that I remember at all clearly is a small seventeenth-century monastery at Calpulalpan. In the sun-filled cloister a frieze of black and white arabesques run around the downstairs wall, while upstairs, ranged along a brickwork balustrade, is a collection of plants flowering in miscellaneous pots and tins. It was here, incidentally, that I saw my first friar, the only friar, as it turned out, that I was to meet during my entire stay in Mexico. They are regarded as *personae non gratae* by the present government and, like nuns and priests, still may not wear their habits in public.

The last miles to Mexico City seem endless. One's attention is drawn again to the altitude, this time with a certain breathlessness, as the climb rises to over ten thousand feet. Abruptly the road sweeps into the dim silence of great pines. They soar from thirty to forty feet and are packed so closely together that the sun, striking through them, is splintered fan-wise into blades of filtered light scarcely sharp enough to penetrate the all-prevailing black-green gloom.

Madame Calderón tells us that this particular tract of forest had been a favourite haunt of the *banditti* who plagued the country from early on in its history. They were at their worst immediately after independence and remained a public danger until the rise of Díaz in 1876. Lyon, a young Englishman with mining interests in Mexico, reports that, while travelling by coach in 1826 from San Luis Potosí to Zacatecas, a distance of forty miles, they passed no fewer than fifteen crosses 'set up by the roadside, to mark the spot where an assassination had been committed'.[1] Admittedly Lyon was in the middle of the silver country, where robberies would have been more frequent than in most places; but there were incidents enough throughout the country to make travelling a highly hazardous undertaking. Crime, in general, seems to have been treated with indulgence: murderers were confined for only a few days and then set at liberty 'to commit further enormities'. Madame

[1] *Journal of a Residence and Tour in the Republic of Mexico.*

Calderón writing from Mexico City reports, not without certain trepidation one feels, 'that men and women could stab each other with impunity'. Another witness testifies to being lassoed and corded like a package by ruffians. 'This system of lassoing in the public streets of the capital is still pursued; although the authorities pretend to prohibit riding on horseback at night.'[1] A highwayman convicted of murder, if not hanged outright, would be imprisoned for a year or two in Vera Cruz. True, he only stood a fifty per cent chance of living out a sentence there, but this was the hand of God rather than of man.

Eventually the pines thin out and we start, at last, our descent, negotiating a series of sharp bends to reach a cleft in the great heights from which one can look down upon the celebrated valley. It is an extraordinary sight. Cortés, in his march from the Gulf, approached the city over a high saddle between the snow-capped volcanoes of Popocatepetl and Iztaccihuatl. From where I stood, some twenty-five miles due north, I could see exactly where he must have appeared. It was November and snowing when he wound down out of the pass and a cold wind moaned in the pines. I stood higher and closer to the city than Cortés had been but not as high as Ordaz, one of Cortés' officers who had actually ascended Popocatepetl. 'We asked him what he had seen,' writes Fray Aguilar, and in his excitement, Ordaz could hardly phrase his words. He had been vouchsafed a glimpse of another world whose magnitude struck terror into his heart, 'a world of large cities, of towers, and a sea and in the sea a very large city'. Díaz, when writing his memoirs many years later, recalled it vividly. 'It is impossible to speak coolly . . .' He remembers long causeways joining the city to the land. He is amazed at the architecture 'all in massive stone'. This tough old veteran marvelled at the buildings 'that resemble fairy castles'. Like Ordaz, his pen fails him and he takes refuge in adjectives – 'magnificent', 'splendid'. It must have been an extraordinary sight and indeed, still is, for although the years have brought about many changes, they have failed to dim the magic.

As luck would have it, my arrival in Mexico City coincided with the opening of the recently constructed Museum of Modern Art which was being inaugurated with an exhibition of paintings by José Maria Velasco,[2] a Creole landscape painter. His generous canvases show dramatic views of the countryside and amongst them are many of the

---

[1] R. H. Mason, *Picture of Life in Mexico*, London, 1851.

[2] Velasco is known as the father of Mexican landscape. He painted roughly between 1860 and 1912, and was the pupil of an Italian, Eugenio Landesio. Four other men painted landscapes in Mexico: Conrad Wise Chapman, an American contemporary of Landesio; Daniel Thomas Egerton, an Englishman; a French diplomat called Baron Jean Baptiste de Gros; and Johann Regendas, who was a companion of Humboldt. Velasco's paintings are far superior to the others in quality.

Valley of Mexico City. One large canvas of the Valley dated 1877 struck me in particular, for although its view is from the opposite side to where I had been standing, it gives very much the impression I myself had of the Valley when first I came upon it from the hills. The city is barely visible, faintly suggested by a tracery of vertical lines in the distance. Away to the left are the two volcanoes. Below them, a dark line of hills is reflected in the waters of a lake, or perhaps it is a mirage, a shimmering of heat thrown up by the great salt flats, all that now remains of Cortés' two lakes 'which nearly fill the whole valley'. In his day there would also have been dense forests, but nothing of this remains either. Even Díaz, during his lifetime, wrote that 'the whole face of the country is completely changed. One would scarcely believe that waves had ever rolled over the spot where now grow fields of fertile maize.' The forests were cut down when the Spaniards rebuilt Tenochtitlán and the lakes were gradually siphoned off by an elaborate programme of draining. Perhaps, when there are heavy rains, the waters return, a ghost-like tracery of the watery world known to the Aztecs. The lakes, though much diminished, were still in existence, however, when Empress Carlota arrived in 1864. She drove in from Puebla and Cholula, a little to the east of the route Cortés took, and saw '*haciendas* with alleys and gardens and lakes gleaming in the distance'. She was reminded of Lombardy and was surprised by the number of poplars. These slender trees with their trembling leaves still exist, but now for the most part only in the floating gardens at Xochimilco. Countess Kollonitz, accompanying the Empress, speaks of 'the verdant plain broken by single hills, rising like mole-heaps'.[1] Indeed they can be seen in Velasco's painting. But this transformation, the gradual change that came over the land and the rebuilding of the city will be dealt with later. This is the moment for first impressions and it is difficult for me to supplement those recorded by earlier travellers, for I saw with eyes only too willing to take in more than was actually there.

[1] *The Court of Mexico.*

4

Mexico City, First Impressions

Mexico City, like the climate of the country, presents itself in layers. Because the Spanish pursued a policy of total destruction – a policy not unusual at the time – there are few tangible remains of the pre-Columbian era. Yet, despite the Spanish holocaust, it is surprising how obstinately the legend of Tenochtitlán lives on, invisible, but in some strange way always present and asserting itself. The presidential palace, once the palace of the viceroys, is still, in memory, Montezuma's glittering mansion 'wrought of jasper with veins of red', its cedar roofs 'curiously carved'. There were courts, fountains and baths and some twenty gates; a palace so dazzling that Cortés dared write to his king 'there is nothing to equal it in Spain'. The cathedral also has its ghosts. The stones used in its building once formed part of the great *teocalli*, or temple, and constantly one's thoughts wander back to Huitzilopochtli, that fearful god of war who was once enshrined high up in the temple, nearly as high up as the cupola topping the cathedral's dome. Cortés, with the Prince of Texococan, an Indian ally, headed the assault against the great temple. When they gained the upper sanctuary Cortés ripped off the jewelled mask covering the idol's face while the Prince struck off its head with one blow of his sword. In 1887 Ober reported that the great image had been unearthed in the Plaza Major, or Cathedral Square, in 1790, 'and then again interred for fear that he might tempt the Indians to their ancient worship'.[1] But Ober must have been confused, for no representation of the god of war has come down to us. It was the frightening *Coatlícue*, the Lady with the Serpent Skirt, the earth goddess, that was exhumed and not Huitzilopochtli.[2] As mentioned in the previous chapter, Huitzilopochtli was modelled from perishable material and thus the idol could be decapitated, an impossible feat had the war god been carved in stone.

[1] *Travels in Mexico.*
[2] *Coatlícue* was eventually re-excavated in 1821 and now stands in Mexico's Museo Nacional de Antropología.

11 The Condes de Santiago de Calimaya's house, now the City of Mexico Museum (page 41)

12 'What impressed me most was the grandeur of the former private houses' (page 41)

13 'I admired their balustrades and gates all of Biscay iron ornamented with bronze' (page 41)

14, 15 Marqués del Jaral de Berrio's house built by the Creole architect Francisco Guerrero y Torres (page 41). (below) Detail. The House of Tiles (page 42)

16 Manuel Tolsá by Rafael Jimeno y Planes (page 44)

17 *The College of Mines from a nineteenth century painting. Artist unknown* (*page 44*)

18 '*shafts of golden sunlight slanting between clusters of Ionic columns make a striking impression.*' (*page 44*)

19 *Tolsá's equestrian statue of Charles IV 'the first important statue in bronze to be cast in the Western Hemisphere'* (page 45)

20 *'When first commissioned by the Viceroy, Tolsá's equestrian statue of Charles IV was placed, very properly, on a high plinth in the middle of the Plaza Major'* (page 45)

21 *Escuela Nacional de Bellas Artes. The foundation's collection of plaster casts cost
Charles III over ten thousand pounds (page 43)*

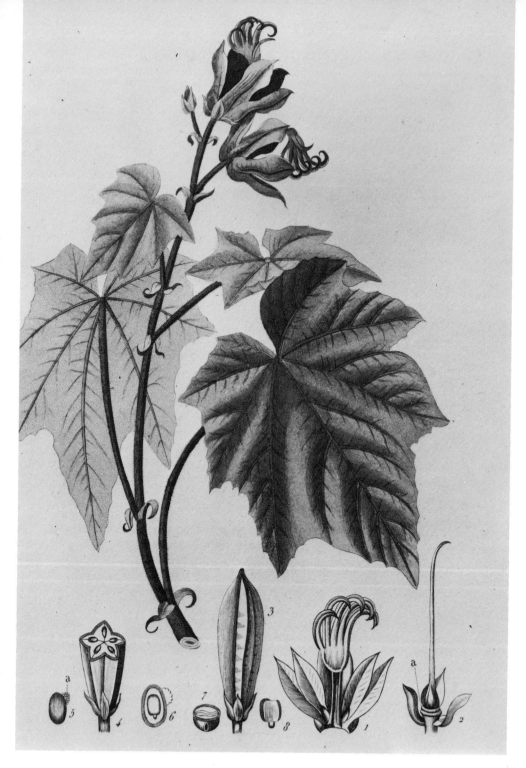

22 *Cheirostemon platanoides* or 'tree of little hands' (*page* 47)

For the first few days I found it hard to settle down. Having studied for my visit in advance, I knew more or less what to expect, but as always in such cases, there was an adjustment to be made between my preconceived ideas and what I actually found. Much of my briefing had depended on old engravings and lithographs of buildings and of places that, though still existing, had undergone drastic changes and many additions.

Walking back across the Alameda to my hotel I remembered Madame Calderón's description of these famous gardens, 'so pretty and shady . . . but no one walks in them, only foreigners'. Now the largest trees are dying and the brown-tiled paths are one continuous stream of people; the lawns, if one can call them that, are much in demand during the lunch hour. Framing the Alameda to the east is the unfortunate Palacio de Bellas Artes, a massive edifice of white marble with yellow domes built by Porfirio Díaz to celebrate the centenary of Mexico's Independence. The city's subsoil, once the bottom of a lake, is so spongy that few buildings of any size have kept their original levels. The Palacio has already sunk a good five feet. Fluid cement by the barrel-load has been pumped into its foundations, but all to no effect – it still continues to lurch and, as Mrs Bedford writes, 'there are still some three hundred feet to sink'.[1]

On a par with the Bellas Artes is the over-elaborate Juárez monument, which, considering his background, is rather a poor joke. Here is Juárez, Mexico's national hero, a full-blooded Zapotec Indian, a New World peasant, who harboured deep-rooted prejudices against all foreign influences and who was openly antagonistic to the Church, enshrined with lions crouching at his feet amidst Doric columns in the company of winged angels. It would be hard to imagine a more inappropriate tribute. Far more interesting are the rooms occupied by Juarez in the Palacio Nacional during his presidency. They have remained exactly as they were the night he died of apoplexy in 1872: small and dark, papered in bottle-green and curtained in wine-red velvet. Dark, elaborately carved furniture only increases the gloom. One wonders why, with the whole palace at his disposal, he chose these particular rooms.

Photographs of him help one to understand: they show a little man, neatly dressed in black with a stern face, an unsmiling mouth and forceful, heavily lidded eyes – the true son of his mother, Doña Josefa Juárez, who, in another daguerreotype taken when she must have been well on into her seventies, is seen to have been an old Indian woman with snow white hair. The President was of the humblest origins, born and brought up in an *adobe* hut and thus quite obviously more at home

[1] Sybille Bedford, *A Visit to Don Otavio*, Collins, London, 1960.

in these cramped quarters, with their brass beds and porcelain cuspidors, than in the viceroy's state apartments.

Conspicuously absent among all these memorials of Mexico's past is any monument to Cortés. No town, village or even street bears his name. A grudging tablet has been recently unveiled behind the Hospital of Jesús Nazareno, which he founded, but this only commemorates the approximate position of his first meeting with Montezuma, when the emperor was carried out in his litter to salute the Spanish advancing along one of the causeways. No word in the inscription mentions that Cortés lies buried in the hospital's church, not a stone's throw away. One guide-book printed in 1964 goes so far as to say that there is nothing of particular interest in the church, other than the sacristy ceiling. Even Terry, usually so well informed, wrote in 1935 that 'it is generally believed that his relics now lie in the family vault of the Duke of Terranova at Palermo, albeit some persons insist that they are still in Mexico, hidden in some place unknown to the people'.[1] Had I not been fortunate in my friends, I would never have found the great man's resting place, which lies in the thickness of the wall to the left of the altar, and unless pointed out passes completely unnoticed.

The history of Cortés' remains is a complicated one. He died in 1547 near Seville, at the age of sixty-two, on his way back to Mexico, and was first buried in the family vault of the Duke of Medina Sidonia. Fifteen years later, Don Martín, his eldest son, fulfilling the terms of his father's will, removed the body to New Spain and buried it not, as directed, in Coyoacán, but in the monastery of San Francisco in Tezucuco, then a small town on the shores of one of the three lakes encircling Mexico City. Some sixty years later Cortés was given yet another funeral and moved to the church of San Francisco in the capital itself. The ceremony was intended as a tribute, conducted in great pomp by the archbishop and attended by all the dignitaries who followed the cortège 'to the sound of mournful music and the slow beat of the muffled drum'. The next move, in 1794, is not easily explained, unless the church's foundations slipped, for, as Gage wrote, 'the ground in the city was so soggy that to be buried was to be drowned'. Whatever the reason, the mouldering relics were transported to the hospital chapel where they now lie, and deposited in a crystal coffin bound in silver and surmounted by a bronze bust by Tolsá. For twenty-nine years the curious were allowed to peer at the remains but in 1823, with the rise of the Mexican Republic, they were again moved, this time surreptitiously at night to forestall the extremist zeal of some patriots who planned to desecrate 'the tyrant's' remains. The historian Lucas

[1] A newer edition of the guide, out of print and unavailable to me, may possibly correct this information.

Alaman anticipated the deed and took it upon himself to hide the relics, immuring them in the thickness of the chapel wall. For years their whereabouts remained a closely guarded secret and it was only in 1946 that their hiding place was finally divulged. I spoke to one of those present when the wall was reopened. Within two metal caskets, one inside another, the bones reposed in a glass urn wrapped in a cloth with Cortés' arms embroidered in red silk. Before the caskets were replaced, a doctor inspected the bones and declared them to be those of a very small man with a little head. One of the limbs had an old fracture. There seems to have been no doubt of their authenticity. Only twelve people in all took part; Mass was said but there was no official ceremony. Those present subscribed to the modest plaque one now sees: anything more elaborate was judged unwise.

Gradually, piece by piece, I plotted out the city. I had various maps pinned up on the sitting-room walls of the little hotel in which I was staying and on these I would mark my progress. Slowly, as the days passed, I lost the frenzied feeling that things were escaping me. With familiarity came calm. The different churches were no longer just an intimidating jumble of saints' names. Many streets had changed names and some of the churches or monasteries no longer existed. The Spanish *convento*, from the Latin *convenire*, to come together, also presented a problem. We use the word incorrectly, solely to imply a religious establishment for women. The Spaniards, and now the Mexicans, use it more accurately to signify both monastery and convent. No distinction is made between the two, which can sometimes be muddling.

To photograph buildings and architectural details took patience. It is wearying to have to dodge hoardings and telegraph poles. The clutter of our modern civilization is at its worst in the Latin American countries where technology has not yet caught up with the requirements of modern living. Pipes are everywhere and wires seem to collect in dense tangles just where one does not want them to be.

There are, happily, constant surprises. Perhaps what unexpectedly impressed me most was the grandeur of the former private houses, many with magnificent stair halls and ample interior patios. Like Humboldt, I admired their balustrades and gates 'all of Biscay iron ornamented with bronze'. A particularly fine example is the Condes de Santiago de Calimaya's house built by a cousin of Cortés but completely remodelled during the eighteenth century. Another is commonly known as the Iturbide Palace, so called because Iturbide, the first emperor of Mexico, lived there from 1821 to 1823 after the War of Independence. Built for the Marqués del Jaral de Berrio during the first half of the eighteenth century by the Creole architect Francisco Guerrero y Torres, the same architect who also designed the house of the Condesa San Mateo

Valparaíso, now the National Bank of Mexico, as well as the enchanting *Capilla del Pocito*, or Chapel of the Well, the Iturbide Palace is one of the best preserved Baroque mansions in the city. For many years it was a hotel, one that Ober in 1887 described as being grand and gloomy, with dirty manservants and chambermaids. It did, however, have the reputation of serving very good drinks at the bar.

Of all the houses my favourite is the Casa del Condes del Valle de Orizaba, better known as the 'House of Tiles'. It is entirely glazed over with an arabesque of blue and white *azulejos* from Puebla – a tiled palace, writes Obregón, 'as blue as the blood that once ran in the veins of its old occupants'.[1]

There is so much to be seen in Mexico City but little of it is where you expect to find it, for the Ministry of Fine Arts has been indulging recently in a major reshuffle. Now paintings of the Mexican school, once exhibited in the eighteenth-century Academy of San Carlos, are found in the Pinacoteca Virrenal, a remodelled church. The nation's remarkable collection of archaeological remains is now dramatically housed in a new museum at Chapultepec. These changes, admittedly, are generally for the better, but nevertheless disconcerting, especially for someone like myself who had gathered much of his information from long defunct sources. It took me a whole day to locate the choir-stalls commissioned for the San Agustín Church. Considered the finest wood carving in Mexico, they were executed during the early years of the eighteenth century by Salvador de Ocampo, an Indian sculptor. I eventually found them lining the council hall of Mexico's leading preparatory school, the former Jesuit College of San Ildefonso, where they make a magnificent room.

I do not complain of these moves for I doubt whether I should, for instance, have visited San Agustín had I known that Ocampo's stalls were no longer there. This church is now the National Library. Its airy proportions and its walls lined with vellum-bound books are a splendid sight. The sun pours through octagonal, clerestory windows, flooding the great vaults and striping the length of the nave crowded with black-haired students. But what really impressed me was the angle at which the building leaned; the whole imposing structure has lurched a good eight feet into the mud. Finding one's way to the head librarian's desk in the apse was like walking the deck of a ship badly listing in a storm.

The Academy of San Carlos, or more precisely, the *Escuela Nacional de Bellas Artes*, is well worth a visit. For despite the fact that it has lost its prize exhibits, the paintings of the Mexican school, the place itself is full of interest, as were its first two directors: the talented Valencian painter Rafael Jimeno y Planes and his successor, the sculptor and architect

[1] Don Luis Gonzales Obregón, *The Streets of Mexico*, George Fields, San Francisco, 1937.

Manuel Tolsá. Tolsá was director at the time of Humboldt's visit to the
Academy, when the enthusiastic young German described a large well-
lighted room, attended every evening by hundreds of young people:
'some draw from relievo or living models, while others copy drawings of
furniture, chandeliers or other ornaments in bronze'. There were no
class distinctions, 'Indians and mestizos sit happily alongside the
children of the great lords of the country . . . some of the most promising
pupils were found amongst the least civilized of the Indian population.
They seemed to draw by instinct and to copy whatever was put before
them with utmost facility.' Humboldt does not tell us, however, that
they had no powers of concentration and disappeared after a few lessons.
Of interest also is the foundation's collection of plaster casts, 'a collection
more complete than any to be found in Germany' and one that cost
Charles III over £10,000.

Although the Academy was eclipsed during the Revolution, it somehow managed to weather the storm and even seems to have benefited
from the political unrest. It was noticed, when things had quietened
down, that quite a few paintings mysteriously missing from people's
houses, from cathedrals and small parochial churches, had found their
way to San Carlos and were hanging in its galleries. One can only
suppose that the members of the staff, when there were no pupils to
occupy them, had indulged in a little judicious looting. While these
light-fingered gentlemen fared admirably in choosing Mexican painters,
they did less well in selecting European masters. It is unfortunate for the
Academy that the latter have been allowed to remain. The collection
today is a galaxy of illustrious artists' names, but hardly one of the
bituminous daubs bears any relation to the names attached to it. Not
even the Zurbaráns are real and one cannot help wondering if the
'silver kings' and high ranking ecclesiastics who originally owned the
paintings were really so completely lacking in discrimination. Much of
their buying must have been done through agents, some of whom were
certainly unscrupulous, but this I feel is not entirely the answer. Independence had spelt financial ruin for certain collectors, the best of
whose paintings undoubtedly found their way back to the salerooms of
Europe. Santa Anna is known to have sold some Murillos to procure
funds for his war with the United States and, according to Terry,
Napoleon III's troops under Marshal Bazaine swept Mexico clean of
every picture they could lay their hands on. There is also the sad story
of the paintings in the Santa Domingo Convent at Oaxaca which were
destroyed for the sake of the canvas, 'the soldiers soaking them in water
and beating the paint off against the stones'.[1]

But to return to Tolsá, the second director of the Academy: Planes'

[1] *Terry's Guide to Mexico.*

portrait of him is so intriguing that one wants to know more about him. Tolsá is shown by his predecessor as a handsome man in his middle thirties, fashionably dressed in a gold-brown suit edged with embroidery that might have been traced by the Adam brothers. He has a strong chin, a sensitive mouth and a far-away, dreamy look in his eyes. Crossed legs and a red cloak thrown carelessly over the back of the chair speak of a certain elegance. His left arm rests on a bust of Socrates and in his left hand he holds a chisel, certainly two allusions to his art. On the whole, one would judge him from his portrait to have been a man of considerable charm, if somewhat obstinate, but never the fanatic that, in the final analysis, he turned out to be. 'A presumptive, blatant egotist' one critic called him and I am afraid, despite his talents and his looks, this censure stands.

During his term as director of the Academy, Tolsá was appointed *maestro mayor* of the cathedral where he was responsible for the forty-five-foot lantern crowning the dome as well as the balustrades, urns and finials that lend a certain grace to the otherwise plain cupola. His also is the immense classic College of Mines with its interior staircase of converging ramps, a building that Kubler describes as 'the most grandiose colonial structure of its kind in America'.[1] Tolsá was an indefatigable worker, producing during the sixteen years he spent in Mexico after his arrival in 1791 a quantity of buildings and one important piece of sculpture. Why, then, was he so severely criticized? Along with Ortiz de Castro, a Creole born in Vera Cruz State, Tolsá was the New World's first exponent of neo-classicism. Trained in that cold classical correctness at the Academy in Valencia, he was incapable of appreciating the taste of the previous generation for the gilded exoticism of the Mexican Churrigueresque, whose exuberance far outran the prototypes from the mother country. If only Tolsá had been content to ignore what he disliked, but no, he set about attacking this architecture with fanatical rage. In church after church, even in the cathedral itself, Churrigueresque *retablos* (the screens behind the altars) were ripped out and treated like so much kindling wood. To make matters worse, these gilded flights of fancy were replaced by lifeless compositions in cold grey marble flanked by naked columns; forlorn structures that Sanford describes as ill fitting and affected.[2] But some credit is due to Tolsá for his College of Mines. The first view of the central courtyard with its double stairs and shafts of golden sunlight slanting between clusters of Ionic columns makes a striking impression. The scale is unexpected,

---

[1] George Kubler and Martin Soria, *Art and Architecture in Spain and Portugal and their American Dominions, 1500 to 1800*, The Pelican History of Art, Penguin Books, London, 1959.
[2] Trent Elwood Sanford, *The Story of Architecture in Mexico*, W. W. Norton & Co., New York, 1947.

but this too was criticized. The College was finished in 1797, but as early as 1827 Ward complained of radical defects in the foundations that were causing the whole structure to fall into ruin. Supposedly the piles upon which the foundations were laid were not driven to the depth specified in the contract. 'It is quite melancholy to see magnificent rows of columns, windows and doors completely out of perpendicular, with walls and stairs cracking in every direction.'[1] Fortunes have been spent in keeping the building from tumbling down, and though in a better condition than when Ward saw it, the College is still far from secure. Viewed from the exterior, the sagging is already very marked; from the inside, it is positively alarming. Many of the ground floor doors and windows have subsided so much that there is hardly space between lintel and paving for a cat to crawl through.

It is only when judged as a sculptor that Tolsá atones, as it were, for the enormities he perpetrated in some of the churches. His spirited equestrian statue of Charles IV, the last Spanish king to rule over the Colonies, is very splendid, being the first important statue cast in bronze in the Western Hemisphere. Humboldt thought the monument second only to the Marcus Aurelius in Rome. Like so much in the city, the statue has suffered a number of moves, almost as many as the relics of Cortés. Originally it was placed, very properly, on a high plinth in the middle of the Plaza Major, or *Zócalo*, facing the palace. Lines inlaid in the pavement led one's eyes to the statue which Tolsá encircled with a stone balustrade interrupted at the cardinal points of the compass by gilded-bronze gates capped with crowns, laurels and palms. The whole composition was eminently satisfactory and the Plaza had never looked so well. Everyone was happy, including the King who, garbed as a Roman emperor, even managed to look noble, not an easy effect to produce in the case of Charles IV who was 'sluggish and stupid to the verge of imbecility'.[2]

The statue took over a year to cast, during which time a gilded wooden model was used as a substitute. The official unveiling occurred in December 1803, only five years before Charles IV abdicated in favour of his son Ferdinand VII, who, in turn, was forced to step aside for Joseph Bonaparte. During Mexico's subsequent struggle for independence Tolsá's work disappeared from view. It was not actually moved, but hidden under a high wooden globe washed a dark navy-blue. Feelings against Spain ran so high, however, that eventually it was thought wiser to remove the statue altogether. Accordingly it was stowed away in the courtyard of the Academy where it remained half-forgotten for thirty years. Not until 1852 was it set up again at the head

[1] *Mexico in 1827.*
[2] *The Cambridge Modern History*, Cambridge University Press, 1907.

of the *Paseo de la Reforma* where it joins the *Avenida Juárez*. The statue is now called *El Caballito*, the little horse, but no mention is made of the rider's identity.[1]

The day to day life of the city no longer centres around the *Zócalo*, having moved westwards towards the *Paseo* where buildings rise vertically, bright and shining, into the sky. In the old days the spongy subsoil obliged Mexico City to spread horizontally, but now, owing to modern techniques, it can grow in any direction. Thus everywhere skyscrapers break the flatness of the roof line. People in smart clothes and sleek cars prefer the new quarter, yet in a strange way the real heart of the city still remains the *Zócalo*. It was the centre under the Aztecs and the Spaniards, and regardless of the changes, it continues to be in spirit. It is bare and treeless, having for the major part of the year the appearance of a vast, deserted parade ground. Melancholia seizes one if left alone in its glaring emptiness. There is even a note of squalor, hard to define, but nevertheless there. It is, for all this, very splendid.

As we have seen, the *Zócalo* did not always present so bald an aspect. During the seventeenth century markets were held there. Cows were milked on its cobbles. There was even a slaughter house, a public latrine and a gibbet, encumbrances effectively swept away by the energetic Conde de Revillagigedo, Mexico's fifty-second viceroy. Under the Emperor Maximilian the square was filled with trees, but as trees interfered with the aim of the revolutionaries bombarding the National Palace, these too were cleared away. One definite advantage of the present bleakness is the magnificent view it allows of the various buildings: the cathedral, the palace and the national pawnshop, where Cortés lived before moving to what is now the palace.

After Cortés left his first residence on the square it was occupied for a short while by the viceroys and later used by the *Audiencia* as an official residence for its judges. In 1775 it was acquired by the fabulously rich Conde de Regla, owner of the famous Real del Monte silver mines, in order to establish a pawnshop, the *Monte de Piedad*. The restrained Baroque exterior was left more or less as we see it today, but the interior was completely gutted to accommodate offices and auction rooms. Subsequent 'improvements' have further defaced the interior.

Municipal pawnbroking, run on a non-profit basis, was a widespread institution in the eighteenth century. Those in need could exchange personal property for cash advanced at a low rate of interest. Articles so pledged and not redeemed were eventually auctioned and the proceeds applied to charitable purposes. This anyhow was the theory, but judging

[1] It is interesting to see that Tolsá's ornamental balustrades have not been wasted but now run, in a rather pointless fashion, under the great trees shading the *Paseo*.

from the sales catalogues, it was not only the poor who had recourse to the *Monte de Piedad*. Scanning these lists one finds a plethora of saddles and swords, of rich garments and gold ornaments, even of diamonds and pearls. A story is told of an Englishman who was held up one day in broad daylight by two brigands who divested him of his cloak. His cloak gone, the man naturally thought that the robbers had finished with him and made to leave. The vagabonds gestured to him, however, to stay. 'Have patience,' they said, 'and you will find the result more agreeable than you expected.' One of the vagabonds departed, returned in a short while and, politely bowing, handed the Englishman a pawn-broker's ticket. 'We wanted thirty *pesos*, not the cloak,' said the villain. 'Here is a ticket with which to redeem it; and as the cloak of such a *caballero* is unquestionably worth at least one hundred *pesos*, you may consider yourself as having made seventy by the transaction. Vaya con Dios!'

The Viceroy's Palace, now the *Palacio Nacional*, extends along the entire east side of the *Zócalo* and is likewise much changed. The scant ornamentation that relieves its monotonous, seven-hundred-foot long façade is concentrated around the three entrances. The building bears little resemblance to the fortress-like house erected by Cortés on the site of Montezuma's imperial palace. Early engravings show that the original building was a square divided into four equal courtyards, with small towers at the corners and with loopholes at regular intervals in the walls. The second storey was more or less as one sees it today with dozens of windows and a continuous row of balconies. Above the central door rose a curvetting cornice carrying the king's coat-of-arms. During the riots of 1692 the palace was severely damaged by fire and subsequently entirely replanned. It now rambles around a dozen or more patios, added as occasion dictated. The whole third storey is a recent addition dating from 1927.

My interest in the palace was largely horticultural. Both Ward and Ober visited a botanical garden hidden away in one of the courtyards where one tree in particular, the *árbol des los manitos*, or tree of little hands, struck them both as being very curious. Native to Mexico, it was practically extinct when Ward wrote, there being only three known specimens, two in the palace garden and the mother plant in the mountains of Toluca where it was discovered. Intrigued, I made a point of finding out about the tree. *Cheirostemon platanoides*, its correct name, is tall-growing with leaves something like those of a plane. It is deciduous but flowers from November through February when the branches are bare. These brownish-red blooms with tulip-shaped calyces and brick-red stamens are the tree's remarkable feature. The five stamens join at their bases, the wrist of a claw-like hand whose fingers bend a little inward. Humming birds are said to feed on the nectar exuding from the finger tips. Helen O'Gorman notes 'that *Cheirostemon platanoides* was well known and highly venerated by the Aztecs, not only for the form of the flowers but for its tonic effect on the heart'.[1] In fact the bloody little hands are a palliative against a variety of ills. Dried they can be drunk as an infusion to calm the paroxysms of epilepsy. Used as a lotion they are good for inflammations of the eyes and also for the pains occasioned by haemorrhoids. In old codices Mrs O'Gorman found that the Aztecs mashed the bark together with datura leaves to reduce 'the swelling, burning and eruption of the genitalia'. Ober reported that Montezuma even went to war expressly to obtain the tree.

Such a plant was certainly something not to be missed, but whether I would find the tree was dubious. Already in 1827 Ward mentioned that barracks had been put up in part of the garden. Still more disquieting were stories of one presidential wife's passion for European vegetables. In order to indulge her epicurean tastes she had most of the valuable plants dug up to make room for rows of cauliflowers and spinach. Had it not been for Mrs O'Gorman's assurances that a tree still existed I would not have persevered. Alas, when finally located, the 'jardino' proved a sad disappointment: no sign of the 'hands', or for that matter, of any other botanical rarity. Quite obviously I am not alone in my curiosity, for the head gardener made it clear that he was heartily tired of having to ward off anxious inquirers.

The tree, incidentally, though rare, is not as rare as Ward would have us believe, so perhaps there is hope for the future. Several specimens have been sighted in recent years in and around Mexico City. Its red flowers may even be a not unusual sight in the mountainous country round Oaxaca where the tree originated.

From the garden, the janitor to whom I had been assigned took me to see Diego Rivera's monumental frescoes thronging the walls of the grand staircase. On our way we hurried past a modest flight of stairs which I recognized from photographs as those used by Maximilian and Carlota during their brief residence in the palace before they moved their court to Chapultepec. I remembered descriptions of their rooms, unused since the departure of the last viceroy and hurriedly refurbished for the Emperor and Empress with borrowed pieces of furniture and improvised curtains. In their sad state of dilapidation they looked like a suite in a second-rate European hotel, and even worse, were alive with vermin. The Empress wrote how they were routed out of bed their first night and were obliged to take refuge on a billiard table. But my

[1] Helen O'Gorman, *Mexican Flowering Trees and Plants*, Ammex Associates, Mexico City, 1961.

janitor-guide knew nothing of all this; either the rooms were closed or else completely transformed, in any case they were not to be visited.

We were headed for Rivera's great work, the eminent Rivera who, with Orozco and Siqueiros, led Mexico's flourishing school of fresco painting in the 1920s. Aldous Huxley found Rivera's frescoes in the palace remarkable only 'for their quantity'. 'There must be,' he writes, 'five or six acres of them.'[1] D. H. Lawrence speaking through Kate Leslie, the central figure of his novel *The Plumed Serpent*, censured Rivera's work, his hate and his strident caricatures of the Spanish:

'Oh No!' she said. 'They are too ugly. They defeat their own ends.' 'But they are meant to be ugly,' said young Garcia, the Mexican teacher showing her around. 'They must be ugly, no? Because capitalism is ugly, and mammon is ugly, and the priest holding his hand to get the money from the poor Indians is ugly. No?' He laughed rather unpleasantly. 'But,' said Kate, 'these caricatures are too intentional. They are like vulgar abuse, not art at all.'

Proof of the aptness of Lawrence's criticism is Rivera's tiresome conception of Cortés as a livid, cross-eyed hunchback. The official guide to the fresco cycle reprints an article by the artist himself in which he goes so far as to say that the Conquistador was so ugly that he never allowed himself to be painted. According to Rivera the surviving pictures of Cortés 'are slightly modified copies of paintings of Charles v'.

But if one ignores the strident class-consciousness, what remains in Rivera's frescoes is very splendid. The man knew his craft and the palace stairs glow with earthy pigments ranging from yellow to orange to vivid flame. The whites are wonderfully pure, and his palette, when cold, has the sharpness of steel – the hardness of obsidian or jade. A marked Italian influence is recognizable in Rivera's simplification of line and in his juxtaposition of colour against colour with no gradation of shade; detailed and yet at the same time broadly conceived. There are moments when Rivera comes very close to the wonderful Piero della Francescas at Arezzo.

He is at his best portraying his own people, the smooth, brown-bodied Indians. Round the corner from the stairs, down one of the corridors, are fascinating murals depicting the Aztec, Huaxtec, Tarascan, Zapotec and Totonac civilizations. Here, carefully studied, is the vanished world destroyed by the Spanish, a far more serious indictment, if one must be made, than the 'vulgar abuse' shown us on the stairs. No dropsical, grasping, pasty-faced foreigners in these panels, but proud princes in full enjoyment of their land – spacious lands of irrigated

---

[1] Aldous Huxley, *Beyond the Mexique Bay*, Chatto and Windus, London, 1934.

fields green with maize and of gridded canals tapering towards the distant, dry, flat-topped hills or towards the deep forests of the south where the Zapotecs lived. The trees in the frescoes are so tall that one only sees their limbs, huge, sinuous and cinnamon-coloured, in the full light. Within all is darkness, an inky depth wreathed in nets; elaborate snares set for the elusive Quetzal bird whose long tail-feathers were prized beyond jewels. Rivera painted the feathers for us, the palest arsenic green, nodding from elaborate head-dresses and sweeping majestically from the standard of a royal messenger.

There is a sequence of panels and one passes from province to province, all vassal states, for as Fray Durán wrote, 'the Aztecs were the lords of all creation; everything belonged to them, everything was theirs!'[1] Here are the files of porters winding over the hills laden with tribute from the hot countries: pineapples, anonas, mameys, guavas, yellow, black and white sapotas, avocados and two or three kinds of yams. Some provinces sent cloth as tribute: bundles of white and yellow cotton, mantles 'embroidered in many coloured threads and enriched with the down of ducks, all beautifully and curiously marked'. Live birds were also collected: green, red, blue parrots, large and small, splendid eagles, buzzards, hawks, sparrow hawks, ravens, herons and white geese. Fierce ocelots, jaguars and wild cats were brought in cages. Snakes, especially sacred to Quetzalcoatl, arrived curled up in baskets. 'Vassals even paid tribute in centipedes, scorpions and spiders!' Provinces unable to supply articles of commerce 'paid in maidens, girls and boys, who were divided among the lords – all slaves'.[2]

In one panel men pan a river for gold dust that was poured into lengths of transparent quill and sold in the markets. An Aztec General, recently returned from the wars, offers a lady his prize trophy: the right arm of a slain enemy lord. Rivera, carried away by his subject, forgets to preach his usual proletarian nonsense, and revels instead in the sophisticated details of a highly privileged world. A high-ranking Aztec official with pointed, lacquered nails appears in a silver mask, while in the background is a rich merchant sunk in the depths of his litter borne over the heads of the crowd. Slaves shield him from the sun with great circular lemon-coloured fans, or is it perhaps the gaze of the vulgar he wishes to avoid?

Rivera's scenes depicting the Conquest cover the lower section of the principal mural on the great stairs. It is a harassing tale of a half war, waged to stave off what the Aztecs believed already to be their inevitable end predicted in their sacred books. Strategically at a disadvantage, and further handicapped by superstition, they were vanquished before

[1] *History of The Indies of New Spain.*
[2] *Ibid.*

the battle even began. The struggle lasted two years. The Aztecs and their allies died by the thousands while the Spaniards lost but a handful of men in comparison. On the stairs of the palace one looks down on the holocaust, a pathetic mêlée of crushed feathers and skins.

An eyewitness wrote that to see the proud jaguar-knights and eagle-knights in their battle array, young, handsome and walking in perfect formation was one of the most beautiful sights in the world. 'Their suits are all of one piece and of heavy cloth . . . covered with feathers of different colours. One company of soldiers will wear them in red and white, another in blue and yellow . . .' The lords wore smock-like coats 'which among us are of mail, but these are of gold or gilt silver'. Helmets were 'heads of serpents, or tigers, lions or wolves and the man's head lies inside the animal's jaws as though it were devouring him'.[1]

But the fierce, beaked masks and the horrifying yells were but so much bluff, utterly ineffective once the Spaniards had recovered from their initial shock. The proud knights were just stuffed nursery toys when measured against foreigners armed to the teeth in mail. What good were fishbone spearheads, and wooden swords edged with obsidian, or reed shields covered with feathers when matched against biting steel? Their quilted armour was like down when exposed to the Spanish artillery. Furthermore, they were completely bewildered by the silence in which their enemy fought. The Indians' attitude towards battle was diametrically opposed to that of the Spaniards. The aim of the Aztec soldier was to capture his opponent alive so that later he could be offered up in sacrifice. This necessarily put the Indian warrior at a terrific disadvantage.

[1] *The Chronicle of the Anonymous Conquistador*, translated by Patricia de Fuentes. Extract from *The Conquistadors*, Cassell, London, 1964.

5

The Past

The Spanish chroniclers have left us vivid descriptions of all that concerns the Conquest. However, they were at a disadvantage in accurately describing the earlier history of the people their countrymen vanquished, because records prior to the Conquest were kept only in a primitive hieroglyphic writing on deerskin vellum or on cactus paper. Such pages, folded together, did not form books as we conceive of them but were a kind of 'aide-mémoire'. Ignacio Bernal, director of Mexico's new Anthropological Museum, explains that these codices were 'essentially only lists of events which certain well trained individuals were taught how to "read" out loud'. Details impossible to convey in picture writing were supplied by a commentator who had learned his text by heart. As can be imagined, this mixture of written and oral history preserved much that must be regarded mainly as mythology.

After the Conquest several missionaries wrote about the Indians' history: the Franciscan Toribio de Benavente, better known as Father Motolinía;[1] the Jesuit Juan de Tovar; the scholarly Franciscan Bernardino de Sahagún; and finally the Dominican Diego Durán. Durán was born in Seville in 1537 but was brought up in Mexico. He spoke Nahuatl fluently and made a great effort, as witnessed in his *Historia*, to understand the Indian point of view. Bernal said of him, 'though he writes in Spanish, he seems to be thinking in Nahuatl'. It is thus to Durán that we must turn for much of our information about the indigenous culture.

The Indian civilization was born among those wandering tribes 'from strange and remote regions' that had gradually settled the Mexican central plateau. Their legends 'show that they themselves are ignorant of their origins or beginnings'. The Aztecs, pre-eminent among the New

[1] Benavente was among the first missionaries to arrive in New Spain. Landing at Vera Cruz in 1524, Benavente with other Franciscan Fathers walked barefoot to the approaches of Mexico City where they were met by Cortés. The Indians were impressed by their poverty-stricken appearance and kept repeating *moto linia*, meaning so poor, so poor Benavente adopted the epithet as a name.

World nations at the time of the Conquest, had the most accurate knowledge of their past, but even this did not date back much further than the thirteenth century.

'Aztec' means 'people of Aztlan', that is 'people of the land of the heron', the location of which is lost in garbled legend.[1] The Aztecs were the last of the tribes to reach the valley, appearing in small groups from the north-west sometime during the thirteenth century. Not powerful enough to impose themselves, they had been pushed into the swamps on the shores of the principal lake, reedy quarters despised by the other inhabitants of the valley. Thus isolated and concentrated, they eventually emerged as a formidable military power, the terror of all around them.

The founding of their capital Tenochtitlán, later Mexico City, in 1325 on a deserted island in the middle of a lake was obviously dictated by the need for security, but the later legends of the proud Aztecs ascribed the choice of the site to divine intervention. The god Huitzilopochtli came to the priest-king in a dream, so says the legend, and spoke to him of an island and of a cactus tree there 'so wonderously tall that it bears the nest of an eagle'. Searching for the omen, the king immediately found 'a huge cactus and on which stood the eagle with his wings stretched out towards the rays of the sun'. Here, at Tenochtitlán, the 'place near the prickly pear', the wandering Aztecs were to settle and prosper.

The city began as a small island surrounded by a collection of wattle rafts spread over with mud scooped up from the lake, floating gardens on which the Aztecs lived in rush huts. The lake was so shallow that trees planted on the rafts soon took root, anchoring the islands to the bottom as they grew. Further islands were added as the need for living space increased. 'There now followed,' writes S. K. Lothrop, the distinguished American archaeologist, 'a series of wars, at first with the Aztecs as minor allies of more powerful neighbours. From these wars there emerged a confederacy of three cities which later dominated and held tributary most of central and southern Mexico. At first the three partners, Tenochtitlán, Texcoco and Tlacopan, were of equal rank,' he continues, but very soon Tenochtitlán took the lead and 'Aztec leadership was unchallenged by the time the Spaniards arrived'.[2] In less than two hundred years Tenochtitlán had grown from a rush hamlet into a vast complex of stone, an urban area with over a million inhabitants. Imperial Rome was scarcely any larger. It really was a most remarkable

---

[1] All authorities seem to agree that the American Indians are originally of Asian extraction, having emigrated in neolithic times from north-east Asia by way of Bering Strait. One source claims that Aztlan is Vancouver Island on the North American coast.

[2] *Treasures of Ancient America.*

achievement. The city is supposed to have numbered some sixty thousand houses and 'the main temple alone was as large as a city, surrounded by a high wall with four main entrances. At each entrance was a building like a fortress.'[1] Aldous Huxley compared the great temple with Pisa. 'The Aztecs had the wit to leave a wide open space all round the monument. One could see the great *teocalli* as an architectural whole, just as (and the case is almost unique in Europe) one can see the Leaning Tower, Cathedral and Baptistry of Pisa.'[2]

Early maps show how the city was joined to the mainland by a series of causeways, the longest nearly five miles in length. Their breadth, as measured by the Spaniards, was the width of eight horses ridden abreast. The city proper had three main streets and was criss-crossed with waterways bordered by sidewalks. 'Houses belonging to the lords,' writes the Anonymous Conquistador, 'had lofty rooms and roof top terraces.' Some had gardens planted with flowering shrubs. Four times the Conquistador made the rounds of Montezuma's palace 'and each time I walked so much that I became tired'. He never saw all of it. Large halls opened off the central courtyard, 'one large enough to hold three thousand people comfortably'. On the roof of the upper gallery thirty men on horseback could play *canas*, a game in which the players, armed with leather shields, threw spears at one another.

More details about the palace are provided by Francisco de Aguilar, one of Cortés' companions-at-arms, who wrote:

there were many rooms, chambers and antechambers and fine halls. There were canopied beds with mattresses made of large mantles, and pillows of leather and kapok; good quilts and admirable white fur robes; also very well-made wooden seats, and fine matting. His household service was large, befitting a great prince.[3]

Three thousand people lived in the palace, not counting the vast garrison of picked warriors who accompanied Montezuma as his personal guard. We know from both Díaz and Durán that the guards and the attendants had to be of noble birth. Díaz writes that the King 'never held any conversation unless to give them orders or to receive some intelligence from them'. Even high-ranking officials were obliged to slip off their sandals on entering his presence where they addressed their emperor as 'Lord! my Lord! sublime Lord!' Communication with him was concise, one imagines almost telegraphic in style, and on leaving his presence the visitor walked backwards out of the room, with eyes downcast. Only the emperor's immediate relatives were permitted to

[1] *The Chronicle of the Anonymous Conquistador.* Extract from *The Conquistadors.*
[2] *Beyond the Mexique Bay.*
[3] *The Chronicle of the Anonymous Conquistador.* Extract from *The Conquistadors.*

look him in the face. Durán once questioned an Indian who had served in the palace about the King's height and his general appearance. 'Father, I will not lie to you,' answered the Indian, 'or tell you about things which I do not know. I never saw his face.'

Fortunately various people's impressions of Montezuma were recorded. Díaz, who admired him and knew him fairly intimately, supposed him to be about forty, while Maurice Collis, in his book on Montezuma,[1] supposes him to have been twelve years older on the grounds that he had succeeded in 1502 and had been reigning seventeen years when the Spaniards landed. Contemporary reports, however, certainly suggest a much younger man. Díaz tells us that he was tall and thin and that the 'symmetry of his body was beautiful'. His complexion was a light honey-colour, and he had fine eyes and a rather long face dressed with a small beard. His hair was black and worn fairly short except over his ears 'which were quite hidden by it'. Aguilar found that his head was on the large size and that he had somewhat flat nostrils. He was very *soigné* in his habits and took a bath every day. Cortés tells us that he was for ever changing, 'always putting on new clothes which were never worn more than once'. Jacques Soustelle, the French pre-Columbian specialist, adds that only the emperor was allowed to wear the famous *xiuhtilmatli*, 'the turquoise cloak', whose blue-green colour was Mexico's equivalent to Rome's Imperial purple.

The emperor ate twice a day, every conceivable dish being served to him, including all kinds of game and maize bread baked with eggs, followed by fruit. To quench his thirst he was served 'frothy cocoa'. He ate alone at a low table spread with a white cloth, seated on a beautifully carved chair upholstered with cushions. Surprisingly the dishes were not gold but pottery, the variegated black and brown glazed pottery still seen in Mexican markets. If the weather was cold a large brazier of charcoal was carried in, 'a kind of charcoal made of the bark of trees, which emitted no smoke but threw out a delicious perfume'. A gold fire screen shielded the emperor from too immediate a heat, while yet another larger gilt screen was drawn forward 'so that no one might see him while eating'.

Montezuma appears to have been a fairly sober man in character. He had two lawful wives of royal extraction and a number of concubines. 'He visited them secretly without anyone daring to observe it, save his most confidential servants.' 'He was perfectly innocent,' Díaz adds, 'of any unnatural crimes.' He obviously had a very definite personality, and all those who came into close contact with him were struck by his charm. After Cortés took the Emperor prisoner, the permanent guard detailed to watch over him all grew to admire their

[1] *Cortés and Montezuma*, Faber & Faber, London, 1954.

charge. Díaz writes that in everything he did 'he showed his excellent breeding'. Always well-disposed he nevertheless maintained his dignity 'and never for an instant forgot his high station'. Aguilar remarks that he was very astute, discerning and prudent, learned and capable but also harsh and very fierce in his speech when necessary. 'If any of the soldiers, or anyone else no matter who he was, spoke loudly or disturbed him, that person was immediately sent out.' On the other hand 'he was very considerate with those of us who were respectful and took off our caps and bowed to him; he gave us presents and jewellery; and dishes of the food that he ate'. He appears to have been very generous, for Díaz says that he often gambled with Cortés 'and always divided his gains amongst us'. He was forever ordering his steward to bring in some gold trinket, 'which he gave to his guards; the value of these gifts generally amounted to some two hundred pounds'. When he died the Spaniards missed him. 'The guards, all young men, mourned him as if we had lost a parent. Even Father Olmedo, who in spite of all his efforts had failed to convert him, could not refrain from shedding tears.'

As Cortés and the men with him knew nothing of the Aztec language, their only means of communication with the Indians being through interpreters, their descriptions of Montezuma, though immediate and vivid, were somewhat superficial; the same does not apply to Durán's writings. Although born after Montezuma's death, Durán had the advantage of speaking fluent Nahuatl, and his Mexican upbringing led the Indians to consider him one of themselves; thus they confided far more in him than they would ordinarily have done to a stranger. Many of those questioned by Durán had held important posts at the time of the Conquest and from them he gathered material that, pieced together, makes strange reading. His *Historia* rings a chill note, the atmosphere is heavy with foreboding and shows Montezuma under quite a different light, as a man haunted by presentiments, a victim of his own god's dour predictions.

Before the arrival of the Aztecs, Mexico's great central plateau had been dominated by the Toltecs. Tula was their capital and Quetzalcoatl, the Feathered Serpent, one of their principal gods. Legend had it that Quetzalcoatl was opposed to human sacrifice and as a result had been banished. Travelling to the Gulf Coast he had disappeared somewhere towards the east, probably towards Yucatan, but not before foretelling his own return. The prediction of a foreign god would not have worried the Aztecs unduly had not their own great Huitzilopochtli himself confirmed the prophecy, also predicting the downfall of the Aztec nation. 'The children of the sun will come from the east. They will rise up against me, take me by the feet and cast me down.' With the 'children' would be the vengeful Quetzalcoatl. Even the date of the catastrophe was anticipated. It would occur in a 'One Reed Year' which in the Aztec calendar fell at irregular intervals: in 1363, again in 1467 and thirdly by some extraordinary stroke of fate, in 1519. When leaving, the Feathered Serpent had embarked on a magic raft, and it was supposed that he would return in some equally impressive manner. Tradition also said that Quetzalcoatl was white skinned and had a full black beard.

The years preceding the Spaniards' arrival were strangely troubled. A large comet was seen to streak across the sky and plunge suddenly over the city. Old people dreamt strange things. They saw the royal palace tumbled by a mighty river. One old man dared to tell Montezuma that 'the Lords of Sleep had shown him the temple of Huitzilopochtli burning with frightful flames. I also saw the God himself fallen, cast down by the flood!' Priests, sorcerers, soothsayers, diviners and astrologers were consulted and more often than not were jailed whatever their predictions, even if they claimed to have seen nothing. The Emperor's own sister Papantzin, 'after lying in a coma for four days, a condition that was taken for death, revived in her grave and on being carried back to the palace declared that she had seen strange beings entering the country and bringing it to ruin'.[1]

As Montezuma had served as high priest in the great temple before ascending the throne and was therefore obviously fully acquainted with the legend, there can be little doubt that Quetzalcoatl's supposed return preyed on his mind. What must his feelings have been when his spies on the coast reported 'a terrible round thing in the midst of the waters. It moved to and fro and within it there were men who appeared from time to time'. White men with black beards!

The rest of the story is history. Not only had Cortés arrived in a 'One Reed Year' but also he had actually landed at San Juan de Ulúa, or Vera Cruz, on a day predicted for Quetzalcoatl's return. And if this was not proof enough, there were pictures in the sacred books of Quetzalcoatl clothed in black. Cortés stepped ashore on 22 April, a Good Friday; he was dressed in black!

Montezuma, deeply religious, a staunch supporter of his country's beliefs, had no choice but to accept Cortés as a god. But how did one treat a divinity? Certainly one could not use force. Perhaps a little tactful dissuasion might work. Montezuma sent ambassadors loaded with gifts. Cortés and his men were more than welcome but given to understand that the journey to Tenochtitlan was long and tedious and food difficult to get. There were more gifts and more solicitous messages, the gifts increasing in value with each train load of porters. Little did Montezuma realize that the more splendorous the gifts the more certain

[1] *Cortés and Montezuma.*

he was of attracting that which he was trying at any cost to avoid. If only he had been warned, been advised to adopt a more energetic attitude, been convinced that it lay within his power to fend off the evil hour, he could easily have resisted the Spaniards. They would have returned, but possibly not during his lifetime. At least he would have lived out his reign in peace. But it was not to be.

For three months the Emperor procrastinated while Cortés, feeling his way cautiously, remained camped in the dunes. Cortés' genius lay in his ability to manipulate people, and these long weeks of waiting for an invitation from Montezuma gave him a chance to ingratiate himself with the coastal tribes tributary to the Aztecs. He worked on the smouldering resentment they bore their overlords and with diplomacy and honeyed words argued them round to his side. Together they would march on Mexico City. It was not long before Cortés had acquired a large army of Indian allies: the Totonacs from central Vera Cruz and eventually several thousand Tlaxcalans, sworn enemies of the Aztecs. An invitation was no longer necessary, and Montezuma finally had to prepare to meet with as much good grace as possible the Feathered Serpent come to depose him.

The march inland, a distance of two hundred and fifty miles, took Cortés exactly eleven weeks. He filed out of Vera Cruz on 15 August and it was already the first week in November by the time he reached Xochimilco, the first of the three lakes in the middle of which floated Tenochtitlán. The march had been through hostile country and there had been a series of pitched battles on the way.

The night of 7 November was spent at Ayotzinco, 'a little town', as Cortés described it, 'lying on the shores of a great lake, half of it being in the water'. It was here that Cortés met with Cacamatzin, the Prince of Tetzcoco, Montezuma's nephew, 'a youth of some five and twenty years to whom all showed great respect'. Díaz writes that his appearance was more splendid and magnificent than any of the chiefs they had yet met. 'He was seated in a beautiful sedan, which was decorated with silver, green feathers, and branches of gold, from which hung quantities of precious stones.' The sedan was supported on the shoulders of eight distinguished nobles. 'When the procession had arrived in front of Cortés' quarters, they assisted the prince out of the sedan, and swept clear every inch of ground before him.' Díaz and his companions were very impressed; if this was only the Emperor's nephew, 'what indeed must be the power and majesty of the mighty Montezuma himself?'

The prince had been sent to deputize for his uncle who was indisposed. The youth, Cortés writes, 'begged me to pardon their lord for not coming in person . . . his city, however, was close at hand . . . and they would journey together'. Díaz writes that they continued their march 'and so vast were the crowds assembled to see us that we could scarcely move'.

Tenochtitlán was still invisible, hidden behind a promontory jutting out into the lake. Crossing over the first of the causeways they came to Ixtapalapa on the shores of Texcoco, the great salt lake. This was to be their last night before reaching the city. Cortés was lodged in a newly built palace with 'cedar and other sweet-scented woods' lining its walls. The different diaries give a delightful impression of silvan glades crossed by paths lined with fruiting trees and of flowering gardens stocked with sweet-smelling flowers. Cortés noticed the quantity of fish in the lake. Wild duck, and other water fowl 'are in such numbers that often they almost cover the surface of the water'. Humboldt writing centuries later imagined the shores of Texcoco as they used to be and compared them with the marshy delta of the Nile. Díaz described canoes converging on the advancing Spaniards from every direction 'for all were curious to catch a glimpse of us. And who can wonder at this, as neither men like unto ourselves, nor horses, had ever been seen here before!'

Tenochtitlán could be seen now in the distance, its buildings mirrored in the lake, their reflections rippling a mile, two miles out over the water towards the towns built along the banks. Díaz wrote that 'when we gazed upon all this splendour we scarcely knew what to think, and we doubted whether all that we beheld was real. . . . I do not believe that a country was ever discovered which was equal in splendour to this; for Peru was not known at that time.' He adds that at the moment of writing[1] 'there is not a vestige of all this remaining, and not a stone of this beautiful town is now standing'.

But we are anticipating; for the moment all is a splendid pageant. A short march had brought the Spaniards to a branch of the main causeway. It veered west to a junction with a side causeway from the town of Coyoacán. 'Innumerable crowds of canoes were plying everywere around us'; and at regular intervals they came to wooden bridges made of heavy beams that could be removed if necessary, a form of sliding drawbridge. The Spaniards had been warned by their Indian allies to be wary of the Aztecs. Montezuma, it would appear, had been advised by his gods to allow the strangers to enter the city and then fall upon them. 'We became more thoughtful on seeing the bridges', writes Díaz. They were doubly on their guard, but there were no threatening signs and anyhow there was no question of turning back. Cortés says that nearly a thousand important officials came out to greet them at the junction of the causeways, 'all richly dressed with mantles knotted over one shoulder'. Sahagún described similar mantles made of feathers or

---

[1] Díaz was sixty-eight and living in Guatemala when he decided to write his history. He is describing events that occurred more than forty years previously.

rabbit fur dyed different colours. 'Some had bright red sea-shells on a background of pale blue whirlpools, others had a tawny background and scattered upon it butterflies woven from white feathers.'[1]

'On coming to speak with me,' writes Cortés, 'each performed a ceremony very common among them, that of placing his hand on the ground and then kissing it'. Cortés stood for over an hour receiving them. Continuing their progress over the causeway they came to a fortress, and the last bridge before entering the city. Here the ground widened, they were now marching down a road lined with houses. Crowds watched in awed silence from the rooftops. Cortés remarked the breadth of the street, 'so straight that one can see from one end of it to the other, though it is some two-thirds of a league in length'. Away in the distance could be seen an approaching crowd. It was the Emperor. 'Here we halted for a few minutes,' writes Díaz, 'while the princes with us hurried forward to meet him.' Montezuma borne in a litter advanced between a column of guards and nobles, the guards keeping close to the walls of the street. When within hailing distance Montezuma descended from his litter and leaning on the arms of his brother and a cousin came towards Cortés. Cotton carpets had been spread on the ground, but Montezuma's tread scarcely touched them, for the royal weight reposed on those supporting him. All three, Cortés noted, were dressed in a similar fashion except that Montezuma wore shoes whereas the others were barefoot. Díaz describes the shoes as 'a species of half boot, richly set with jewels, and whose soles were made of solid gold'. The canopy carried over their heads was 'of exceedingly great value decorated with green feathers, gold, silver, precious stones, and pearls'; the pearls forming a fringe. Cortés dismounted and advanced alone to embrace the Emperor; 'but the two lords prevented me from touching him, and they themselves made me the same obeisance as did their comrades, kissing the earth: which done, Montezuma commanded his brother to stay with me and take me by the arm, while he with the other lord went on a little way in front'.

While communicating with Montezuma through an interpreter, Cortés:

took off a necklace of pearls and crystals which I was wearing and threw it round his neck; whereupon having proceeded some little way up the street a servant of his came back to me with two necklaces wrapped in a napkin, made from the shells of sea snails, which were much prized by them; and from each necklace hung eight prawns fashioned very beautifully in gold some six inches in length. The messenger who brought them put them round my neck and we thus continued up the street in the manner described until

[1] Bernardino de Sahagún, *Historia general de las cosas de Nueva España*, Editorial Porrúa, Mexico, 1956.

we came to a large and very handsome house which Montezuma had prepared for our lodging.

It was a palace and had belonged to Montezuma's father.

'The Mexican grandees were greatly astonished,' writes Díaz, 'at all these uncommon favours which their monarch bestowed upon our general.' They were probably not aware that to Montezuma, Cortés was the metamorphosized Quetzalcoatl, the Feathered Serpent. Montezuma, no doubt, had considered it wiser not to divulge this catastrophic news. Considering the circumstances, Montezuma seems to have behaved with remarkable self-control.

Arriving at the palace, Montezuma led Cortés into the great hall and taking him by the hand set him on a dais. Díaz quotes Montezuma, or anyway gives us the gist of his speech welcoming the Spanish to his city. He imagines that they must be fatigued after their journey. 'You and your brothers must now do as if you were at home. Take some repose and after you have rested I will return. With these words he left us and went to his own palace'. Díaz, a practical soldier, adds a few technical details: 'we allotted the apartments according to the several companies, placing our cannon in an advantageous position, and made such arrangements that our cavalry, as well as the infantry, might be ready at a moment's notice'. A splendid meal was then served to the 'gods', 'and thus ends', writes Díaz, 'our bold and memorable entry into Tenochtitlán-Mexico. Praise be to the Lord Jesus Christ for all this.'

6

The Phoenix City

The peaceful reception of Cortés at Tenochtitlán provides a glimpse of the city as it was under the Aztecs, before its total obliteration and its immediate, phoenix-like resurrection. The destruction of Tenochtitlán is one of history's most harrowing tales: a terrible and sickening but apparently unavoidable catastrophe, for Cortés wrote 'I know not how to free ourselves without destroying the city – the most beautiful city in the world.' This was the course of events leading to its fall.

All had gone unbelievably well for the Spaniards. It was not until Cortés confiscated the imperial treasure and seized the Emperor as a hostage against any possible uprising that the Indians began to manifest an active hostility. Even then, despite these drastic provocations, the nobles, persuaded by their Emperor to remain passive, expressed their resentment only by closing the city market.

Then followed a series of misfortunes for the invading army. The Governor of Cuba, the King's immediate representative, jealous of Cortés' success, sent a squadron of eighteen vessels and a large number of men under the command of Narváez with orders for his arrest. Hearing of their arrival at Vera Cruz and immediately marching to the coast, Cortés with his usual good fortune defeated Narváez, won over his men, annexed their equipment and started back to the capital with the reinforcements. The capital, however, was on the verge of rebellion.

In his absence Cortés had delegated command of the city to one of his officers, the handsome Pedro de Alvarado. Impulsive and hot-headed Alvarado proved entirely unworthy of the trust. At a large gathering of nobles held in a temple court next to the Spanish quarters to celebrate the festival of the Aztec war god, Alvarado and his soldiers, invited as spectators, rushed upon the unsuspecting Indians in the midst of a wild dance and slaughtered the lot. Now provoked beyond patience, the Aztecs laid siege to the palace where Montezuma was imprisoned

Cortés begged the Emperor to intercede on the Spaniards' behalf. The General wanted free passage for himself and his troops to leave the city. Montezuma agreed and mounted to the roof to address his people. It was to no effect, and in the mêlée that ensued he was struck by stones from a sling. The wounded monarch was carried back to his apartments. 'We were immediately going to bandage up his wounds,' writes Díaz, 'and begged of him to take something strengthening; but he refused everything, and, contrary to all expectation, we soon heard that he had expired.'

The death took place on 29 June, the fifth day of the siege; then followed a melancholy scene reported by Aguilar. 'In the quarters where Montezuma was lodged there were other great lords being held with him, and with the approval of the captains Cortés had them killed.' The bodies were then carried down and deposited in the street. 'At about ten o'clock a hysterical mob of women appeared carrying torches and flaming braziers. They came for their husbands and relatives . . . and they came for Montezuma too.' On recognizing their men they raised a terrifying wailing and screeching, 'a hell of flood and tears. In truth never in all the wars and the difficulties I went through was I so afraid as when I saw that awful lamentation.'

Having failed to secure a truce, Cortés decided to fight his way out of the city. The Spaniards made several sorties and even scaled the great temple of Huitzilopochtli to set fire to the Mexican idols, but all to no effect. 'In this way,' writes Díaz:

our strength daily diminished while that of the enemy increased. Several of our men had been killed, and most of us were wounded. Our courage was of no avail against such vast crowds, who kept up a constant attack upon us both during the day and all through the night. Our powder was fast diminishing and provisions and water were beginning to fail.

The day following Montezuma's death was chosen for the flight. They would take the Tacuba causeway to the west, this being the shortest and having the least number of bridges. Anxiously the Spaniards waited for darkness to fall, the darkness of the famous *Noche Triste*, the 'sad night'. It was a tragic affair. 'A wind storm had risen,' writes Aguilar, 'so that by midnight it was thundering and hailing as if the heavens were bursting.' Silently the Spaniards filed out of the gates. The great square before the palace was deserted. 'It seemed truly that God wished to work a miracle to save us.' The city was sleeping and the Spaniards had already reached the causeway before the alarm was given. From then on all was utter confusion, the bridges had been destroyed by the Mexicans which meant swimming the horses and the men over the gaps. 'The number of Indians pursuing us,' writes Aguilar, 'must have been about five or six thousand.' 'Does any believe,' adds Díaz, 'that there was a man amongst us who still observed the order of retreat as it was first regulated? That man would, indeed, have been a fool who had thought of anything else but of his own safety.' Aguilar even mentions some of the soldiers 'fainting away from fright'.

Reaching Tacuba a halt was called to regroup the men, and it was here, on the outskirts of the town, that Cortés watched the file-past of his bedraggled troops. He had lost over half of his small army: some eight hundred men, about fifty horses, all the guns and the bulk of Montezuma's treasure, which had been melted down into ingots. Legend has it that he retired to the shade of a great tree and wept under the famous cypress of the *Noche Triste*.

This landmark is still pointed out to tourists, but some authorities discredit the legend. Obregón, one time director of the Mexican National Archives, was of the opinion that events precluded any delay. But he is wrong about the time element, for Cortés stressed in his dispatches that he waited in some ploughed fields for the rearguard to catch up with him. Whether he wept or not is of little importance, and in any case it is not the kind of detail a campaigning soldier might confide to his king. What is interesting though, is that the tree shown to tourists is indeed old enough to have witnessed the Spaniards' defeat. Directly behind it stands a chapel built in the sixteenth century to commemorate the night.

I drove out to Popotla and found the tree fenced in to protect its reddish-brown fibrous bark from souvenir hunters. Experts have done what they can to prolong its life; all dead matter has been removed and its gaping, twisted trunk has been sealed against further rot. What little vegetation remains hangs in sad dusty tufts and is barely recognizable as the light, feathery plumes of the proud *Taxodium distichum*, America's deciduous cypress, a first cousin to California's gigantic sequoias. The tree, I am afraid, is a mere spectre of its former self and can survive but a few more years.

From Tacuba a roundabout retreat to Tlaxcala. The Tlaxcalans, the Aztecs' hereditary enemy, were now Cortés' only friends. The Spaniards fortunately had a Tlaxcalan guide 'who said he would bring us to his country providing they did not stop us on the way'. Tlaxcala is due east of Mexico City, which meant that Cortés was obliged to march north to the top of the lake and then cut across in a north-easterly direction in the hope of eventually finding shelter among his allies. In all it was a march of some one hundred miles.[1]

Half-starved and fighting off incessant attacks, the Spaniards reached Zumpango where after climbing some low-lying hills, they would head south to the plains of Otumba. It was while they wound up the last of the inclines that the advanced guard came galloping back with the news

[1] See map of Tenochtitlán, its Causeways and the Five Lakes.

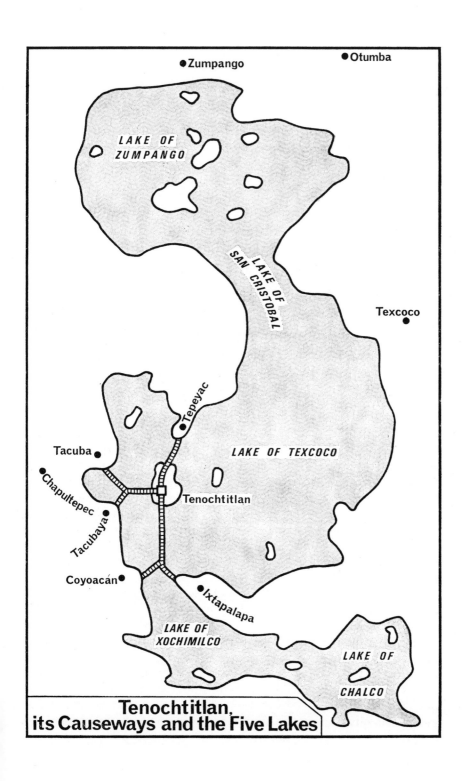

Zumpango •

• Otumba

LAKE OF
ZUMPANGO

LAKE OF
SAN CRISTOBAL

Texcoco
•

Tepeyac

Tacuba •

LAKE OF TEXCOCO

Chapultepec •

Tenochtitlan

Tacubaya

Coyoacán •

Ixtapalapa

LAKE OF
XOCHIMILCO

LAKE OF
CHALCO

Tenochtitlan,
its Causeways and the Five Lakes

that the whole of the Aztec army, more than half a million men according to Aguilar, lay in wait, lined up in magnificent array on the sandy flats below. They had rowed across the lake and marched the fifteen miles to Otumba and were now quietly waiting, certain at last of the sequel.

What actually happened was little short of a miracle. 'And in truth,' writes Cortés, 'we thought our last day had come, the strength of the Indians being overpowering, and our own powers of resistance almost at an end, seeing that we were worn out and almost all wounded and faint with hunger.' Their only food for the last forty-eight hours had been the flesh of a dead horse. Despite this, they massed for attack and 'struggling thus we continued a greater part of the day until by God's will one of their chieftains was killed who must have been so important that with his death the battle entirely ceased'. They had, in fact, killed the commander-in-chief.

Aguilar writes that no sooner had the Aztecs heard of their defeat at Otumba than they 'sent ambassadors to the lords of Tlaxcala, bearing many presents and gold necklaces, and other valuable jewels, to persuade them to intercept and kill us'. It was another extraordinary stroke of luck that the Tlaxcalans remained loyal to the Spaniards 'and came out to receive our captain and his men, who arrived shattered, wounded and dying'.

For nearly a year Cortés made Tlaxcala (eighty-four miles from Tenochtitlán) his headquarters. 'My men,' he writes, 'begged me to return to Vera Cruz. But I considered that to show signs of weakness to the Indians, especially to our friends, would result in their abandoning us and going over to our enemy.' Calling to mind that fortune always favours the brave, he dug himself in and set about reconquering the central provinces. It was a decision that showed remarkable courage, for Cortés had received severe wounds, so also had most of his men. Some had even died of fatigue. 'Others,' he writes, 'remained maimed and lame, for the wounds were very severe and there was very little in the way of effective treatment. I myself lost the use of two fingers of my left hand.'

In less than a month after Otumba he was back in the saddle and off on different campaigns. He still had enough of his old magic left to convince his Indian friends that he would yet prevail. They flocked around him, their numbers increasing with each victory gained. News came from Tenochtitlán that Montezuma's brother, Cuitlahuac, had been elected Emperor. Of the late Emperor's sons two who had been held as hostages were killed in the flight from the city. 'Of his remaining sons,' Cortés writes, 'one was reputed to be mad and another paralysed.' The city, it was also said, was being fortified. 'In particular I learnt that they were making extra-long lances to use against our horses.'

Cortés sent ships to Haiti and Cuba for reinforcements and, most important of all, he set about building twelve brigantines for action on the lake. Fortunately there was a ship's carpenter amongst the troops, a man called Martín López. 'The decking and other parts,' writes the Captain-General, 'were being made in Tlaxcala so that they can be carried overland and assembled close to the lake.' Their construction was a remarkable *tour de force*.

Events moved quickly. Next, the important towns in the immediate vicinity of the lake were methodically reduced. The first to be occupied was Texcoco, the second largest city in the valley. They entered it without any difficulty, for the lord of the city had withdrawn all his troops and evacuated to Mexico. It was here that Cortés assembled the brigantines. 'A deep canal was dug along a gully that went all the way to the lake,'[1] a distance of about two miles.

The year 1521 opened with three months of manœuvring and a series of skirmishes. Cortés had succeeded in destroying all the Mexican garrisons in the valley and had marched completely round the lake. It was obvious by now that the troops occupying Tenochtitlán were not planning an offensive but relying rather on a defensive action. Cortés planned accordingly, drawing the net ever closer, and thus completely surrounded the great city that considered itself impregnable. The brigantines were launched on 28 April; everything was now ready for the attack. There remained one last hope of staying the holocaust. Montezuma's brother had died of smallpox (a disease not known in Mexico prior to its introduction by a Negro serving in Narváez's army) and had been succeeded by Cuauhtémoc, his nephew, a youth of about twenty-four married to Montezuma's daughter. Cortés sent him a last minute overture. It was just conceivable that the young Emperor might reconsider Cortés' terms and accept Charles v as his overlord. But the Emperor did not even deign to answer Cortés, and the Indian who had acted as intermediary was put to death for having presumed to deliver such a message. There was to be no reprieve; the die was cast. Within four days every causeway leading from the city to the mainland had been cut off, so also had the aqueduct at Chapultepec, thus depriving Tenochtitlán of its main water supply. It must be remembered that the lake, or rather that part of it directly surrounding the city, was salt. The few wells situated in the city proper were brackish, but fortunately for the besieged it was the rainy season.

Cortés divided his land force among three commanders. Gonzalvo de Sandoval was stationed at Ixtapalapa and Coyoacán to guard the

[1] *The Chronicle of Fray Francisco de Aguilar.*

southern causeway. Cristóbal de Olid's command overlapped Sandoval at Coyoacán and extended northward to Tacubaya. Alvarado held Tacuba. Sandoval was later moved to the little town of Tepeyac to thus control the northern sector. The besieging army numbered some six hundred Spaniards and about eighty thousand mercenaries.

Cortés occupied himself with the brigantines. 'I myself,' he writes, 'had been anxious to go by land and arrange the details of our camps, but as the captains were men to be trusted with the latter, and the management of the ships was of paramount importance requiring great nicety and care, I decided to go with them, more especially as the greater risk and adventure were expected on the water.' Each vessel was allotted twenty-five men, 'in addition to the captain and six musketeers and crossbowmen and a small field gun'.

There was a major encounter the very first day when Cortés was anchored at Ixtapalapa. 'The Indians in the capital and the other island cities aware that I had entered the lake immediately gathered a great fleet of canoes to oppose us,' four thousand of them according to Díaz. 'At this moment,' Cortés continues, 'when we were regarding each other face to face it pleased the Lord that a light breeze should spring up from the land enabling us to close with them. I immediately ordered the commanders to bear down on the fleet of canoes and follow them right up to the walls of the capital.' Turning tail the Indians jabbed at the water with their paddles but could not make sufficient headway. 'We bore right into the middle of them smashing an infinite number of canoes.' Those that escaped, Díaz tells us, 'took refuge between the houses built in the lake where they could not be followed by the brigantines. Thus ended our first naval engagement, and Cortés gained a victory.'

Left free for a spell to manœuvre his brigantines, Cortés landed on the Coyoacán causeway 'and captured two towers. I determined to pitch my camp there.' It was at the juncture of the causeway leading to Ixtapalapa and seems to have been a small fortified island, an ideal vantage point from which to oversee the three sections of his army. The siege proper, the battle of the causeways, had now begun and lasted two and a half months: 'for seventy-five days we lay before the great and strong city'. Díaz adds, 'We were compelled to fight day and night almost without intermission'.

The enemy was perfectly organized. 'The troops which lay in the other towns of the lake merely awaited the morning dawn, when the signals were given from the summit of the great temple of Huitzilopochtli to rush out upon us both by land and water.' The Spaniards were sometimes sorely pressed and there were moments of extreme peril. Twice Cortés narrowly escaped being taken prisoner. Had the

Aztecs been content with killing him instead of capturing him alive for sacrifice, there is little doubt that they would have succeeded in raising the siege. Losses were far heavier than either of the combatants admitted. Cortés seldom mentioned numbers when reporting on his operations but one day fifty-three Spaniards were captured, another time eighteen, and yet another time seven horses and twelve men. Díaz wrote that the great snake drum was continually booming out from the top of the temple, each beating signifying the death of a Spaniard. 'We could plainly see the platform, with the chapel in which those cursed idols stood.' The Christians, naked and white, crowned with plumes, were made to dance in front of the idols, 'and then we saw how they stretched them out full length on a large stone and ripped open their breasts with their flint knives'. Afterwards the bodies were thrown down the steps 'at the bottom of which other executioners stood ready to receive them'. Arms, legs and heads were severed. 'They drew the skin off their faces, which were tanned with the beards still adhering to them, and produced as spectacles of mockery and derision at their feasts.'[1] The legs and arms were eaten. Before an attack Díaz was haunted 'with terror at the thought that I might have to share a similar fate! . . . It was then I fell on my knees, and commended myself to the protection of God and the Blessed Virgin; and from my prayers I rushed straight way into the battle, and all fears instantly vanished.'

Rations were an acute problem; the Spaniards subsisted largely on herbs, cherries and wild figs. Díaz writes that there were times when even the wounded were obliged to go without maize cakes. Their Indian allies fared better, for, as Cortés reported, 'all those who were killed they cut to pieces and took off with them to eat'.

Advancing up the causeways proved to be a slow, arduous undertaking. The Spaniards had no room to manœuvre and would have made little or no headway were it not for the brigantines. Flanking the troops they protected them from attack by canoe. Cortés writes that 'the brigs also went round the city burning all the houses they could, and managed to discover a canal by which they could enter into the very heart of the suburbs'. The suburbs consisted of small colonies of detached buildings, many of them standing right in the water. Díaz explains 'those in the water were difficult to burn' and had to be knocked down. The rubble, however, came in very handy for blocking up the canals. Cortés adds that 'we advanced not a step without leaving everything desolate behind us, blocking up every single waterway'. This work was delegated to the Indians and since 'over a hundred and

---

[1] In another part of his narrative Díaz draws attention to the fact that 'the hair of their heads and beards was much longer than when on the living body'. Among the heads 'I recognized those of three of my companions'.

fifty thousand warriors marched with us not a little was accomplished'. 'Our allies,' he explains, 'seeing the steady progress we were making were swelling daily to such an extent that they could not be counted.' Often the Spaniards heard the deep notes of Cuauhtémoc's royal horn 'which', says Díaz, 'was always a signal to his troops that he allowed them no choice but death or victory. With this at the same time was mingled the melancholy sound of the drum from the temple.' Goaded on by fanatical priests 'the Mexicans charged in fury, running headlong against our swords. It was really a horrible sight . . . in this way we continually kept advancing nearer and nearer the centre of the city, though the enemy constantly renewed their attacks upon us . . . and it was with difficulty we could repulse them'.

The siege had begun on the last day of May and by the end of July Cortés and Alvarado met in the great market place and were converging on the main square. Gaining the principal street of the city a cannon was placed at the entrance 'and thus did great damage to the enemy'. Cortés had sent repeated peace offerings 'that the city might not be totally destroyed'.[1] Cuauhtémoc was offered the regency under Spanish rule but the proud young Emperor replied that he preferred to be buried sword in hand under the ruins of his capital. Díaz intimates, however, that Cuauhtémoc would have ceded had it not been for the priests.

In the last stages of the siege the great temple was stormed 'and I ordered', writes Cortés, 'the large houses surrounding the square to be set on fire', including Axayacatl's palace where the Spaniards had been lodged as guests when first arriving in Mexico. 'We also burned several smaller palaces, one more elaborate than the others and very finely worked, in which Montezuma had been wont to keep all his birds. I was much grieved to do this.'

Cuauhtémoc and what was left of his army were now confined to the north-east corner of the city, pushed into an area built out on piles in the water. Cortés paints a pathetic picture: the Spaniards, hoping that the Aztec would sue for peace, had not attacked for several days. The inhabitants were dying of hunger and could be heard at night creeping out in their canoes to fish. In the morning they found the streets 'full of women and children and other wretched beings . . . moving about listlessly outside their defences in the most pitiable manner'. They were pulling up weeds and even gnawed the bark off the trees. 'Not a single warrior had advanced into the open, but we saw them sitting wrapped in their mantles on the flat tops of the roofs and without arms.' The stench in the street was intolerable. Thousands had been crammed in one small corner of the city; 'it was beyond the wit of man to understand how they could endure it'. They learnt afterwards, as Cortés

[1] *The Memoirs of Conquistador Bernal Díaz del Castillo.*

23 Popotla's ancient tree of the Noche Triste painted by José Velasco in 1885. It is now one-tenth of the size shown in this picture and the church of San Esteban has disappeared to be replaced by an ugly little brick chapel (page 64)

24 Hernán Cortés created Marqués del Valle de Oaxaca (page 77)

25 (opposite) Antonio de Mendoza, Conde de Tendilla, the first viceroy (1535–50) (page 78)

26 *Detail of Cortés' palace at Cuernavaca* (*page* **77**)

explains 'that the drinking of salt water, hunger and the stench of the dead bodies had worked such havoc upon them that, in all, more than fifty thousand souls had thus perished. And in order that we should not realize their plight their bodies were neither thrown into the water where our brigs would have come across them nor taken out of doors and exposed in the streets where we should have been able to see them. I myself visited some of the streets which remained to them and found the dead heaped one upon the other, so that one was forced to walk upon them.'

Finally, on the evening of 13 August, Cuauhtémoc was taken prisoner, having been intercepted by one of the brigs while trying to escape across the lake. His canoe had been singled out, writes Díaz, 'by the beautiful carved work with which it was ornamented, by the tent, and other decorations'. With him on board, the Emperor had his wife and children and immediate members of his suite. Díaz describes his wife as young and very beautiful. The Emperor 'could in all truth be termed a handsome man, both as regards his countenance and his figure'. He had great dignity and appeared to have been several shades paler than is usual among the Indians.

When led into the presence of Cortés, the Captain-General 'received him with utmost respect and embraced him affectionately'. The Emperor replied with a moving speech. 'I have done what I was bound to do in the defence of my metropolis . . .' He made no excuses but instead, Cortés tells us, 'drew a dagger which he had in his belt, bidding me dispatch him with it at once'. We know Cortés' reaction, for the Emperor lived on for several years.

Díaz adds an interesting postscript, the only mention of the noise the Spanish had endured during the siege: the constant yells, piping and war-whoops of the enemy, and the hellish music of drums and shell trumpets. 'Day and night did all this din and noise continue without intermission.' So intense had it been that 'we soldiers were deafened by it and could scarcely hear anything'. When the hostilities ceased, they were dazed by the lack of noise. Díaz compared the sensation to that of someone who, standing in a belfry with all the bells ringing at once, is suddenly faced with complete silence.

Cuauhtémoc after his surrender 'requested Cortés to allow the whole of the inhabitants, with the remaining part of his troops to leave the city. This our General readily granted, and the causeways were crowded for three days and nights with men, women and children, on their way to the mainland'.[1]

Mass was said, 'to offer up our thanks to the Almighty' and afterwards 'Cortés ordered a banquet to be prepared at Coyoacán, to

[1] *The Memoirs of Conquistador Bernal Díaz del Castillo.*

celebrate the conquest'. A ship had conveniently docked at Vera Cruz with a cargo of port and barrels of Spanish wine. The allies disbanded and returned to their provinces, but not without 'many gracious words of promise', and considerably enriched with 'cotton, gold and various spoils – amongst which were portions of the bodies of their enemies salted'.

Coyoacán became the Spaniards' headquarters since there was no question of inhabiting Tenochtitlán. Now came the all important problem of where to rebuild the new capital. As the lake had no natural outlet, the island city had suffered whenever the rains were abnormally heavy. The Aztecs had thrown up earthworks in an attempt to control the floods, but they had proved only partially successful. All things considered, it was thought advisable that Cortés build on higher ground: at Coyoacán where he was quartered, or then at Chapultepec, or Tacubaya among the foothills. Ignoring this counsel, he decided eventually to rebuild on the original site, 'because', as he wrote, 'the city had acquired celebrity, because its position was delightful, and because in all times it had been considered as the head of the Mexican provinces'. He must also have been influenced by the vast quantity of available building material from ruined temples and palaces.

As it developed later, it would have been better had Cortés settled on the foothills, for the new Tenochtitlán-Mexico City suffered a series of disastrous floods, one in 1607 and a succession of them from 1629–34. 'The streets,' Humboldt wrote, 'were passed in boats . . . as had been done before the Conquest in the old Tenochtitlán and wooden walks were constructed along the sides of the houses for the convenience of foot passengers.' Already in 1607 Philip III had passed an edict for the removal of the city but the magistracy had protested. The value of the buildings condemned to destruction amounted to millions of pounds. 'Madrid,' they wrote firmly, 'seemed to forget that the capital of a kingdom founded eighty years ago, is not a flying camp which may be destroyed at will.' Again in 1629 Madrid ordered the move, and again the magistracy refused. The value of the buildings had doubled in twenty-two years.

The fall of Tenochtitlán must have produced a deep impression. Travelling merchants and wandering huntsmen spread the tale. No doubt all Central America soon knew that the great city of the Aztecs had been captured. Díaz says that 'the inhabitants of the provinces would not at first credit that Mexico had fallen'. When convinced of the fact:

they sent ambassadors to congratulate Cortés on his victory, and to declare themselves vassals of our Emperor . . . Each of those ambassadors brought with them valuable presents in gold, and many had their young sons with them, to whom they pointed out the ruins of Mexico, just as we would show our children the spot where Troy once stood.

Cortés, a first-class soldier, also proved to be an excellent administrator. He wrote to his king that he did everything in his power to encourage the former inhabitants to return. Cuauhtémoc he kept prisoner, but 'I put a captain-general of his in charge of the repeopling', and in order that he might have more authority, 'I conferred upon him the same office which he had held in the time of his lord. To other principal persons I gave offices of government in the city, which they had been accustomed to hold.' Later he is able to write 'that they have worked in such a manner that there are already thirty thousand inhabitants in the city, and the same order that there used to be in their market places.' Indian masons, stonecutters, carpenters and silversmiths were also employed. Cortés also mentions the 'persons who live by fishing, which was a great branch of commerce there'.

Five months after the fall Cortés could already refer to the new city as being very beautiful 'and your Majesty may believe that each day it will become nobler'. Díaz says that 'in the opinion of those who have travelled through the greater part of Christendom, Mexico, after its restoration, was a larger and a more populous city than any they had seen'. The style of its architecture was considered magnificent.

Father Motolinía, an eyewitness to the rebuilding, paints a less rosy picture. According to him, Mexico's solid splendour was nothing but a monument to human suffering. Thousands of Indians had been put to work 'and their songs and shouts did not cease day or night'. The streets were wide 'but the work was so busily carried on that a man could scarcely make his way through them'. A stone, or beam of wood 'which should have taken a hundred men only, was dragged by four hundred'. The loss of life among the Indians working on demolition was very high. According to Gómara,[1] food was also scarce and workmen died of hunger. The mortality rate during the first years was appalling. Forced labour killed a good many, but the majority died from epidemics. Twice before 1580 the indigenous typhus plague, *mazahuati*, swept the country. More widespread still were the ravages of the newly imported European fevers, smallpox and measles. Hundreds of years of exposure had given Europeans a relative tolerance to these diseases, but 'to the American Indian they were death with no reprieve'.[2] In 1576 over two million Indians perished in Mexico alone from smallpox.

But to return to the reconstruction of the city: a look at the plan of

[1] Francisco López de Gómara, who became Cortés' secretary on his return to Spain in 1540. His *Historia general de las Indias* was published in 1552.
[2] *The Ranks of Death. A Medical History of the Conquest of America.*

Tenochtitlán shows that the great temple and the main palaces were grouped around the central island and this obviously was to remain the pivotal point of the new city. The first church was begun in about 1524 just south of the present Cathedral's location, for which the foundations were laid in 1562. The new city grew southwards and westwards as a grid of square blocks, but its extension, owing to the nature of the terrain, was slow. For years all important buildings were confined to the limited space which today encircles the Plaza Major. Cortés claimed for himself the site of Montezuma's two palaces.

We learn little from the conquistadors themselves about the actual planning; they are, in fact, annoyingly vague on the subject. Gage says that Cortés 'separated the buildings of the Spaniards from the Indians'. Montezuma's son was given an entire section in which to build and other nobles were allotted some of the islands. The part reserved for the Indians lay to the east, on the far side of a broad canal, and it is remarkable that it is in this district that the Aztec language is still spoken.

The Spaniards used the same stone as the Aztecs for building material: a porous stone composed of silica and volcanic ash, a kind of harder pumice, and known locally as *tezontle*. Extensive quarries of it exist not far from the city. While it varies a good deal in colour, as a rule it is deep maroon mottled with what looks like flecks of cinders. Sometimes the maroon pales to apricot, as though burnt in the intensity of long-extinct volcanic fires. When seen on the walls, the constant variation in colour produces a very pleasing effect. In conjunction with *tezontle*, the Spaniards used a grey-white limestone called *chiluca* to trim doorways and windows.

It is not known what year Cortés left his whitewashed house at Coyoacán to take up quarters in the new city. Presumably he moved straight to the building which is now the national pawnshop, on the site of Axayacatl's palace, where he was first entertained by Montezuma. In 1535 this same building was serving as a residence for the first viceroy, Antonio de Mendoza, Conde de Tendilla. By this time Cortés was already at work on what is now the National Palace, where he probably moved on the viceroy's arrival. This was much larger than his previous house and after his death was bought from the Cortés family to serve ever since as the seat of government.

The rebuilding of the city appears to have been achieved in record time, for already by 1524 Cortés was planning a campaign which he hardly would have dared had the city not been well advanced. The campaign was a punitive expedition against his officer Cristóbal de Olid who, after founding a settlement on the Gulf of Honduras, had declared his independence. It proved to be a long and hazardous march through the swamps and jungles of North Guatemala. Of greater interest than the expedition itself are the luxurious details of its organization. One wonders how the Spaniards were able to evolve so complex a pattern for living, following so immediately the incredible rigours of the Conquest. Cortés took with him a large service of plate fashioned by native silversmiths after Spanish models. 'Plates of various sizes, spoons, cups and other vessels for drinking, all of which were imitated with the greatest exactness.' He travelled with a retinue consisting of a physician, a surgeon, his chief equerry, two stewards, lance bearers, three Spanish mule drivers, two falconers, a number of pages, also his own orchestra and 'lastly a buffoon and a juggler, who likewise entertained the men with puppet-shows; further, he took with him a large herd of swine in order that the troops might have a constant supply of fresh meat on their march'.[1]

On his return to the city, a year and eight months later, he gave a fête for Luis Ponce de León, a representative sent over by the King. His palace was hung with beautiful tapestries. 'Everything was served in gold and silver, and the whole table was beautifully arranged.' Díaz writes that León was heard to remark in an undertone to his secretary that 'Cortés, in his manner and conversation, had every appearance of a man who had lived like a grand señor for many years'.

This love of splendour got Cortés into trouble. His success made him many enemies and incurred much jealousy. The envious used every means to blacken his reputation. The death of a government official recently arrived from Spain was attributed to him. It was also rumoured that he had poisoned his wife, who had appeared unbidden from Cuba. It was well known, according to gossip, that the King was not receiving his full share of revenue. Slander poured in from every direction, and Charles v, already suspicious by nature, was thoroughly alarmed by the stories. Inquiries were made, and in the end Cortés decided that the wisest course was to appear in person to allay his master's fears. Cortés left for Spain in March 1528, and was received by the King in the autumn of the same year.

'The two vessels in which he sailed,' writes Díaz:

were so plentifully provisioned that they had sufficient victuals for a voyage of two years. With him went one of Montezuma's sons who had been baptized, and several young Tlaxcalan nobles, a quantity of gold and jewels, Mexican birds and animals, rope-dancers, dwarfs and various other curiosities. Landing in Palos he made his way to Seville where he was received by the Duke of Medina Sidonia. From there he travelled to Guadalupe and here charmed the distinguished Doña María de Mendoza and the ladies of quality in her suite. He was possessed of sufficient wealth to bestow with an

[1] *The Memoirs of Conquistador Bernal Díaz del Castillo.*

unsparing hand; and to the whole of these ladies he presented the most valuable presents. Gold and panaches of green feathers looped with pearls.

Doña María was suitably impressed and wrote to her husband at court that 'all the fame of his deeds of arms were really nothing when compared with his own personal qualities'. She mentioned 'the charm of his conversation', the 'noble frankness of his disposition', and 'the grace of his every action'.

This is perhaps the moment to correct Diego Rivera's absurdly distorted portrait of Cortés. Both his secretary, López de Gómara, and Díaz describe Cortés as being well proportioned with a rather small head, slightly bowed legs and fine ankles and feet. Both refer to his complexion as 'ashy'. His hair was black and long, and he wore a beard. Díaz tells us that the rigours of the Honduras campaign turned his beard grey and immediately on returning to Mexico Cortés had had it dyed. He was on the lean side until constant campaigning eventually affected his digestion. Unless he rested after every meal he was seized with violent nausea. 'We therefore took the precaution as soon as he had dined to spread a carpet for him underneath some tree or elsewhere in the shade.' This necessarily affected his figure so that towards the end of his life he became 'excessively fat and big-bellied'. His clothes were elegant and he was very neat of person. Díaz continues:

he always dressed according to the fashion of the day; wore very little silk, satins or expensive damasks . . . he never bedizened himself with heavy gold chains, but always had the same one, which was of exquisite workmanship and had attached to it a medallion of the Virgin with, on the other side, St John the Baptist. On one finger he wore a valuable ring set with a most splendid diamond.

It seems he was impervious to the weather, 'it mattered not whether it was oppressively hot, or that the rains came down in torrents, it made no difference to him'. He was an excellent horseman, 'remarkably expert in all martial exercises, both as a foot and cavalry soldier', also remarkably brave. Gómara tells of his weakness for women and his love of gaming, 'he was a wonderful dice-player, skilful and good natured'. Díaz remarks that his eyes generally 'were kindly in expression but that he could also look very grave'. 'But laughing,' adds Gómara, 'was one of the things he enjoyed most.' He seldom lost his temper, but when he did, he had a curious habit of throwing off his cloak. 'He never,' writes Díaz, 'made use of low or unbecoming expressions to his officers or soldiers. His strongest language when out of humour was "upon my conscience!", "may the plague take you!", or "hold your tongue!".'

The son of a country squire of Estremadura he had attended university at Salamanca, had studied law and could speak Latin fluently. 'His bearing,' Díaz adds, 'his gait, his conversation and the taste he showed in his dress, all bespoke the cavalier of distinction and good breeding.'

With his very definite charm added to his remarkable achievements Cortés probably had little difficulty in persuading the Emperor that the charges against him had no foundation.

The imperial court was being held at Toledo, where the day following his arrival he was received in audience. The Emperor created him Marqués del Valle de Oaxaca, a high rank, second only to a duke, and also awarded him the Cross of the Order of Santiago. With the marquisate came a number of townships which Díaz described as some of the richest land in the country:

> the valley of Toluca, the province of Cuernavaca, Coyoacán, the province of Cotaxtla and Tuxtla (Vera Cruz), a large part of the valley of Oaxaca and the isthmus of Tehuantepec – an estimated twenty-five thousand square miles, yielding something more than eighty thousand gold pesos a year in Indian tribute alone.[1]

Cortés was fêted, and reinstated as Captain-General, but he was not made governor of New Spain. Although he had cleared his name, Charles v and the Council of the Indies were wary of delegating any more power to him. It was thought unwise to let him rule alone and he was never to regain his former authority. From thenceforth New Spain was to have a civil government. Cortés was to be consulted, but the laws were to be administered by the royal *Audiencia*, a judicial and administrative court composed of a *presidente* and four *oidores*, or jurists. In 1535, five years later, the first viceroy arrived.

Shorn of any real power but master of vast estates, Cortés set sail again for the flat coastline he knew so well. The Indians cried when they saw him. 'His arrival,' writes Simpson, 'was the signal for an outburst of rejoicing among the Spaniards and Indians alike.' He brought back with him a new wife, married in Spain, Doña Juana de Zúñiga, niece of the Duke of Béjar.

In eclipse but still full of energy, Cortés' last ten years in Mexico were far from idle. At his own expense he built a fleet of ships to explore the Pacific. He also erected a large winter palace at Cuernavaca and founded a Franciscan monastery whose impressive, Romanesque style church with its fortress-like walls was eventually ranked as a cathedral. The palace, sitting on the edge of a *barranca*, or gorge, retains, in spite of various alterations, many of its original features, notably the columns and arches of the loggia at the back from which there is a sweeping view of the snow-covered Popocatepetl. In Cortés' day the country

[1] Lesley Byrd Simpson, quoted in *Many Mexicos*, University of California Press, Los Angeles, 1961.

around was planted with sugar cane that he had introduced from Cuba. Added to all his other talents the great conqueror seems also to have been a very capable farmer, tireless in his attempts to improve the land. Under his management Tehuantepec became an important centre for mule breeding. He imported hundreds of sheep and cattle from Spain, planted mulberry trees and encouraged silk culture, even alternated crops.

When in town, living in what is now the National Palace, Cortés entertained lavishly. Díaz compared the fêtes in the Plaza Major celebrating Charles v's visit to France and his meeting with François i at Aiguesmortes to the festivities of ancient Rome. One day the Plaza was a forest with Indians treading its glades, hunting with bows and arrows. On another occasion four ships in full sail rocked their way across the square. Indians dressed as Dominican fathers cast nets over an artificial ocean and so realistic was this seascape that the crowds burst into thunderous applause. There was no end to the ingenuity displayed; Turks in crimson silk and 'with voluminous turbans' laid siege to the turreted walls of Rhodes. Following this bellicose scene was a horse race in which women took part, run from the Plaza de Tlaltecolco, the Aztec market place, to the Plaza Major: 'Prizes for the winner consisted of jewels of gold.' Two elaborate banquets terminated the proceedings; the first given by Cortés and the second by Mendoza, the Viceroy.

Díaz mentioned the strained relations between Cortés and Mendoza arising from questions of precedence at public functions. At a church ceremony at which both men were to be present, 'seats were brought by the valets and', writes Obregón, 'Cortés' seat was placed ahead of the Viceroy's. The latter's valet took it away and substituted the Viceroy's chair in the position of honour'.[1] Clearly if an open clash were to be avoided, some protocol had to be devised. Therefore it was agreed that when hearing mass together they should both kneel on the same cushion. When on horseback in the city Cortés would yield the right side of the street to Mendoza. When the Viceroy dined in Cortés' house he would sit at the head of the table, and both would be served simultaneously. But when Cortés went to dine with the Viceroy, seats were to be placed not at the head of the table but alongside each other. Luckily Mendoza, a grandee of Spain, was a remarkably enlightened and able man, beyond petty bickerings. So fortunately was Cortés. Indeed, Cortés, had he wanted to stage a revolt, was most certainly in a position to do so. A god still to the Indians, and looked up to by the majority of his fellow countrymen, he would have had eighty per cent of the country behind him. Although somewhat resentful of playing second fiddle to a representative of the King, he was nevertheless loyal.

[1] *The Streets of Mexico.*

Mendoza, for his part, was obliged to manœuvre the great conquistador into the background while at the same time keeping on amicable terms with him. It was a situation fraught with danger. Small wonder that care had to be taken about the niceties of their coexistence.

The two banquets were well organized and a general conviviality helped clear the air. Cortés entertained the Viceroy and then Mendoza, temporarily installed in Cortés' original house, reciprocated. The guests were bidden early and the banquet lasted until the early hours of the morning. The sombre Renaissance palace had been completely transformed: fountains splashed in the courtyard and the long corridors were trellised with flowering trees, gaudy parrots screeching from their interlacing branches. Díaz, always exact, tells us that places had been laid to accommodate five hundred people. Don Hernán Cortés and Don Antonio de Mendoza presided at the table of honour in two high backed chairs. Dish followed dish, all on service of silver and gold: hogs' heads, whole venison and a new indigenous delicacy, 'turkey hens with silver-plated feet'. The cloths were then changed and immense meat pies were brought in. 'In some of these were live rabbits, and others were filled with partridges and doves and other living birds. The pies were served together and as the tops were lifted off, rabbits ran out on to the table and the birds flew into the trees amid laughter, cries and jests.'

For drinks the guests were served an Indian beverage called *aloja*, a mixture of water, honey and spices; cold frothy chocolate; and a claret *sangría* sweetened with sugar and perfumed with cinnamon.

Díaz, commenting on the morals of some of the guests, notes that at the dinner given by Cortés over a hundred marks' worth of silver was stolen. The Viceroy, thanks to his major domo, fared better, losing only a few salt cellars and some table linen. The major domo 'saw to it that an Indian guarded each place at the table, and when dishes with uneaten food were taken by the guests to their various houses, the Indian followed and brought back the platter. It is easy to see that those who delivered the food were much more honourable than those who received it'.

These fêtes occurred in 1538. Ten years later Cortés left again for Spain, on what he hoped would be a short visit. Convinced that he still had the King's ear, he was going to solicit a more responsible position. His Great South Sea expedition had failed to reveal 'secret and wonderful things' and he was far too restless and ambitious a character to devote himself entirely to farming. But the situation at court was no longer the same: new conquerors had appeared on the scene, Balboa and Pizarro. Already the treasures of Peru were rivalling those of Mexico. Pizarro was actually in Spain when Cortés arrived and, like Cortés, had been made a marquis. 'It was in his deeds, his treasure,' writes Collis, 'that people were interested. Cortés seemed a tiresome figure out of the past, a man whose fame belonged to history and who had nothing new to tell or give.'[1]

For seven years Cortés dogged the King's footsteps, joining him in Flanders, and then embarking on an elaborate crusade against the Moors at Algiers in order to draw attention to himself and to gain one word from his sovereign. The Council of the Indies were willing to accommodate Cortés, were they so directed by the King, but the word never came. Weary at last of vague promises Cortés decided to return to New Spain. He had waited too long. Ready to embark at Seville he was suddenly struck down with dysentery accompanied by a high fever. They carried him to the little town of Castilleja de la Cuesta where he had a house and where it was hoped he would rally. But at sixty-two, worn out by a hard life and in a depressed mental condition, he had no will to fight. He lingered a few days and died on 2 December 1547.

[1] *Cortés and Montezuma.*

7

Of Viceroys and Floods

Mendoza ruled New Spain for a little over fifteen years. The Council of the Indies had chosen their representative wisely, for in deposing Cortés they might well have jeopardized the future of the country that was eventually to prove their prize colony. Cortés had been remarkably humane and just in his treatment of the conquered native population and had been vehemently opposed to their being completely subjugated as they had been in the West Indies. He wrote to the King, 'I have lived twenty years in the islands and have experience of the evils wrought there. Here I have ordered matters in a very different way.' Mendoza continued Cortés' policy of conciliation and proved both capable and energetic in organizing further exploratory expeditions, following the precedent set by Cortés who had encouraged the penetration of Honduras and Guatemala because it was from Central America that Montezuma had derived the greatest part of his wealth. Mendoza for his part pushed out towards the west founding the future cities of Guadalajara and Morelia.

Mendoza's management of New Spain was so adroit that he was offered the troublesome viceroyalty of Peru. Don Luis de Velasco was posted to Mexico City in his stead. Mendoza and Velasco were men of the same school, trained in the great tradition of the Renaissance; humane, informed and open-minded, fully aware of their responsibilities. Velasco distributed Crown Lands amongst the Indians and established a university and the *Ospidale Real*. In the north he founded Durango, Sombrerete and Fresnillo as frontier posts to ward off the predatory raids of the Apaches, Comanches, Mimbrenos and Yuts whom the Spaniards lumped together under the general name of *Chichimecas*. Rich silver deposits had been discovered and already worked under Mendoza to the south of these posts, at Zacatecas, San Luis Potosí and Guanajuato. They lay miles away from any Spanish settlement and it was important to guard their lines of communication. Velasco, married to Mendoza's niece, was, like his predecessor, fond of good living.

Simpson tells us he was 'exceedingly proud of his superb horsemanship' and was also a practised bull fighter, a sport performed on horseback in those days. He died in office, a pauper, after thirteen years of rule.

The areas of Spanish occupation had gradually extended over the continent, fitting together on the map like pieces in a gigantic jigsaw puzzle. In 1513 Balboa had crossed the isthmus of Panama and sighted the great *Mar del Sur*. Seven years later came the news of Magellan's discovery; but Magellan, a navigator by profession and hardly concerned with the land, had sailed away across the seldom pacific Pacific to the far islands of the East. Cortés' probings in the new sea had proved disappointing – one expedition reached the arid peninsula of Lower California – but Pizarro had hugged the western coastline of South America and thus discovered Peru. From Peru further explorations were made northwards to Bogotá and south to Chile where Santiago was founded in 1541. The Spaniards also built powerful strongholds along the Venezuelan and Colombian coasts, mighty fortresses such as Santa Marta and Cartagena. By 1538, operating from European bases, they were at Asunción, far up from the Plata.

Having thus extended their power in the southern and central portions of the continent they pushed their way upwards to all the northern regions of Mexico and then to large areas of what was to become the United States. Narváez followed Ponce de León on the Florida coast. Hernando de Soto explored the Mississippi basin ten years later, while Cabeza de Vaca penetrated farther west. Mendoza, excited by de Vaca's tales of 'Seven Golden Cities', organized another expedition under Francisco Vásquez de Coronado only to find that the gold was an effect of light, the sinking sun washing over the pale *adobe* walls of pueblo settlements in the present state of New Mexico. Two years later Mendoza sent out another expedition under Juan Rodríguez Cabrillo who sailed up the California coast as far north as Oregon.

Early on these vast holdings were divided into the two viceroyalties of New Spain and of Peru. The viceroy of Mexico nominally controlled all the Spanish dominions in North and Central America plus the Philippine Islands. In point of fact only the kingdom of New Spain was directly subject to him. The Philippines, Guatemala and the provinces of Yucatan and of New Biscay (California) were separately ruled by captains-general. The viceroy of Peru had control over the entire extent of Spanish South America. As we shall see, further divisions took place within the framework of the government, but not until the first quarter of the eighteenth century.

The viceroy was endowed with almost all the prerogatives of royalty. There were only two checks upon his authority. The first was the *residencia*, a legal investigation of his conduct which might be instituted at the king's pleasure on a viceroy's return to Spain, but which seldom, if ever, was held. The second was the *audiencia*, the resident court of appeal which the viceroy as its honorary president could usually manage. Ward describes the *audiencia* as a body 'possessed of considerable power and influence; it had a control over all other tribunals ecclesiastical as well as civil and had enjoyed the privilege of corresponding directly with the sovereign, and with the Council of the Indies'[1] (which was the Crown's agency in Spain for administering the American colonies). 'This right to communicate directly with this formidable tribunal gave of itself great weight to the *audiencia*; and this was increased by the care with which its members were usually selected, and the pains that were taken to keep them distinct from the natives.' The *oidores*, the jurors, were forbidden to marry Creoles, as were the viceroys and their children, or to engage in trade or even to hold property in the country in which they resided. Even their dress was prescribed. J. H. Parry writes that they led a semi-monastic life housed in a building adjoining the court and were forbidden to attend bull fights or any similar public amusement. 'The only relaxation allowed them was attendance at religious festivals.'[2] To compensate for all this their salaries were much higher than those of any other colonial officials except viceroys, who received about twelve thousand pounds a year save 'that a few court favourites obtained as much as sixteen thousand pounds'. Both Humboldt and Ward claimed that a majority of the viceroys were hopelessly corrupt. Men of modest income when they took up office they were reputed to have returned to Spain worth millions. Humboldt and Ward have been much quoted, but one should consider that Humboldt was writing just before the Revolution and Ward just after it, when the Spaniards' reputation was at its blackest. The material now available throws a different light on the subject. Of the sixty-two viceroys who ruled Mexico surprisingly few turned out badly. They were, for the most part, honourable hard-working men, 'administrative public servants', as Simpson puts it, 'trained for their profession, and possessing a high degree of personal responsibility'.

A letter written by Bucareli, the forty-sixth viceroy, gives an idea of the viceroy's daily life: it was not a sinecure. 'I spend ten hours at my desk, and still cannot complete what I would like . . . Some Sundays I go to the theatre, more to comply with the public expectation than because it entertains me. At ten I am in bed.'[3] He had no family, and ate alone, which he thought a martyrdom.

[1] *Mexico in 1827.*
[2] J. H. Parry, *The Spanish Seaborne Empire*, Hutchinson, London, 1966.
[3] *The Viceregency of Antonio María Bucareli*, by Bernard Bobb, University of Texas Press, Austin, 1962.

Scanning three centuries of names, a succession of nobles, prelates and court politicians, one finds that only one viceroy was American born, the Peruvian Don Juan de Acuña, Marqués de Casafuerte. Others stick in one's memory because of some peculiarity: the Duke de Veraguas, for instance, who died a few days before taking office; or José Valladares, the thirty-second viceroy, who married a direct descendant of Montezuma and was given the title of Conde de Montezuma. One can see their portraits in Chapultepec Castle where they are represented three-quarter length, standing stiff and erect, bedecked in all their finery, and all posed indoors with no distracting backgrounds. The light, Soria writes, is usually clear and even, as in a cloudless Mexican day: 'the likeness', he continues, 'is linear rather than sculptural'.[1] Each viceroy is identified by his coat of arms, full name, and titles of nobility and office painted at the bottom of the picture or appended in a decorative Rococo shield. The names and titles can confuse the visitor, for sometimes one viceroy held office twice or, like Luis de Velasco, was succeeded by his son.

Count Gálvez is the only viceroy not portrayed in the usual manner. Instead he prances off on a calligraphic steed executed in delicate black and white scrollwork. His body is also of scrolls, except for the head, the hands and his lace jabot. This lively portrait was painted by two monks, Fray Pablo de Jesús who did the head and Father San Gerónimo who provided the calligraphy. Gálvez, who ruled from 1785–7, belonged to a family that had risen to power under Charles III. He was young, amiable and rich, and lived in great style, converting Chapultepec into his summer residence. His wife, the Vicereine, was a celebrated beauty, and one of the first blondes to be seen in Mexico.

Following close on Gálvez came Juan Vicente de Güemes, the second Conde de Revillagigedo, well known as a model viceroy. 'His reign,' Simpson writes, 'was the triumph and final flowering of benevolent despotism.'[2] He was an energetic reformer and an excellent administrator. During his tenure of office the Crown revenue reached the highest point in its history. Revillagigedo gave the city a proper lighting system, replacing the flaring torches servants or slaves had to carry on dark moonless nights. He paid 'sedulous heed to the public welfare', and in order to discover and correct hidden abuses he wandered incognito about the city at night attended by one or two aides-de-camp. One such Haroun Al Raschid-like expedition was described by Madame Calderón. Late one night his Excellency encountered a good-looking damsel walking briskly and alone on the outskirts of the city. Suspicious of her motives, though she was 'quiet and modest in her demeanour',

[1] *Art and Architecture in Spain and Portugal and their American Dominions, 1500 to 1800.*
[2] *Many Mexicos.*

the Viceroy decided to 'try the temper of her steel – or brass'. His officers were told to drop behind while the grave and severe Revillagigedo made his advances which were instantly rejected:

'Come!' says his Excellency, 'give over these airs – you, a *mugereilla*, strolling alone in search of adventure.' For answer he received a well applied box on the ear. The staff rushed forward and were astonished to find the Viceroy smiling. 'What! your Excellency – such insolence! such audacity! such—' 'Come, come,' said the Viceroy, 'she has proved herself worthy of our favour.'

Inquiries were made about her birth and parentage, and above all about her reason for being on the streets so late. It turned out that she was a poor girl who supported a dying mother by giving music lessons. Among her pupils was the daughter of an old lady who lived outside the city gates. 'On being informed of these particulars, his Excellency ordered her a pension of three hundred dollars per annum, to be continued to the day of her death.'

The Chapultepec portraits, hanging in chronological order, offer an excellent survey of the evolution in fashions. In the sixteenth and seventeenth centuries, viceroys mostly wore the black Hapsburg court dress: short black capes with collars, doublets, breeches, black stockings and low shoes. Only Cortés, included among the viceroys, is portrayed, quite appropriately, in armour. Mendoza and Velasco are shown in those circular woollen caps worn by their king and familiar to us from the paintings of Titian, Clouet and Corneille de Lyon. The cap is jauntily tilted to one side and pulled slightly forward over the forehead. In the early portraits the shirt gatherings are just visible above the outer garment, forming a modest ruff at the neck. These grow in size with the years until starched linen stands out in bold flutings, forming an entirely separate garment, as seen in the portrait of Don Luis de Velasco II. Hats grew with the ruffs so that by the beginning of the seventeenth century they were high-crowned and made of straw. An abrupt change occurred when the Bourbons introduced French fashions into Spain. Then the viceroys all dressed in rich lace and heavily embroidered silks 'often with an Oriental flavour, reminders that the Spanish trade with the Far East went via Mexico'.[1]

The first hundred years of the city's history is poorly documented pictorially. There are a few rather schematic bird's-eye views and a small collection of maps. A hand-coloured engraving dated 1580 shows the city still linked to the land by causeways like a medieval Venice. The next document, dated from forty-eight years later, already shows considerable differences. Much of the ground had been filled in and a

[1] *Art and Architecture in Spain and Portugal and their American Dominions, 1500 to 1800.*

great dike ran round the eastern perimeter. Mexico City now looked like a Dutch city in the fens. The total absence of any fortification throughout its history is striking, and led Gage to write in the middle of the seventeenth century, 'the Spaniards live so secure from enemies that there are neither gates, wall, bulwark, platform, tower, armoury, ammunition nor ordnance to secure and defend the city from a domestic or foreign enemy; from the latter they think San Juan de Ulúa (the fort of Vera Cruz) sufficient and strong enough to secure them'.

Secure as it might have been from attack by man, the city was certainly not safe from the elements. The first flood in 1553 led to the construction of a great dike. These dikes, modelled after those erected by the Aztecs, were often more than fifty feet in breadth, consisting of a wall of stone and clay, supported on each side by a range of palisades. Even so they were adequate only if the rains were not exceptionally heavy.

A study of the relevant water levels in the valley reveals the seriousness of the problem. At normal water level the pavements of the city were exactly three feet above Texcoco, the principal lake, but the two northern lakes, San Cristóbal and Zumpango, lay twenty-five feet above the city, while Xochimilco and Chalco to the south were ten feet higher. In other words the city lay in a watery hollow, protected in normal times from the overflow of four other lakes by a complex system of dikes. The southern lakes, fed by mere streams whose flows were barely affected by the rains, presented no real danger except in the unlikely event that Popocatepetl should erupt and melt the snow on its peak. The main problem lay in the northern lakes. Zumpango was fed by the powerful Tula river which in heavy rains became a raging torrent emptying into Zumpango to swell its volume to bursting point. The excess spilled over into San Cristóbal, and the waters of the two combined would on occasion burst the dikes separating them from Texcoco, a lake with no outlet.

The floods increased in severity with the years, occurring in 1580 and again in 1604. Indiscriminate deforestation for timber to construct the city was one of the causes. Cortés' palace alone absorbed nine thousand heavy wooden beams. In 1607 the whole valley was flooded and the city almost abandoned. It was at this point that the Council of the Indies ordered the city removed to higher ground. The citizens refused to comply; but in order to validate their stand they were obliged to cope with the floods. Tired of constructing dikes which the water periodically destroyed, they decided to adopt another hydraulic system, and to dig canals.

Enrico Martínez (probably of German extraction and born, it is thought, Heinrich Martin), a Royal Cosmographer to the Court of

27 *Luis de Velasco, Marqués de Salinas, the eighth viceroy (1590–95) who returned from Peru and became viceroy for the second time (1607–11). His father, after whom he was named, had been second viceroy after Mendoza (page 85)*

28 (far left) Juan Vicente de Gümes, the second Conde de Revillagigedo (1789–94) (page 84)

29 Count Bernardo de Gálvez (1785–87) (page 84)

30 'A hand-coloured engraving dated 1580 shows the city still linked to the land by causeways like a medieval Venice' (page 85)

MEXICO.
Anno 1580.

MEXICO, REGIA
ET CELEBRIS
HISPANIÆ NO-
VAE CIVITAS.

31 San Angel (page 92)

32 A monastic retreat built by the barefoot Carmelite friars (page 92)

33 Desierto de los Leones, surrounded by tall murmuring pines (page 93)

34 The hacienda of Santa Clara (page 95)

35 Farm buildings at Santa Clara (page 95)

Madrid, proposed the opening of a canal six miles long from Lake
Zumpango to Nochistongo. To achieve this, a subterranean tunnel had
to be cut four miles straight through the mountains, which fortunately
for the Indian workers were composed not of rock but of loose and
crumbling earth. On the other side of the mountains another canal two
miles in length would drain the Tula river. It was a stupendous task.
On 28 November 1607 the Marqués de Salinas, in the presence of the
audiencia, applied the first pickaxe. Fifteen thousand Indians had been
drafted, and the work, carried out in a number of shafts simultaneously,
was finished in a record eleven months. To commemorate the occasion
the Viceroy entered the tunnel on horseback and according to Martínez
who accompanied him 'he advanced to the depth of two miles'. The
gallery, only ten feet wide and just over fifteen feet high, was the first
tunnel of its kind in the modern world. Pliny describes one constructed
in Italy to drain Lake Fucino but that was only half the length. The
Viceroy must have been a man of steel nerves.

The tunnel achieved its purpose, siphoning off a good part of
Zumpango together with the troublesome river, so that for a while the
city was entirely free from apprehension. But as Ward pointed out, 'an
enterprise of such magnitude, conducted with such extraordinary expedition, could hardly be free from defects' and it was not long before they
became apparent. The interior of the tunnel had been lined with mud
bricks that began to corrode immediately. A facing of wood proved
equally ineffectual and masonry was at last tried. This succeeded for a
time but the vaulting had insufficient foundations and also fell in.
When the next abnormally heavy rains occurred in 1629 the tunnel was
too silted up to be of any assistance. Overnight Texcoco splashed over
its embankment. A golden head of a lion at the corner of Avenida
Madero and the Alley of the Holy Ghost marks the height, about six
feet, reached by the water. The floods persisted for five years until the
Council of the Indies again called for a move. Their order was again
sidestepped; this time because a series of earthquakes in 1634 opened
great rents in every direction that allowed the water gradually to seep
away.

The tunnel was eventually converted into an open trench, but this
latter undertaking was not finished until 1789, nearly two centuries
after its commencement. It is known as the *Tajo*, or Cut of Nochistongo,
and Mexico's National Railway now winds through it.

Canals survived well on into the eighteenth century, for mention is
made of the viceroy and his family in the viceregal barge with pennants
flying. One canal, the Viga (now known, what little of it exists, as the
Canal Nacional), was still functioning as late as 1850. It ran from just
behind the Plaza Major clear out to Xochimilco, and a road of sorts

skirting one side and lined all the way with poplars constituted one of Madame Calderón's favourite rides. 'We would go to the Viga at six in the morning, before the sun was high, to see the Indians bringing in their flowers and vegetables by the canal. The profusion of sweet-peas, double poppies, gilly-flowers and roses, I never saw equalled.' The women in their canoes seemed to be seated in a floating garden of flowers. In the evening they wove garlands of the roses and poppies they had not sold, 'and are constantly crowned. The same love of flowers distinguishes them now as in the time of Cortés'.

Already by 1625 the city had streets broad enough to accommodate six coaches driven abreast. The cathedral must also have been well under way, for the corner-stone was laid in 1573 and the dedication performed eighty-three years later, in 1656. By 1667 the great central arches of its three aisles were finished, the scaffolding removed and the cathedral open for public worship. Only the façade and its details, the tower tops, and the drum of the cupola over the crossing were later embellishments. Begun in Philip II's reign, the building had been overtaken during its construction by the Baroque and terminated in the Neo-Classical manner of the late eighteenth century. Indeed, looking at it now 'it is hard to determine', as Sanford writes, 'whether the building is Baroque trying to hide its severe classic spirit or classic trying to dominate the Baroque superimposed upon it'. (He refers to the Renaissance classicism of its original plan and not to the later eighteenth-century classical detailing.) Notwithstanding its hybrid style, the cathedral imparts a feeling of lordly grandeur, and even while still in construction it must have impressed the spectator who as the years passed saw the buff lime-stone drums piling up in great clustered piers to terminate eventually in stiff, correct Doric capitals. When finished the cathedral dominated the whole square, indeed the whole continent, for until quite recently it was the largest church in the Western Hemisphere.

Mexico was one of the richest cities in the world, 'to which by the North Sea', wrote Gage, 'cometh every year from Spain a fleet of near twenty ships laden with the best commodities not only of Spain but of the most parts of Christendom'. In the south was the commerce with Peru and above all the trade from the East Indies as well as 'from those parts which are inhabited by Portuguese and from the countries of Japan and China'. 'In my time,' he continues, 'the population was thought to be between thirty and forty thousand Spaniards, who are so proud and rich that half the city was judged to be keeping coaches. The coaches do exceed in cost the best of the court of Madrid' – they were encrusted with silver and upholstered with cloth of gold and flowered Chinese silks. Even the horses were shod in silver! 'Both the men and the women are excessive in their apparel, using more silks than stuffs and cloth.' Jewels were prominently displayed, 'a hat-band and rose made of diamonds in a gentleman's hat is common, and a hat-band of pearls is ordinary in a tradesman'. The gallants when they stepped abroad had a train of blackamoors, 'some a dozen, some half a dozen waiting on them, in brave and gallant liveries, heavy with gold and silver lace, with silk stockings on their black legs'. Ladies 'also carry their train by their coach's side'; jet-black damsels in light apparel, 'who, with their bravery and white mantles over them, seem to be, as the Spanish sayeth, *mosca en leche*, a fly in milk'. The train of the viceroy 'some say is as great as the train of his master, the King of Spain'.

The religious houses had incredible wealth:

There are not above fifty churches and chapels, cloisters and nunneries, and parish churches in the city; but those that are there are the fairest that ever my eyes beheld, the roofs and beams being in many of them all daubed with gold, and many altars with sundry marble pillars, and others with hazel-wood stays standing one above another with tabernacles for several saints richly wrought with gold.

Gage mentions a hundred-branched chandelier of solid silver hanging in the church attached to the Dominican Monastery. The Augustines were also heavily endowed, 'having riches of infinite price, such as copes, canopies, hangings . . . and a tabernacle of solid gold and crystal to carry about the sacrament in procession'. Their monastery, however, had already suffered severely from poor foundations, too hurriedly laid on recently reclaimed land. The cloister was falling, and 'I was credibly informed that that was the third time that new pillars had been erected upon the old, which were quite sunk away.'

Gage was also very impressed by the streets: the *Calle del Aguila* was one of the finest 'where live gentlemen, and courtiers and judges'. St Austin was also 'rich and comely and here dwell all who trade in silks'. Off the main square 'is a beautiful street called *La Platería*, Goldsmith Street[1] . . . In less than an hour one may behold many millions worth of gold, silver, pearls and jewels'.

The jewellers themselves were for the most part Aztecs aided by skilful Chinese silversmiths who had arrived in the country at Acapulco on the Manila galleons. One particularly talented worker was a protégé of the Viceroy, the Marqués de Cerralvo, who commissioned this anonymous Fabergé to fashion a fabulous popinjay 'as a present unto the king'. It was the size of a pheasant, cast in gold with its feathers inlaid with precious stones, and of such 'exquisite art and perfection that it was prized to be worth in riches and workmanship half a million of ducats'.

[1] Later known as *Calle de San Francisco* and now named *Madero*.

Although Gage admired the breadth of the streets, 'those of Christendom must not compare with them in cleanness'; others found them ill-paved and strewn with garbage thrown from windows and balconies. Obregón writes that 'broken pots and old clothes, dead dogs and cats litter the streets', but so they did in any European city during the seventeenth century. What must have struck the traveller was the exotic character of the place and the curious aspect of its inhabitants: a mottled crowd of Indians some in native costume, others in Spanish dress, a fashion adopted by the rich *caciques* and Indian women of noble birth. A strange law had been passed forbidding all mestizos, mulattos and Negroes to dress themselves in anything except Spanish attire.

A number of Negroes had been imported to circumvent the prohibition against Indian bondage. The majority remained in the hot coastal region where they worked the lands. Some, however, came to the cities, especially during the early years of colonization. Prior to 1575 they probably outnumbered the whites, but as time passed they were gradually absorbed or else bought their freedom and disappeared. In any case the mixture of blood had produced a colourful variety of hybrids: the mulattoes, descendants of white and Negro, and the zamboes, descendants of Negro and Indian. Sub-divisions went on *ad infinitum* producing quadroons and quintroons. Indians and Chinese or Malays from the Philippines produced a caste known as *chino cambujos*. The dominant caste were naturally the mestizos or mixed breed of whites and Indians. As few Spanish women came to America during the early years, it was not considered a *mésalliance* to marry a well-born Aztec girl.[1]

Gage was intrigued by the mulatto girls, 'more like roaring boys than honest civil maids . . . Their carriage is so enticing that many of the Spaniards even of the better sort disdain their wives for them . . . When they go abroad they cast a white mantle of cambric over their shoulders', more often than not just over one shoulder, swaggering and swinging the free arm 'to show off their broad sleeves bordered with silver lace hanging down almost unto the ground.' Their dresses he describes as being of the flimsiest kind clasped with 'broad girdles of great price stuck with knots of gold'. Low-cut bodices frogged with more silver lace cupped their 'tawny breasts' which were 'covered with bobs hanging from their chains of pearls'. 'The profaner sort' tottered through the streets on stilts or many-soled shoes plated in silver. He adds that 'most

---

[1] Humboldt points out that the principal Indian families were badly hit by the Conquest. The rich Indian women preferred marrying their Spanish conquerors to allying themselves with the remnants of their countrymen: the poor artisans, workmen, porters etc., whom Cortés describes as filling the streets of the great cities, were considered little better than beasts of burden.

of these women are, or have been, slaves though love has set them at liberty to enslave souls to sin and satan'.

There would have been few soldiers about as New Spain had no regular army until much later in its history. What units existed would have been stationed in the north to police the wild Chichimec country. There would, however, have been a variety of religious orders abroad in the streets: Discalced Carmelites; friars of the Order of Mercy, of St João de Deus and of St Anthony; Dominicans in their white habits with black capes; the black-robed Augustinians and Jesuits, the latter in their strange horned and fluted hats. One would not have easily recognized the Franciscans who, unable to procure the right dye in Mexico, had abandoned their familiar brown habit and taken to wearing clear, azure-blue.

For diversion the people flocked to the *Plaza del Volador*, a small square to the left of the palace, where provisional wooden bullrings were erected. Here also they witnessed cockfights, coursing with rabbits and, most diverting of all, the terrible *autos-da-fé*, 'acts of faith', staged by the Inquisition. The Holy Office had implanted itself in Mexico in 1571. Its investigations, as Pál Kelemen points out, were concerned especially with freethinkers, Protestants, Freemasons, and converted Mohammedans and Jews who had reverted to their former faiths.[1] Those with suspicious riches were also subject to scrutiny. Indians, it is interesting to note, were outside the jurisdiction of the Holy Office on the grounds that they were too simple-minded. The tortures practised by the Inquisition were of a fairly rudimentary nature. One consisted of attaching the victim to the rack and shoving a funnel down his throat into which were poured jugs full of water. Simpson tells us that the water torture was so painful that few were able to support it. 'Those who lasted out the course were declared "to have vanquished the torment" and pronounced innocent.'[2] The other torture, the cord treatment, consisted of twisting knotted ropes round the accused's arms and legs; each turn of a stick inserted in the loop tightened the cord which eventually bit into the flesh. These tortures were carried out in secret, within the depth of the Inquisitional Palace. It was only the burnings and strangulations and scourgings that were performed in public. The accused who confessed and repented were obliged to march through the streets as penance, sometimes for months on end, wearing the *sambenito*, a penitent's garb consisting of an open tunic painted with flames, devils and crosses and the diagonal cross of San Andrew. The tunics were worn over striped, tightly fitting combinations. They carried green candles and were coifed in mitres painted to match the tunics.

[1] Pál Kelemen, *Baroque and Rococo in Latin America*, Macmillan & Co., New York, 1951.
[2] *Many Mexicos.*

The Holy Office was not only concerned with heresy but had jurisdiction also over a variety of minor offences such as witchcraft, the casting of spells, bigamy, polygamy, sodomy, and the possession of pornographic and other prohibited books. There were many less concrete misdemeanours leading, as can be imagined, to not a few denunciations that were quite ludicrous. One poor woman in the Canary Islands was reported to the Inquisition for having smiled when she heard mention of the Virgin Mary.

An *auto-da-fé* was by no means a frequent occurrence. A fairly important one, attended by a long line of eighty-four victims, occurred in 1574; another seventy years later. A majority of the victims in the first *autos-da-fé* were the Englishmen taken prisoner when the pirate John Hawkins attacked Vera Cruz in 1568. Two of the men were burnt and the others whipped. The latest victim was the revolutionary hero José María Morelos, burned in November 1815. The Dominicans founded the Holy Office in Mexico City and their last tribunal, erected in 1732–6, was situated in the *Plazuela de Santo Domingo*, where the National School of Medicine is today.

What of the houses and their appearance; how were they lived in? Few have remained as they were originally built. D. H. Lawrence describes the typical conquistador's house with its studded, fortress door and its square, inner patio as:

dark, with sun lying on the heavy arches of one side . . . ponderous, as if dead for centuries. A certain dead, heavy strength and beauty seemed there, unable to pass away, unable to liberate itself and decompose. There was a stone basin of clear but motionless water, and the heavy reddish-and-yellow arches went round the courtyard, their bases in dark shadow.[1]

Beyond was a glimpse of a tall-growing garden, Aztec cypresses rising to strange, dark heights, 'and dead silence, like the black porous, absorptive lava rock'. One can still have fleeting glimpses of the atmosphere he evokes. I found it in the patio of the *Ospidale de Jesús Nazareno* founded by Cortés and again under the colonnades giving on to the *Plazuela de Santo Domingo*, but it is at its strongest in the outlying districts, places such as San Angel, or Churubusco, where the conquistadors lived while the city was being rebuilt. Tlalpa, Tacubaya and Coyoacán – names already familiar – although overtaken by, and now part of the city, still retain the quiet air of a village. It is here that one will find Lawrence's falling of thick plaster from cracked walls, the ponderous still beauty of dead centuries. Another place is a monastic retreat built by the barefoot Carmelite friars at the very beginning of the seventeenth century, some fifteen miles from the capital on the road

[1] D. H. Lawrence, *The Plumed Serpent*, Martin Secker, London, 1926.

to Toluca. It is known as the *Desierto de los Leones* and is surrounded by tall murmuring pines, cedar and oak; a beautiful, silent place of tiled domes and gently crumbling ruins.

The houses in the centre of the city have all been rebuilt with an urban elegance and airy eighteenth-century grandeur. From the roof of my hotel, itself an old building, the ghost of a silhouette, an outline of the city as it must have been, can still be seen: flat-roofed with mountains in the distance. The houses are low and only the cathedral and the domes of the churches stand out against the turquoise sky. 'Few of the public buildings,' wrote Ward in 1827, 'attain the height to which the European eye is accustomed in such edifices.' This was owing partly of course to the difficulty of laying good foundations and partly to the frequency of earthquakes. Although the lakes by this time had been drained, water was, and still is, uniformly found at a very few feet from the surface. Hence all the larger buildings were raised on piles. As to earthquakes, while the shocks are seldom severe in the valley, it was thought unwise to attempt 'too lofty edifices'. A majority of the travellers found the low roofs attractive, reminding them, no doubt, of the Orient. William Bullock, a naturalist and antiquarian, writes that 'seen from a certain distance the city presents a far more beautiful appearance than those of Europe where deformed roofs and shapeless stacks of chimney are the principal features in the prospect'.[1] Mark Beaufoy, a young Guards officer travelling in Mexico in 1828, mentioned that the roofs were bricked and ornamented with flowering shrubs 'effecting a pleasant place of resort on a fine evening'.[2] He writes of the gleaming stars and of the soft moonlight 'flooding the sea of roofs on every side'. He also remarked on the ferocious dogs 'which effectively deter thieves from attempting to swing down on to the balconies of the inner court'. Countess Kollonitz described the Mexican women walking up and down on the roof tops 'to dry their long hair which falls like a mantle over their shoulders and reaches almost to their feet'.

On the whole the houses were well adapted to the climate, which is perpetual spring. The rooms were large and high-ceilinged with no fireplace since there was little change of temperature. Even glass in the windows was often dispensed with.

Madame Calderon on first arriving in Mexico City lodged in the suburbs of Buenavista:

By daylight we find our house very pretty, with a large garden adjoining, full of flowers and rose bushes in the courtyard, but being all on the ground floor it is somewhat damp and the weather though beautiful is so cool in the morning that carpets, and I sometimes think even a soupçon of a fire would not be

[1] *Six Months Residence and Travels in Mexico.*
[2] Mark Beaufoy, *Mexican Illustrations*, London, 1828.

amiss. There are neither chimneys nor grates, and I have no doubt a fire would be disagreeable for more than an hour or so in the morning.

Such lower apartments, however, were generally occupied by the porter and his family and a miscellaneous collection of servants. Very often they were let off as shops or offices. The first floor above it was also rented. The *piano nobile* inhabited by the proprietor was the top one. These houses were seldom more than three-storyed (the four-storeyed Iturbide Palace being a rare exception), and the stairs leading to the family apartments were always of great magnificence.

Madame Calderón says that most of the large houses lacked a fine finish in details. The door would not shut properly and rain washed in under the windows 'making these residences appear something like a cross-breed between a palace and a barn'. I can find no contemporary accounts describing colonial interiors, but Madame Calderón's much later comments give a vague idea of what they must have been like. In general the houses seem to have been richly furnished, for she mentions 'cabinets inlaid with gold', 'fine paintings and hundreds of rich and curious things'. If Madame Calderón found the appointments lavish in 1839, what must they have been before the Revolution, before the closing of the mines and the expulsion of the rich Spanish families – 'before', as Bullock writes, 'the superb tables, chandeliers, and other articles of furniture, of solid silver, the magnificent mirrors and pictures, framed in the same precious metal, had passed through the mint, and in the shape of dollars circulated over Europe and Asia'.

Madame Calderón, with her genius for elaborating just those details about which one is curious, declares that the servants were universally indolent and indifferent to earning money. The porters originally assigned to them were so dishonest that the Calderóns eventually procured two soldiers from the *Invalidos*, old Spaniards who had no worse foibles than being constantly drunk. 'We at length found two others, who only got tipsy alternately, so that we considered ourselves very well off.' She adds that:

one of the most disagreeable customs of the women servants is that of wearing their long hair hanging down at its full length, matted, uncombed, and always in the way. I cannot imagine how the Mexican ladies who complain of this, permit it. Flowing hair sounds very picturesque but when it is very dirty, and suspended over the soup, it is not a pretty picture.

The servants, however, did possess some redeeming qualities. 'They were the perfection of civility – humble, obliging, excessively good-tempered, and very easily attached to those with whom they live.' She also notes that 'notwithstanding the enormous size of Mexican houses they generally are the perfection of cleanliness'.

The same observer also had some interesting things to say about the country *haciendas*, explaining that they must not be equated with English country houses. The *haciendas* were mostly run by major domos, or managers; the owners rarely lived on their estates:

The house is merely used as an occasional retreat during the summer months and is generally a large empty building, with innumerable lofty rooms, communicating with each other and containing the scantiest possible supply of furniture – a deal table and a few chairs; a complete absence of the luxurious furniture which in Mexico seems entirely confined to the town houses.

The eighteenth-century inns appear to have been even bleaker than the *haciendas*. Pages, a French naval officer, travelling round the world between 1767 and 1771, described them as 'large handsome buildings' but says that 'one is not a little mortified on entering them to find they contain nothing but empty apartments, destitute of both furniture and provisions'.[1]

[1] P. M. F. Pages, *Travels Round the World*, London, 1791.

8

A Creole World

The population of New Spain appears to have varied considerably, fluctuating between some five and twelve million people. At the turn of the nineteenth century Humboldt estimated that forty per cent of the whole population were Indians of pure blood. Whites and mestizos accounted for the remaining sixty per cent, mulattoes by this time having almost entirely disappeared. Humboldt reported that Mexico City had some 137,000 inhabitants of which 2,500 were white Europeans, 65,000 Creoles, 26,500 mestizos and 33,000 Indians, with 10,000 mulattoes. He added that a great number of the mestizos were almost as white as the Europeans and the Spanish Creoles. The pure white population further decreased during the following years. Eventually the whole hybrid question became so complex that by 1921 the Mexican census officials had given up the traditional terms Indian, white and mestizo as meaningless and misleading. This, however, was not the attitude adopted by the colonial government, quite the opposite.

The Conquerors and the first colonists were natives of the poorer regions of the Peninsula, the regions that had always furnished Spain with her soldiers. These were the dry, windswept highlands of León and the Asturias, the stony stretches of Castile and the rock-convulsed horizons of Estremadura. As François Chevalier writes:

many said that they hailed from Seville; but by various tokens it appears that frequently they were Andalusians only by adoption, who had made prolonged stays in Seville . . . the meeting place of all those looking for work, service in the army, expeditions, or a change in luck. Most of the soldiers claimed to be *hidalgos*. In point of fact a good number of poor second sons and younger sons of large families did emigrate to the Indies. But among the emigrants were more whose origins were obscure: rustics who had left their villages under a cloud, orphans . . . they all converged on Seville, or wandered off in the wake of companies of soldiers. Charmed by the wonders told of the Indies.[1]

[1] *Land and Society in Colonial Mexico.*

Hidalgo is a contraction of *hijo de algo*, son of somebody, in other words a gentleman. Gage said that all Spanish Americans claimed to be *hidalgos*, 'for everyone will call himself a descendant from a conqueror, though he be as poor as Job. Cobblers or even muleteers, if he be called Mendoza or Guzman, will swear that he descends from those dukes' houses in Spain and that his grandfather came from thence to conquer.' Velasco, the second viceroy, ridiculed such pretensions and complained in his private correspondence that the country was being populated by *gente común*. In any event, whatever their social status, Spaniards considered themselves far superior to the indigenous inhabitants of the country who found themselves bound over in serfdom as manual labourers or, at best, tillers of the soil. While the Indians' lot was to improve slightly, never at any moment in colonial history were they to attain positions of any importance. It was forbidden, for instance, to instruct an Indian in the use of firearms, and no native was allowed to ride a horse unless a special order had been obtained. To the Indians the white man was *gente de razón*, 'people who were in the right', while the Indians themselves were persuaded that they were *gente sin razón*, 'people who were not in the right'.

The second wave of settlers were men of an entirely different calibre from the Conquerors. These were the Officers of the Crown who took over power from the soldier adventurers: jurists and theologians, lawyers, attorneys, notaries and missionaries plus a few merchants, shopkeepers and craftsmen. A century later, still further determined to keep a firm hold on her colonies and suspicious of her colonists, the Crown decreed that all important political posts and offices in the Church be held by Spaniards born in Spain rather than by Mexican-born Creoles, Creole designating a white person of pure European race born in Latin America.[1] Ward writes:

Europeans of every description were united amongst themselves. It became a passion which induced them to prefer the ties of country to the ties of blood. The son, who had the misfortune to be born of a Creole mother, was considered as an inferior in the house of his own father to the European bookkeeper or clerk for whom the daughter, if there were one, and a large share of the fortune were reserved.

'*Eres Criollo y bzsta*', 'you are a Creole and that is enough', was a common phrase among the Spaniards when angry with their children.

Humboldt bears out Ward, saying that 'the most miserable European without education and without intellectual cultivation, thinks himself superior to the white born in the new continent'. The Spaniards born

[1] Although not always admitted, many of the best Creole families have Indian blood which betrays itself in a certain obliquity of the eyes and small hands and feet.

in Spain became known as *Gachupines*, or 'beret-wearers' as opposed to the Creoles.

The viceroy, and the governors, the judges, archbishops and bishops were all *Gachupines* and no doubt were rigidly snobbish towards the rest of the inhabitants of the colony. But however jealously they might have protected their alleged superiority, they were too few to control the social life of the city. Many of the Creole families were well-to-do, owning either silver mines or large *haciendas*. Some, despite the stringent rules, even held the lesser salaried positions in the government. In any event it was the Creoles who effectively set the tone of the city. It was to their houses and to their receptions that one went. It was the Creole way of life that lent the city its particular flavour.

The Creoles were described as generous and warm-hearted. Beaufoy, a handsome young Guards officer, enjoyed their lavish hospitality and commented on their punctilious manners. Taking leave after a visit:

you advance close to the ladies and bow, they must not leave their seats. If very polite you endeavour to gain the door without turning your back, but at all events you pause there and bow. The master of the house accompanies you out, and you bow to each other at the top of the stairs; six steps down you turn and bow again; on the first landing this is repeated, and again at the foot of the staircase. Be sure likewise, if you value your reputation, not to quit the courtyard without turning to see whether your persecutor has still kept you in view. I once gave serious offence by this last omission.

On another occasion he recollected how one distinguished señorita, wishing to show him particular attention, 'put her hand into her bosom, pulled out a number of *cigarritos* and entreated my acceptance of one. Even I who abhor tobacco, have been thus forced to make myself sick more than once; for who could reject a cigar from such a place!'

It is difficult to tell exactly when ladies took up smoking. It is known that smoking became so popular among men at the end of the sixteenth century that Pope Urban VII was obliged to issue an edict excommunicating those who smoked in church. It is from this time that priests began to take snuff. It was said 'to discharge the head' and in Spain was known as *yerba santa*.

Snuff, however, was not for the ladies. John Stephens, the nineteenth-century explorer-archaeologist, was amazed at the amount of clicking of flint and steel that went on in Yucatan among the ladies. 'It was the first time that we had smoked with the fair sex and to begin with we found it rather awkward to ask one for a light.'

There are numerous references to smoking at the opera in Mexico City. The theatre no longer exists, but it must have been pretty with its 'boxes supported by delicate columns; and garlands of flowers,

delicately cut and gilded, twined over a white ground'.[1] The Countess
Kollonitz described the ladies all in black 'with a fan in one hand and a
cigar in another'. There was so much smoke that it was difficult to see
from one side of the house to the other. 'The whole pit smoked,' writes
Madame Calderón, 'the galleries smoked, the boxes smoked, the
prompter smoked, a long stream of smoke curled from his box, giving
something oracular and Delphic to his promptings.'

The Creole women of the fashionable world were pale, coffee-
coloured odalisques with charming manners but little intelligence.
Countess Kollonitz, whose sniffing was so fiercely resented that Empress
Carlota found it advisable to ship her back to Trieste, described their
ignorance as complete. 'They have not the smallest idea of geography
and history. Europe to them is Spain, from whence they spring; Rome
where the pope rules; and Paris from whence come their clothes.' The
only books she ever saw them read were their prayer-books. Ober also
noted their want of intellect and complained 'that sensuality easily
obtains the upper hand' – one wonders what particular experience
prompted these confessions. Madame Calderón was much kinder,
admiring the Mexican women's eyes, their fine dark hair, their beautiful
arms and hands and their little brown feet shown off so well by the
white satin slippers they all wore. 'Their defects,' she writes, 'are that
they are frequently too short and too fat.' When seated they had an air
of great dignity and the most perfect repose of feature. 'They are always
to be seen to the most advantage on their sofas, in their carriages, or in
their boxes at the theatre.' But they did not compare favourably with
the Indian women, many of whom were very beautiful. Madame
Calderon particularly admired their graceful upright figures and the
way they strode out when they walked. The Creoles abroad in the
streets 'seem to feel pain in putting their feet to the ground', probably
through want of practice, for walking was frowned upon in the city:

A few ladies in black gowns and mantilla do occasionally venture forth on
foot very early to shop or to attend mass. But the streets are so ill kept, the
pavements so narrow, the crowds so great, and the multitude of *léperos* in rags
and blankets so annoying that all those inconveniences, added to the heat of
the sun in the middle of the day, form a perfect excuse for their non-
appearance in the streets of Mexico.

'Instead,' commented another traveller, 'they pass the days among
themselves in *négligée* and careless freedom.' Madame Calderón wrote
that there was too great a difference 'between the full dress style of toilet
adopted by the ladies when they pay their visits and the manner in
which they receive their visits at home'. No Mexican lady ever called

[1] *The Court of Mexico.*

on Madame Calderón in the morning without diamonds. 'The Dowager Countess of C——, a very distinguished woman, one of the true ladies of the old school of whom not many specimens now remain in Mexico, was dressed in black velvet, lace mantilla, diamond ear-rings and brooch.' A splendid *parure* of diamonds was worn on another morning by the Marquesa de San Roman, 'an old lady who has travelled a great deal in Europe, and who is of a noble Venetian family'. Madame Calderón remarked that she and her contemporaries, the last survivors of the days of viceroyalty, were fast fading away. One gathers that other callers were of less *bon ton*, such as an extremely rich general's wife, mistress of the handsomest house in Mexico. Her mantilla was fastened by three diamond aigrettes, and she wore diamond ear-rings of extraordinary size as well as 'a diamond necklace of immense value and beautifully set. A necklace of pear pearls. On every finger two diamond rings, like little watches. Dress of purple velvet, embroidered all over with flowers of white silk.'

The morning, even among the ladies of the diplomatic corps, seems to have been the accepted time for calling, for we find Madame Calderón having breakfast with 'a young and beautiful Countess lately married, and of very low birth. She looked very splendid, with all the family diamonds, and a dress of rose-coloured satin.' Hot chocolate, highly spiced with cinnamon, was served on these occasions. The etiquette sounds tedious beyond words. When the newcomer had been embraced and seated on the right side of the sofa, the following dialogue was *de rigueur*:

'How are you? Are you well?'

'At your service, and you?'

'As usual (*sin novedad*) at your service.'

'I am rejoiced, and how are you, Señora?'

'At your disposal, and you?'

And so it went on.

In another letter Madame Calderón mentioned that 'it is considered more polite to say señorita than señora even to married women, and the lady of the house is generally called by her servants, "*La niña*", "the little girl", even though she is over eighty'.

If the *Gachupines* were haughty towards the Creoles, both groups were appallingly insular in their treatment of foreigners. It was not even a question of foreigners being able to converse in Spanish, but literally whether or not they *hablan Christiano*. The English, French, Germans and North Americans were all lumped together and, along with the Jews, condemned as heretics and unbelievers whom no good Catholic could frequent without contamination. It was almost impossible for a Mexican to obtain permission to visit a foreign country. The situation, however, improved after the separation from Spain. By Madame Calderón's day the city, as we have seen, had a *corps diplomatique*.

She described a ball given by the British Minister to commemorate Queen Victoria's twenty-first birthday. It was held in the School of Mines and went off with great éclat. 'Nothing,' she wrote, 'could be more splendid than the general effect of this noble building, brilliantly illuminated and filled with a well-dressed crowd.' Although this ball took place somewhat later than the viceregal period, customs being so slow to change, it resembled a viceregal occasion. 'We ladies of the *corps diplomatique* tried to flatter ourselves that we made up in elegance what we wanted in magnificence! for in jewels no foreign ladies could attempt to compete with those of the country.' One countess wore pale blue, with garlands of pale pink roses, and a *parure* of most superb brilliants. Madame Calderón compared a certain señora's tiara with the one she had seen Lady Londonderry wearing at Covent Garden. The Marquesa de Vivanco wore a *rivière* of brilliants of extraordinary size and beauty. Another woman had a dress '*garnie* with plumes of ostrich feathers, a large diamond fastening each plume'. There was a profusion of large pearls, generally pear-shaped. 'Diamonds are always worn plain or with pearls; coloured stones are considered trash, which is a pity, as I think rubies and emeralds set in diamonds would give more variety and splendour to their jewels.'

According to the same description, no man, however modest his fortune, married in Mexico without presenting his bride with at least a pair of diamond ear-rings, or a pearl necklace with a diamond clasp. 'They are considered a necessity of life; quite as much so as shoes and stockings.'

Thinking back on the ball the Englishwoman came to the conclusion that the women on the whole were overdressed, or 'over loaded' as she puts it, 'a common fault in Mexico; and many of the dresses though rich, were old fashioned'.

From the College of Mines let us move to the cathedral. Hardly a day passed that I did not slip quietly into its dim, beautifully proportioned interior. On each visit I was impressed by its size and by the magnificent sweep of its side aisles. The floor dips towards the centre, propelling one forward towards the great choir that occupies two bays of the central nave and interrupts the vista. The choir is very splendid with large elaborately encased organs and richly carved stalls. A heavy wrought-iron grille, or *reja*, shuts the choir off from the high altar, but when the doors swing open one steps into the *via de crujía*, or processional walk, leading onward between solidly wrought metal balustrades that support metal angels carrying wax candles. The balustrades were cast in Macao and shipped to Mexico via the Philippines. The metal is known as *tumbaga* and is a special alloy of brass and silver, silver that probably came from the mines of New Spain. Considering the rather dull effect of the final result, one wonders if it was really worth all the trouble. The cost of production and shipping must have been considerable and the balustrades must literally be worth their weight in gold.

In the apse, at the far side of the high altar, is the remarkable *Capilla de los Reyes* built for the use of the Spanish sovereign if ever he had come to Mexico, a visit often projected but never actually undertaken. The chapel is the work of Gerónimo Balbas and contains a duplicate of the large *retablo* he did for the Sagrario[1] of Seville cathedral (now replaced). This took nearly twenty years to carve, being finished in 1737 and gilded in 1743. It is, as Sanford describes it, 'a resplendent maze of wood carving, gilding, and painting, filled with a host of saints, angels and cherubs'. Despite its vast scale it has the elaborateness of a Renaissance enamelled jewel and is the first example of the Churrigueresque style in New Spain.

Both Madame Calderón and Ober were awed by the magnificence they found in the cathedral. She refers to bishops arrayed in white velvet and gold, 'their mitres literally covered with diamonds'. Ward wrote of treasures which 'seemed to burn with an almost intolerable brightness'. After a century and a half of plundering, few of these treasures remain. Their absence, however, hardly diminishes the effect made by the interior. The organ is playing and smoke curls up from the censers. High above, where Huitzilopochtli once sat enthroned, blazes the hot Mexican sun, its brightness filtered by the clerestory windows. In long diagonal shafts it falls in dancing motes, probing the cool depths below where the flames of devotional candles flicker.

The Altar of Pardon at the back of the choir and the chapel of St Philip of Jesus, born in Mexico and martyred in Nagasaki, are both very popular, but it is Our Lord of Poison who claims the most attention. He hangs from his cross limp and pitch black, skirted with *ex voto* silver hearts of all sizes, one overlapping the other. Legend says that a certain nobleman, particularly devoted to this image of Christ, was poisoned by his enemies. On realizing his plight he dragged himself to the cathedral and in his last agonies managed to draw himself up to kiss the crucifix, which thereupon turned the ebony colour we now see it. Christ, drawing the poison unto himself, had saved the nobleman.

In the past, during special services, men were allowed to sit on chairs or benches, while women were obliged to sit on the ground. The floor was so dirty wrote Madame Calderón 'that one kneels with a feeling of horror'. Countess Kollonitz accused the congregation of showing

---

[1] According to Joseph Baird, a *sagrario* is a 'building where the consecrated Host is kept – often a kind of parish church for a cathedral'.

36 A Mexican lady of about 1790 painted by Ignacio María Barreda (page 99)

37, 38 (above) *The Cathedral, Mexico City. A great choir occupies two bays of the central nave (page 101). (below) 'The hot Mexican sun, its brightness filtered by the clerestory windows of the Cathedral' (page 102)*

39 *The girl when she appeared 'was arrayed in pale blue satin, with diamonds, pearls, and a crown of flowers'. Note the escudo de monje (page 105)*

40 *Sor Inés de la Cruz* (*page 108*)

little true piety. 'High and low are very much under the thumb of the clergy, and kiss with humility the hands of these pious gentlemen.' People surrounded the altar 'like a herd of pasturing sheep'. Distinguished ladies, closely veiled in heavy silks, knelt beside some 'filthy disgusting *lépero*'. Indians crowded about, half-naked, some carrying long poles on which perched brightly coloured parrots. Others huddled at the base of a pillar, threading one another's hair with bony fingers in eager search of lice. Madame Calderón added that except on special occasions and at certain hours, few ladies performed their devotions in the cathedral.

Everywhere were the *léperos*, homeless, half-naked beggars that for generations had thronged the streets of the city, a sinister underworld, a mixture of the worst of the Spanish with the worst of the Aztec races, their progeny exhibiting all the vices, without a single virtue. Humboldt compared them to the *lazzaroni* of Naples. Passing storms were their only toilet. Their clothes were a tattered blanket begrimed with abominations and leather breeches donned at puberty, a second skin that was never peeled. Wild eyed, with long lank hair, their features pinched by famine, they haunted the shadows, limped down the side alleys and sheltered in the churches.

They are often mentioned in letters and diaries. Madame Calderón's experiences with the *léperos* send chills down one's spine. She had scarcely settled in the city and was still living out at Buenavista in a large one-storeyed country house:

Whilst I am writing a horrible *lépero*, with great leering eyes, is looking at me through the windows, and performing the most extraordinary series of groans, displaying at the same time a hand with two fingers, probably the other three tied in. 'Señorita! Señorita! For the love of the Most Holy Virgin! For the sake of the most pure blood of Christ!' . . . the wretch! I dare not look up, but I feel that his eyes are fixed upon a gold watch and seals lying on the table. That is the worst of a house on the ground floor . . . There come more of them! A paralytic woman mounted on the back of a man with a long beard. A sturdy-looking individual, who looks as if, were it not for the iron bars, he would resort to more effective measures, is holding up a deformed foot . . . What groans! What rags! What a chorus of whining!

Madame Calderón tried to write on, to take no notice as if she were deaf but the agitation outside the window was too much for her. 'There are no bell-ropes in these parts. I must walk out of the room, without looking behind me, and send the porter to disperse them.' Hardly had she returned and started writing again, 'when I heard a footstep near me, and, looking up, lo! there was my friend with *the foot*, standing within a yard of me, his hand stretched out for alms! I was so frightened

that for a moment I thought of giving him my watch to get rid of him.'
But gliding past him while mumbling a few unintelligible words she
rushed to call the servants, 'sending him some money by the first person
who came . . . the porter, who had not seen him pass, is now dispersing
the crowd. A—— has come in and drawn the curtains, and I think they
are going off.'

Another striking aspect of life in Mexico City were the number of
nunneries. Young girls, whether *Gachupines* or Creoles, were all educated
in the convents, where many stayed as lodgers until of marriageable age.
The nunneries also became sanctuaries for dowerless daughters, 'plentiful', writes Chevalier, 'in a country where there were frequently fifteen
or twenty children to a family'.[1]

The usually critical Gage was impressed by the care lavished on these
jeunes filles. They were taught the most delicate needlework and the
subtleties of the difficult and complex Mexican cuisine. 'They are also
taught to make all sorts of music, which is so exquisite in that city that
I dare be bold to say that the people are drawn to the churches more
for the delight of the music than for any delight in the service of God.'
Nuns, gathered in their elaborate balconies where they were invisible
behind iron or wooden grilles, sang in the different convent churches.
One anonymous traveller described such a scene in the convent church
of Santa Clara, a small and elegant interior with white marble columns
wreathed round with gold. It was quite empty 'and in the midst of a
vast death-like stillness a voice of angelic sweetness was singing behind
the grating, alone'.

By the close of the sixteenth century there were twenty-two nunneries
in Mexico City, most of them generously endowed by pious donors who
left them large sums in their wills. Chevalier tells us that certain convents were reserved for high Creole society, 'in these each nun had
personal serving-women and companions. A number of Immaculate
Conception convents quartered several hundred of these servants. The
cloister rule was so lenient that civil and religious authorities sometimes
had to intervene and ban performances of plays and concerts . . .'[2]

Not all the orders were lenient. The Santa Teresa Convent, for
instance, practised the most gruelling penances. Madame Calderón
visited the convent in the company of Monseigneur Madrid, 'a good-
looking man, young and tall, and very splendidly dressed' whose purple
robes, fine point-lace and cross of diamonds and amethysts must have
struck an almost jarring note against the bare convent walls. The nuns
had permission to put up their veils, a thing rarely allowed in the strict
orders in the presence of strangers. The Mother Superior led the party

[1] *Land and Society in Colonial Mexico.*
[2] *Ibid.*

into the refectory, a large room with narrow deal tables and benches ranged all round. 'Before the place of each nun, an earthen bowl, an earthen cup with an apple in it, a wooden plate and a wooden spoon; at the top of the table a grinning skull, to remind them that even these indulgences they should not long enjoy.'

The visitors were shown an iron crown of thorns with nails pointing inwards that was worn by the nuns on special occasions during which a penitent, with her mouth gagged with a wooden bit as well, would lie prostrate on the floor of the refectory until the meal was ended. Further self-inflicted penances were practised by the nuns in their cells. They slept on wooden planks with a wooden pillow, holding a cross in their hands and with their feet sticking out over the end of their pallets which were purposely made too short. 'Round her waist she occasionally wears a band with iron points turned inwards; on her breast a cross with nails.' Sometimes they scourged themselves with nail-studded whips. Each nun kept these instruments of discipline in a little box beside her bed.

Madame Calderón was surprised at their cheerfulness but noted that many looked pale and unhealthy. Among them was one strikingly beautiful novice. 'She was as pale as marble, and though still young, seemed in very delicate health.' Her eyes and eyebrows were as black as jet, the eyes large and soft, the eyebrows two pencilled arches; her smile so resigned and sweet that 'she would have made the loveliest model imaginable for a Madonna'.

After the rounds the Bishop and Madame Calderón were served an elegant supper, 'a profusion of custards, jellies and ices', the ices made from the snows wreathing Popocatepetl.

Few writers on Mexico can approach Madame Calderón. Observant and alive, she tells us more in one letter than others can pack into several chapters. 'The finest monastery in Mexico,' she writes, 'is that of San Francisco.' Built in 1531 and now, alas, demolished to make way for a road, it was founded by Fray Pedro de Grante, a great benefactor of the Indians and an illegitimate son of Emperor Charles v. No woman, of course, may enter the monasteries, but one vicereine, insisting on her prerogative, forced her way into San Francisco. 'Immediately the gallery and every place her footstep had desecrated were unpaved. *Peu galant* to say the least of it.'

Of all the different episodes recounted in Madame Calderón's letters, those dealing with girls about to take the veil are perhaps the most arresting. At one ceremony the Mother Superior gave Her Excellency an honoured place, beside the godmother of the future nun, who appeared 'arrayed in pale blue satin, with diamonds, pearls, and a crown of flowers; the corsage of her gown entirely covered with little bows of ribbon of divers colours'. On her chest she wore an *escudo de monje*, an oval tortoiseshell plaque painted with a religious scene, usually a representation of the Virgin. Worn high, almost touching the chin, these *escudos de monje* seem peculiar to Mexico for I can find no reference to them in Spain.

At another such ceremony the new nun was flushed in the face 'as well she might be, for she had passed the day in taking leave of her friends at a fête they had given her, and had then, according to custom, been paraded through the town in all her finery'. Apparently her laughter verged on hysteria. The poor girl was laughing to impress the spectators with:

her perfect happiness; for it is a great point of honour amongst girls similarly situated to look as cheerful and gay as possible – the same kind of courage that makes a Hindu widow mount the funeral pile without a tear in her eye ... the girl was very young, but by no means pretty; on the contrary, rather *disgraciée par la nature*; and perhaps a knowledge of her own want of attraction may have caused the world to have few charms for her.

At one point in the service the girl lay prostrate on the floor, despoiled of her finery and covered over with a black cloth, while the nuns, black figures kneeling round her, chanted a hymn. Before, all had been a blaze of light, a mass of crimson and gold drapery. Now all was darkness. 'Even the sunbeams had faded away, as if they would not look upon the scene' symbolic of the nun's withdrawal from the world. When she was raised 'all the blood had rushed to her face and her attempt at a smile was truly painful'. Blessed by the Bishop she then 'went round alone to embrace all the dark phantoms as they stood motionless, and as each dark shadow clasped her in its arms, it seemed like the dead welcoming a new arrival in the shades'.

More poignant still was the reception of a beautiful girl of good family into the Convent of Our Lady of Incarnation. She was just eighteen, could not possibly have known her own mind (we are told), and had been persuaded to enter a convent by her confessor against her family's wish. The mother looked on pale and sad, her eyes almost extinguished with weeping. In the future she would be allowed to hear her daughter's voice speaking to her only as from the depth of the tomb, the only contact she would ever again have with her. The most terrible thing to witness was the last, straining, anxious look which the mother gave her daughter through the grating. 'Suddenly, and without any preparation, down fell the black curtain like a pall.' The family dissolved into tears. 'One beautiful little child,' the nun's brother, 'was carried out almost in fits.'

Two personalities emerge from this cloistered woman's world. One, the Nun Alférez, rose to fame masquerading as a man. The other, the elegant and witty Sor Inés de la Cruz, was 'more beautiful than any nun should be' and is now considered Mexico's most talented poet.

The Nun Alférez, Doña Catalina Erauso, was born in Spain in the province of Guipúzcoa in 1592, the daughter of an officer. While still very young she decided to take the veil, a hasty decision, for on reaching maturity she realized that she was hopelessly unsuited to the monotonous cloistered life. Escaping in male attire she enlisted in the army, volunteered for service overseas, and was garrisoned eventually in Vera Cruz! It is not quite clear whether the officers realized that she was a woman. Certainly her companions at arms must have known, for they referred to her as Monjita Alférez, 'Little Nun Ensign'. Contemporaries described her as large of stature for a woman, with a swarthy complexion, black hair worn short like a man's and affecting a thin moustache. The painter Francisco Crecencio, who is supposed to have painted her portrait, wrote that 'she carries her sword well-guarded and gives every appearance of a soldier'. Only by her hands was it possible to recognize that she was a woman, 'they are massive and fleshy and the way she moves them is typically feminine'. She journeyed to Rome and, in an audience with the Pope, obtained official sanction to continue wearing men's costume. From Italy she moved to Spain where the King awarded her a pension for services rendered abroad. By 1630 she was back again in New Spain driving mules between Mexico and Vera Cruz. Many stories relate to these years: she is said to have fallen madly in love with a rich magistrate's daughter from Jalapa. She died in 1650 while journeying to the coast, just short of her sixtieth year.

A contrasting tale is that of Sor Inés de la Cruz, or Doña Juana Inés de Asbaje y Ramírez de Santillana, as she was known before she joined the Jeronymite community. She was born in Nepantla, a small hamlet within the shadow of Popocatepetl, in 1651, and went at the age of eight to live with relatives in Mexico City. It was found out afterwards that she had been illegitimate, though this was not generally known at the time, her confessor probably being the only person to share her secret. She must have been a precocious child, for already at the age of three she had begun to read. At any rate it was not long before the Vicereine, Doña Leonor Carreto, wife of the Marqués de Mancera, herself a beautiful and talented woman, heard of the gifted girl. Probably she was about fourteen when she became lady-in-waiting to the Vicereine. Quite a few of her poems written at this period survive, witty and affectionate verses dictated to 'Laura', as she called her patroness. It seems that 'the admiring Viceroy, himself, on one occasion, had arranged that a group of leading professors at the University of Mexico should examine the precocious girl in various branches of learning'. The professors 'marvelled at the erudition and composure of a maiden who hardly seemed more than a child'.[1]

The Marqués de Mancera's court was polished, sophisticated and reputedly somewhat fast. It was rumoured that the Marqués was much taken with Doña Juana's charm. Whether to escape his attentions, or perhaps preferring her books and a life of contemplation to the agitations of the palace, Doña Juana suddenly decided to retire to a convent. Some months short of her sixteenth birthday she entered the stern Order of Discalced Carmelites. The transition from a worldly court to the harsh confinement of a convent proved too abrupt and severe, for she suffered a general breakdown. Persevering, however, in her vocation, she moved from the Carmelites to the less austere convent of St Jerome and here, in a comfortable book-lined cell, she spent the remaining twenty-six years of her life.

A posthumous portrait of her was painted by Miguel Cabrera, a Zapotec Indian born in Oaxaca the year she died. Cabrera is Mexico's best portraitist and had great elegance of manner. His portrait is said to be based on a self-portrait by Sor Inés, a copy of which is in the Philadelphia Museum of Art. The Philadelphia copy of the self-portrait shows a more lively, intelligent face; but Cabrera's picture, hung at Chapultepec, is the more decorative.

Sor Inés's poetry, published in Spain, was highly esteemed. It included love lyrics that might be thought to border occasionally on the erotic:

> To those who tarnish most I give my soul;
> The would-be worshippers I but despise.
> I scorn the man who would my honour prize,
> And favour him who goes away heart-whole.
> If I reproach myself for slighting one,
> The other takes offence at my misdeed.
> Between the two I finally am undone;
> They vex me with a torment cruel indeed,
> The one asking that of which I've none,
> The other lacking that for which I plead.[2]

But there are those who claim that the love she courted in her poems stood for a new concept of thought, whereas the love she spurned represented the old order of things.

Sor Inés also wrote religious and secular plays, indeed one of her three-act comedies was being performed while I was in Puebla, but it was impossible to get tickets.

---

[1] Irving A. Leonard, *Baroque Times in Old Mexico*, The University of Michigan Press, 1959.
[2] Translation of sonnet, by Pauline Cook in *The Pathless Grove*, Decher Press, Prairie City, Illinois.

One reads of Sor Inés receiving in her cell, where she was visited by all the cultured men of her time, including Don Carlos de Siguenza y Gongora, professor of mathematics at the University of Mexico. Her erudition seems to have exasperated her fellow nuns and she rebukes them in a ballad:

> Why, people, do you persecute me so?
> In what do I offend, when but inclined
> With worldly beauties to adorn my mind,
> and not my mind on beauty to bestow?

The Bishop of Puebla, although an admirer, chided her for 'her neglect of religious literature and her fondness for profane letters'. He admonished her 'to apply herself to better books'. The rebuke must have preyed on her mind, for two years later, in 1693, she signed a confession with her own blood and renounced all her possessions, 'the gifts, and trinkets of her admirers, the mathematical and musical instruments that she had so long studied and used, and – most painful wrench of all – those silent and precious companions of her cell, her beloved books'.[1] Her library numbered about four thousand volumes, when it was sold at public auction and the proceeds distributed among the poor.

Time must have hung heavy on Sor Inés's hands. She spun out the day occupying herself exclusively with religious duties and excessive acts of penances. 'See how death eludes me because I desire it,' she cried in one of her poems, 'for even death, when it is in demand will rise in price.' She had not long to wait. In 1695 the convent was invaded by one of the frequent pestilences that swept the city. Sor Inés, ministering to her sisters, soon caught the dreaded infection and died a few days later, a wan reflection of what she had once been.

Another distinctive feature of city life was the custom of riding out in the evening. Already in Gage's day, 'the gallants show themselves daily, some on horseback but most in coaches, about four of the clock in the afternoon in a pleasant shady field called la Alamada, full of trees and walks'.

Another very popular ride was along the Viga, where people were especially employed to water the dusty road bordering the canal and where soldiers were posted to prevent any disturbances. An engraving shows us long lines of carriages going and returning as far as the eye can see. The sidewalks are crowded with people selling fruit and sweets. The carriages would not have disgraced Hyde Park. Madame Calderón, always present with the details but discreetly mentioning no names, singled out the handsome carriage belonging to a man of her acquaintance, the owner of one of the finest houses in Mexico. 'His wife wears a

[1] *Baroque Times in Old Mexico.*

velvet turban twisted with large pearls, and has at this moment a cigar in her mouth. She is not pretty but her jewels are superb.' More carriages are spotlighted and then Madame Calderón breaks off excitedly '. . . but here come three carriages *en suite*, all with the same crimson and gold livery, all drawn by handsome white horses. Is it the President? Certainly not; it is too ostentatious. Even royalty goes in simpler guise, when it condescends to mingle in the amusements of its subjects.' In the first carriage 'there is much crimson and gold, much glass and well-stuffed cushions'. The second is another splendid coach containing the children and servants, 'while in the third equally magnificent, are the babies and nurses'. In complete contrast 'is an old hackney-coach . . . in it are six figures, closely masked, their faces covered with shawls'. It is impossible to guess whether they are women or men. 'It *was* impossible, but as the carriage returns, the wind suddenly blows aside the shawls . . . and discloses the gowns and hoods of friars!'

Later on, as the city grew, the Calles de Bucareli, now known as the Paseo, became the fashionable place to drive. Here also there was much parading in open carriages. The ladies in evening toilet with bare shoulders, their heads uncovered and white flowers in their hair, waved to each other with their fingers or fan. It was considered proper to wave, 'the ladies', Ober says, 'doing it very gracefully but at the same time in such a way that you are puzzled to know whether they are merely giving you recognition or beckoning to you'. Finger tips were raised to the level of dark, limpid eyes and then fluttered.

But far more conspicuous on these occasions were the men in the crowd, *charros* mounted on fine Arab horses with rippling manes and tails. Equipped in the full riding dress of the country, they looked like medieval knights caparisoned for the tourney, the difference being that the Mexicans were encased in stamped and gilded leather hung with silver, not in tempered steel arabesqued in gold. The horses had leather coverings on their hind quarters, saddle flaps and stirrup guards. The saddle fitted the rider Moorish fashion, an inlaid pummel rising in the front. The curiously worked leather, generally from Guadalajara, was fringed all over with little tags and tassels of silver that jingled with every step. The headstall of the bridle was also inlaid. The rider wore a broad brimmed, low-crowned hat edged in gold or silver, an embroidered jacket and a pair of breeches open at the knee, terminating at two points considerably below it. The lower part of the leg was protected by a pair of stamped leather boots worked with silver. The spurs were of preposterous size, weighing as much as a pound and a half. A hundred or so solid gold or silver buttons were sewn down the sides of the trousers. The effect was exceedingly picturesque.

The horse ridden on these occasions was called a *brazeador*, the name being taken from the peculiar action of the forelegs, the *brazos*, which doubled up at every step. This remarkably high action showed off the horse and the rider to the greatest advantage. The mount was either walked or paced. To trot was considered almost a vice. Pacing, or the *paso*, is a queer shuffling run, first the two legs on one side together, then the other two. You jolt gently up and down without rising in the stirrup. It is much less tiring than trotting, especially on long mountain journeys.

These splendid figures paraded up and down between the carriages, rarely saluting the ladies as they passed and never venturing conversation with them. But they were well aware to whom each carriage belonged, and when it behoved them, they made their horses curvet and otherwise showed off their horsemanship. Black eyes were upon them and well they knew it.

The Creoles were inveterate gamblers and they bet heavily at cockfights and *monte*, a Spanish game of chance played with a pack of forty-five cards. *Monte* tables were to be found in almost every house, and immense sums of money were won and lost in the course of an evening.

The popular gaming rooms were at San Agustín de la Cuevas, a pleasant morning's ride due south of the city. San Agustín, now the suburb of Tlalpan, had long been popular with the nobility and the great merchants of the city who had built themselves houses there. Gradually it had taken on the air of a resort, a place of singular beauty according to Humboldt. In the distance rose the misty slopes of the two volcanoes, Popocatepetl and Iztaccihuatl – *la Mujer Blanca*, 'the White Woman'. Silver poplars shaded the roads and the gardens were full of sweet peas, jasmine and roses.

Spring and early summer were the popular months at San Agustín. A great annual fair was held in May, its object, Ward says, being exclusively amusement. 'It is attended by every creature in Mexico who can save, beg, or borrow a dollar for the occasion.' Houses were taken months ahead of time for large sums, just for three days. 'Amongst the ladies it is the etiquette to change their dresses four or five times in the course of the day; once for the early promenade before breakfast; again for the cockpit, which opens at ten o'clock . . .' Dinner served in the middle of the day was the occasion for another toilet, the last change occurring for the public ball. Embroidered muslins were much in vogue and it all sounds charmingly airy and pretty.

Every night there were balls in the cockpit which underwent a complete transformation, refurbished with carpets, cushions, mirrors and chandeliers. The walls and ceiling were entirely lined with green branches and swathed with garlands of flowers, 'the whole forming an agreeable circular room, in which the élite and the refuse of Mexican society may be seen assembled at the same time. The *hoi polloi* are excluded from the centre of the gathering, into which no one improperly dressed is admitted',[1] the rabble thus being obliged to take their seats on the higher tiers behind. The crowds slept *à la belle étoile* or in temporary huts made from boughs and mats and a profusion of flowers.

The gambling was divided between silver tables for the modest players and others where nothing but gold was seen. The lowest stake at a gold table was a doubloon, worth in those days about three guineas. The bank at the high tables varied between fifteen hundred to three thousand doubloons, and the stakes averaged about £300 at the turn of the card. There was no limit to the stake. With such enormous sums involved, the high road back to Mexico was heavily patrolled by soldiers.

Madame Calderón unfailingly gives also her impressions of the fête. Gone are the viceroys, replaced by the president in a carriage-and-six attended by his aides-de-camp. 'Time has made no change only the fashions alter, the graceful mantilla gradually gives place to the ungraceful bonnet. The old painted coach, moving slowly like a caravan, with Guido's "Aurora" painted on its gaudy panels, is dismissed for the smart London-built carriage.' She also commented on some of the startling shop signs seen along the way. 'Religion is called in to sanctify everything, as the robber will plant a cross at the mouth of his cave so do the *pulque* shops seek the protection of the Holy Virgin', *pulque* being a fermented drink made from the fleshy leaves of a certain cactus. Lyon, a compatriot of Madame Calderón, noted down some of the tavern names: 'Shop of the Deity', 'Drinking house of the Holy Trinity'. 'Jesus Christ' quite calmly designated a *pulquería* in the way 'Don Jesús' was a common christian name.

Madame Calderón went to a dinner given by the Dowager Marquesa de Vivanco in her *hacienda* at San Agustín. The courtyard was entered through a deep archway; the great outbuildings, stables and granary – the remains of feudalism – were on a magnificent scale. 'The great hall was lighted with coloured lamps and everything was of solid silver; even the plates.'

No gambling resort is without its bad luck story. Madame Calderón of course picks on a particularly telling episode:

A very rich Spaniard, proprietor of several *haciendas*, attended the fête and having won three thousand ounces, ordered the money to be carried in sacks to his carriage, and prepared to return to Mexico. His carriage was just setting off when a friend of his came out of an adjoining house, and requested him to stay to breakfast.

[1] *Mexico in 1827.*

The inevitable happened. There was a *monte* table and at it several of the rich man's acquaintances. What could have been more natural than to have an idle bet before leaving?

He put down two ounces and lost. He continued playing and losing, until he had lost the three thousand ounces, which were sent for, and transferred to the winner. He still continued playing with a terrible infatuation, until he lost his whole fortune. He went on blindly, staking one *hacienda* after another, until the sun, which had risen upon him as a rich and prosperous man, set leaving him a beggar!

Madame Calderón met the man's son, earning his living as one of the croupiers at the gaming tables.

Whitsun is no longer celebrated at San Agustín de la Cuevas, but the Feast of the Dead is still a longed-for holiday that can have changed but little over the years. The cemeteries are heaped with paper flowers, candles and marigolds. Temporary booths are erected in every plaza through the country. In them dark-eyed Indians trade in death: chocolate funerals and bread in the form of shrouded corpses – crisply cinnamoned and glazed. A plastic skeleton rides astride the boiler of a biscuit locomotive, and grown men find it quite normal to wear dancing skeletons in their buttonholes. I saw a child walking down the street munching away happily at a life-size skull – in sugar. There are rows and rows of these skulls, iced in every conceivable colour. Looking at them, one remembers the ancient gods and their terrible appetites: Tlaloc, god of storm, who was fed on drowned children, Centeotl, the Mexican Ceres, who claimed only female victims, and Huitzilopochtli who existed on a glut of human hearts. For years the Spanish clergy laboured to abolish any remembrance of this bloodthirsty pantheon. When the Indian did finally transfer his allegiance to the foreign god, it was natural enough that the more dramatic incidents of the new religion were what appealed to him most.

Holy Week is another popular holiday; and the Mexicans have a special spite against Judas. Images are made of him in papier-mâché filled like a firecracker with explosives and a fuse. On Good Friday, Ober tells us, 'a peculiar apparatus housed in the tower of the cathedral makes a loud, cracking noise, which is supposed to represent the breaking of the bones of the thieves on the cross'.

On the road map of Mexico City the Lago de Texcoco is still marked as a lake, shown as an extensive area of blue adjoining the city. I drove out one evening in search of it and found instead a barren track covered with a white crust of soda, miles of sterility without a sign of a tree. Squatters from the provinces had claimed a part of it and built themselves a shanty colony roofed in old tins. Another morning I drove out to

Chalco, once famous for its marsh-fly cakes. The fly, *Ahuatlea Mexicana*, deposited its eggs, which resemble fine fish roe, in incredible quantities upon flags and rushes. The Indians used to gather them and pat them into cakes which they presumably baked, for Gage compared them to 'brickbats'. The insect itself was also considered a delicacy and was pounded into a paste and then boiled in corn husks. The larvae, yellowish-white worms, are said to be delicious fried.

Chalco, like Texcoco, has now completely disappeared, but Xochimilco still exists. I had hoped that *Ahuatlea Mexicana* still haunted its shores, so curious was I to add the fly to my list of exotic dishes, but I was disappointed. I was equally unlucky with a salamander, *Siredon lichenoides*, that resembles a fish but has legs, webbed feet and a long compressed tail. It is black and white with gills like feathers on each side of the neck, a strange creature indeed, in the engraving I saw of it. Ober writes that 'this most hideous protean' was yet another Indian delicacy, 'its flesh being white and resembling eel'.

It is difficult to pin-point the exact date when Texcoco finally ceased to exist. At the turn of the nineteenth century Humboldt already regretted the greenery of the beautiful gardens bordering the lake 'which is now but a crust of efflorescent salts, smelling of sulphur' – exactly as I found it myself. But the map I am looking at is quite modern, and there is Texcoco quite blue. Perhaps Texcoco returns with the rains, a faint ghost of its former self. Ober's description in 1887 suggests such a possibility, for then a single shower lasting but an hour or so was enough to inundate the streets. 'On the occurrence of such sudden squalls, the porters of this city transform themselves into beasts of burden, and for a few *centavos* carry ladies and gentlemen pick-a-back from one crossing to another. They are rascals, many of them, who have been known to suspend an unlucky passenger above the water until he agreed to a generous *douceur* for the privilege of landing.'

9

Silver Mines and the Churrigueresque

Spain had good reason to regard Mexico as the most valuable of her American possessions. The Peninsula's main concern in her colonies was for precious metals. Little heed was paid to any possession that did not produce them. The mother country made no attempt to develop a balanced trade between the goods she supplied to a colony and those rich raw materials she extracted in return. Nor did Spain conceive her role to be that of a carrier of trade between her colonies and other nations. A colony existed simply to feed the royal coffers with a constant flow of silver and gold, and in this respect Mexico acquitted herself admirably. Two-thirds of the world's entire silver production came from Mexico, an amount that over three centuries totalled some £1,000,000,000. Half of this metal left the Mexican mints as glittering *pesos* and pieces-of-eight; the remainder was exported from Vera Cruz as ingots. Accurate tallies of the quantities of silver mined in each district are to be found in the archives of the mint; and the figures are amazing. The famous Guanajuato vein alone yielded £57,000,000. (I quote the sums in sterling, having made allowances, as far as it is possible to do so, for the changing values.) The Rosario mine in the Real del Monte group at Pachuca produced £90,000,000 in a period of thirty years. A lump of pure silver weighing 425 pounds was taken from the El Carmen mine in the state of Sonora and yet another of 2,750 pounds. The mines disgorged huge loads. The 'king's fifth' alone amounted to a prodigious sum, 'twice as much', Humboldt reckons, 'as the revenue Great Britain derived from her possessions in India'.

Through centuries of change, of discord and of war the mint went on stamping out the likenesses of successive rulers upon the uninterrupted stream of silver pouring from the mines. The first *Casa de Moneda*, or mint, was completed in 1537. The earliest Spanish money, roughly hammered out and marked with a cross, castles and lions, and the initials of the king, replaced the 'T'-shaped copper plaques, the cocoa beans, and the transparent quills filled with gold dust used until then in trade with the Indians. Later in the sixteenth century the mint moved to the Palácio Nacionál adjoining the royal treasury. Finally it moved to its present site on the south-west corner of Calle del Apartado. From these two last locations issued the well-known *peso* divided into eight reales, whence 'pieces-of-eight'. On one side were stamped the arms of Spain, on the other two globes showing the New World suspended between the Pillars of Hercules. Both pillars and globes were blazoned with royal crowns. This so-called *moneda columnaria* was replaced by the *moneda de busto* which bore an effigy of the king. After independence had been achieved, the king's likeness was superseded by the profile of the first Mexican emperor, Agustín de Iturbide. In quick succession there then followed the Mexican eagle, the Phrygian cap and again an imperial bust, that of the Archduke Maximilian.

One enters the mint by way of a sombre patio, occupied on the day of my visit by an armoured truck and uniformed guards come to fetch away a load of white canvas bags bulging with coins. Beyond the patio are the smelting rooms, vast halls veiled in blue vapours that rise from the molten streams of silver and of zinc and nickel alloys with which the silver is now mixed. Smelting techniques have obviously been improved, but the surroundings remain much the same. A smudged light heightens the dramatic effect of the scene, which reminded me of Piranesi's vast prison halls echoing to the creaking of winches and the clank of metal rings. The heads bending over the crucibles can have changed little too, for the Mexicans of today still have their ancestors' dark, slanting, centreless eyes, and black, gleaming hair 'like wild, rich feathers'. Only their skin has perhaps paled to a lighter tone of bronze. Bare to the waist, the men wear their trousers tightly belted. Though after thirty their bodies become less smooth and over bulky, they are nevertheless a handsome race, square-shouldered and erect with a slight swagger to their walk.

I watched freshly minted fifty-*centavos* pieces being shovelled into wooden boxes. Heaped together, they shone a pale copper-pink. In contrast, the *pesos*, with their coating of pure silver, had a dusty sheen, a false transparency resembling moonstone. Beaufoy said that the old brick flooring of the mint absorbed so much silver that every few years it was taken up, ground to powder and profitably smelted. The floors are now lined with great square plaques of iron to minimize such waste. In another room I found a series of cubicles, each with a tester whose job is to sound the coins. These men are fed a constant supply of *pesos* which are kept neatly stacked to one side. With a dexterity and precision that are almost mechanical they run through stack after stack, bouncing each coin on a small square of marble. Flawed coins let off a dull ring and are immediately discarded. This kind of testing is unusual in modern mints; but the Mexican government is obliged to do so because the country people invariably test a coin on some hard substance to assure themselves of its validity. Trouble would ensue if the ring were not true.

In the days of Spanish dominion there were some three thousand mines. Many, like those in Taxco to the west of the city, were taken over from the Indians, but the most important veins were found shortly after the Conquest in the wild north lands. A Basque, Juan de Tolsa, discovered the rich silver deposits at Zacatecas in 1548. Those at Guanajuato were found ten years later and soon afterwards followed the discoveries at San Luis Potosí and Catorce.

Towns sprang up in the wake of the prospectors. After only two years Zacatecas with five churches and fifty-odd refineries ranked as the second most important city in the country. Henry Hawks, an English merchant travelling in Mexico towards the end of the sixteenth century, commented on the 'pomp and liberality' enjoyed by the Zacatecans. Rich miners, he told his Queen, kept such lavish open house that a bell was rung at meal times to invite passers-by under their roof. He also saw a miner's wife set out for Mass 'with a hundred men and twenty gentlewomen and maids'.

These *provincias internas*, as the northern central provinces were called, were in a state of constant warfare with the Indians, and the roads were infested with brigands, even to within ten miles of Mexico City. The silver towns had to be heavily policed by local militia. It was not unusual for a visitor to find a colonel of such a militia grandly sitting in his shop selling vegetables in full uniform. The battlements, parapets and observation towers on the one-storeyed, thick-walled and narrow-windowed buildings were not always ornamental. The Victorian Gothic offices of the Real del Monte Company at Pachuca were altered inside when taken over by an English company, but the austere exterior remains as it has always been, flanked by crenellated towers and its approaches guarded with solid steel doors pierced by squint holes.

There were many incongruities in the *provincias internas*. Lyon[1] travelling to Zacatecas in 1828 paid his respects to the governor of the state, a cobbler by profession. His Excellency was ailing. So Lyon was received instead by his lady, a thin, talkative, little woman, and her large, greasy sister, a half-dressed maiden 'with black moustachios and nut-brown teeth'. The ladies sat huddled in a corner, smoking. 'The tiled floor was strewn with extinguished cigars and their ashes, cabbage and lettuce leaves, and other filth which had fallen from five birdcages hung along the centre of the room.' Also present were two unwashed

[1] *Journal of a Residence and Tour in the Republic of Mexico.*

and unshaved cavaliers paying their morning compliments to *La Presidenta*.

I hired a car to explore the silver country. Driving north from Mexico City one comes to Queretaro, where, on a rise just outside the town, Maximilian was executed. Here his brother, the Emperor Franz Joseph, erected a small chapel. The headstones of the two Mexican generals shot with Maximilian mark the exact spot, facing the altar, where the bodies fell. It is a sad place but interesting for the daguerreotypes on the chapel walls. One is of the Empress when young, in a billowing crinoline, almost pretty save for her eyes which were 'dark in the centre, and about the edges a strange, unholy green'. In another she is seen on her deathbed, an old woman of eighty-six who had survived the 1914 war and was dying, not quite mad but very deranged, in the gloomy Gothic castle of Bouchout in Belgium. Next to the dead Empress hangs a faded daguerreotype of the mummified Emperor. The embalming had been perfunctory, and his eyes, damaged by a shot in the face, had been replaced by a glass pair taken from a statue of the Virgin in Queretaro cathedral.[1]

Leaving Queretaro one continues north-west through Celeya and San Miguel Allende. The country grows drier and drier: pale earth, burnt grass and dust-green cacti. The only trees are the peppers that seam the fields and look like weeping willows. Originally from Peru, they are a poor relation of the black pepper of commerce and of no economic value. They bear no fruit; and the wood, useless for building, smokes too much to be used for fuel. They are, however, very useful for shading the roads, and the farmers plant them also to divide their land.

Between León and Aguascalientes the desolation increases. The peppers give way to mile upon mile of thorny acacia and patches of pink, feathery grass with a small flowering marigold splashed in amongst it. In the opaline distance one can just make out the mountains beyond Catorce. The plateau then lifts to hundreds of miles of semi-desert: an endless stretch of cacti, mesquite and sage, an arid landscape once inhabited by wild Indians and the domain of the Franciscans whose mission was to convert all the northern tribes. In this instance, however, one feels that the missionaries absorbed more than they imparted, for it was the Indians who taught them how to survive. Life was impossible in these desert lands unless one knew such secrets as how to get water from cacti. Every cactus has its own reservoir of water, but one must know how to extract it. Sometimes burning drives it out; other times, as with the tall-barrel cacti, the top must be cut off and the white pulp pounded into the standing trunk with a blunt stake. The

[1] Bertita Harding, *Phantom Crown*, George Harrap, London, 1935.

41 *Great flying buttresses and towering walls give the Guadalupe shaft the appearance of a castle* (*page 119*)

42 (*below*) '*For the actual appearance of the mine we can turn to Egerton's coloured wash*' (*page 120*)

43 *A silver hacienda showing the patio, or amalgamation court (page 122)*

44 *Guanajuato. The house of the Conde del Rul (page 122)*

45 *(opposite) San Martín at Tepotzotlán. Façade built in 1760–62. Architect unknown (page 123)*

47 (opposite) San Cayetano de la Valenciana. Side portal (page 124)

46 Mexico City. Detail. Façade of the Sagrario Metropolitano built by Lorenzo Rodríguez (page 123)

El Fiel Retrato del Señor
Conde de Valenciana Don
ANTONIO de Obregón

48 Antonio de Obregón, Conde de la
Valenciana (page 120)

50 Pedro Romero de Terreros, the first
Count of Regla (page 128)

49 Don José de la Borda
(page 125)

51 Taxco. The Church of
Santa Prisca and San
Sebastián (1751–58)
(page 124)

52 (below) Santa Prisca. The
heavy corbels supporting the
balconies in the towers
(page 126)

53 Santa Prisca. 'The bold
sculptural surrounds of its
doors' (page 126)

54 *San Miguel Regla. 'Vines trail over great scalloped doors that lead into roofless halls'* (*page 127*)

55 *San Miguel Regla. 'The grounds are crowded with viaducts and old chimney stacks shaped like pyramids'* (*page 127*)

flesh thus treated can then be squashed to produce some two or three quarts of clear, slightly bitter water.

The light in this fascinating countryside is peculiarly pure and transparent. One can gaze out over immense distances wherein every detail, even down to the stones, is clear and accentuated. Dawn is brittle and sharp, the sunsets quite extraordinary. They begin as a suffusion of dusty copper under a prismatic sky shot with all the fires of an opal. The colours blaze before the horizon darkens to the burnt orange of dying embers. Then the sky pales to a cold electric-blue. Slowly, slowly the blue deepens, dampening out the glow, and then, suddenly, comes the dark, a luminous blackness ringed round by the silhouettes of velvet mountains.

The first mine I visited was Nuestra Señora de Guadalupe, one of the many shafts of the fabulous La Valenciana mine at Guanajuato. La Valenciana itself is part of the *Veta Madre*, the mother vein, discovered thirty years after the Conquest but abandoned as unpromising after having been worked for several years. It was not until the second half of the eighteenth century that the really great strike was made, turning La Valenciana into the most important mine of its day. But it was so neglected during the subsequent political upheavals that the shafts became flooded. Only recently, with the assistance of improved drainage techniques, has the government been able to reclaim the district.

The approach is through a dramatic, sunblasted landscape grown over with prickly pears. Veins of ore are generally found in ravines or along mountain slopes, but the *Veta Madre* on the contrary runs along the crest of a mountain. The precipitous hills round about are dotted with mining shafts, winches, ore dumps and the varied paraphernalia of deep mines. Great flying buttresses and towering walls give the Guadalupe shaft the appearance of a castle. It is only the chimney-stacks and a newly formed slag pile that betray its real character. The original entrance to the mine was a gently sloping shaft, but now the descent is made in an open metal lift. I happened to arrive just as one of the eight-hour shifts was changing. The foreman set the hoisting machinery in motion, and after about three minutes the men appeared, steel-hatted and sweating, in a cloud of sulphuric smoke raised by the explosions below. Over a thousand feet under the earth, subterranean networks of tunnels cross and recross each other for a distance of some twelve miles.

The story of La Valenciana is almost forgotten but for what Humboldt and Ward recorded. After the cursory exploitation during the latter part of the sixteenth century, it was not until 1760 that a Señor Obregón, a Spaniard of small fortune but of immense tenacity, started to dig at a point believed to be destitute of 'mineral riches'. For six long years he persevered until, having exhausted his own means, he had to take a local shopkeeper called Otero into partnership. Further long months of search followed, Obregón and Otero themselves wielding the pick. They reached a depth of 250 feet without the slightest sign of encouragement. Then, suddenly, one morning they struck an enormous mass of rich ore. The yield continued to increase in value the farther they tunnelled. In no time the shaft pitched down into the soft clay-slate to a depth of 1,640 feet and thus became the deepest mine in existence. The two proprietors were then netting £500,000 a year. In 1803 Humboldt cited La Valenciana as the rare instance of a mine whose yield had not diminished for nearly forty years. By 1808, even after others had joined the company, a partnership in the mine netted £800,000 a year.

Although we know nothing of Otero, a few meagre facts can be gleaned about Obregón, 'a man as dedicated', wrote Humboldt, 'to mining as some people are to gaming'. He was well liked by his countrymen, for despite his great wealth he 'preserved the same simplicity of manner, and the same freshness of character, for which he was distinguished previous to his success'. His 'simplicity', however, did not deter him from spending a few thousand *pesos* to purchase a title, borrowed from the name of the mine. It is with his newly acquired quarterings that we see the Conde de la Valenciana posing in his portrait.

The actual appearance of the mine is recorded in Egerton's coloured wash which accentuates the cavernous vaulting that measured from thirty to thirty-six feet across. Engineers of the time had the mistaken idea that the larger the shaft, the fresher the air would keep. The mine was also famous for its fine walling and for the facility with which it could be entered by a flight of commodious stairs, 'which even ladies could descend without difficulty'. From Egerton's watercolour one can readily understand the enormous expense involved in sinking the shafts and running drifts. Only too often subterranean water deposits were pierced and the galleries flooded. In a period of fifteen years the annual expenditure at La Valenciana rose from £90,000 to a figure double that amount simply to maintain drainage operations. Still the profits came rolling in.

Humboldt described the day-to-day operations of the mines in the Guanajuato district. About five thousand men worked in gangs on a day or night shift the whole year through, supervised by an administrator, an overseer and nine master miners. A master miner ran the subterranean operations, carried to his job by men 'who have a sort of saddle fastened on their backs and go by the name of "little horses", or *cavalitos*'. In Europe wheelbarrows were harnessed to dogs, but in the

Mexican mines all the manual labour was performed by Indians known as *tenateros*, 'half-naked beings who carry the minerals in bags'. Through long training the *tenateros* were able to shoulder loads weighing anything from 225 to 350 pounds. For light they had tallow candles set into hats that looked like inverted cones. 'We meet with fifty or sixty of them in single file, men over sixty and boys of ten or twelve years of age. In climbing the stairs they throw their body forward and rest on a staff, walking in a zigzag direction.' Humboldt admired their endurance, admitting that he felt tired just ascending the shaft 'carrying nothing heavier than my own weight'. Ward was not especially impressed with the *tenateros'* physique, but did remark that their neck and back muscles were 'developed much beyond those possessed by any other member of the body'. The men were well paid: five shillings a day plus a share of every eighth bag they bore. In spite of this, 'honesty is by no means so common among the Mexican as among the German and Swedish miners', Humboldt wrote, 'and they make use of a thousand tricks to steal the minerals'. Wearing practically no clothing, the Indian miner needed a certain cunning to hide fragments of crude silver. It was concealed in hollowed handles of the hammers which they were allowed to carry with them, or the ore was pulverized and rolled up in cigarette papers. They hid it in their hair or under their arm pits and between their toes, but a clay cylinder, a *longanas*, lodged in the anus was the safest place. Humboldt was shocked by the rigorous search the men were subjected to on leaving the mines. A complete record is available of the quantities filched from the mines. The losses from the Guanajuato district alone amounted over a period of ten years to the astonishing sum of £380,000.

Silver is hardly ever found in a directly usable form. Consequently the most complicated operation in the arduous mining process was amalgamation, the mixing of mercury and quicksilver into the ore to isolate the silver content. Nowadays silver is separated from base ore by treatment with cyanide, a great improvement technically on amalgamation, but so recent that it is no concern of ours. The amalgamation process required endless experimentation before it was finally perfected in the sixteenth century by a Mexican miner from Pachuca named Bartolomé de Medina. It is almost impossible for the layman to comprehend the chemical reaction that takes place, but by following engravings illustrating its successive stages one can at least get a rough idea of the mechanics involved in freeing the silver.

First the ore was crushed, usually in a covered shed, or *galera*, in a series of mills worked by blindfolded mules. It took days to reduce the ore to the required fineness, whereupon it was sprinkled with water and further churned until it became a muddy paste that was scooped up, removed to a patio, or amalgamation court, and spread out on what were technically known as *tortas*. A mixture of salt, mercury and copper sulphate was now added as preparatives, and once again the mules, this time harnessed in teams, were driven backwards and forwards across the amalgam. Then came the crucial point in the process, when the *capitán de galera*, or overseer, had to decide what dosage of mercury was needed. This depended on what quantity of silver he thought could be drawn from the ore; the amount of mercury required was generally six times the quantity of silver estimated to be in the paste. When the mercury was added and began to become lead-coloured, the chemical reaction had begun, in other words, the silver, freed from its compound, was uniting with the mercury. To hasten the process the mass was often given an extra stirring by the mules, aided sometimes by barefoot workmen who spent hours each day sloshing around in the metallic mud. The entire processing took about a month.

The vital mercury came, in large part, from the Almadén mines in Spain. Austria, China and Peru supplied the rest. Enormous quantities were needed. Between 1760 and 1780 the amalgamation works of New Spain used up twenty-five million pounds of mercury valued at £2,500,000.

When Obregón first started to work the vein in 1760, La Valenciana was a lonely spot grazed over by goats; by the end of the century it had become a thriving settlement with seven or eight thousand people. But La Valenciana was never more than the mine's administration centre. The city proper, Guanajuato, 'The Place of Frogs', as the Indians called it, grew up below, pushed into a narrow gorge through which tumbled a river. Picturesque bridges spanned its turbulent waters but floods caused so much damage that a tunnel was eventually built to divert the river's flow. The original river bed is now the city's main thoroughfare into which narrow and crooked side streets converge like so many sloping tributaries. Despite the cramped space the city has many fine buildings, 'houses', Humboldt wrote, 'that would be an ornament to the first streets of Naples or Paris'. The house of the Conde del Rul, husband of the third Countess of Valenciana and thus proprietor of the renowned mine, 'is fronted with columns of the Ionic order, and the architecture is simple and remarkable for great purity of style'. It was built by the Creole architect Tresgueras, who, after Tolsá, was the leading neo-classicist and the last great architect of the viceregal period. It cost the Count £33,000, a considerable sum, Humboldt pointed out, 'in a country where the price of labour and materials is very moderate'.

It is the same Conde del Rul, a flamboyant character whom Humboldt hardly mentions, who must be credited with having built one of Mexico's most beautiful examples of Churrigueresque architecture, the church of San Cayetano.

Agricultural expansion and improved mining techniques brought to eighteenth-century Mexico a new wave of prosperity that was reflected in the new buildings erected in the Churrigueresque style. Cities and towns competed in raising public monuments. The smallest village in a successful mining area boasted several churches, one of which was generally much larger than the others and had high towers flanking a tiled dome. These glinting domes and the dazzling interiors above which they floated were, as Joseph Baird[1] points out, the Mexican *genius loci*. Mexican Churrigueresque churches are all cross-shaped in plan with a dome atop the crossing. At the foot of the cross, so to speak, two towers flank an elaborate façade. On the inside an altar screen with polychrome saints gesticulating between twisted columns of burnished gold repeats the drama of the façade.

The Churrigueresque, a Spanish offshoot of the Baroque, reached its height in the colonies, achieving flights of fancy that the Old World never dreamed of. Lorenzo Rodríguez seeded the style in Mexico, notably in his two façades of the Sagrario Metropolitano in Mexico City designed in 1749. After that Churrigueresque spread throughout the country. One of the most striking examples is the lovely Sanctuary of Ocotlán near Tlaxcala. One should also mention San Martín of Tepotzotlán and the fantastic Casa del Alfeñique, or 'Sugar-Cake House', at Puebla built towards the end of the eighteenth century as a guest house for the viceroys, as well as the handsome rusticated stone façade of the unfinished Casa de Mascarones in Mexico City designed by Francisco Antonio Guerrero y Torres. Another building by Torres is the lovely Pocito Chapel, Chapel of the Little Well, in the suburbs of the city, at Guadalupe where the Virgin first appeared in the New World to the Indian Juan Diego.

My first experience of the Mexican Churrigueresque was the façade of the Balvanera Chapel, erected some forty years later than the Sagrario in a quiet little square off Avenida Madero, the busiest street in Mexico City. Its richly carved stone façade first gave me a feeling almost of discomfort, so tortured are its columns, like barnacled posts encrusted by the sea. Much as a Baroque column may be twisted or overlaid with decoration, it still reads as a column; not so in the Churrigueresque. Here columns are a complete jumble of unrelated forms piled atop one another – circular blocks, squares and inverted pyramids – capped by elaborate foliated capitals. Broken pediments and curvetting cornices, whole areas of curling and uncurling scrolls, festoons of fruit and flowers, rinceaux and tasselled *pinjante* further confuse the eye

[1] Joseph Armstrong Baird, *The Churches of Mexico*, University of California Press, 1962.

as it darts from detail to detail, incapable of reading the composition as a whole. After one's initial wonder at the apparent jumble, it does eventually become apparent that the component parts are carefully integrated. The elements of the façade work together well, the whole sweeping upwards with great verve and conviction to a cartouche that once bore the royal arms.

By the time I reached Guanajuato I had become quite used to the architectural pyrotechnics of the Churrigueresque and was well ready to look at Conde del Rul's church of San Cayetano with a sympathetic eye. It caps the brow of a treeless hill grown over with organ cacti; the church is an elegant mass of rose-buff stone rising above these fluted hexagonal columns of the vegetable world. The visitor immediately notices that a belfry on one of the towers is missing, the result of jealousy on the part of the church officials at Guanajuato. Watching the building of the church progress, they had decided that it was altogether too grand and appealed to the authorities in Mexico City on the grounds that a licence had been given to build a chapel, not a basilica. A compromise was finally reached when Rul agreed to complete only one tower.

Various stories are told in the district about the church, most of them to do with the lavishness of the decoration on which no expense was spared. It was said that silver had been built into the foundations and 'fine wines brought over from Spain to be used in mixing the mortar'.[1] Rumours circulated that the church covered a rich mineral deposit and that the Count had refused a large sum for the property. It was even suggested that the church be moved to another site.

The archives of the church were destroyed during the War of Independence. Consequently its architect is unknown, but whether Spaniard or Creole he was a man of infinite refinement. Every detail in the church is of extraordinary quality even down to the craftsmanly elegance of its geometrically panelled doors. The interior painting is also unusually delicate: the walls are a creamy white, while the ornamental elements in relief are picked out in white against a pale straw-coloured ground. Baird thinks that it was the work of a city-trained man who had come north, drawn by the newly rich mining communities. He considers the side portal one of the loveliest pieces of ornamental stone carving of its time, 'a technical exercise as only that era could do in perfect taste . . . worthy of Cuvilliés at his best'.[2]

Despite the elegance of San Cayetano, I personally prefer the church of Santa Prisca y San Sebastián in Taxco. It was founded by yet another

[1] *Baroque and Rococo in Latin America.*
[2] *The Churches of Mexico.*

mining magnate, José de la Borda, and is named after two Roman martyrs: one a virgin of thirteen who was thrown to the lions, the other a youthful Christian soldier in Diocletian's legions. It antedates San Cayetano by some thirty years, is more robust and ebullient in style, and above all has a remarkable homogeneity.

The road to Taxco leads south-west out of Mexico City and winds through a tawny-green countryside that rolls out in fold after fold of mountain. We are back again in the *tierra templada*, a corrugated landscape that collapses eventually into the Pacific. Taxco is an untidy collection of whitewashed houses roofed with red tiles and terraced one above the other on the slopes of a hill. The cobbled streets are narrow and twisted, skirting steep ravines filled with banana trees. Dominating the scene rises Santa Prisca, a delicious faded pink. The yellow, blue and white tiles of the octagonal ribbed dome mirror the sun's own image in star-like bursts.

The stone of which Santa Prisca, and a majority of the eighteenth-century churches, is built looks like pumice tinged with ashes of roses. I have watched it being quarried where it is cut into squares like slices of a gigantic cake. A piece of it lying in front of me here as I write is soft enough to notch with my nail. The stone hardens after long exposure to the air and fades under the strong Mexican sun. When it becomes too bleached it is washed with a solution of a similar colour, obtained from pulverizing new stone and mixing the powder with lime.

We know considerably more about José de la Borda than about either of our two previous mining potentates at La Valenciana. Doctor Antonio Peñafiel, the leading authority, tells us that Borda was born in Pau, the son of a French officer in the reign of Louis XIV. The family's name may originally have been Laborde. At sixteen José emigrated to Mexico, following an elder brother who had opened a mine at Taxco. La Lajuela, the family mine, did not prove particularly remunerative, and so José wandered about the country working a number of different diggings. But when his brother Francisco died and he inherited La Lajuela, José decided to sink shafts in a new direction. Almost immediately, in 1748, he struck the San Ignacio vein. It started to produce enormous amounts of silver and very soon Borda found himself the owner of a vast fortune equivalent to several million pounds.

Borda's oft-quoted motto was 'God gives to Borda and Borda gives to God', but pious gratitude was not Don José's only motive for building a church. He wished to keep near him his son Manuel, a priest studying in the Royal University of Mexico, and so obtained permission from the Archbishop of Mexico to demolish the old parish church and erect a new one, worthy of the Borda name and handy for Manuel to serve in. Licence was given and Borda's condition 'that he alone should direct the works and control the funds' was accepted. The fact that one person presided over its construction must certainly account for the building's remarkable unity of style.

From the outside Santa Prisca is not strictly speaking Churrigueresque, but rather a Spanish Baroque that is almost Rococo, spiced, as Baird points out, with classicism and Mudéjar geometry. The interior, however, is wonderfully Churrigueresque. It has a dazzling sequence of twelve *retablos* carved with a bravura that at times is almost excessive. Not one inch of their soaring height is without decoration. No surface is at rest. The eye moves up, down, across, and deep into gilded caves peopled by apostles, evangelists, popes and saints. Polychrome figures are enveloped in a riotous convulsion of carving that almost swamp them. Round the edges hover winged cherubs struggling with mitres and keys that are far too large for them. Along with the cherubs are recurring symbolic motifs like the clusters of grapes representing the blood of Christ and the scallop shells signifying baptismal grace. Another favourite is the pomegranate, the fruit which when ripe bursts open to spread its ruby beads, each bead signifying a pearl of wisdom from the Gospel. Bewildering in their detail, the *retablos* are unified at least in their overall theme, the glorification of the church. The paintings in them too are all by one hand, which is unusual. They are the work of Miguel Cabrera, a Zapotec Indian born in Tlalixtac in 1695 and considered one of Mexico's ablest painters.

Again and again I returned to Santa Prisca, hypnotized by its beauty. Its large handsomely framed windows and the elaborate finials distributed along its dipping walls look, as Kelemen said, like 'festive bouquets'. How bold are the sculptured door surrounds and the heavy corbels carved with grotesque faces that support the balconies in the towers! How well the pink stone shows off the burnished gold of the *retablos*! There is no detail that does not please. The walls of the aisle are coffered like Chinese wood carving. Directly above the door is a red and gold Baroque organ. Leading off the aisle is a small chapel dedicated by Borda to the Acayotla Indians from whom he acquired the land on which the church is built.

Santa Prisca was begun in 1751 and completed seven years later. The year the church was dedicated the San Ignacio vein gave out. Don José, who had spent a large part of his fortune on the church, was bankrupt. With what was left of his capital he sunk further shafts, but all without success. As a last resort he sold the precious ecclesiastic objects intended for Santa Prisca, among them a beautiful monstrance, one of the richest jewels of Hispanic Colonial America. The monstrance was wrought of solid gold and studded with precious stones, over five thousand diamonds alone without counting the emeralds and rubies. It fetched a handsome sum which Don José immediately put to good use. Moving north he started working the Vita Grande at Zacatecas. Within a matter of months he had struck another vein, the famous La Esperanza.

When he made his second important strike, Borda was over sixty and already worn out by his mining activities. He retired to Cuernavaca where he occupied his declining years with laying out a garden on a steep hillside behind the town, not far from Cortés' palace. Though sadly neglected, the garden is still one of the attractions of the town. It is reached through an empty, rambling house. The windows of a long denuded salon open onto the main terrace. There are steps and massive walls and more terraces. When Borda first made the garden it must have been a blaze of colour, but now all is dank and moss-grown. The mangoes, sapotes and Indian laurel have long since outgrown their proper scale and roof out the sky overhead. Intended to be decorative features of the garden, they are now the garden itself. The dark coolness, however, is very soothing and lends an air of mystery to the place. Right at the bottom of the garden there is a large tank with open pavilions at each end. Here, one is told, the Empress Carlota and the ladies of her court bathed on moonlit nights.

Borda is supposed to have had two sons and a daughter. One son was in the Church; the other lived in Peru. Humboldt said that before dying Borda compelled his daughter to enter a convent so that he could leave his entire fortune to his sons. Whether this is true or not, neither of the sons was interested in the garden. At the old man's death it passed out of the family.

After visiting mines in the north and south-west, I went to the mining town of Pachuca in the east. The Aztecs mined here long before the Spaniards came and the hills are honeycombed with their old workings. According to my guide-book, Pachuca still produces more silver than any other place in the entire world. Its citizens tell of a man who offered to macadamize the main avenue, an act of philanthropy that paid off in the end. By processing the old paving stones he extracted enough silver to make a profit as well as pay for the new road.

I stayed at the *hacienda* of San Miguel Regla, the former *hacienda de las minas* of the Counts of Regla. The present owners have dammed the river flowing through the property so that the old amalgamation yards are now weed-grown lakes, planted round with cannas and bordered with clumps of arum lilies, the haunt of bright-feathered ducks and flocks of wild geese. The grounds are crowded with viaducts and old chimney-stacks shaped like pyramids. Vines trail over great scalloped doors that lead into roofless halls. Above the ruins, tracing the contours of the hill, runs a twenty-foot-high cyclopean wall. Humboldt wrote that the *hacienda* cost the first Count £400,000 to build. One can well believe it.

Pedro Romero de Terreros, the first Count of Regla, started life as a muleteer. His rise to riches is an interesting story. A friend of his named Bustamante bought the old Biscaina mine which had been abandoned on account of flooding. The mine was not very deep and was known to hold rich ores at lower levels but the difficulty of keeping the water out had discouraged prospective bidders. Bustamante, an old hand at mining and more enterprising than most, experimented with various methods of drainage. He eventually hit on the idea of digging adits below the water level, horizontal passages tunnelled through the rock to the surface, but this was so costly a procedure that he was obliged to borrow funds. Terreros, infected by his friend's enthusiasm, invested all the savings earned by his mules, a fairly modest sum, as can be imagined. Bustamante took sick and died just after the draining had begun. Thereupon Terreros inherited the mine and finally completed the work. The moment the mine was dried out there came immediate success. Terreros found himself netting profits of a million pounds a year. Like others before him he set about obtaining a title. 'Never,' as Sir Henry Ward wrote, 'was a title more dearly bought.' It cost Terreros 'two ships of the line, one of 112 guns constructed at Havana of the most costly materials, entirely at his own expense.' Added to this he was obliged to lend Charles III £500,000, 'no part of which', Ward writes, 'was ever repaid'.[1]

Terreros, now Regla, did not build himself a church, but he did found the Monte de Piedad in Mexico City. He seems generally to have enjoyed his money. At his son's christening the whole party walked from the house to the church upon ingots of silver. One of his dearest wishes was to induce the king to visit Mexico. He assured His Majesty that his horse should touch nothing but solid silver from Vera Cruz to the capital. His apartments, like those of the Inca, should be lined with the same precious metal. The Countess de Regla also had extravagant tastes. From Madame Calderón we learn that the Countess sent the Vicereine 'a white satin slipper entirely embroidered with large diamonds'. One wonders why only one slipper.

We have dealt with the silver nobility very cursorily. There are many other names frequently met in letters and memoirs, Guadiana for example or the Marqués of Vivanco. Madame Calderón knew one of the Vivancos and said that she had never seen the equal of her diamonds. What fascinating stories a search through the archives would reveal.

Nature has endowed Mexico with seemingly inexhaustible mineral

[1] *Mexico in 1827.*

resources. For centuries now vast quantities of precious metals have been wrested from the soil, yet Mexico is still the world's largest single producer of silver. From the time of the Conquest to about 1850, Mexico, Bolivia and Peru were the principal producers. Peru dropped to a lower position after 1850, while the United States alternated with Mexico as leader between 1871–1918. Canada assumed third place in 1908. Of the total world output in recent years, Mexico mined nineteen per cent, United States seventeen, Canada fourteen, the USSR eleven, Peru ten and fifty-four other countries twenty-nine per cent. The value of Mexico's annual output of silver amounts to twenty million pounds.

10

South to Guatemala

Reluctantly I had to leave Mexico City and begin my southward journey with the long drive via Puebla, Oaxaca and San Cristóbal de las Casas to Guatemala. Beyond Guatemala my route lay towards Central America and the Panama Canal; beyond the canal awaited the vast pear-shaped *Tierra Firme*.

Looking at the map I felt apprehensive about what the months ahead would bring. Mexico is a strangely seductive country and even now I am still attached to the memory of its beauty, regretting that a lack of space obliges me to pass over certain districts like Patzcuaro, a somnolent lake town, whose name means 'Place of Delights'. It is at Patzcuaro, with its sympathetic and homespun quality, that one feels closest to the conquistadors. Its cobbled streets and *adobe* houses with projecting roofs supported by crudely hewn beams remain exactly as they must have known it. And how picturesque also is San Miguel Allende with its doorways, balconies and its covered market! Mérida too has its charms, and Yucatan, apart from its famous ruins, is little known. Men go armed there, for the puma lurks in the thorny scrub. The oval, thatched huts, walled with stone, in the villages of this dry land are quite different from those in any other part of Mexico. The Yucatecos all sleep in hammocks woven from *henequin*, the fibrous sisal thread obtained from the bayonet-like leaves of a cactus. These cacti cover so many thousands of acres of gently swelling plantation land that they look like the reaches of a heaving, blue-green sea. I learned from one of the planters that the cactus takes eight years to mature before it can be harvested for a further twenty-five. It is cropped three times a year, each plant yielding an average of eight leaves a crop.

I spent a night at a plantation and rose with the dawn to make the rounds of the estate. Afterwards breakfast was served – *tortillas, frijoles,* eggs, oranges and chocolate – but there were no chairs. These *haciendas* never have any surplus furniture as they are visited only once or twice a year, and then only for a few days, when the owner brings with him whatever he needs. One of John Stephens' party visiting Yucatan in 1841 had exactly the same experience when he misguidedly asked for a bed. 'He might as well have asked for a steamboat . . .'[1]

The Yucatan sisal is a cousin of the famous *maguey*, or *Agave americana*, that is grown in plantations on Mexico's great central plateau and from which the Mexican national drink, *pulque*, is obtained. *Agavos* in Greek means noble and the plant well merits the name. Leaving Mexico City for Puebla we had driven through miles of it in serrated ranks. The Mexican plant is much larger than its Yucatan relative, the leaves curving upwards to the height of a man. If not cut, the flower-stalks can be as high as twenty feet. I need hardly describe the plant, for although native to Mexico, it is well known in Europe where it has been cultivated for purely decorative purposes since about the middle of the sixteenth century. In many instances, it has escaped the garden and established itself as part of the natural flora, particularly on the rocky shores of the Mediterranean.

Maguey grows slowly and flowers but once after a number of years, when a tall stem, or 'mast', shoots up like a gigantic asparagus from the centre rosette of thick, fleshy leaves. The plant dies after flowering. D. H. Lawrence saw them as black-tarnished swords bursting out of the Mexican soil, 'a great unfolded bud . . . thrust at the sky'.[2] Indeed there is something sinister in the arrogant way the plant grows. One feels almost anxious for the harvester passing on his rounds to collect the sap.

Those who cultivate the plant know almost the very hour at which the central shoot, the flower, is about to appear. This they anticipate by extracting the whole heart of the bud, leaving the thick outside rind as a natural basin to catch the oozing sap that would have fed the flower. A good *maguey* yields from eight to fifteen pints of sap a day and can be tapped for two to three months. The harvester collects the liquid twice and even three times a day, siphoning it up with his mouth into a large gourd which he empties into a pigskin bottle. From the fields it is carried to a central depot where it is fermented into *pulque*.

Pulque smells rather disagreeably, something like sour milk, or slightly tainted meat. The taste I would describe as a dulled sharpness with an after-flavour of mustiness. 'It is said,' writes Madame Calderón, 'that when one gets over the first shock, it is very agreeable.' I cannot say that I ever found it so. This is not the opinion, however, of many Mexicans, whose feelings are expressed in the following lines:

[1] John Stephens, *Incidents of Travel in Yucatan,* John Murray, London, 1842.
[2] *The Plumed Serpent.*

Know ye not *pulque*
That liquor divine
Angels in heaven
Prefer it to wine.[1]

Pulque was also known to the Aztecs who called it *octli*. It was sacred to Tepoztecatl, a rustic god of the harvests, a kind of Indian Bacchus. According to Sahagún, it was very strictly rationed; only old people were allowed to drink it. Drunkenness among the Aztecs was a severely punishable crime.

We know already that the Aztecs made paper from *maguey* leaves. The plant also has other uses, for like the coconut of the Pacific, no part of it is wasted. The pointed thorns on the gigantic leaves are used as nails, and I have seen women sewing with them too. They strip off the thorn and with it comes long strands of fibre, a pre-threaded needle. The fibre of the plant was woven into a coarse resilient material used by the common people for clothing. It did not, however, always play so humble a role. One of the viceroys, the Marqués de Cruillas, had his wigs made out of it and he wrote that they were 'highly satisfactory'. Gage noticed that the rind roasted 'healeth hurts and sores and from the top boughs issueth a gum which is an excellent antidote against poison'.

All morning long we drove through cactus plantations. Mark Beaufoy, viewing them in 1828 with the romantic eye of his period, judged them 'stiff and disagreeable'. I, in a different age, found them rather beautiful.

We were still at seven thousand feet where the transparency of the air lends a false impression of nearness. Objects at a distance seem close at hand and stand out with a clarity of etched glass. Always in the background were the pleated hills and clumps of trees that indicate a village and, of course, a church. Each house was a small fortress with the windows to the street heavily barred.

Puebla is the only Mexican city founded by the Spanish colonists; all the others had been rebuilt on the rubble of their former greatness. Bullock, travelling in Mexico just after the rise of the First Republic, found the churches and monasteries of Puebla among the most sumptuous he had ever seen. 'Those of Milan, Genoa, and Rome scarcely surpass them,' and the splendours of their religious ceremonies 'yield to no city in America or Europe.'[2] He exaggerates, naturally, but nevertheless the cathedral is very impressive. The original plans are said to have been drawn up by Juan de Herrera, one of the architects

---

[1] *Revista Científica Mexicana, Vol. I, No. 6*, article by Señor José C. Segura, Mexico, 1885.
[2] *Six Months Residence and Travels in Mexico.*

of the Escorial. However, it is predominantly the work of Juan Gómes de Mora, who was also employed on the Escorial. Indeed it was Mora who prepared the plans for the Mexico City cathedral, but his façade at Puebla is more severe than the sister cathedral's, more aloof, and more in the academic taste associated with Charles v's reign. The emphasis on vertical lines, the cold bluish-grey stone and the severity of the ornamental detail carefully picked out in white marble combine to give the Puebla cathedral a unity of design and a simplicity of statement that is altogether lacking in Mexico City.

Not far from the cathedral, on the top floor of the Governor's palace, is the library of Juan de Palafox de Mendoza, bishop of Puebla from 1639 to 1653. This remarkable legacy is one of the oldest libraries on the continent. The immense vaulted hall in which it is housed dates from the eighteenth century and is reminiscent of similar rooms in Austrian Baroque monasteries. The brick flooring is pointed with blue and white Puebla tiles. The cases are unpainted pine meshed over with gilt wiring, behind which glimmers gold tooling. Balconies run the length of the top storeys. Great square-topped tables are inlaid with plaques of local onyx, the colour of mutton-fat jade flecked with flaws of brown and green. It is a beautiful room and, warmed by the morning sun, was redolent of leather, dust and age; a comforting smell.

One is supposed to admire the ornate, profusely foliated decoration of the Rosario Chapel in the church of Santo Domingo. Polychrome and lavishly gilt strapwork curls from the ceiling in interlacing waves, engulfing the entire chapel. However, to me it was more a deluge of glutinous seaweed than a 'miracle'. I much preferred the delicious meringue effect of the stucco squeezed over the brick and tile façade of the elegant Casa del Alfeñique.

Cities in this country each have their individual colour effects, determined largely by the geology of the neighbourhood. Mexico City is brown-red pumice and whitish limestone; Oaxaca is a green-brown; the Guanajuato-San Miguel area varies from grey-pink to a pinkish-yellow. Here, in Puebla, to counteract the sad effect of its grey stone, men have devised an alternative: glazed tiles of pied gaiety. The Puebla clay proved so particularly suitable for making tiles that every church tower and dome is covered with them. Façades of palaces and private houses, wainscotings, stairs, kitchens, balustrades, columns and fountains shine with dark blue, white, yellow, green, orange and dark brown glazes. Tiles baked in thick uneven pastes are set in every conceivable combination of pattern: in herringbones alternating with brick; in solid floral motifs; or in little blue and white triangular pointings set with unglazed hexagonal tiles.

Three buildings vividly impressed themselves on my memory: the church of San Francisco, the Convent of Santa Mónica and La Concordia, which is a late eighteenth-century retreat unmentioned in any of the guides. To my mind, it has the most fanciful use of tiles in the entire district. There is something almost heraldic about the pilastered façade set with candy bar twists and sharply accented, stylized bursts of pattern. Along the rooftop runs a flat-sided balustrade entirely glazed in blue and white tiles.

Sanford best describes the church of San Francisco, 'across the little river which winds through the centre part of the city and set at the back of a garden'. It has a carved Churrigueresque stone portal 'planted against a wall of red brick relieved by great panels of glazed tile in four storeys'. In the centre of each panel 'is a huge blue and white vase out of which great conventionalized floral groups project and twist' forming a pattern of 'green, yellow and blue against a white ground'.[1]

Santa Mónica has a charming, flower-filled patio, the walls entirely covered with blue and white tiles criss-crossed over an inlaid trellis of bricks. It is hard to believe, but the convent community continued to function long after the Reform Laws of 1857 abolished all religious institutions in Mexico. For nearly a hundred years Augustinian nuns lived here undisturbed. The entrance, hidden behind sliding shelves in a parlour, remained a closely guarded secret until 1934. An altar swings silently to the side, exposing a dark gap through which one passes to find long corridors, apartments, cells, and even a private cemetery. It seems that the nuns were denounced to the authorities by a drunken antique dealer who had unsuccessfully tried to acquire some of the paintings in the convent.

Love for ceramics spread to the neighbouring villages: three of which have tiled churches – Santa María Tonantzintla, San Bernandino Tlaxcalalcingo, and the most dazzling of all, San Francisco Acatepec. The Acatepec church was finished about 1750. There is not a detail of the busy façade that is free of tiles; they even spiral round its belfry, twisted into shiny blue columns. The effect is wonderfully gay, like a field in summer sprigged with flowers.

The Dominican friars, who settled in Mexico soon after the Conquest, imported potters from Toledo, famous for its talavera ware. The Indian makers of the Mixtec polychrome pottery known as Cholula ware, which Montezuma used at his table, were quick to learn the craft of Toledo. Soon they were masters of the fanciful arabesques, conventionalized flowers, figures, animals and saints. Puebla still produces this talavera ware, but the formulas for many of the old glazes have been

[1] *The Story of Architecture in Mexico.*

56, 57 San Miguel Allende (page 130)

58 The famous maguey or Agave americana (page 131)

*59 Puebla tiles
(page 133)*

60 Puebla tiles
(page 133)

61 Convent of
Santa Mónica
(page 134)

62 San Francisco
Acatepec
(page 134)

63 Casa del Alfeñique. Legend has it that the stucco was mixed with the white of egg (page 133)

64 La Concordia (page 134)

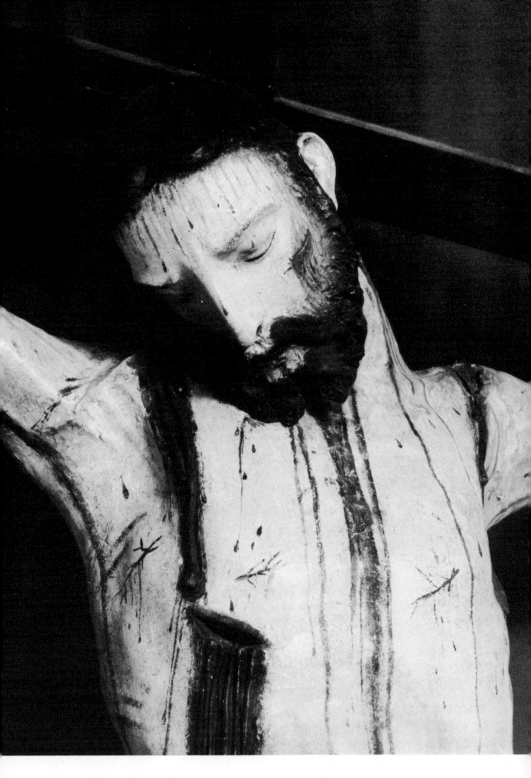

65 Sixteenth-century crucifix in papier-mâché at Acolman (page 138)

66 Sixteenth-century fresco at
San Nicolás Actopan
(page 138)

67 The sixteenth-century
Dominican monastery at
Cuilapan (page 138)

68, 69, 70 Franciscan
monastery of San Luis Obispo
at Tlalmanalco; Detail;
Battlemented silhouettes
(page 138)

71 *Oaxaca. The Dominican monastery of Santo Domingo begun in 1575 and completed in 1675 (page 139)*

72 *'The next morning we drove to Cuauhtemoc and over the border into Guatemala' (page 140)*

73 *(left) Oaxaca, a place of infinite charm (page 139)*

74 Oaxaca. Detail of carving on cathedral (page 139)
75 Mitla. Entrance to the Palace of the Columns (page 139)

lost and the quality of the pottery in the markets is inferior. Compared to the wonderful Mixteca-Puebla ceramics in the museums, modern efforts are paltry.

In Mexico I always ate in the small, popular restaurants, the only places, apart from private houses, where one finds genuine Mexican cooking. Tourists seldom realize that this is difficult and very complex. Most of the dishes are composed of a bewildering number of ingredients and delicately balanced flavours, the supreme example being Puebla's turkey *molé*.

The turkey is fattened on chestnuts and walnuts and is consequently deliciously succulent, but what really counts is the *molé*, its unctuously soft, rich mahogany-coloured sauce. I once watched a voluminously skirted, pigtailed old woman preparing it in the pretty tiled kitchen of a friend's house. *Molé*, meaning 'ground', is an apt name, for all morning long she ground and stirred. I noted down what I could, but certainly many of the reportedly twenty to half a hundred ingredients escaped me. A variety of carefully arranged piles surrounded the mortar and over these her old gnarled hands darted, snatching cloves, sesame seeds, peanuts, cinnamon, nutmeg, almonds, aniseed, slivers of bitter chocolate, and at least three different kinds of peppers, the small variety of which is much hotter than anything we know in Europe. I could only guess at the contents of the large earthenware pot simmering away on the coals. The base must have been a stock made from what remained of the turkey, for only the white meat is served. Into the pot she had thrown tomatoes, garlic and onions browned beforehand in olive oil. Judging from their skins, I thought bananas must also have gone into the stew, and the grated peel of an orange. I went back to watch several times, and always she was pounding and stirring. On each visit the sauce had thickened, until at last it was reduced to a slow, lazy-bubbling consistency.

When the *molé* is served it is sprinkled lightly with sesame seeds. One eats it with a fork and a *tortilla* rolled up to serve as a pusher; a quantity of these pushers disappear, well dunked in the ambrosial sauce.

Tortillas are prepared now in precisely the same way as at the time of the Conquest, when Cortés' major domo Francisco de Terrazas listed them as an Aztec food along with *tamales*, quail, turkey, venison, rabbit, dog and 'a kind of pepper for seasoning that is called chili'. To make *tortillas* maize is first parboiled in lime-water until cleansed and soft enough to mash with a stone roller on a great inward curving block. Worked in with a little water, the grain soon becomes a paste that is then patted into flat cakes and laid on the griddle to bake. The great art is not to break the edge of the pancakes, nor should they be allowed to brown in the toasting. It is most important to serve them up hot, when they are generally passed round in a folded napkin. In Madame Calderón's day '*tortillas* were considered unfashionable, though they were to be met with occasionally in some of the best old houses'. Captain Lyon, her predecessor by several years, found that 'most respectable houses' had a special woman whose sole job it was to make *tortillas*. 'It sounds very oddly to the ear of a stranger during mealtimes to hear the rapid patting and slapping that goes on in the kitchen.' For my part, the houses I most enjoyed going to all served *tortillas*, though I must admit that they were far too grand for one to hear any 'slapping'.

In Madame Calderón's day every dinner included *puchero* on the menu, a kind of mixed stew with a herb sauce, served immediately following the soup. She also mentioned a delicious cream cheese made by the Indians and eaten with honey in the comb. I was never given the cheese but often had the honey which comes from Yucatan. There they boil it with yucca root and serve it as a pudding. The yucca is of a starchy consistency like a yam and is rather tasteless, but the honey has a very pungent flavour, like the odour of some tropical flower.

I tasted black zapotes, candied marrow and sticky squares made from *camotes*, the Mexican sweet potato. I tried the stringy pad of the nopal cactus stewed as a vegetable which was not unpleasant and rather comparable to okra. One also eats the red and yellow pears of the same plant. Gage knew them as *nochtli*, their Indian name, and warned one, thank heavens, against their effects on one's bladder 'for they dyeth the urine the deepest red'. Without his warning I should certainly have believed myself to be dying of a haemorrhage.

The pineapple, a native of tropical America, was unknown in Europe until the end of the seventeenth century. Gage tackled it warily, for 'there is nothing more dangerous than to eat much of it'. Even the Spaniards took precautions and before eating it 'cut it in round slices, and lay it awhile in salt and water which taketh much of the rawness from it'. Quite understandably Gage preferred his pineapple as a preserve.

Much of my time was spent in the markets. Only once did I regret my curiosity, when I tried fried grasshoppers. Their taste stayed with me the whole morning: a nauseating, copper greasiness. Perhaps the most *recherché* of my Mexican delicacies was a dish called *huit la cochi* made from sweet-corn that has been attacked by a fungus. The grain swells up and turns a milky charcoal and in this condition is sautéd in cream – delicious.

The markets do a lively trade in a variety of drinks sold by the glassful, among them the milky *atole*, popular already in pre-Columbian times. Gage thought it 'like unto our almond milk but much thicker and made of the juice of young maize which they so confection with spices, musk and sugar'. These days *atole* is much in demand following First Communions, and generally drunk flavoured with strawberries.

After *pulque*, *tequila*, a local *eau de vie*, is the most popular drink. The Mexican first sucks a quartered lime, then taking a pinch of salt tosses the *tequila* down in the way Russians drink their vodka. Lawrence thought little of it and writes that 'the Mexican burns out his stomach with these beastly fire-waters and cauterizes the hurt with red-hot chili. Swallowing one hell-fire to put out another.'[1] *Tequila* is also the product of a cactus, a small, sharper-leafed plant than the *maguey* from which *pulque* is drawn. *Tequila* is prepared differently from *pulque*, the juices being extracted from the amputated leaves only after these have been roasted.

From Puebla we drove to Oaxaca, a run of just over two hundred and fifty miles. The road is boldly cambered and winds through wooded mountains at altitudes between five and six thousand feet. The clouds were especially remarkable. Great cumuli, their contours accentuated by luminous shadows, sailed majestically across the horizon. Against their whiteness, smaller, looser clouds of grey drifted raggedly by in the foreground. Suddenly a curtain of rain cut across the titanic skyscape, springing a rainbow and soaking the baked earth so that it smelt of wetted potsherds. All day we were among the mountains, but they were less impressive than the clouds that played so dramatically across them. In the afternoon the vegetation changed. First, elegantly slim cacti appeared among the trees and then the monster *Cereus candelabrum* took over, a dinoceras of the vegetable world from whose single vertical thick stem grow thirty or forty spikes each twenty feet in length. So large are they that an entire herd of cattle can shelter in their shade.

It was dusk by the time we reached the Dominican monastery of Santo Domingo at Yanhuitlán, set on a small rise in an isolated setting. According to Baird, the church was begun about 1543–50. The façade is late seventeenth-century but the nave is rib-vaulted, perhaps the purest Gothic vaulting in all Mexico. It contrasts splendidly with the superb seventeenth-century *retablo mayor*. The high soaring nave of pale, coloured stone was beautiful in the obscurity. One could just discern the faded gold of the altars and the dusty pink of the bricks lining the floor. A grim figure of death, a crowned skeleton in painted wood armed with a scythe, was fast melting into the walls. Standing there in the cool silence I had a feeling of immense peace.

The nostalgia of twilight brought memories flooding back to me,

[1] *The Plumed Serpent.*

and in the stillness I recalled deliciously crowd-free expeditions to other sixteenth-century monasteries: Actopan, Acolman and Tlalmanalco in the vicinity of Mexico City. Shortly to be added to these was the Dominican monastery south of Oaxaca at Cuilápan, which looks more Romanesque than Gothic, and resembles the kind of ruin one might expect on the coast of Brittany.

These monasteries were founded by the Mendicant Orders. The Franciscans' sphere of influence extended over the central and western provinces, while the Dominicans established settlements to the south of Mexico City. The mountainous regions to the north-west were left to the Augustinians to evangelize. Tlalmanalco, some forty-five miles south of Mexico City, is Franciscan. Actopan and Acolman to the north are Augustinian.

To reach both Actopan and Acolman one must pass over dusty roads until suddenly, above some pepper trees, their buttressed and crenellated walls appear. Each monastery was self-contained, a walled complex of buildings that dominated the countryside like a small castle. In general such churches are high box-like structures without aisles and with the simplest of openings placed as windows high up under the vaulting. As the friars were their own architects and the Indians their masons, 'the buildings put up by the Mendicant Orders were of the simplest plans . . . the necessary result of untrained labour and of amateur design'.[1] During the first years of settlement the friars had to assume that they might need protection, and it was therefore natural that their monasteries resembled forts. As it turned out, this was unnecessary, except in the northern provinces. The watch towers and the crenellated walks between sentry posts may have provided a feeling of security, but otherwise were merely decorative.

The cloisters in the monasteries of the Mendicant Orders were nearly always two-storeyed. Many of them had walls frescoed in black and white with religious subjects. The scenes depicted, like the black-and-white technique, were obviously inspired by the woodcuts and book illustrations brought over by the friars from Europe. Acolman has some good examples of such work. Also at Acolman, in one of the long corridors leading to the cells, hangs a naïve and poignantly touching life-size crucifix modelled in papier-mâché by the Indians. There are many of these Christs. Over a foundation of branches and peeled cornstalks, the Indians moulded the layers of moist paper with their fingers. Once dried the figure was coated with plaster and painted.

An architectural novelty peculiar to the New World is the open chapel sometimes adjacent to a monastery church. Sanford explains this 'by the necessity of saying mass to huge crowds of Indians who

[1] *Art and Architecture in Spain and Portugal and their American Dominions 1500 to 1800.*

could not be accommodated'.[1] Already by 1531 the Franciscan Juan de Zumárraga, Mexico's first bishop, reported the conversion of over a million Indians by members of his order alone. One reads of a simple Franciscan friar baptizing so many Indians a day that he used 'his left hand when the right one got cramp'. Aguilar did not have a very high opinion of the converted Indians' faith: 'most of them come to church by force, and with very little fear and reverence; they gossip and talk, and walk out during the principal part of the sermon'. Commenting on the same subject, Humboldt felt that the missionaries paid little attention to the Indians' motive for accepting Christianity; 'their great object was to get as many baptized as possible'. They were concerned 'when a parting soul could not be snatched from hell's powers for want of a drop of water!' It is hard to gauge the Indians' reactions on the matter. According to François Cali: *'ils ne craignaient pas de se faire baptiser plusieurs fois tant cela les amusait'.*[2] If true, this would help to explain the startling statistics given out by the missions.

It was dark by the time we finally reached Oaxaca, or more correctly Huaxyaca, an Indian word meaning 'place covered with trees'. Morning revealed it to be of infinite charm, a characteristically southern city in every respect. The air was warmer, the sun more golden, and the light clotted and heavy as it fell, sifting through the leathery verdure of dusty trees.

In spite of three major earthquakes Oaxaca remains a stately city full of impressive buildings. One is struck immediately by the quality of its stone work. Wherever one looks the soft green-brown, pistachio-coloured stone has been masterfully handled – in the filigree of carving on the sculptured panels at the base of the columns that flank the entrance to the cathedral, or then again, in the sharpness of detail in the angled, screen-like façade of La Soledad. Kelemen[3] gives the credit for this to the Zapotec and Mixtec Indians of the region, traditionally excellent masons as their nearby ruins testify. At Monte Albán the Zapotecs levelled the hill-top to raise their altars and shrines, while at Mitla the Mixtecs built themselves palaces inlaid with mosaic murals of such intricacy that Huxley called them 'petrified weaving'.[4]

The Santo Domingo monastery is certainly one of the most beautiful of the conventual structures in the Republic. Both church and monastery are very grand in scale. One mounts to the second floor of the cloisters by a splendid double stairway worthy of the finest Roman palaces. Although it suffered considerably from Napoleon III's troops at the time

---

[1] *The Story of Architecture in Mexico.*
[2] *L'Art des Conquistadors*, text by François Cali, B. Arthaud, Paris, 1960.
[3] *Baroque and Rococo in Latin America.*
[4] *Beyond the Mexique Bay.*

of the French intervention, its scars are being effectively dealt with by the Department of Antiquities.

Another of Oaxaca's highlights is the Monte Albán treasure. Unearthed in 1932, it is one of the most spectacular finds in New World archaeology. Although found in a tomb at Monte Albán, a Zapotec site, the treasure is of Mixtec origin. Before the Aztec ascendancy, and long before the Conquest, Oaxaca Valley was dominated by the Zapotecs, but 'Mixtec groups drifting down from the north gradually took over and introduced their own cultural patterns'. While there is no evidence that the Mixtecs ever occupied Monte Albán permanently, 'they did, however, bury their dead within the city limits, and in some cases they made use of the beautifully painted Zapotec tombs of an earlier period'.[1] Such a burial was Tomb Seven which, when opened, revealed nine bodies, one of them a woman. My memory of a room in the State Regional Museum set aside to display these treasures is one of dark walls and brilliantly lit cases containing objects of transcendental beauty.

Dr Alfonso Caso, the first to enter the tomb, described how a magnificent goblet of rock crystal caught the rays of his flashlight. 'The floor shone with jewels; beads, bells, pectoral plates, gold ear-rings and bracelets, silver vessels, innumerable objects of jade, shell, jet, obsidian and amber.' There were piles of turquoises which, when reassembled, made handsome masks. Pearls literally covered certain parts of the tomb. Their lustre, I noticed, is surprisingly unimpaired, and their size quite remarkable, some of them being as large as doves' eggs. But it is not so much the intrinsic value of the objects that strikes one as their excellent quality and fine execution. The Mixtecs, the 'People of the Clouds', were superb craftsmen.

Alongside the pearls stands an alabaster bowl cut so thin that it looks as if it might blow away if you breathed on it. There are obsidian ear-spools whittled down to the thickness of paper, and objects of the clearest rock crystal without a trace of a flaw. Perhaps the most beautiful of all are the series of jaguar bones carved with fantastically delicate traceries of figures and arabesques. The contours of the bones have been carefully exploited so that the carving moves and undulates over their surface. In another case is a wide collar, a gossamer mesh of fine gold linking pale turquoises, coral and pearls; its outer edges are fringed with gold beads from which hang tiny golden bells. Ranged in a second room is a collection of stylized figures in terracotta representing the people who wore these jewels and square built-up headdresses of feathers and flowers. The sophistication of their apparel is almost beyond belief. Their physical features have been so skilfully tortured into a stylized

[1] *Treasures of Ancient America.*

geometry that they look more like architectural motifs than human beings.

After a short stay in Oaxaca we drove on down to Tehuantepec. Not far from Oaxaca the road winds past the gigantic cypress of Tule which completely overtops a chapel in an explosion of green plumes. Known to the botanists as *Taxodium mucronatum*, it is about 160 feet high, and according to Humboldt, is 'the oldest organic monument on the globe'. He cut his name into its bark, but this has long since disappeared.

From the Gulf we again started climbing. San Cristóbal de las Casas, where we spent a night, lies at seven thousand feet. It is beautiful country, bewildering in the diversity of its flora that includes bright red broom and a deciduous tree that first puts out a mass of egg-yellow, cup-like flowers. By midday we were twisting through verdant hills looking down onto the yellow glinting waters of the Grijalva river. Thatched huts with smoke seeping through the reeds nestled in banks of fern. I picked some blackberries and a bunch of deep blue salvia. Later we met groups of Indians returning from market, pure bred Zinacatáns of Mayan stock, who dress as they must have dressed under the Spaniards, in flat straw hats with ribbons floating down their backs. If the ribbons are tied it indicates that they are married. The women are less spectacularly garbed than the men in long wrap-around skirts dyed a deep indigo. Indian boys sold us pale yellow passion-fruit from which we sucked out the delicious, seedy, musk-flavoured fruit through a hole bit in the hard shell.

We had climbed into clouds when, dipping down two thousand feet, we reached Las Casas, named for the famous bishop, protector of the Indians. The town lies in a hollow surrounded by pines and marshy grazing land. The dark, earth-coloured tiles, the raised pavements and cobbled streets reminded me of places I have seen in the Himalayas. The night was cold and I slept under a wooden ceiling painted with flowers.

The next morning we drove to Cuauhtémoc and over the border into Guatemala, through a wall of serrated mountains, piled one behind the other. They became more abrupt, more precipitous, as we advanced, a series of cones. The air was much warmer, and we were again among bananas and flowering canes with their silken plumes.

11

The Pompeii of America

Having been almost completely destroyed by a series of earthquakes between 1917 and 1918, Guatemala City has little to offer the traveller, and indeed, seems never to have been particularly prepossessing. Henry Dunn[1] in 1827 found it of an unbearable dullness, while Robert Dunlop not many years later complained of the lodgings. 'Apartments when found, are mostly but bare walls . . . Window glass is only used in the better houses and in the smaller towns all description of windows are considered superfluous, hence in doing anything requiring light it is necessary to open the door, when dogs, pigs and fowls are always ready to rush in.' The sophisticated young Dunlop also noted the number of saints 'stuck upon the walls of every house. They are the general remedy employed for all kinds of sickness, each complaint having its patron saint'.[2] This must have been most useful, for we know from other sources that the medicine practised in Latin America was usually of the most primitive kind. There is Captain Lyon's story of an old lady 'to whom I gave a couple of pills in order to remove her headache. Very deliberately she poked one up each nostril as being nearer the seat of pain.'[3] Fray Navarrete's cure for scorpion bite was equally eccentric. To escape them the brothers 'would rub about the beds with garlic', and once stung 'a try'd and certain remedy against the pain of it is to stroke the part that was hurt with a child's private member which immediately takes away the anguish and the venom exhales'.[4] In explaining such ignorance, José Gabriel Navarro wrote that 'medicine was not in the required programme for the American colleges and universities . . . It was considered a plebeian art proper for mulattos and unworthy of gentlemen.'[5]

There are various references to Guatemala City itself, nothing, however, of much importance. Montgomary, an American travelling at

[1] Henry Dunn, *Guatemala*, Nisbet, London, 1839.
[2] Robert Glasgow Dunlop, *Travels in Central America*, Longmans, London, 1847.
[3] *Journal of a Residence and Tour in the Republic of Mexico.*
[4] *The Travels and Controverses of Friar Domingo Navarrete 1618–86.*
[5] *La Medicina y los Médicos a Quito durante la época virreinal*, by José Gabriel Navarro.

more or less the same time as the two Englishmen, singled out the double door-knockers, 'one considerably higher than the other, the under one, for persons on foot, the upper, for those who are on horseback'.[1] Some of these, I noticed, still exist. Montgomary also commented on the thick-walled shelters found in the patios of most private houses, a wise pre-caution certainly, given the country's appalling record of earthquakes.

Guatemala has had three capitals, all blasted by earthquakes. The first, Santiago (after St James the Apostle, patron saint of Spain) de Guatemala, was founded in 1524 by Pedro de Alvarado, Cortés' second in command. He unwittingly chose a terrifying site, at the base of a towering volcano 'from which flowed a quantity of trickling streams. On this account the Spaniards called it *Volcán de Agua* to distinguish it from another mountain close by which they called *Volcán de Fuego*, out of which belched a continual sheet of flames.'[2] When Santiago, or *Ciudad Viejo*, as it is now called, was destroyed in 1541, the settlement was moved to what was believed to be a more favourable site, a pleasant valley five miles to the north but still slung like a hammock between the giant cones of these two very suspicious-looking mountains. Twelve times, between 1541 and 1773, this second city was badly shaken and as many times rebuilt by its persistent citizens. It took a succession of severe shocks, from May to December 1773, to convince the authorities that another move was imperative. But again they made the mistake of not moving far enough. The modern day Guatemala City is only twenty-seven miles from its namesake, now known as Antigua, meaning ancient.

In the fateful year 1773 Antigua had a population of sixty thousand inhabitants, besides thirty thousand who farmed the surrounding districts. A map of the period shows just how important it had become. It was a big city with thousands of houses, thirty-five churches and sixteen large monasteries and convents. Its end must have been a harrowing experience. Frequent tremors were experienced during the early months of 1773; by June they had become so severe that work of every kind had stopped. The Indians of the outlying villages were afraid to bring in supplies; food became scarce. 'People moved into the open, preferring the rain to falling walls and roofs. The archbishop himself fared no better than the rest,'[3] for he had to spend several nights in his coach which had been dragged to the security of the Plaza de Armas, known then as the Plaza Real. There followed a week of comparative calm, and then on 29 July the city was shaken so violently that people rushed

[1] A. W. Montgomary, *Narrative of a Journey to Guatemala*, New York, 1838.

[2] Arthur Helps, *The Spanish Conquest of America*, London, 1857.

[3] Dorothy H. Popenoe, *Santiago de los Caballeros de Guatemala*, Harvard University Press, Cambridge, 1935.

out screaming into the streets. Ten minutes after the first shock, there followed a second, much more violent. An eye-witness, Fray Felipe Cadena, described how clouds of dust suffocated the city and how roof tiles were flung in every direction. The only refuge was to lie down in the streets. Those trees that were not uprooted were bent double, their branches sweeping the ground. Above the general clamour, the shouts and yells, the crashings and rumblings, the church bells clanged incessantly, set in motion by the swaying of the ground, 'swelling up like an agitated sea'.

I have never experienced an earthquake; however, other travellers have recorded their impressions of them. Ward described the motion as a perpendicular one that cracked doors and rattled windows, having been preceded by a 'melancholy howling of dogs who are usually the first to feel and to announce its approach'.[1] In Madame Calderón's experience, 'suddenly the room, the walls, all began to move, and the floor to heave like the waves of the sea. All Mexico was on its knees while it lasted.' She felt seasick for days afterwards and found the worst thing to have been 'the heaving of the solid earth. It makes one lose confidence in its security.'

By 1 August almost the entire city of Antigua, except for a few buildings in the centre, lay tumbled to the ground. Among the few exceptions were the yellow and white church of La Merced, the façade of the Cathedral San Felipe Neri, and part of the exterior of San Francisco. An anonymous manuscript quoted by Mrs Popenoe described the ensuing pestilential conditions:

the bodies of the dead and of the many animals that have died within the stables have corrupted the air. The fountains have dried up and there is a shortage of water, which adds still further to the suffering . . . The Dominicans are the only ones who have not fared so badly, for they still have rich farms and convents in the province, but the rest, having lost all, are reduced to begging.

All lament their misfortune . . . The father seeks his daughter, the son his mother, the husband his wife, and so with all of them. The dead bodies are buried without shrouds . . . and without public attendance, for there is none to see to these matters . . .[2]

Still the Antiguans were so reluctant to leave their city that the authorities were obliged to evacuate it forcibly. They were given one year to move. For a decade or so Antigua stood empty, until people then started gradually creeping back. With a large abandoned city at their disposal they settled themselves in the least damaged of the buildings and pastured their cattle and mules in the grass-grown courts of the

[1] *Mexico in 1827.*
[2] *Santiago de los Caballeros de Guatemala.*

convents and monasteries. Eventually the Indians were persuaded to venture in with their wares; they found the abandoned Jesuit monastery of La Compañía de Jesús better protection than the open plaza and established in its roofless church the market that exists there today. By 1838 Antigua had a population of twelve thousand. A year later John Stephens, on an archaeological expedition to Guatemala, visited the city. 'On each side were the ruins of churches, convents and private residences, large and costly, some lying in masses, some with fronts still standing richly ornamented with stucco cracked and yawning, roofless, without doors and windows, and trees growing inside above the walls.' The cathedral's gigantic walls were standing but it was roofless, 'the interior was occupied as a burying ground, and the graves were shaded by a forest of dahlias',[1] the giant *Dahlia imperialis*, six to eighteen feet high, that is found growing wild all over the Guatemalan highlands.

The graves have now been trodden underfoot and the weeds routed. Two chapels at the entrance of the cathedral have been roofed in, but otherwise the great nave stands exactly as Stephens saw it, suggesting 'even in decay, its former grandeur'.[2] It sweeps majestically upwards, an interplay of bricks, mortar and sky. Many of the stucco mouldings and friezes, of remarkable workmanship, are still in place. In the cupola the blotched and crumbling arms of Spain can still be distinguished, while on the pendentives below the main dome, four red-headed angels in voluminous robes stand swinging censers to perfume a void.

During one of my visits I met a family of Indians carrying baskets of flowers on their heads. They disappeared silently down some crumbling steps leading to a stucco crucifix on the walls of the crypt. Above the crypt used to stand the main altar described by Domingo Juarros, Archbishop of Guatemala, as having a baldachin 'supported on sixteen pillars sheathed in tortoise-shell and bearing medallions of finely wrought bronze'.[3] The cathedral had been very splendid.

What struck Stephens more than the ruins was the fact that the city was still inhabited. 'It presents a strange appearance . . . the inhabitants, like the dwellers over the buried Herculaneum, seemed to entertain no fear of renewed disaster.'[4]

In 1850 an enterprising mayor restored the Palace of the Captains-General and the church of La Merced. Large-scale coffee cultivation undertaken during the latter part of the century encouraged further settlers; more and more of the old houses were restored. The restoration

---

[1] John Stephens, *Incidents of Travel in Central America, Chiapas and Yucatan*, Harper Bros., New York, 1841.

[2] *Baroque and Rococo in Latin America.*

[3] *Historia de la Ciudad de Guatemala*, edition by the Museo Guatemalteco ,Vol. I, Guatemala, 1857.

[4] *Incidents of Travel in Central America, Chiapas and Yucatan.*

still goes on, but under the watchful eye of a board of architects, since the government has wisely declared the city a national monument.

Antigua became my headquarters while in Guatemala. I stayed in what used to be the monastery attached to the El Carmen church, 'once famous for its orchestra and choir'.[1] The proprietor has shown great restraint in converting the ruins. Our shower dripped onto a tiled court overshadowed by a giant philodendron. The cold starlit nights were warmed by roaring fires of timbers and old beams from some nearby ruin. At the end of the street Fuego rose 12,582 feet in a great symmetrical cone outlined against the sky.

Fuego last erupted in 1932 when a fine shower of ashes so veiled the sun that it was necessary to work by artificial light. This light, buff-coloured lava dust is ingrained in the seams of the tiled roofs, providing an ideal habitat for a species of *Kalanchoe*, a semi-succulent plant with an erect head of yellow-pink flowers.

Again and again Antigua reminded me of Pompeii. Fuego is Vesuvius – their silhouettes are much the same – and there is something of the broken grandeur of Pompeii in Antigua's cracked and blackened walls with vegetation pushing out among the crevices. But just as Piranesi peopled his eighteenth-century views of the Roman ruins with contemporary figures and vignettes of their lives, so too does Antigua seem to be a Pompeii still alive. When I was buying air-mail stamps for a postcard to England, the postboy disappeared through a plywood door beyond which I caught a glimpse of the ruined cloister of the cathedral behind the post office. Against one of the columns, painted a chequered red and white design, leaned a bicycle. Ducks waddled across the grass-grown cobbles. Over the top of a lattice gate into the hulk of the roofless church of Santo Domingo I saw earth and rubble piled up to the height of the cornice. On top there was a wooden lean-to occupied by a family of Indians. It was here in Santo Domingo that Gage saw 'a lamp of silver hanging before the high altar so big as requiring the strength of three men to haul it up with a rope'.

And what about Fuego? Although it never actually buried the city under flows of lava, its explosions seem always to have heralded the terrible earthquakes. Gage, if no one else, showed a healthy respect for the flaming mountain, writing of Antigua as being 'seated in the midst of a Paradise on the one side and hell on the other'. Fuego was more active in his day, for then the air stank of brimstone and 'castles of smoke rise to such heights as to out-dare the sky'. Plants and fruit were shrivelled by its heat and the volcano spewed forth stones and rocks 'which had they fallen upon the city would have crushed it to pieces'. Sometimes the flames were so bright 'that my friend, Mr Cabannas,

[1] *Baroque and Rococo in Latin America.*

confidently avowed that standing one night at his window he had with the light of that fire read a letter, the distance being over three English miles'.

Nothing now remains of the first capital, *Ciudad Viejo*, except some moss-grown foundations and a few tumbled walls hidden in rank volcanic vegetation. But Díaz described its destruction, and there are also a few details regarding the founding of the city to be gleaned in the dispatches Alvarado sent to Cortés.

Cortés in his third letter to Charles v informed the Emperor how, after the fall of Tenochtitlán, he sent Alvarado south to subject the Mixtecs in the Oaxaca region. The expedition penetrated as far south as Tehuantepec. On Cortés' orders Alvarado further embarked on the conquest of Guatemala. His troops left Mexico City in December 1523 along with several hundred Aztec mercenaries. They were of course outnumbered by the Mayas, who were, however, always terrified by the Spaniards' horses and who could never match the Spanish in cunning. The Mayas also lacked political unity, and Alvarado played one tribe against the other, thus managing ultimately to subdue both. Alvarado's major engagement was won on the road to Quezaltenango. By July 1524 the army had arrived at a spot which the natives called Panchoy, meaning 'great lake'. 'Not,' as Arthur Helps writes, 'that there was any lake there, but the form of the ground, surrounded by mountains, suggested the idea of one. The soldiers were delighted with the beauty of the place. The freshness of its foliage, the gentleness of its streams.' Here it was declared should stand their city. It would have been difficult to choose a more dangerous site, 'but this was not yet suspected by the Spaniards, who, weary by months of harassing warfare found in this green place something which must have reminded them of the most beautiful parts of Andalusia'.[1]

We know from one of Alvarado's dispatches to Cortés that he was not insensible to the awesome sight of a volcano in action. But the Spaniards had no experience as yet of a severe earthquake, and from a safe distance must have regarded an eruption as a rather splendid spectacle. 'From its mouth it hurls rocks as big as a house, burning in flames, and when they fall they shatter in pieces, covering the mountain with fire . . . Sixty leagues beyond this,' continued Alvarado, 'we saw another volcano which throws terrible smoke that rises to the sky, in a mass half a league wide.'[2] Díaz, on an expedition in the vicinity some months later, was the first to experience an actual earthquake, 'so violent that a number of soldiers were thrown to the ground'. But it was too late; Santiago de Guatemala was already half built.

[1] *The Spanish Conquest of America.*
[2] *The Chronicle of the Anonymous Conquistador.* Extract from *The Conquistador.*

Before recounting the terrible destruction of the city, it is important to know the chief characters involved in the drama: the handsome Alvarado and his proud wife Doña Beatriz.

Alvarado was thirty-four when he joined Cortés and was a man 'whose countenance was particularly graceful and noble', according to Díaz. He had, as certain Spaniards do, reddish-blond hair. This the Aztecs immensely admired, christening him *Tonatiuh*, meaning the Sun, son of the Sun.[1] Díaz's description of Alvarado ignores his reprehensible behaviour when left in command of Tenochtitlán during the Conquest. Díaz has nothing but praise for him, his splendid horsemanship and his 'open and agreeable conversation. He was remarkably neat in his dress, which was always of the richest stuffs.' Helps delves deeper into Alvarado's character and is far less complimentary, feeling that his qualifications for command were not of the highest order. 'He was brave, daring, restless, crafty, devout but without any true policy. He was a great talker, a man of considerable force, if not skill in action . . . but it can hardly be said that he governed.' He was absent most of the time, 'and absent not for the good of his colony but for the promotion of his own interests'.[2] Certainly he was restless, one of the most restless of those restless men, the conquerors of the New World.

Having subdued Guatemala, Alvarado, like Cortés, left for Spain. His plan was to persuade the King to bestow upon him directly the stewardship of the south, rather than hold the office by virtue of Cortés' appointment. In this he was successful, being named governor of all the lands he had conquered. These included modern Honduras, El Salvador, Nicaragua, Costa Rica and most of the Mexican state of Chiapas. He managed also to contract an advantageous marriage with Doña Francisca de la Cueva, niece of the powerful Duke of Albuquerque, and a relative of Francisco de los Cobos, the Emperor's Secretary of State. Doña Francisca died, however, on landing at Vera Cruz. History does not specify what her fatal malady was, but it could not have been the dreaded yellow fever, which, as it will be remembered, is thought to have been of African origin and thus could not yet have been imported on the slave ships.

Although the governor of Guatemala was technically subject to the viceroy of New Spain, only in moments of great stress or in the event of an unexpected vacancy in the office did the viceroy ever interfere. Besides being named governor, Alvarado was also designated Captain-General and *adelantado*, or 'frontier commander'. An *adelantado* was

---

[1] A full-length portrait of Alvarado is in the municipal building of Guatemala City, but it was painted long after his death and has been considerably retouched in the nineteenth century.

[2] *The Spanish Conquest of America.*

legally required to found at least three towns. A royal decree, outlined by Professor Kirkpatrick, concisely defined the form these new towns were to take:

The plaza or central square was marked out; round it was set the public buildings – *cabildo* (town hall), church, hospital and prison; the streets were traced intersecting at right angles and enclosing equal blocks; every man received a rectangular building-site within the town and a piece of land without, thus becoming a *vecino*, or householder in the civic community; every *vecino* became an *encomendero*, receiving an *encomienda*, a trust or fief of one or more villages of Indians who were to pay him tribute or fixed labour in return for protection and Christian instruction.[1]

This was the *encomendero* system mentioned in a previous chapter.

There was plenty to occupy the handsome *Adelantado* had he taken his responsibilities seriously, but his attention was drawn elsewhere. When stories began to circulate about the wealth of the Incas and about Pizarro's 'golden' successes in Peru, Alvarado hurriedly equipped a small expeditionary force and sailed southward for his share of the spoils. But Pizarro, reluctant to share either spoils or honours, sent two of his lieutenants to head him off. They met at Quito where Pizarro's men persuaded Don Pedro to accept 100,000 gold *castellanos* for his fleet and his armament. This seemed a sizeable sum – until Alvarado discovered on his return that copper had been added to the alloy.

In 1536 he returned again to Spain and married his sister-in-law Doña Beatriz. While in Spain Alvarado, like Cortés, pledged himself to provide thirteen vessels to explore the Southern Ocean, always with a view to discovering a western passage to the Spice Islands. To fit out the promised ships Alvarado had to spend a fortune, because, as Díaz explains, 'the harbour lay eight hundred miles from Vera Cruz and all the iron work, and the greater part of the building materials had to be transported thither by land'. Díaz estimated that he might have built eighty vessels of the same size at Seville for an equal sum of money.

Despite the large amount contributed by Alvarado, it was not possible for him to finance the expedition entirely from his own purse. To raise further funds he turned to the Council of the Indies who advanced him the requested amount, but in return stipulated that Mendoza, the viceroy, should be admitted as a partner in his adventure. It was a form of control should the expedition prove a success.

When the armada was fully equipped with 650 men and 200 horses, Alvarado hoisted the imperial flags, attended Mass and set sail. But before turning westward across the uncharted Pacific, he sailed northward along the coast to Colima where Mendoza, journeying down from

[1] *The Cambridge Modern History*, Cambridge University Press, Cambridge, 1907.

Mexico City, came in person to interview him. Here fate intervened: an Indian uprising coincided with Alvarado's arrival. The wild northern tribes laid siege to Guadalajara in such great numbers that the Spanish commander of the district found himself hopelessly outnumbered and called upon Alvarado for help. In a rocky and mountainous terrain, while attacking up a steep incline, Alvarado met with his fatal accident: a falling horse rolled on top of him. Not killed outright, he was carried to Guadalajara where he lingered on for several days of anguish, physical and moral, 'weeping over his errors, cruelties, and acts of injustice'. One day, when the pain was at its worst, a friend who was standing by inquired, ' "What part is it which Your Lordship suffers from most?" . . . "El alma – the soul," he answered.'[1]

Alvarado died in July 1541. The news soon reached Santiago de Guatemala (*Ciudad Viejo*), but Doña Beatriz refused to believe it until it was confirmed in an official dispatch from Mendoza. His family's grief at his death knew no bounds. Doña Beatriz and the ladies of the household all lopped off their hair. In his often quoted account, in his *Historia General*, of Doña Beatriz's hysterical behaviour, Gómara gives the impression of a woman who has taken leave of her senses. Her face bruised with self-inflicted beatings, Doña Beatriz hid away in a darkened room, refusing all contact with the outside world. Orders were given that the entire house should be daubed in black. Her confessor tried to reason with her, talking of the various evils with which God chastises men, pointing out that it was a small evil when He deprived them of temporal things such as estates, children, wives and husbands. 'She sprung up like a viper that had been trodden on. "Get out, Father, and come not hither to me with these sermons; peradventure, has God any greater evil to afflict me with, after having deprived me of my Lord the *Adelantado*?" ' It was Doña Beatriz's blasphemy, Gómara maintains, that brought on the ensuing holocaust.

Díaz sprang to Doña Beatriz's defence, claiming that Gómara, who was Cortés' chaplain in Spain and who had never set foot in the New World, was guilty of pure improvisation. 'I have often been assured,' he writes, 'since I have resided in Guatemala, that this lady never gave utterance to the sinful expressions of which she has been accused.' He also avowed that it was Alvarado's major-domo, not Doña Beatriz, who had all the walls plastered with black bitumen, 'which stuck so fast that it could never after be taken off'.

I favour Díaz's version of the story for it seems improbable that Mendoza would have appointed Doña Beatriz *Gobernadora* in her husband's place had she been the hysterical character that Gómara paints her. In any event her tenure of office was of the briefest duration.

[1] *The Spanish Conquest of America.*

76, 77 *Antigua. The ruined monastery of La Recolección, and Nave of Cathedral (below)* (*page 145*)

79 *El Carmen church with the volcano Fuego in the background* (*page 146*)

78 (*opposite*) *Antigua. Stucco mouldings in Cathedral* (*page 145*)

82 (opposite) Antigua. Plaza Real showing the Palace of the Captains-General (page 145)

80 Antigua. Church of La Merced. Detail of façade. Built 1760 (page 157)

81 Antigua. View from my bedroom (page 146)

83 Antigua. Hospital church of San Pedro built in 1654–65 (page 157)

*84 Cloister of Las
Capuchinas convent
1726. A good example
of the heavy, squat
architecture developed
to resist the earthquakes
(page 157)*

*85 Lake Atitlán
(page 154)*

*86 Antigua. Great
fountain in the
monastery of the
Mercedarians (page 157)*

87 Antigua. Patio of San Carlos University built in 1763 by the mestizo architect José Manuel Ramírez (page 157)

Elected *Governadora* on 9 September, she had met her death by the thirteenth.

On the morning of Doña Beatriz's appointment a hurricane started blowing accompanied by torrents of rain which lasted for three days. It is not quite clear whether an earthquake or the vast quantities of water collected in its crater caused the *Volcán de Agua* to burst its sides with an effect of a huge dam giving way. Volumes of water came hurtling down the mountain carrying boulders and uprooted trees. It happened during the early hours of the morning and Santiago, or *Ciudad Viejo*, lying directly in the path of the tidal wave, was taken completely by surprise. Nearly six hundred in all perished, amongst them Doña Beatriz. She had fled to the chapel on the roof with her ladies-in-waiting and had been engulfed by a wave of mud and water. Doña Leonor, one of Alvarado's daughters by a Tlaxcalan princess, was more fortunate than her stepmother. She was swept out of the palace into the kitchen garden where she clung to an uprooted orange tree and managed to weather the flood.

The following morning Doña Beatriz was found lifelessly embracing the cross that had stood on the chapel altar. The *Governadora* was given a temporary burial until 'some years later, at the instigation of Doña Leonor her remains were removed to a place of honour beside that of the *Adelantado* in the cathedral of the new capital'.[1] When Díaz died fifty-seven years later, he was buried alongside them, but no trace of the three tombs has ever been found. Excavations during the 1930s under the main altar in the *Capilla Real* failed to uncover any remains, and as Kelemen writes 'it must be assumed that the bodies . . . were removed, but when and where no one knows'.[2]

What does remain, however, is the immense gash cut into Agua's crater. It is still, as Stephens put it, 'fearfully visible', an awesome monument to the force of the flood waters that engulfed *Ciudad Viejo*.

One should add to this account of the *Adelantado* and his wife some information about Díaz who spent his old age in Antigua. Here, in his fiftieth year, he started writing his *True History of The Conquest*.

Although Díaz had been allotted an *encomienda* in the *tierra caliente* south of Vera Cruz after the fall of Tenochtitlán, he decided to move to Guatemala following the Honduran campaign with Cortés. His brief glimpse of the country on the march back from Honduras must have attracted him. He was in his late forties when he first arrived in Antigua, which was then in the process of being built. 'The cathedral,' writes Herbert Cerwin, Díaz's biographer, 'had almost been completed, the

---

[1] *Santiago de los Caballeros de Guatemala.*
[2] *Baroque and Rococo in Latin America.*

streets and the plaza had been laid out.'[1] While in Mexico, Díaz had lived with an Indian mistress who had produced a son and two daughters. One of the daughters came with him to Antigua while the rest of the family remained behind on the *encomienda* in the state of Vera Cruz. Once installed in Antigua, he is said to have taken a second Indian mistress, but 'as the government continued to frown on land-holding Spaniards who did not have legal wives' he married a Spanish widow, Teresa Becerra, the only daughter of one of Alvarado's men. By her he had eight children.

Díaz was never what could be called prosperous but lived quite comfortably on the income his three *encomiendas* derived from maize, wheat and cocoa beans. Cerwin's picture of him is that of a country squire and a respected member of the town council. 'Most of the colonists lived in large houses, dressed in imported materials, ate of the best food, had servants to do the slightest chore for them and prayed in churches whose altars were ornamented with heavy gold and silver. They attempted to make of the country they had conquered another Spain and they almost did.' Díaz seems to have enjoyed robust health, riding over the rough mountain trails to his distant *encomiendas*, preferring to sleep on the floor on these trips rather than in a bed. 'After the Conquest of New Spain, it was my custom to lie down dressed and without a bed and I slept better than on a mattress', he wrote, and then added, 'now when I go to the towns of my *encomiendas* I generally do not take a bed, and if sometimes I do, it is not because I wish to, but because I must keep up an appearance as there are men who might believe I do not even own one'.

One of my first visits in Antigua was to the so-called Díaz house. He had, no doubt, owned the property on which it stands, but the actual building is of a much later date; the original in all probability was levelled by one of the many earthquakes.

It is impossible not to have an affection for Díaz. He was rather full of himself at times, but only because he felt that the contemporary histories written by Gómara, Paolo Giovio and Gonzalo de Illescas had a tendency to emphasize the heroic achievements of Cortés and to pass over those of the men who served under him. Díaz praised the other soldiers 'equally deserving of remuneration'. 'Yet I myself,' he writes, 'was not one of the least among them, and I had always the reputation of being a good soldier.' He fought in 119 battles and nearly got killed on several occasions.

'If anyone wishes to know anything further about us I can tell him that most of us were men of good families.' Díaz was, indeed, an *hidalgo*, though this signified little more than a man's descent from Christian

[1] Herbert Cerwin, *Bernal Díaz*, University of Oklahoma Press, Norman, Oklahoma, 1963.

forefathers, without any mixture of Jewish or Moorish blood. We know nothing of his appearance, but his Antiguan nickname 'the gallant' leads one to suppose that he had pleasing manners and a certain elegance.

As mentioned already, Díaz was fifty when he started writing his *True History*. He wrote a few chapters and then locked them away in a cupboard, perhaps as a result of the remarks two scholars made when allowed to read them. 'With respect of my style,' Díaz writes, 'both remarked that it was plain old Castilian, which was more agreeable at that time than those embellished sentences which are generally affected by historians . . . they were, however, of opinion that I had written too conspicuously about myself.'

'The old warrior,' Cerwin writes, 'appears to have written slowly and painstakingly, a few pages at a time, and sometimes for weeks and months he would not touch the manuscript.' It was Gómara's *Crónica de la Nueva España* that spurred him to action again. He was sixty-eight and one of the few remaining conquistadors alive. He must have felt that if he was ever to finish his work he must press on, sixty-eight in those days being a goodly age. It is quite remarkable how accurately he recalled events that had occurred more than forty years previously. Cerwin observes:

When he began to write the years fell away and the past became the present; one little incident led to another until the whole drama of the Conquest lay before him. 'Now that I am an old man,' he wrote, 'I often entertain myself with calling to mind the heroic deeds of early days . . . they are as fresh as the events of yesterday. I think of the seizure of the Indian monarch (Montezuma) and his confinement in irons, and the execution of his officers, till all these things seem actually passing before me. And as I ponder on exploits I feel that it was not of ourselves that we performed them but that it was the providence of God which guided us. Much food is there for meditation.'

The first draft of the history was finished in 1568 but the manuscript was not sent to Spain until 1575. Even at that time Díaz was still amending his copy. By now Díaz was an old man in his eighties. At eighty-eight he died, deaf and almost totally blind.

Díaz's amended copy of his manuscript is kept in a safe at the National Archives whose director allowed me to leaf through the fine vellum pages, tidily written over in faded sepia ink. One cannot but admire the straight margins and the beautifully formed lettering: its free sweeps curl and flow across 598 pages, amounting to a total of more than three hundred thousand words. Only the corrections are in Díaz's own hand. Cerwin with the help of a handwriting expert established that at least three different persons served as amanuenses. 'Díaz first wrote what he called a *borrador*, or draft, of his history' so full of corrections that 'he would never have sent such a copy to Spain. He therefore had a clean one made, and this is the one which was forwarded to the Council of the Indies. At a later time he had a second copy made, probably destroying his *borrador*, which was entirely in his handwriting.'[1] The second copy, the one on which he continued to work for so many years, is the one I saw. The first copy, the one sent to Spain, lay around the Council offices for nearly half a century until finally published in 1632, forty-eight years after Díaz's death. The Spanish copy has since disappeared. The Guatemalan manuscript stayed in Díaz's family until 1840 when it was bequeathed to the government by Mariano Larrave, a descendant of the old conquistador.

One can readily understand why Díaz preferred Guatemala to all the other countries he had seen in the New World. The gentleness of its rolling hills and soft clouds and its greenness induced by plentiful rain are of such an extraordinary, intimate beauty that it is easy to disregard the potential danger of the suspicious-looking mountains whose curves add yet more grace to the landscape. I never tired of exploring the countryside, either on ponyback or in a Land-Rover. The various roads leading out of Antigua are narrow lanes mostly lined with *adobe* walls behind which are dense acres of vigorous evergreen coffee shrubs shaded by the lacy foliage of one of the tall-growing grevilleas. Antiguan coffee, a crop dating back only about a hundred years, is considered the best on the market. The higher-up coffee grows, the better its quality; and the high slopes around Antigua lie close to the maximum altitude at which coffee can grow. Up in the forest behind the coffee plantations one can sometimes find the *Lycaste skinneri alba*, the *monja blanca* or white nun orchid, a frail ethereal thing now almost extinct. If extremely lucky one might catch a glimpse of the Quetzal (*Pharomacrus mocinno* or Gould's *Trogen resplendens*), the royal bird of the Quiché so proud of its tail that it excavates a nest with two openings in some worm-eaten tree in order to pass in and out without turning. It is timid by nature and frequents only the densest forests where, in the shade of heavy foliage, its brilliant colours are surprisingly inconspicuous.

We drove to Lake Atitlán whose surface shines like a sheet of molten silver. Here, too, there is an interesting bird, the Guatemalan grebe. It has speckled-brown and grey plumage, clear amber eyes, a yellow beak streaked with black, and webbed feet. Atitlán is the only place in the world where it can be found.

The country on the way to Chichicastenango is a patchwork of different greens, tidy squares of wheat, corn and maize. As Humboldt

[1] *Bernal Díaz.*

pointed out 'the fewer mines a colony has, the more the industry of the inhabitants is turned towards production in the vegetable kingdom', a kingdom that in Guatemala takes on the aspect of an undulating counterpane. It was market day at Chichicastenango and Indians crowded the plaza, their attention divided between buying and selling and offering up prayers. Two churches, facing one another across the open square, stand higher than the plaza and are approached, like the Mayan temples before them, by steep flights of stairs. A constant ebb and flow spilled over the steps of Santo Tomás, the larger of the two. The men carried tins of hot coals in which to burn copal incense, made from the resin of a coniferous tree widely found in the temperate and cool areas of Central America. Also the incense of their ancestors, it wreathed their comings and goings in blue opaque clouds of sweetness.

The large and barn-like interior of Santo Tomás looked like a dimly lit cave. As there are no benches, the Indians were squatting on the floor around tin trays of lighted candles. These clumps of flickering light spread right up the middle of the nave to the steps of the altar. It was a place of dim gold, blackened by smoke and inhabited by gesticulating Baroque saints. The supplicants mumbled their prayers – arguing, cajoling, giving angry voice to their complaints – all the while throwing crushed roses and wallflowers in among the candles. The warm glow over which they bent threw their dark heads into relief; their beaked noses and slanting, half-shut eyes were exactly the same as those found on the Mayan stelae at Tikal or in the splendid murals from Bonampak.

The men's clothes, one suddenly realizes, are modelled on those of the Spanish conquerors of the sixteenth century: split trousers and short jackets of brown wool, with a gay woven sash and an embroidered kerchief tied round the head. It is almost, as Huxley said,[1] the costume of Sancho Panza. The women's clothes are less distinctive. Their skirts are plain pieces of cloth simply wrapped around their bodies and their blouses, or *huipils*, have no particularly Spanish character. But their hair is prettily braided with strands of coloured wool, and on their heads they carry a kind of shawl, similar to certain Italian head-pieces, that serves every conceivable purpose, and which, when not in use, is folded up like a napkin. What is really fascinating is the complexity of the Indian woven stuffs. Their colours and patterns change from village to village; in one, reds and bright yellows predominate, the colours of the former Spanish flag. In Santa María de Jesús, for instance, a geometric pattern of blue and plum-red lozenges is favoured. The effect is highly stimulating to the eye. From Mrs Osborne I learnt that there is usually a fault in the pattern, for 'no human was supposed to produce

[1] *Beyond the Mexique Bay.*

a perfect piece of weaving, this being only the privilege of the Gods'.[1]

Santa María is typical of many small Guatemalan villages and is comparatively unspoilt. Its *adobe* huts are still roofed in weathered thatch, and they stand in clearings of beaten earth fenced in with palisades of corn stalks. About fifty-four per cent of the population in the country is pure Indian; and Spanish is unknown to literally thousands. The Guatemalan Indians, in fact, are more nearly aboriginal in their habits and life than those in any other section of Latin America, with perhaps the exception of Bolivia and Paraguay. As late as the beginning of the eighteenth century the Indians still wore loin cloths, which must have been a strange sight in Antigua's market. Even Indian officials wore loin cloths, but they could be distinguished by the black top hats they wore set at a rakish angle and bedecked with ribbons. This stylish effect was further heightened by their large staffs with enormous silver knobs and many coloured tassels which they carried to indicate their office. It was, incidentally, in Santa María de Jesús that the villagers collected ice from the crater of Agua to send to Antigua.

In Antigua itself, there were pleasant mornings spent with Dr Wilson Popenoe, a distinguished botanical explorer who has spent a lifetime propagating the avocado, *Persea americana*, indigenous to Southern Mexico and Guatemala. An old tree he used for many of his grafts stands at the bottom of the garden and in it he hangs spiny nopal leaves to keep away the bats. His house, expertly restored, is perhaps the most splendid in Antigua. In time it will undoubtedly become a museum, for it has all the distinguishing features of the colonial period, including handsome medallion windows typical of Antigua during the seventeenth century. Hidden away at the back, in a second patio, are raised flower beds bordered with fluted masonry, again a local peculiarity. On one of my visits I admired a statue found, Dr Popenoe informed me, thirty-five years ago in *Ciudad Viejo*. I asked him about it:

There was an old boy in those days, half-Indian, a kind of guardian. He lived in the ruins and I was pottering around not really paying much attention to him. You know how sometimes, when people are standing near you, you can feel them without actually seeing them. Thinking it was the Indian behind me I questioned him about something or other. They pass things on in the family and sometimes come up with interesting details dating back several generations. Not getting an answer, I turned to find that I had been addressing this statue, miraculously preserved in a niche.

It was of a tonsured monk in his robes, one hand uplifted in blessing.

The most striking thing about Antigua is the squat, massive architecture of its buildings, a style Kelemen describes as 'Earthquake

---

[1] Mrs Osborne, *Guatemalan Textiles*, Department of Middle American Research, University of Louisiana, New Orleans, 1935.

Baroque'. In Guatemala the Spaniards had their first experience of serious seismic conditions. Antigua's almost fortress-like architecture with its massive ten-foot walls was their solution to the problem. Antigua is said to have been planned by Juan Bautista Antonelli, an engineer and the elder brother of the man who in fact designed the fortress of San Juan de Ulúa at Vera Cruz and the great fortress of Cartagena on Colombia's coast. George Kubler has explained that the heavy rainfall in Guatemala's highlands made masonry architecture indispensable. 'Here Central American buildings became thicker, heavier, lower and flatter, as if growing scar tissue after each disaster. As the proportions became more ungainly, ornamental effects of greater animation were invented.'[1] Elegant examples of this ponderous, squat building style relieved by lively decoration are the hospital church of San Pedro and the neo-Mudéjar arches in the main patio of San Carlos University, which in its day was the greatest seat of learning in Central America. Another of my favourites is the façade of La Merced covered with a naïve rendering in shallow white and yellow stucco of vines laden with ripening bunches of grapes. The great fountain in the centre of its patio is perhaps the most impressive of Antigua's remains, mute testimony to the grandeur of other times.

[1] *Art and Architecture in Spain and Portugal and their American Dominions 1500 to 1800.*

12

Panama

My next important stop was Panama. The 'S'-shaped isthmus, at its narrowest only thirty miles across and at its widest no more than 120 miles, is the point where the two halves of the New World met. To the north lay the Aztec kingdom subjugated by Cortés and to the south the Inca Empire conquered by Pizarro. Moving southwards I was thus entering another sphere, the vast territories that comprised the viceroyalty of Peru.

Panama and the isthmus were of vital importance to Spain. As Peru on the Pacific coast was virtually inaccessible to Atlantic shipping, the isthmus ports of Puerto Belo on the Caribbean and Panama on Balboa's 'Great South Sea' formed a vital overland link for transhipments between Spain and the southern viceroyalty. (Puerto Belo replaced an earlier Caribbean port, Nombre de Dios, abandoned after Drake burned it in 1596.) Just as Vera Cruz in the north was the sole gateway to Mexico, Puerto Belo became the monopoly port for galleons plying the Atlantic south of the Great Antilles.

On my own journey to Panama, we made a brief stop in Nicaragua to visit Granada and León. To reach these towns we flew to Managua and from there took a car. I did not expect too much of León, the capital until 1852, because already in 1854 the city was decaying and the finest houses had been burned or torn down. Although it has vestiges of a certain grandeur, León is a sad, lifeless place, inhabited by young men of sallow complexion and listless *señoritas* who lounge in hammocks all day long, stuffing themselves with *dulces*, a confectionery made from the sugar of the country. John Stephens' experiences here had been more lively. While riding between Granada and León, he fell in with a woman and two men plus their servants. 'The younger man accosted me . . . and from the style of his dress and equipment I supposed him to be a gentleman.' He carried a gamecock under his arm 'rolled up carefully as a fractured leg'. It was journeying to fight a challenge. The parties spent the night at the same *posada*. The woman was an itinerant merchant 'travelling in horn combs, beads, ear-rings and rosaries'. She 'entrapped the daughter of the host into the purchase of a comb'. 'For supper,' Stephens writes, 'we had poached eggs and beans, without plate, knife, fork or spoon. My companions used their *tortillas* to take up an egg, and also, by turning up the edges, to scoop out *frijoles* from the dish; withal, they were very courteous.' After supper 'the younger of the two dressed his bird in its *robe de nuit*, a cotton cloth wound tight around the body compressing the wings, and then, with a string fastened to the back of the cloth, so that the body was balanced, hooked it to the hammock'. Poor Stephens, on the other hand, slept on a 'log chest made from the trunk of a tree, which in every house in Nicaragua serves as a sort of cupboard'.[1]

Granada lies to the east of Managua, on the shores of Lake Nicaragua. The morning of my expedition was overcast and there were moments when the landscape looked almost English. This was but a momentary illusion, irrevocably dispelled when suddenly there appeared a palm, then several palms, until finally the leaden sky cleared and a hot tropical sun turned the drizzle to steam. Then I could clearly perceive that the cattle were Brahmin and not Jersey, the herbage was too lush for England and the clumped trees, if one looked carefully, were obviously mango.

Granada, when we reached it, had a strong nineteenth-century flavour. Little remains of the original town founded by Hernández de Córdoba. The Alhambra, our hotel, fascinating as were its cast-iron railings and its bent-wood rocking chairs, was not exactly what I had come to see. The place, however, has its own character, a nostalgic, unreal quality. The empty arcaded streets and the jetty where a double-decked lake steamer fretted at her moorings were swept of all life by a blinding afternoon sun. Did anyone ever cross the lake? It certainly had been crossed often enough the other way. Three times Granada had been invaded by British and French pirates coming up from the Caribbean.

Granada had once been a rich city surrounded by sugar plantations. For the purposes of trade, it was, as the guide-book puts it, 'most advantageously placed' on the shores of a lake drained by a navigable river that flows into the Caribbean. It was up this river, the Río San Juan, that the buccaneers had sailed, among them Sir Francis Drake and John Hawkins. When Henry Morgan in his turn raided Granada, he rounded up quite a number of priests and nuns, and being a good Protestant, shot the lot of them. When Nelson was an officer in his twenties he too was scheduled to 'visit' Granada but was recalled the day before the expedition sailed. The American freebooter William Walker was the last to sack the place in 1856.

[1] *Incidents of Travel in Central America, Chiapas and Yucatan.*

Granada is certainly rich in associations. Hernando de Soto, the discoverer of the Mississippi, was once held prisoner here, and the famous Las Casas often preached from its pulpits. But gone are all traces of so distant a past.

Arriving in Panama I found, as in Guatemala, that there have been two cities of that name: the old and the new. Panama La Vieja is, however, really a ruin and so can in no way be compared with Antigua. It was founded in 1519 on a flat strip of coast which, because it lay on the Pacific side of the isthmus, was not thought to require fortification. Thus in 1671 Henry Morgan, crossing the isthmus with an army of two thousand men, was able after a pitched battle to win ready access to the city and sack it. The Governor, however, had taken the precaution of shipping a greater part of what bullion happened to be in the treasury out to sea, and before finally surrendering he had set fire to the city. Morgan made his entrance between walls of flame.

Gage landed at Panama a little over a quarter of a century before this sack and commented upon the town's flimsy construction. 'The houses are of the least strength of any place that I had entered.' Lime and stones were hard to come by 'and therefore for that reason, and for the great heat there, most of the houses are built of timber and boards', the president's house included. 'The heat is so extraordinary that a linen cut doublet, with some slight stuff, or taffeta breeches is the common clothing of the inhabitants.' For once the settlers seem to have made allowances for the climate, most unusual in those early days when it was a common rule to overdress and over-eat, irrespective of the temperature. 'Fish, fruits and herbage for salads are more plentiful than flesh,' Gage wrote, 'and the cool water of the cocoa is much drunk by the women.' For the men there was wine from Peru. Gage made his usual dig at the Spaniards: the city is 'much given to sin, looseness and venery and there is much lusting after blackamoors'. He was impressed, however, by the wealth. 'It is held to be one of the richest places in America.'

Eleven years after the founding of old Panama, Francisco Pizarro discovered Peru. This retarded the development of the city considerably, for after the arrival of the first shipments of Peruvian gold, it was everyone's ambition to sail on down the coast. 'I dare not let them go,' wrote the Governor to his King, 'for they then leave us without anyone to till the land. But it is unjust to make them stay, as many of them live in misery and see those who had recently worked for them return from Peru laden with gold while they themselves have hardly enough to subsist on.' Despite its slow beginning the city grew in importance. The whole of western South America depended on Panama to ship out the Spanish provisions that had been loaded on mule teams at Nombre de

Dios – later at Puerto Belo – and transported across the isthmus. There was a vital heavy traffic in the opposite direction. Silver bars from Potosí were carried by llama to the port of Arica, thence by ship to Callao, the port of Lima, and from there to Panama. Incredible sums then travelled from Panama to Puerto Belo, through the jungle on a cobbled road known as the King's Highway. Besides Bolivian silver there were caskets full of Inca gold. The arrival of the Atlantic galleons at Seville must have been an exciting moment. One report described a shipment of silver so huge that for six days mule wagons shuttled constantly night and day between the docks and the *Casa de Contratación* unloading treasure.

Pearls were also in the treasure of the New World. For several decades after its discovery Latin America was called the 'Land of Pearls'. Christopher Columbus on his third voyage in 1498 was the first to mention them: one of his sailors traded a piece of broken Málaga ware for some strings of pearls. In his *Historia general de las Indias* Gómara writes that Columbus 'ordered others to go with buttons, needles, scissors, and fragments of the same Valencian earthenware, which they seemed to prize', in order to be sure that these necklaces had not been given in exchange through pure chance. It had not been chance; the men brought back 'more than eighty-four ounces of pearls, large and small, with many good pearls among them . . . Of the numerous women there, not one was without rings of gold and necklaces of pearls'.

Records show that in 1597 Spain received 350 pounds weight of pearls from the Venezuelan fisheries. They were shipped, unpierced, in caskets. Kunz and Stevenson write:

It is to be regretted that the Spaniards so frequently reported the yield of pearls by weight. The value of three hundred and fifty pounds of pearls might have been anywhere from £7,000 to £700,000. Assuming that they were two grains each in weight and of good quality the total value would approximate £200,000 according to the valuation of that period; and on a basis of eight grains each it would be £3,200,000, or sixteen times as much.[1]

The Panama fisheries in the Pacific proved even more remunerative than those in the Caribbean. Balboa sent a special gift of two hundred magnificent pearls to the Queen. Fortuno Ixmines, an officer under Cortés, while writing of pearls found on the west coast in the state of Sonora, described native chiefs living in primitive huts with quantities of beautiful pearls lying carelessly around in the sand. They were obviously not considered of any great value, for on Pearl Island, thirty-six miles south-east of Panama, the Indians strung them around their

[1] George Frederick Kunz and Charles Hugh Stevenson, *The Book of the Pearl*, MacMillan & Co., London, 1908.

paddles. Balboa boasted that the oysters on Pearl Island were the size of sombreros. It must have been oysters such as these that produced Balboa's pearls, which, according to Gómara, 'were like filberts, the others like nutmegs'.

In his *Historia Natural de las Indias* published in Toledo in 1526, Gonzalo de Oviedo mentions the weights of some of these fabulous jewels. One pear-shaped pearl weighed 124 grains. La Peregrina, The Incomparable, the most celebrated early American pearl, weighed 134 grains. Jacques de Treco, the court jeweller, valued it at 100,000 ducats, adding that it was in fact so remarkable as to be beyond any standard valuation. Garcilaso de la Vega,[1] who in 1597 saw it in Seville, said that it was found in Panama in 1560 by a Negro who was rewarded with his liberty while the Negro's master was appointed mayor.

All the best pearls found their way to the Spanish court. The rest, according to the Italian traveller Gemelli-Careri who visited the Panama fisheries in 1697, were sent to Lima 'where the demand for them is very great. They are not only universally worn there by all persons of rank, but also sent from thence to the inland portions of Peru'.[2]

But to return to Panama. Morgan left it a total ruin, yet its citizens were reluctant to abandon the place. Called on to mediate, the Viceroy of Peru finally persuaded the people to choose some other site, better suited for defence. A position was chosen five miles to the west, at the foot of a hill, on a promontory which, it was planned, should be rendered impregnable. Much of the rubble of the old city went into the walls of the new Panama. Little was left standing except the cumbersome remains of La Merced monastery and the tower of the cathedral, a fitting tombstone for a once flourishing city.

It was always low tide when I visited old Panama. A murky sea insipidly nibbled the shore. Cormorants perching on the rocks looked like rotting stumps in a shiny wetness of mud rimmed by a sky of troubled clouds. Great pelicans came winging in from the direction of Pearl Island, barely skimming the water and carrying their large beaks proudly like figureheads on a ship. It was a melancholy scene but grand – a proper setting for the ruins, many of them almost inaccessible in the swamps, submerged in reeds and overgrown with creepers. Much of the terrain is dense jungle, the habitat of wild pigs and iguanas which scuttle across your path.

New Panama was fortified so effectively that it was never successfully attacked. The walls, thirty feet high and ten feet thick, cost a vast sum to build. A portion still stands, confining the city and compressing its

[1] Garcilaso de la Vega, *Historie des Incas, Roi du Pérou*, Amsterdam, 1704.
[2] Gemelli-Careri, *Giro del Mondo*, Venice, 1719.

streets. The houses are frame structures with first floor balconies cast in iron, attenuated copies of those in New Orleans. In many cases an entire family occupies one room. The place is a blend of the atmospheres of Spain and of the Eastern bazaar. I remembered La Condamine's reaction to the Panamanian women. A geodesist and a member of the *Académie des Sciences* of Paris, Charles-Marie de La Condamine was on an expedition to Quito to test Isaac Newton's theory that the globe was flattened at the poles and bulged at the middle. Measurements had to be taken on the Equator and Quito was the most convenient place for such an undertaking. Panama was a necessary stop on the way. Used to the polished manners of eighteenth-century France, La Condamine must have been taken aback by the ladies of mark who received him 'lolling at ease in their hammocks'.[1] 'They wear a kind of petticoat,' La Condamine wrote, 'and on their body a very thin waistcoat . . . which, however, they always lace to conceal their breasts. On their heads they put a cap of fine white linen in the shape of a mitre. Instead of shoes . . . they wear a kind of slipper large enough to contain only the tips of their feet. The ladies,' he continued, 'and other white women smoke in their houses, a decency not observed by women of the other castes.' Their manner of smoking must have surprised him, 'for they palm the tobacco into slender rolls and put the lighted part into their mouths and there continue it a long time without its being quenched, or the fire incommoding them.'[2]

One reason for my coming to Panama was to journey across the isthmus to Puerto Belo which nowadays is as inaccessible as an island. I had learned from John Minter that the jungle has reclaimed the 'Kings Road' except for a few isolated stretches and that 'the once important city has reverted to what it was when Columbus discovered it – a fishing village'.[3] The only way to reach Puerto Belo is by sea, a twenty-mile run north-east from Colón, the Caribbean terminus of the Panama Railroad. There was no regular transport, and I had been warned that it would be difficult to find any small craft, as the trade winds had started blowing. They blow from the end of November to the beginning of March and can swamp a boat in an instant. I had to get to Colón and from there on just take a chance.

We caught the train at Ancon in the Canal Zone. How tidy and neat everything is in this narrow strip of land leased by the United States from the Panamanian government! The stucco houses built for the specialists and the personnel working on the canal are as white as the

---

[1] Victor Wolfgang von Hagen, *South America Called Them*, Little Brown & Co., Boston, 1955.
[2] *Journal du Voyage fait par ordre du Roi à l'équateur*, Paris, 1751.
[3] John Easter Minter, *The Charges, River of Westward Passage*, Rinehart & Co., New York, 1948.

whitewashed stones that used to border the parade grounds of the vanished British Empire. There is a distinct flavour of the 1920s about the buildings with their wired-in verandahs and red-tiled roofs. They stand on rising ground surrounded by shaved lawns and are approached up curving roads bordered with palms. The old carriages of our train clattered noisily over the rails. The coaches with their hard wooden seats were all empty until, at frequent stops, we began to take on some wives of the canal personnel. Mercifully they were not sensitive to draughts and made no objection to the open, screened windows. We passed through a cutting and gathered speed and I fell to wondering about the railway.

Each epoch has used a different means to cross this narrow spit of land: road, then railway and finally the canal. It was the California gold rush of 1849 that led to the construction of the railway. 'Many gold seekers,' writes Minter, 'journeyed across North America in covered wagons. Others afraid of the fierce Plains Indians took passage on ships going round the Horn. Some travelled the Panama route.'[1] The difficulty in negotiating the old Puerto Belo trail, or in following an alternative river route along the Charges, gave rise to the scheme for a rail link. This took six years and a heavy toll in human lives to realize. An original plan to build the line between Panama and Puerto Belo was not pursued because the inhabitants of Puerto Belo asked such exorbitant prices for their land. Instead it was decided to run the line from a small island, across some swamps to the mainland. The swamps, alive with alligators and infested with malaria and yellow fever mosquitoes, had to be filled in with rocks. Irish labourers were employed originally, but they proved incapable of the task. Chinese were imported to replace them, but these too were decimated by the fevers. To keep the survivors fit for their work, the company was obliged to dose them with opium, the supply of which gave out. The wretched coolies, half-crazed with fear and misery, resorted to suicide. Some buried themselves in the sand waiting for the tides to drown them; others looped their pigtails around their necks and hung themselves from trees. Jamaican Negroes finally completed the task: the last rail met at midnight on 27 January 1855 under pelting rain. The official estimate of deaths during construction was about six thousand. The true figure may be twice as large. The railroad is said to rest on human bones instead of wooden ties. This cannot be a gross misrepresentation.

In many places our tracks ran parallel with the canal. We clattered through dense palmetto scrub splashed here and there with what seemed to be the red-flowering *Hedeychium coccineum*, 'a spike of scarlet flowers', as Taylor describes it, 'thrust from the heart of a convolution of

[1] *The Charges, River of Westward Passage.*

unfolding leaves'. Bayard Taylor, a world traveller, paddled down the Charges River in 1850 and left a vivid description of the country: a deluge of vegetation smothered in parasitic vines that wash against the trees in enveloping waves, leaping into the air and breaking eventually into a froth of green spray. There were parakeets, and 'brilliant butterflies circle like blossom blown away'.[1] When these walls of jungle receded, one caught glimpses of the canal, its course traced by channel markers through the man-made Gatun Lake. Skeletons of trees, dead fifty-two years, stuck up through the calm waters, a convenient roost for snowy egrets.

If the railroad cost dearly in human life, the canal took an even heavier toll. But what an amazing achievement, probably the greatest engineering feat the world has ever seen. Ever since Balboa's discovery of the Pacific there had been talk of a canal across the isthmus. The problem was to dig a ditch joining two rivers, as had been done in Holland and Italy, and in China even before the birth of Christ. The Charges River cuts south-eastwards from the Caribbean across the isthmus to within some twelve miles of Panama City. Here, because its run southward is interrupted by the mountains of the Continental Divide, the river takes an abrupt turn to the north. There is a gap in the Divide on the far side of which the Río Grande drains into the Pacific. The canal now threads its way through this gap at precisely the point chosen by the Spaniards.

Early in the sixteenth century, military engineers were sent out to examine the possibilities of constructing a canal. A report favouring the project was sent back to the King, but here, writes the historian Antonio Herrera, opinion became divided. 'Some are against it, saying the land would be flooded because one ocean is at a lower level than the other, but the wise think this is nonsense.' This idea that water levels varied from sea to sea came from ancient Greece. When Strabo, the geographer, was asked to advise on the Corinth Canal, he recommended that it was better not to attempt it for that reason. Although such fears still persisted, Charles v was not convinced and ordered the Governor of Panama to instigate a yet more detailed survey. Pascual de Andagoya, who was this time responsible, reported that a canal was indeed possible, but that no monarch existed with sufficient riches to finance the undertaking. If that did not fully deter the King, the Church's attitude would have finally dissuaded him. 'Man,' they proclaimed, 'must not separate what God had united,' a sentiment completely opposite to the Canal's present motto: 'The land divided, the world united.'

'For over two centuries,' Minter writes, 'the fear of God's displeasure

[1] Bayard Taylor, *Eldorado, or Adventure in the Path of Empire*, Putnam, New York, 1850.

was a factor in Spain's hesitancy about attempting a canal.'[1] Humboldt, reviewing the same problem in 1803, was incensed at this lack of enterprise. Referring to Balboa's crossing the isthmus, he wrote, 'since this memorable epoch in the history of geographical discovery, the project of a canal has occupied every mind; and yet at this day, after a lapse of nearly three hundred years, there neither exists a survey of the ground, nor an exact determination of the position of Panama and Puerto Belo'.

But this state of affairs was not to endure for long. In 1869 the world's newspapers were full of Count de Lesseps' extraordinary achievement at Suez. Eleven years later the suave Frenchman steamed into the Panamanian port of Colón, intent on repeating in the West what he had achieved in the East. Panama was no longer a Spanish possession but a province of the Republic of Colombia. Fully aware of the benefits that could be derived from a canal, Colombia had granted the French a concession to build the waterway.

Work began in 1881, but nine years later the company crashed. De Lesseps, so successful in Suez, had failed in Panama; the fault lay not in his mistakes as an engineer but in useless squandering of money and above all the terrible fevers. In addition to malaria and yellow fever, cholera and smallpox were rife. The death rate among the labourers was as high as twenty per cent. Bodies were buried two deep in the Mount Hope cemetery near Colón.

When the French pulled out, they left nineteen miles of diggings choked with rusty machines. De Lesseps, ill and failing, and out of his mind, died shortly afterwards in Paris.

France's concession was next offered to the United States. In 1903 the Senate ratified a treaty by which Colombia and the United States were to maintain joint judicial and military control over a canal zone ten miles wide. Washington agreed to an initial payment of $10,000,000 to Colombia plus an annual rent. Everything was settled, until, at the last moment, hoping to extract still more money, the Congress in Bogotá rejected the treaty and suggested another draft. Panama, seeing herself deprived of a healthy source of income, revolted. Whereupon the United States immediately recognized the government of the new country and guaranteed its independence. This, very briefly, was the situation, although there were various side-issues which we need not go into here.

Before even beginning the canal, the Americans had to deal with the crippling fevers and make Panama a healthy place. Colonel William Crawford Gorgas, a medical officer of the United States Army who served in Cuba with Walter Reed, the discoverer of the cause of yellow

[1] *The Charges, River of Westward Passage.*

88 León. It has vestiges of a certain grandeur (page 158)

89 Granada. Church of San Francisco founded sometime in the sixteenth century but last repaired in 1862. It presents a strongly neoclassic aspect (page 159)

90 *Panamá La Vieja. Tower of the cathedral* (*page 162*)

91 *Panama Canal, after a lithograph by Joseph Pennell* (*page 165*)

92 *Puerto Belo. 'Much battered and half camouflaged by the rank vegetation'* (*page 167*)

93 Puerto Belo, 'its clapboarded houses wedged in among the ruins' (page 168)

94 Puerto Belo. 'Sentinel boxes still command views out over the bay' (page 168)

95 Puerto Belo. 'Cannon lie lurching crookedly in their embrasures' (page 168)

fever, was put in charge. Colonel Gorgas performed one of the greatest sanitary operations in history. First sewers were laid to deal with the cholera, and then screens were ordered on every door and window. Stagnant pools were spread over with oil. Gorgas' men even siphoned off the holy water in church fonts where mosquitoes were wont to breed. A curfew was declared and no one was allowed out at night when the mosquitoes were biting. Very soon the Canal Zone became one of the most healthy places anywhere in the tropics.

Disease was not the only problem. Landslides in the immense cuts killed labourers and ruined weeks of work; but the crews would always begin again with more dynamite and new steam shovels. It took ten years, until 1914, to do the job. When the canal was finished, it ran for forty miles from shore to shore in a series of locks, virtually a staircase over the mountains which carries ships between the Atlantic and the Pacific. Columbus's dream of a Westward Passage had come true.

Arriving in Colón and finding no transport to Puerto Belo at the docks, we drove to the office of the Captain of the Canal Zone. He thought someone at the base might be persuaded to make the trip, and there were boats enough, but their owners were all on duty. Then someone suggested Clemente Wong who worked at one of the yacht clubs. He was already booked on a deep-sea fishing expedition. So at least boats were willing to brave the full ocean. Eventually a series of telephone calls procured Gonzales, the owner of a flat-bottomed, twenty-five-foot outboard launch. Gonzales proved to be a cheerful, energetic little man who for a price guaranteed to return us safely to harbour. It would take us an hour and a half to get there.

It rained fitfully and there was a heavy swell that sent us spanking over a jade-green sea, douching us in warm spray. Tongues of land jutted out from the shore, and behind them ran the low-lying ridges of the Cordillera. The country, dripping and green, had a familiar aspect. But for the occasional palm, it could almost have been southern Ireland. Also there was something not quite in keeping about the sky, the angry coils over our heads were far too dramatic.

Three little humps of islands announce the entrance to Puerto Belo bay. No doubt Columbus had so named it in his relief at finding a safe anchorage, for the place has no great claim to beauty. *Puerto malo* Gage called it, but then he was alluding to its detestable climate. It was a supremely unhealthy place, even worse than Vera Cruz, if such a thing were possible.

The bay is square-cut and framed by two fortified headlands that defended the harbour like stout arms. Lesser forts run in a string of walls round the bay. The town lies to the right of the approach and, though now much battered and half-camouflaged by the rank vegetation, it would be recognizable to those who had known it in better days.

We landed and scrambled over the ruins. The coral rock of which the forts are built has grown leprous and hoary with age and is covered with moss and ferns. Slippery, moss-grown ramps led us up onto the walls. Pink flowering, sensitive plants were spread everywhere and banana trees and rushes choked the moats. Sentinel boxes still command views out over the bay, and a row of ten or fifteen cannon, tumbled from their rotted chairs, lie lurching crookedly in their embrasures. No ship could enter the harbour without passing under their threatening maws, some of which were famous for having the largest calibre cast in their day. They were manned 'by picked troops of the Spanish army, veterans with records of bravery under fire in campaigns all over Europe and Africa'. The place was riddled with underground passages reputed to have once 'contained stores of food, ammunition and medical supplies enough for a year of siege'.[1] I dared not venture down the dripping, vaulted tunnels echoing to the faint clickings of the large blue-black land crabs that have appropriated the darkness.

We inspected the Black Christ in what passes for a cathedral. The statue had been commissioned by the viceroy of Peru, but the ship carrying it had been wrecked in the bay and the natives who salvaged the image refused to part with it. The town itself has shrunk to a moderate-sized village of clapboarded houses wedged in among the ruins. The inhabitants are a sullen lot and barely acknowledged our '*buenos días*' with a scant '*buenos*' heavily mouthed by octoroon lips. A party of youths who had watched us disembarking at the jetty did not answer at all, but just stared at us, munching away at fibrous lengths of sugar cane, tearing at it with their strong teeth like animals. 'An independent people,' remarked Gonzales. He explained that various welfare organizations, critical of the way they lived, had wanted to help, but they would have none of it. They were not only independent but also proud, perhaps preferring to dream on amidst their mottled ruins of the days when the mule trains unloaded untold treasure on their quays.

Their past was certainly uppermost in my own mind. I remember Gage's stupefaction as he watched the silver arrive. 'In one day I told two hundred mules laden with nothing else.' The ingots were stacked up in the market-place where they 'lay like heaps of stones in the streets'. No one worried about it, 'only gold and gems were dignified by storage under lock'.

Puerto Belo, like Vera Cruz, was fully occupied only once a year. The rest of the time it was abandoned to a handful of officials, a few Negroes and a small garrison that was relieved every three months on account of the fevers. Its reputation was such 'that cows', it was said,

[1] *The Charges, River of Westward Passage.*

'did not breed there or chickens lay eggs'.[1] Thomas Jefferys, geographer
to George III, compiled a series of eyewitness accounts of the Spanish
settlements in the Caribbean including Puerto Belo. Its population of
toads surprised him the most. 'The streets and squares in the morning
are paved with these reptiles so that you cannot step without treading
on them.' At night they were deafening, 'for there is no bigger, noisier
toad anywhere than those to be found here'.[2]

However, the town must have presented a very fine sight on the day
the fleet arrived from Spain, when great galleons, full to bursting,
manœuvred slowly to their anchorage, poops high and prows low in the
water. In the fleet were vessels bearing seventy guns and such grandiloquent names as *Conquistador*, *Glorioso*, *América*. As a measure of the
importance of their cargo, they carried 'soldiers that came for their
defence, at least four or five thousand'.[3]

The armada was no sooner sighted than a rider was sent off posthaste
to Panama. His message was that the treasure from the Pacific Fleet,
whose arrival in Panama was carefully timed to coincide with the sail-
ings from Europe, should begin moving across the narrow isthmus.
With the treasure train appeared merchants from Bogotá, Quito, Lima,
Popayán, Potosí, Santiago and Buenos Aires, all the cities of the New
World including Santiago de Guatemala and Mexico. Some came from
even as far away as the Philippines. They piled into Puerto Belo by the
hundreds, their mule-packs loaded with 'cocoa, *quinaquina* or Jesuits'
bark, vicuña wool, *canela* or stick cinnamon, and bales upon bales of
ipecac, sarsaparilla and vanilla'.[4] They exchanged these raw materials
for the manufactured products from Spain. Later in history came
shiploads of Negroes from Guinea.

'It was worth seeing,' writes Gage, 'how merchants sold their commodities.' Temporary stalls were built round the customs house and
bargaining went on far into the night. Prices, of course, sky-rocketed,
'a pound of beef was worth two *reals*.' Fowls became prohibitively
expensive; and Gage, short of money, fed on tortoises, 'of which there
are very many'. Business was conducted in an atmosphere of mounting
tension, 'Don Carlos de Ybarra, the Admiral of the fleet, made great
haste to be gone'. Not only were fevers feared, but there were rumours
that 'some three or four Holland or English ships' were 'abroad at sea,
waiting (as it was supposed) for some good prize out of that great and
rich fleet'.

The cumbersome, American treasure fleets threading their way

[1] Germán Arciniegas, *Caribbean Sea of the New World*, New York, 1946.
[2] *A Description of the Spanish Islands and Settlements on the Coast of the West Indies*, London, 1762.
[3] *Thomas Gage. The English American. A New Survey of the West Indies 1648.*
[4] *South America Called Them.*

across the Atlantic were naturally a magnet for North European free-booters and pirates, an international confederacy united against Spain. They had been operating since the sixteenth century. Names such as Coates, Hawkins, Drake, Raleigh and Morgan 'sound', as Father Valtierra put it, 'like warning trumpets in all the islands and bays of the Caribbean'.[1] The Caribbean was ideal pirate country, with miles of indented coastline and uncharted islands where the raiders could hide. The Island of Tortuga, or Turtle Island, off the coast of Hispaniola became a regular pirate republic. Good markets for stolen plunder were found also on the New England coast, in Jamaica and at New Providence Island, as well as in Ireland and certain places on the west of England.

William Parker of Tortuga was the first of the buccaneers to attack the new base of Puerto Belo in 1602. The Port Royal buccaneers under Morgan plundered it again and massacred its garrison in 1668. Finally in 1739 Admiral Vernon stormed into the port with a squadron of warships. The town was taken by surprise and surrendered. Had it been in a proper state of readiness, the Admiral would have met with a different reception, for so elaborate were its defences that the mining and blowing up of the fortifications took nearly three weeks. After Vernon's visit Spain's galleons loaded at San Lorenzo at the mouth of the Charges River.

In 1637, the year of Gage's visit, Puerto Belo would not yet have been concerned with either Morgan or Vernon: they were to be scourges of the future. But Don Carlos, as commander of a silver fleet, had other worries enough. Once at sea, a storm could scatter the ships which once separated were at the mercy of the 'Hollands or the English'. Nonetheless the Admiral must have fretted and been impatient to embark when his thoughts turned to Sir Francis Drake, his country's arch-enemy buried a few miles to seaward. After sacking Nombre de Dios and on his way round the headland to Puerto Belo, Drake had been attacked by the dysentery ravaging his men. Already weak with malaria, he grew delirious and, struggling up from his bed, insisted on donning his armour, 'raving in words that no one cared to record'. 'It was four o'clock in the morning, as the light stole back into the sea beyond Puerto Belo, that, as Hakluyt records it, "Our General, Sir Francis Drake, departed this life".'[2] The next day they enclosed him in a leaden coffin and to the roar of guns committed him to the deep. Even today the nurseries of the New World are stilled by the warning, '*ahi, viene Drake!*'.

[1] Father Angel Valtierra, s.j., *Peter Claver, Saint of Slaves*, The Newman Press, Westminster, Maryland.
[2] Ernle Bradford, *Drake*, Hodder & Stoughton, London, 1965.

The trip back to Colón was for me terrifying. We rode the swell, our propeller lifting and shuddering against a backdrop of deep grey slashed across by diagonal shafts of black. The sea turned a livid green and rose to alarming heights above our tiny craft. Sweeping in over us, it swamped the engine. Gonzales managed to start it up again. In front of us, over Colón, the sky boiled in swirls of gold and flame, an extraordinary mixture of sunset and storm. As a fierce jab of lightning was followed by a sudden, terrific thunder clap, we limped to our moorings, barely able to see for the rain.

13

Colombia

I flew from Panama to Bogotá by *Avianca*, or more correctly, the *Aerovias Nacionales de Colombia*. I was impressed by the line's energetic efficiency, impressed but hardly surprised, for Colombia was the first South American country to develop air travel on a commercial scale. As the Andes, the continent's vast stony vertebrae, taper towards the Isthmus, they divide into three principal ranges that cut diagonally across Colombia, isolating the densely populated interior regions from the coastal districts. Only to the north, in the direction of the Caribbean, is there a natural access to the interior along the precipitous valley of the Magdalena River. In such terrain roads and railways are few and cost a prohibitive price to build. In the early part of the nineteenth century Colonel J. P. Hamilton, an Englishman travelling in Colombia, described the arrival of a pianoforte from England via Guayaquil in Ecuador. From there it had to be transhipped in a small coaster five hundred miles north to Buenaventura, 'whence it had been carried on men's backs over the mountains to Popayán',[1] a provincial capital in the south of Colombia.

Until a hundred years ago people travelled in the same manner as that pianoforte. 'I have been told,' Hamilton wrote, 'that the Spaniards and natives mount their fellow human beings with as much sang-froid as if they were getting on the backs of mules.' At Ibaque, a halfway halt from Bogotá to the Pacific coast, 'there are between three and four hundred porters who subsist entirely by carrying persons and baggage over the mountains'. These men were known as *silléro*, 'men of mixed race, half Indian, partly Spanish'. Captain Cochrane, a young naval officer, described them as 'fine athletic fellows with good features and well limbed',[2] entirely naked but for a breechcloth. A chair with arm

---

[1] Colonel J. P. Hamilton, *Travels through the Interior Provinces of Colombia*, Murray, London, 1827.
[2] Captain Charles Stuart Cochrane, R.N., *Journal of a Residence and Travels in Colombia during the year 1823–24*, Colburn, London, 1824.

rests and a swinging footrest was harnessed to their backs by straps passed round the head, shoulders and across the chest. Linen pads, one for the loins and another between the straps on the forehead, prevented chafing. 'In this manner,' wrote Cochrane, 'they journey on, never stumbling, and seldom halting, climbing up the mountains, and sometimes running when the ground will admit.' They were capable of carrying loads up to 175 pounds, 'but they die young, seldom living beyond forty years, being generally carried off by the bursting of a blood-vessel or by pulmonic complaints'.

Incredible though it may seem, some of the travellers put spurs to their *silleros*. Cochrane's companion, 'a well-informed young Spaniard', recounted an episode he had witnessed on the very path they were traversing, which cut into a cliff face above a 1,500 feet drop into a raging mountain torrent. The ascent was very steep and the brute in question, an officer, had fixed a pair of mule spurs to his boots which he kept digging into his unfortunate carrier's flanks while urging him on to greater speed. The *sillero* remonstrated with his persecutor, assuring him that he could not quicken his pace. Complaint only produced additional aggression. Eventually, maddened with pain and resentment, the *sillero* jerked the officer out of his chair and over the precipice, himself escaping into the mountains never to be heard of again.

But to return to Bogotá. The Bogotans call it the Athens of South America and claim that their reputation for learning goes back to the sixteenth century. They will tell you that the city's founder, Gonzalo Jiménez de Quesada, a lawyer and an intellectual, stamped Bogotá with a special distinction that survives to this day. Perhaps that is so, but at the moment I had eyes only for more tangible things. To begin with, Bogotá is much less of a city than Mexico, like Florence in comparison to Rome, civilized but provincial. It stands at over eight thousand feet on a sloping plain at the base of two mountains. The climate is one of perpetual springtime although it lies only 5° north of the Equator. The temperature at dawn is just above freezing point, but warms up during the day. The mornings are frequently fine and brilliantly sunny, but often about noon there descends on the city a dense and penetrating mountain mist, sometimes attended by driving sleet, rain and even hail. Strangers unused to these sudden changes get soaked to the skin.

The population at first sight appears to be predominantly mestizo; the correct figures, I believe, are twenty per cent white, sixty-eight per cent mixed and only seven per cent pure Indian. There are few Negroes in Colombia, except on the coast. While Indian blood is apt to blunt the features, it does not necessarily darken the skin. Many Bogotans have the russet complexion peculiar to mountain folk.

The nearness of the mountains heaving upwards directly behind the town is not an illusion. There is a hint of the Tyrol about Bogotá and the popular *ruana*, a cloak made of a cloth similar in consistency to *loden*, encourages this comparison. The *ruana* is Colombia's equivalent to Mexico's *sarape*, an aboriginal garment dating from pre-Columbian times which is worn as a shawl or coat with the head passed through a hole in the middle. It is about jacket length in front and rides up high at the back, falling loosely and gracefully over the shoulders and concealing the arms. Sometimes one side is gathered up and thrown over the shoulder, lending an elegant air of swagger to the wearer. *Ruanas* are never patterned and are usually different shades of brown, though I have seen both black and white being worn by the more dashing inhabitants. They are almost exclusively masculine garments whereas felt trilbys, with us worn only by men, are very popular here with the mestizo and Indian women.

Bogotá grows on one. The old houses with their *adobe* walls, tiled roofs and their uniformly dark green wood against whitewash are very pleasing. Square wooden balconies with fragile window grilles look almost Chinese. In the old houses, the downstairs rooms are generally paved with tiles laid over with rush matting and spread with carpets; upstairs the flooring is invariably of wood.

Tyrolean, but there are also features that remind one of Italy, especially the extensive use of brick. Church façades, pilasters, arches and buttresses are often of unplastered brick, beautifully laid in thin layers in the ancient Roman manner. A soft yellow-pink, they glow in the setting sun with an unearthly light as if caught in a conflagration.

The Colombian churches have fortunately escaped the classical revival. Their gilded altars are intact, shimmering softly in the light of multitudinous candles. Tradition says that La Concepción, built as a chapel for the first nuns in Bogotá and the oldest church in the city, is haunted; three blows are heard in the crypt when a nun is about to die. At La Tercera the entire church is lined in natural walnut and cedar, the two-toned woods being worked in a profusion of carving. A quilted ceiling of gilded wooden flowers is to be found at Santa Clara, a pretty effect as the flowers are detached from a ground of white plaster stencilled over with an overall design of dark blue and pink leaves. Rather fine also is the lacerated figure of Christ, standing stripped and bleeding, before Pontius Pilate. Centreless glass eyes weep crystal tears which are inlaid in His darkly polychrome cheeks. Rope binds His wrists and He is kilted in white satin fringed and embroidered in gold.

The religious sculpture in Colombia does not have the frightening morbidity usual in Mexico. In New Spain the hair, tending to auburn, is nearly always real. Blood the same colour as the locks, clots the

96 *Bogotá. Casa de Moneda* (*page 174*)

97 *Bogotá. A town house* (*page 174*)

98 *Bogotá. Courtyard of a town house now the Museum of Colonial Art* (*page 174*)

99 *Puente del Común, over the Bogotá River built in 1792* (*page 183*)

102 (opposite) Passiflora laurifolia. A plate from Flor de La Real Expedicion Botánica Del Nuevo Reino de Granada (page 176) ▶

100 Baron von Humboldt as a young man of thirty-one. From a portrait in the National Gallery, Berlin, by F. G. Weitsch painted in 1806 (page 176)

101 José Celestino Mutis (page 175)

Passiflora laurifolia L.

*105 (opposite)
Highlands landscape
in vicinity of Bogotá
(page 183)*

*103 Typical farm house
on the Sabana
(page 184)*

*104 House in the
village of Leiva
(page 188)*

*106 (opposite) Lake of
Guatavita. The cut is
clearly visible to the
left of the photograph
(page 184)*

107 Cartagena (page 189)

108 Cartagena. Palace of the Inquisition (page 189)

realistic wounds and broken knees. In one Ecce Homo I remember bruised flesh torn back over the ribcage, exposing a wooden heart like some macabre Dali jewel. The sculptors were usually Indians who had no difficulty in depicting the various stages of the Passion. Oppressed by the Spaniards they instinctively identified themselves with the suffering Christ.

By far the most beautiful of Bogotá's monuments is the early seventeenth-century church of San Francisco. I shall never forget my first view of it, not for any aesthetic consideration, but rather because of the taxi ride there. The Bogotá traffic is completely uncontrolled. If there is a right of way, I was not conscious of it, particularly down the narrow side-streets. Concerned as always with the driver's progress, I was not paying much attention to anything else until, suddenly, my eyes caught a swaying object hanging from the windscreen: one of those shrunken heads found among Venezuela's primitive jungle tribes, a tiny black face perfect in every detail even to the silken lashes and the long strands of shining black hair. It was through these strands that I first glimpsed the restrained façade of San Francisco.

The plain, discreet Plateresque exterior does not prepare one for the wealth of detail inside. There the eye travels up the aisle to the two pulpits, one each side of the apse. Turbaned figures surmount each of their heavy domed baldachinos. Beyond rises the high altar. Around it, against the wall, is a gilded and polychrome carved screen with three tiers of panels. The panels above depict virgins and martyrs, but below are 'a number of lascivious, wildly grotesque masks alternating with Bacchic boys emerging from garlands of fruit'.[1] Martin Soria attributes these pushing, exuberant forms in their lush tropical wilderness alive with monkeys, anteaters, macaws and other exotic beasts to an unknown Franciscan lay brother, and points out that he was the first to interpret native flora and fauna in sculpture.

Besides two universities, various schools and colleges, Bogotá also boasts the first observatory in Spanish America, built at the behest of the Spanish scientist and naturalist Don José Celestino Mutis, the foremost Iberian disciple of Linnaeus. A visit to the observatory, now the head-quarters of the Geographical Society, led me to hunt through the National Library for any material on Mutis's *Flora de Bogotá o' de Nueva Granada*, a monumental work which was to run to thirteen folio volumes. Arrangements for only the first volumes were complete at his death in 1808, but Mutis left behind a large quantity of coloured plates, some by himself and others executed by a group of commissioned painters. In these circumstances I had thought it possible that some unpublished material might remain in the city library. I found the three first volumes

[1] *Art and Architecture in Spain and Portugal and their American Dominions, 1500 to 1800.*

of the *Flora* in a recently printed edition brought out by the *Ediciones Cultura Hispánica* of Madrid. In them are tabulated the different passi-floras, begonias and *cinchonas* collected by Mutis. The name 'passion flower', comes from the early missionaries who saw in the plant's blossoms the crown of thorns, the nails and the cross of crucifixion. *Cinchona,* the quinine tree, was named after the Countess de Cinchón, wife of a Peruvian viceroy in the seventeenth century. It was the Jesuits of Lima who discovered about 1630 that the alkaloid essence of *cinchona* bark had a curative effect on malarial fever. The distribution of the approximately forty species of *cinchona* and experiments in the properties of the drug were among Mutis's preferred studies. The result of these investigations attracted the attention of Charles III who sponsored a botanical expedition in 1783 under the direction of this remarkable doctor, priest, botanist and teacher of natural science.

Mutis was born in Cadiz on 6 April 1732. He took his degree at Seville University and afterwards specialized in medicine in Madrid. He lectured in anatomy and studied mathematics and natural science, especially botany – which eventually led him to emigrate to South America, a fruitful field at that time for botanical exploration. At twenty-eight he sailed for New Granada in 1760 as King's physician in the Viceroy's ship. He was fifty when the King appointed him to head the 1783 expedition.

Humboldt was so impressed by the results of this expedition that in 1801 together with Aimé Bonpland, a medical doctor with a passionate interest in botany, he sailed up the Magdalena River to Bogotá to meet Mutis, then aged sixty-nine. On this occasion Mutis presented Humboldt with a hundred finished drawings for the *Flora* volumes. A portrait reproduced here shows Mutis at about the time of his meeting with the admiring young explorer-geographer. We see a heavy-set figure holding a pen and a magnifying glass in one hand and in the other, one of the numerous passifloras he studied. It is an intelligent, sympathetic face with dark inquiring eyes and a domed forehead framed by a thick head of white hair.

Humboldt at thirty-two must have been a dynamic figure; pleasant-looking, romantic, vivacious and highly intelligent. Goethe wrote that he was 'always struck with fresh amazement in his company'. Weitsch's portrait, painted in 1806, two years after Humboldt's return from the New World, must be a good likeness for it tallies well with contemporary descriptions of Humboldt who was short in figure – five foot eight – and had light brown hair, grey eyes, a large nose, full mouth and a well-formed chin. His open forehead was pitted with smallpox, naturally not shown in the portrait.

Humboldt's considerable reputation during his lifetime was well justified, for he accomplished a prodigious amount. He was born in Berlin in 1769, the son of a Prussian officer, aide-de-camp to the Duke of Brunswick. His mother, a well-to-do, intelligent woman of Huguenot descent, was widowed early, and became responsible for Humboldt's education. The young boy was taught languages and sent to the University of Göttingen, then a centre for studies in the physical sciences. In 1790 he visited England in the company of George Foster, the naturalist who had sailed with his father on Captain Cook's second voyage. By the time he was twenty-three Humboldt already held an important post as director-general of mines in Franconia; a post he abandoned at his mother's death in 1796. Then while on a visit to Paris, the Directory invited him to take part in a scientific voyage circumnavigating the world. The expedition was scheduled to join Napoleon and his *savants* in Egypt, but was cancelled at the last moment. As it happened, Humboldt shared the same building in Paris with the twenty-six-year-old Aimé Bonpland who was to have been on the expedition's staff too. They met while talking to the *concierge*. With so many common interests they became fast friends and left together for Marseilles intending to embark independently for Alexandria. Nelson's blockade, however, intervened. From Marseilles the two travellers crossed over the border into Spain where they hoped to find a small vessel that would smuggle them through the British cordon. No vessel was found, but while in Madrid Humboldt was introduced to the Spanish Secretary of State and in the course of conversation suggested that, instead of Egypt, he and Bonpland should visit the Americas and make a full report on what they found there. Charles IV was approached and not only granted them passage but provided a *laissez-passer* bearing the royal seal.

The King and his minister were fortunate in their choice, particularly of Humboldt. Inquiring by nature, he was remarkably erudite and wrote highly readable accounts of his travels and scientific observations, such as his finding the cold current off the coast of Peru, now called after him. He found interest in the most divergent of subjects like the fertilizing properties of guano, whose introduction into Europe was mainly due to his writings. The New World volcanoes were another of his studies. He also surveyed and mapped the course of the mighty Orinoco and established the exact point at which it merged with the waters of the Amazon. Together with Bonpland he scaled the Andes, ascending Pichincha and the vast snow-topped Chimborazo, which rises twenty-two thousand feet above the Pacific. Although they did not quite get to its dome-shaped summit, they reached 19,286 feet, the highest point attained by man up to that time and a record that was not to be beaten for another fifty years.

Humboldt spent three years in South America, one year in Mexico and, on his way back to Europe, stayed with Thomas Jefferson at Monticello. Based on Paris, he then set about arranging all the material collected on his travels, a gigantic task that took him the best part of twenty-one years to complete. He published the results at his own expense. His volumes on Mexico, so often quoted here, were separately printed and appeared in 1808. Following these, there appeared a succession of volumes covering the entire voyage. The completed work numbered thirty volumes, with illustrations and over a thousand diagrams and maps. They formed the first comprehensive report on Latin America available to the general public and had an immediate success.

No sooner finished with the New World than he started on his *Cosmos*. 'I have been seized with a mad idea,' he wrote, 'of representing in a single work the whole material of the world.' The first volume of this project appeared when he was seventy-six, the fifth and last was published posthumously in 1862. Fragmentary though his work might appear in the light of present knowledge, the *Cosmos* gave a strong impetus to scientific exploration, influencing especially young men such as Charles Darwin.

In his last years the worldly scientist spent much of his time at the court of Frederick William III in Berlin, where the King used him as his representative on diplomatic missions. He was ninety when he died, one of the most respected figures in Europe.

If an agreeably peaceful atmosphere of learning envelops one in the octagonal rooms of the Bogotá observatory, the *Museo del Oro* in the vaults of the *Banco de La República* keys one up to a fever pitch of excitement. Begun in 1939 this remarkable collection of pre-Columbian gold now numbers eight thousand pieces, such a hoard that the directors can only exhibit it all on a rotating basis. Guards are posted outside an impressive barrage of gates and admittance is finally gained by registering one's name. The effect of the black velvet-lined cases shining with alloys ranging from the palest yellow to the brilliance of sunshine is electrifying.

The massive, highly burnished, golden flasks of the Quimbaya Indians of Eastern Colombia are perhaps the most arresting objects exhibited. One bottle, a foot high with a bulbous body, tapers gently upwards to a top composed of four globular caps; a design that could quite easily pass as Art Nouveau. There are great golden alligators a foot long that were worn as pendants, as well as necklaces of golden beads and chest ornaments hung with discs and rings that shook and shimmered with the wearer's every movement. When not worn these pectoral plates were hung on fences or doors to catch the sun's rays and to tinkle in the wind. There are the enormous ear-pendants of the Calima Indians on the coast, eight-inch spools that the men inserted into their distended ear lobes and from which hung concave disks the size of porridge bowls. From Calima also come crowns and diadems set with gold foil ribbons that trembled like feathers. There are shells too, among them a natural-sized strombus cast entirely in gold. The same Indians fastened their cotton mantles with long gold bodkins some of which are clustered with bells that contain emerald jingles. They also used nose ornaments which hung from the septum to cover the mouth. Some of these are so pure in line that they look like Brancusi sculpture; others terminate in a fringe of wire that must have had the appearance of a golden moustache. In one case is a large pectoral ornament from Lake Guatavita, famous site of the *El Dorado* legend. Guatavita, a crater lake sunk into the summit of a nameless peak in the Eastern Cordillera, was Chibcha territory at the time of the Conquest. The Chibcha objects, mostly votive figurines, compare rather poorly with the rest of Colombian pre-Hispanic gold work. They are usually flat sheets, rarely burnished, and with facial features and limbs outlined in thin threads of gold wire to give a filigree effect.

The objects displayed in the *Museo del Oro* are nearly all tomb furnishings found within the last fifty years. Systematic grave robbery has been carried out ever since the Conquest, but until recently every-thing excavated was sent to the melting pot. André Emmerich, an expert on the subject of pre-Columbian gold, states that until a very few years ago 'it was still common practice in Panama to sell hard-to-market gold objects to dentists for slightly less than bullion value to be melted down into fillings'.[1] Fortunately, the increasing interest in pre-Columbian art has now pushed prices of ancient gold high enough to make it improbable that any further treasures will be lost in the melting pots.

Of all the advanced cultures in the New World, the Colombian Indians have the most obscure pre-history. It is known that the Chibcha Indians had established their supremacy over their neighbours by the time of the Conquest, and in some ways their civilization appears to have been as advanced as the better known Indian cultures of Mexico and Peru. Jiménez de Quesada wrote a treatise on the people he con-quered but it was never published and has since disappeared. It is from other sources, therefore, that we know that the Chibchas were ruled over by a Zipa, or supreme chief, who was important enough to be carried into battle on the shoulders of his nobles in a gold-encased litter. Local chiefs also lived fairly ostentatiously in houses lined with gold

[1] André Emmerich, *Sweat of the Sun and Tears of the Moon*, University of Washington Press, Seattle, 1965.

plates, but the houses themselves were little more than commodious beehive-shaped huts, as the Chibchas had no stone architecture. There are no remains of cities, of great buildings or roadways, and their historical tradition, which at the time of the Conquest extended back only three generations or about sixty years, dealt almost entirely with local wars fought with neighbouring chiefs.

Spanish association with the country began early: its coast was among the first visited by the explorers. In 1525 Rodrigo de Bastidas founded Santa Marta. The colony grew so fast that by 1535 it had its own *adelantado*, Pedro Fernández de Lugo, under whom Jiménez de Quesada served as auditor and *justicia mayor*. Although a man of letters with no military experience, Quesada must have been a remarkable figure, for the following year Lugo chose him to command an expedition to search out the headwaters of the Magdalena, which is Colombia's largest river, stretching, as the crow flies, five hundred miles inland. Quesada filed out of Santa Marta in the spring of 1536 with an army of 875 men. It was January 1537 before he finally reached the great central plateau of Bogotá, his force reduced to a ragged crew of 167 starving men.

The coastal Indians had been friendly enough. Pedro Cieza de León, one of the conquistadors, described them as clever, clean-limbed men, 'Their private parts covered with heavy gold shells,' and their wives 'some of the handsomest, and most lovely women I have ever seen'.[1] The forest Indians, however, proved far from friendly. They tipped their blowpipe darts with a particularly virulent poison, concocted, according to Cieza de León, from 'short roots of an ill-scent', probably mangrove, 'beetles, large spiders and hairy worms, head and tail of a poisonous fish, snakes and lastly a poisonous apple and various noxious herbs'. The brew was prepared in a remote place far from any dwellings by a slave 'or Indian woman of small value, who boils, and brings the mixture to the due temperature, and I was told that the person so doing was always killed with the steam and stench of it'.

Still more deadly was the poison of a frog known as the *rana de veneno*. Captain Cochrane described it as small, about three inches long, with a yellow back, and very large black eyes. The frog was caught in the jungle and kept in a hollow cane. When its poison was needed the unfortunate creature was taken out and transfixed on a piece of pointed wood. 'This torture makes the frog perspire especially on the back which becomes covered with white froth, and in this they dip and roll the points of their arrows, which will preserve their destructive powers for a year.'[2] A hundred years later another traveller of a scientific turn

[1] Pedro Cieza de León, *Crónica de Peru*, first published at Seville in 1553.
[2] *Journal of a Residence and Travels in Colombia during the year 1823–24.*

of mind established that the poisons were Epinephrin and Bufotalin, 'two powerful drugs which in overdose act fatally on the heart and blood vessels'.[1]

The Spaniards suffered so appallingly from the heat that they soon adopted the armour of the Indians, padded cotton covered with bamboo slats. It was lighter and cooler than steel breastplates, but there was not much the men could do to protect their exposed arms and legs at which the Indians, hidden in the trees, aimed their darts. Added to the Indians were the tropical fevers. Captain Cochrane wreathed himself against the mosquitoes in a 'gauze dress' made according to Humboldt's recommendations, but the Spaniards had nothing like this. Their march must have been hell. For days they slogged alongside the swampy banks of a muddy, fast-flowing river alive with alligators which they thought were dragons. They had big mastiffs with them trained to fight the Indians, but at night the dogs were dragged off into the jungle by prowling jaguars. There were rumours, too, of strange animals like the half-human *mono blanco*, a great white monkey ten feet high with huge round eyes, that was supposed to carry off Indians as mates. There are descriptions of 'swine with navels on their backs' that gave off an appalling odour when the pig was attacked, so appalling that it served to 'put tigers to flight and strikes hunters with vertigo'.[2]

Month after month, their numbers constantly decreasing, the men struggled forward. There were no seasons; only the colours of green changed, from dark green to a grey hoary with age. What a relief it must have been when they finally reached the open grasslands inhabited by the Chibchas!

It was the usual story. Quesada with 167 men and 59 horses prevailed over a population estimated at well over a million. After a series of skirmishes and a final battle the Zipa abandoned his capital and fled the field to disappear from history. With him, according to the Spaniards, he carried a great treasure in gold; a hoard that is still awaiting discovery.

Quesada founded his new city near the site of the Zipa's summer palace, on the foothills of the savanna, or *sabana* as it is called here, by a clear mountain stream. 'The great plain,' writes Mr Veatch, 'reminded Quesada of the Vega round Granada where he had spent his boyhood days and he named the city Santa Fé in memory of the camp which Ferdinand and Isabel maintained in their wars with the Moors.' The *sabana* was known as the '*bogotá*' by the Chibchas, a word that in their language meant 'the great cultivated land'. The new city thus became

[1] A. C. Veatch, *From Quito to Bogotá*, George H. Doran & Co., New York, 1917.
[2] Kathlen Romoli, *Colombia Gateway to South America*, Doubleday, Doran & Co. Inc., New York, 1943.

Santa Fe de Bogotá and when the country became a republic the first part of the name was dropped.

While Quesada was grappling his way up the Magdalena Valley two other expeditions were converging on Bogotá. It is one of the strange coincidences of history that three expeditions should set out independently across unknown country, and from widely separated points, and all end up in the same place. One of Pizarro's lieutenants, Sebastián de Belalcázar, was pushing northward from far-off Quito in Ecuador. At the same time Nicolaus Federmann, on behalf of the German merchant princes of Augsburg who had been granted a colonial concession by Charles v, was approaching up a branch of the Orinoco from Venezuela. Belalcázar reached Bogotá in 1538 and Federmann in 1539, but Quesada successfully maintained the priority of his rights against both of them. In 1546 the King ennobled Quesada. 'We command,' he wrote:

that thou be given for arms a shield in two parts; in the upper most, a golden lion holding a naked sword in a field of red in memory of thy spirit and fortitude in going up the Great River to discover and win the New Kingdom, and in the lower half, a mountain arising out of the sea and covered with emeralds, in memory of the emerald mines thou didst discover.

Quesada saw emeralds for the first time shortly after his arrival in Chibcha territory.[1] A chieftain was wearing the stones on his wrists, but when questioned he proved evasive, 'not caring to reveal any information regarding the source from whence the precious stones came'. A young Indian was made to talk and the mine was found on a high ridge, in a gap formed by two mountains to the north-east of Bogotá, in the present department of Boyacá.

There are no known emerald deposits in South America other than those in Colombia. Long before the Conquest the Chibchas traded the stones. The Chivor, or Indian mines, were working when the Spaniards first arrived. Then, quite by chance, at the end of the sixteenth century, another source was found in the steaming, low-lying forests of the Carare Valley when the Spaniards discovered some small, indifferent crystals in the crops of their chickens. Later, a farmer of the district, while riding into the little settlement of Muzo, found his horse limping. Dismounting, he noticed something embedded in one of its hoofs. On removal it turned out to be an emerald encrusted with stone.

Not far from the Chivor mines is Guatavita, the sacred lake into which *El Dorado*, the 'golden one', flung his yearly offerings. *El Dorado*

---

[1] Fray Pedro Simón, *Noticias Historiales*. The *Noticias* are to be found in Bogotá's National Archives, written in longhand on brown and stained pages that are sometimes badly worm-eaten.

was one of the Chibcha chieftains, the Usque of Guatavita, who prided himself, like the Incas, on divine descent from the sun. Each year, acting as the sun god's representative on earth, he made sacrifice to his ancestor. The rites took place at dawn upon a raft towed out to the middle of the lake. At a given moment four dignitaries, or priests, accompanying *El Dorado* stripped him of his clothes and daubed him with an adhesive mixture of resin topped with a dusting of powdered gold. At the same time the spectators crowded around the lake started chanting sacred hymns to the accompaniment of thudding drums. Glistening like an idol come to life, *El Dorado* slowly unclasped his regalia of bracelets, armbands and leg pieces and threw them into the water. The drums beat louder and just as the sun burst over the horizon *El Dorado* himself dived into the lake to wash off his golden skin.

There is no doubt that this ceremony actually took place. The enthralling story was certainly one calculated to fire the Spaniards' imagination. Indeed, it grew so in the telling that very soon a man sprinkled with gold dust became an entire city of golden streets with houses all studded with gems. The reality was so insignificant compared to this glorious legend that when they faced Guatavita's lonely waters, the Spaniards would not believe that here lay what they were hunting for.

Quesada's brother was the first to be lured farther on in the futile quest. On being questioned about *El Dorado* the Indians had pointed over the mountains, towards the jungles of Venezuela. The Indians were always pointing ahead, hoping in this way to be rid of the invaders. Even Quesada himself, who had actually found the lake, continued the search. He equipped an expedition of three hundred Spaniards and 1,500 native porters. Only twenty-five men remained when he returned two years later.

As far as I could gather, Lake Guatavita lay due north-east of where I was staying, a day's expedition by car. It was not marked on any of my maps and I could find no reference to it other than the material I have already quoted. My host could give me vague directions, but he had never been there himself.

It was one of those delicious mornings one gets in the highlands – green, rolling hills seamed with feathery eucalyptus and low ragged clouds like a golden mist over the sun – when we crossed Bogotá and swung to the north across the imposing Puente del Común built in 1792. Legend would have us believe that this bridge was built by British prisoners of war captured in Admiral Vernon's unsuccessful attack on Cartagena. But this is hardly likely. Vernon's attack was in 1741 so that even the youngest of the prisoners would have to have been approaching his seventies in 1792.

Having crossed the bridge the road threads its way like a ribbon over the *sabana*. The country is thickly settled. *Adobe* farmhouses are everywhere, plastered over, whitewashed and topped with heavy thatching. The thatching is made from the fine grasses that one sees blowing in green-brown waves across the downs. It is a beautiful country where the light is sharply cut with deep shadows.

We had been on the road some hours before trouble started. No one had ever heard of Guatavita. After several wrong turns it suddenly struck me that I should try asking for 'the Lake of the Gilded One'. Our success was immediate. After slithering over some muddy tracks we came to an abrupt halt in a field. From here on the way was on foot. Someone had mentioned ponies, but, of course, there were none. Much more upsetting was the problem of finding the trail leading to the lake. Fortunately we fell in with a couple of farmers, one of whom agreed to be our guide.

The lake, I had read, lay at an altitude of ten thousand feet and climbing to that height is an arduous undertaking for someone who is not in training. The guide filled his lungs deeply and every few minutes blew out audibly. Far too winded to emulate him, I was obliged to slow down the pace. A rough path, scoured deep into the peaty earth by the rain, led us upwards over a series of rolling ridges. The bracken and heath were not unlike parts of north-west Scotland, but among this herbage were unfamiliar flora: small mauve orchids and a larger variety shading from orange to pale yellow, and dark mauve everlastings as well as flowering shrubs, some with branches tipped by pale red leaves, others with clusters of white-green berries – and all of them meshed with strands of almond-green moss.

After about an hour of panting for breath we reached the lip of the crater and there, lying some six or seven hundred feet below us, spread the lake. The sky was overcast and the water had taken on a dark sorrel-green, a mirror-like surface across which the breezes played, feathering it with ripples. I well understood Quesada's refusal to believe that here lay the end of his quest. In his day there had been a small temple beside the lake and in it a life-size golden statue. As the Spaniards wound over the hill the priests had toppled it into the water. But even this fleeting glimpse of gold flashing in the light as it sank to the depths failed to convince Quesada.

The Spaniards might not have accepted Guatavita as the fabled place they were looking for, but neither did they entirely ignore it. The idea that a solid gold statue, and possibly other treasures, lay at the bottom, ensured a degree of attention. Kathleen Romoli in her excellent book on Colombia writes that three attempts have been made to retrieve the treasure. The first was in 1580 when a merchant from Bogotá secured a commission from the Crown together with a loan of working capital. Employing Indian labourers he cut through the mountain rim. The water sank a little, thus bringing to light some of the lesser offerings that had been thrown from the shore. 'But just as discovery of an emerald as large as an egg and a high priest's mitre and staff in wrought gold seemed to promise a bigger catch, funds gave out.'[1]

In 1824 the second attempt was carried out under the auspices of our English friend Captain Charles Cochrane. But the lake again held out longer than the available capital. It must have been a painful experience, for Cochrane actually had a figure for the amount he had hoped to extract. It had all been worked out by a Monsieur de la Kier of the Royal Institute of Paris, a great expert, it would seem, on all that concerned the lake. The sum amounted to an astronomical £1,120,000,000. One wonders how he arrived at such a figure.

The third attempt was made seventy years later. A Colombian company did a little ineffectual excavation and then invited a British concern to take over. But they too met with failure. 'In the course of centuries,' writes Mrs Romoli:

the gold had washed into the funnel-shaped centre of the lake, and when after years of work the water level was lowered, it was found that the bottom consisted of twenty-five or thirty feet of mud that became almost as hard as cement on exposure to the air. Some £40,000 were expended on the venture and after two years' work the company had only recovered some £2,000 worth of adornments.

The 1914 War put an end to the whole affair.

We stood in silence, the three of us. A sheer wooded slope dropped almost down to the ruffled water. To the left was the cleft in the rocky perimeter made by the first prospector. One wondered what lay hidden down there under Guatavita's clouded surface. I questioned the guide about the unsuccessful attempts at emptying the lake. There was no doubt in his mind as to the cause of failure. 'No one will ever succeed, Señor. The place is magic.'

Had it been possible I would also have visited one of the two emerald mines, preferably Chivor because it was the older. The Muzo mines are worked on behalf of the government by the *Banco de La República* and the Chivor mines are American-owned. I had made an appointment with Chivor's American director, Mr Bronkie, a quiet-spoken, direct man who was perfectly willing to arrange my visit. He warned me that it was pretty rugged going, mountainous and densely forested. The roads are mere bridle paths which, in parts, are hazardous and almost impassable in the wet season. But this fortunately had just ended. The company

[1] *Colombia Gateway to South America.*

jeep could take me as far as the township of Almeida and from there I would travel by pack mule. The only drawback was time. A minimum of four days was needed which unfortunately I could not spare. Unable to make the mine, I at least was lucky enough to have Mr Bronkie to myself for a whole morning.

We started with the stones in the safe. Emeralds are not mined in quantity and a flawless Colombian emerald sometimes brings three times the price of a diamond the same size. The best stones had just been sold to New York and those that were left, while good in colour, were heavily flawed. It takes an expert cutter to shape an emerald, to know on which spot to centre for the best light and colour. Since emeralds have little brilliance or fire, much depends on colour, transparency and freedom from flaws. Wholly unflawed raw material of any size is virtually unobtainable.

Adjoining Mr Bronkie's office were a series of small workshops in one of which two girls were busy grading inferior stones, arranging them in little piles. Pounds of these pale green crystals are shipped annually to India, mainly to Jaipur, the centre of the jewellery trade. In another room the cutter sat with a magnifying glass screwed to his eye. In front of him was a tray of minute slivers which he was endeavouring to shape into baguettes, to be used eventually in settings. One wondered how he was able to manipulate such infinitesimal fragments.

I learned from Mr Bronkie that Chivor and Muzo between them are responsible for ninety-five per cent of the world's emerald production. The remaining five per cent comes from Rhodesia, South Africa, Brazil, Austria, Australia, the USSR and Egypt. Records indicate that emeralds were mined in Upper Egypt as early as the seventeenth century BC. During the Alexandrian period Greek miners continued to use the same source. The stone through which Nero is said to have quizzed the burning of Rome was almost certainly of Egyptian origin.

But what of the actual mines? I looked the subject up and found that emeralds are found in thin mother-veins of pale green beryl. Here and there in the powdery beryl are darker green, hexagonal crystals which are the gem stones. Fragile while still in the matrix, they harden after exposure to air. They are elusive stones to find, for the vein is hardly more than a tiny crack in the rock, about a finger's breadth in width. Furthermore, the rock in which this insignificant crack lies is usually several hundred feet below the surface and covered by barren rock formations that give no clue to what may be below. Experts, however, can usually tell when they are nearing an emerald-bearing vein. There the texture of the rock changes. It becomes sharp and jagged with a silky feel and breaks off into chunks that are square or parallelogram in shape.

Many old workings recently brought to light show that the Indian and Spanish methods of mining differed little from those in use today. They all are open mines which, owing to the rugged terrain, are worked in step cuttings, or terracings. These terraces are worked from side to side. The miners line up next to each other and armed with long steel bars they pry the rock loose. Emeralds occur so irregularly that every square foot is carefully turned. They work in gangs of fifteen to forty, each gang is handled by an Indian foreman who is closely supervised by a responsible member of the staff. When a likely looking formation is reached, a careful watch is kept for *morralla*, the emerald mineral, which is picked by hand from the vein as it is uncovered. Annual production is very irregular, depending entirely on the size of the pockets encountered. The labourers, descendants of the Chibcha Indians, are checked for any possible pilferage. A substantial reward is made for any stone found in the streams or discharges below the mines which would otherwise offer a thief an easy means of disposing of his stones. In the last few years only one small stone has been presented for sale in this manner.

The American Institute of Mining commissioned Peter Rainer, a Chivor administrator, to prepare a report on the mine. From him I learned the strange story of how the diggings were abandoned. In 1672 Chivor became the subject of litigation between its Spanish owners who were unable to come to an agreement and referred the case to Madrid. A peremptory order came back that the mine should be closed. Operations ceased in 1675 and immediately the vegetation took over, within a matter of years completely eradicating all trace of the diggings. Incredible though it may seem the mine was then lost for over two centuries. It was found again only in 1896 by a Colombian mining engineer who had stumbled upon an ancient parchment map in the government archives.

Using Bogotá as my base, I made various side expeditions, one of them to Tunja, the oldest city in Colombia after Bogotá. It lies higher than Bogotá and the air is sharp and hard as a diamond. Here also the Chibchas had a settlement with streets at right angles and buildings made of saplings and straw with high stockades. One reads of thin gold plates dangled from temple eaves to give back the sun, of priests with long scarlet robes and of parrots offered to the gods in place of human sacrifice. The Spaniards, when they arrived, wheeled into the temple courtyard and by the end of the day had gathered so much gold that one horseman could not see another over the top of the pile.

The city is approached over a *sabana* with fields of grazing cattle, willow-bordered streams and tall feathery eucalyptus. The landscape rises gently on each side to the surrounding hills, while threaded down the middle of the plain the road dips and turns. One climbs gradually to Tunja situated on a height surrounded by bare, sun-toasted hills swept the year round by cold, harsh winds.

My memory of the town is of its churches. In the early seventeenth-century Rosario Chapel of Santo Domingo the walls are sheathed in wood painted a deep crimson and encrusted with gilding. In others there are patterned wooden ceilings decorated with pendant knobs like stalactites in a grotto. There was a profusion of Mudéjar interlacing: of stars, sun-bursts, and cherubs' heads, framed in petals of wings and looking like catherine wheels pinned up across the rafters. In the house of the conquistador Juan de Vargas the ceilings are frescoed with sixteenth-century arabesques representing Greek gods along with grotesque and savage beasts, among them elephants and rhinoceroses, inspired certainly by Dürer's woodcuts.

On the way home we passed through the charming village of Leiva where the viceroys spent their summers. Carlos, a young native of the place, piloted us around and showed us, among other things, the Royal Distillery with its hallway paved in sheeps' knuckles and black fossilized marine sediments from the bed of an Eocene lake up behind the town.

The next day I flew down to Popayán, the pretty provincial capital of south-western Colombia. I slept in a converted monastery and was woken in the morning by the tolling of a bell famous for its depth and clarity of tone. They say it can be heard all over the valley and when black storms roll down from the Cordillera to menace the crops, the bell is supposed to have the power to drive them away, or at least, reduce them to harmless rain. The citizens attribute its magical tones to the fifty pounds of gold which reputable sources assure one were cast with the bronze at the time of its founding.

Popayán was the administrative seat for the whole province, and was also a main station on the overland route from Cartagena to Lima. The important role it once played is reflected in the stylishness of its houses and the elaborate treasure displayed in most of the churches. No more eloquent example can be found than the elaborate pulpit in the Franciscan church. Carved and gilded with a matching canopy, it is like a large golden chalice standing on one side of the aisle, a goldsmith's masterpiece rather than the product of a sculptor's chisel. Its banisters and stairs are equally elaborate, terminating in what Martin Soria judges to be the finest newel post in the Americas. The figure of an Indian with brown glass eyes reaches one hand up to steady a basket of fruit on his head, the other cups a pineapple. The body below the waist of this exotic caryatid is made up of leafy volutes bound with pearls.

14

The Pearl of the Indies

I then flew north into an entirely different climate in this varied country, to Cartagena on the Caribbean coast where the annual temperature ranges from 80° to 90° fahrenheit. My arrival, winging over the indented shoreline, proved an excellent introduction to the place for the topography is somewhat complicated. The old city lies on a sand bar to the north of an enormous bay, commodious enough, the Spaniards boasted, to shelter all the navies of the world. The bay is almost a lagoon entered by a narrow, heavily fortified passage known as the Boca Chica. Seven fortresses in all cover the harbour and its approaches. Cartagena was the major redoubt on the continent, a key point in the Spanish defences of the Antilles. The other was Havana, on the north shore of Cuba, which in turn was protected by fortifications on the adjoining Florida and Yucatan peninsulas. Behind this formidable barrage lay the trading ports of Vera Cruz and Puerto Belo. Cartagena was thus not a port for the silver fleets but a vital station in the screen of defence for the *Tierra Firme* and for the fleets sailing to Puerto Belo. The military installations were started by Philip II in 1581, and were still being built or enlarged well on in the eighteenth century.

My first impression was of blue-green, transparent water and then, once in the city, of blazing light reflected from white wooden shutters, grilled windows and open, white wooden balconies. Everything white and everywhere wood. Wood, as Kelemen points out, was preferred to iron which was apt to corrode in the moist tropics. Other memories are the philodendrons that snake up the African tulip trees planted in the old Plaza de la Inquisición. Under their shade splash pyramidal fountains built up of conch shells.

The Palace of the Inquisition dominates the square. Passing through its impressive Baroque portal, one enters cool, high-ceilinged rooms striped with latticed shade. In the rooms are exhibits relating to the past, among them a plan referring to Cartagena as the 'Pearl of The Indies', her official title for many years. In another room hangs a portrait of the one-eyed, one-armed and lame Don Blas de Lezo, the commander and gallant defender of the city. For seven weeks he held out against British and American forces. Never had a more imposing fleet entered Caribbean waters: thirty thousand fighting men – fifteen thousand of them sailors – in more than 120 ships. Sir Edward Vernon commanded the fleet and General Wentworth the army, composed largely of Jamaican Negroes and North American soldiers. Don Blas with only four thousand men was outnumbered by seven to one.

The siege opened in March 1740. After a fierce struggle the British eventually managed to storm the fortifications at Boca Chica. When news of this success reached London, medals were immediately struck in anticipation of the city's seemingly inevitable fall. 'Spanish pride humbled by Admiral Vernon' one of the inscriptions boastfully announced. The other medal showed Don Blas de Lezo kneeling, holding out his sword to the Admiral. The rejoicing, however, was premature, for the city never fell and England's conquering hero, instead of receiving a humbled Spanish commander, was forced to beat an ignominious retreat.

I spent all of one morning climbing up and around the sloping ramparts of San Felipe de Barajas, the most important single fortress on the entire continent and a formidable piece of engineering. The whole hilltop has been cased in an immense carapace of masonry. Smooth, inclined walls some sixty feet high and forty feet thick mount from terrace to terrace, each terrace wide enough to accommodate a platoon of a hundred men. Vaulted galleries tunnel down under the walls and connect up, they say, with the centre of the city. I found it very impressive but almost impossible to photograph. There was no shade so I had to shoot from the inside, through openings cut into the thickness of the walls, without being able to compose the pictures properly.

An excellent view of the city is to be had from the ruined galleries of an old monastery on top of La Popa hill. Directly below is the disreputable Chambacu district spread out in a maze of rusted, corrugated roofs. Gay music floated up, and it looked inviting down there amongst the bright-coloured washing and the flowers bedded out in tin cans. Such, however, is the place's reputation that no visitor ventures down unless heavily escorted.

The *costeños*, the people of the coast, are eighty per cent Negro, or anyway mulatto, and are graded into every possible colour combination. There are also those who 'the Cartagenos referred to as "*tente en el ayre*", those "suspended in the air", who knew not whether they were dark or white'.[1]

---

[1] Victor Wolfgang von Hagen, *South America Called Them*, Little Brown & Co., Boston, 1955.

That Spanish America was not converted into an immense slave market has been mentioned in a previous chapter. Africa was not so fortunate, for already while still a young man Charles v granted licences to import Negroes into the colonies. Merchants first obtained these slaves from the Portuguese, but later traded directly with the west coast tribes who made war on each other in order to sell fellow Africans. Black convoys ploughed the seas, averaging an annual importation of ten to twelve thousand. It is estimated that Cartagena absorbed close to a million Negroes in the period that slavery lasted.

There exist harrowing accounts of conditions on these convoys. Not only was food and water in short supply, but leprosy, hookworm, dysentery, the white flux or more exactly amoebic dysentery, sleeping sickness and a variety of eye infections were rife. By the time they reached Cartagena many of the Negroes were suffering from ulcers and frequently they fell victim to the plague. The facilities for nursing the sick once they had arrived were practically nonexistent, only a reed hut near the harbour half-flooded with water. Those considered to be incurable were sent to the lazaret, a collection of hovels outside the gates. A contemporary describes the horrors attending those smitten with the plague. Forgotten and neglected, they were stretched out on the ground without any bedding and the pestilential smell they gave off was so violent that they were literally unapproachable.

In contrast to these reports is the extraordinary story of Father Pedro Claver, the Cartagena Jesuit who devoted his whole life to the welfare of the slaves. Every day he visited the sick and the dying. Claver was reported to have once carried a leper who had come to beg alms and was too weak to return to his hut. He would attend plague patients pretending to feel nothing while others with him would be overcome with nausea from the heat and the stench. The horrified mayor was with him one day when he put his mouth to a slave's ulcer. He flinched from nothing. A brother testified to Claver's extreme acts of self-mortification with scourges, one of them tipped with iron. He wore a hair shirt and lodged a thick cord of hog bristle under his instep, making his every step torture. When not tending the slaves he spent hours on end praying. Negroes who lived with him swear that he levitated. The Slave of Slaves they called him and already during his lifetime he gained a reputation for sanctity. But it was not until 1889, 235 years after his death, that he was finally canonized.

I visited his grave, a glass coffin under the main altar of San Pedro Claver, the fine Jesuit church named after him. His yellowed skull lies on a white satin pillow and his body is vested in a fine yellow cassock heavily embroidered with gold. One is also shown where the saint died in a room in the adjacent monastery, a long, three-storeyed building next to the city walls and overlooking the sea and the harbour.

Father Angel Valtierra has written an excellent life of the saint and it is to him I turn for a description of Claver's death. Aged seventy he caught the plague, but recovered and lived on a further four years in a pitiful state, 'his feet and hands almost useless, his jaws trembling, making a continuous clacking'. He actually died either of the violent palsy of Parkinson's disease or of 'general paralysis perhaps together with chronic malaria which had affected his kidneys'. 'On Sunday morning, 6 September, the sick man refused the offer of receiving the viaticum in his cell.' Making a supreme effort he got two of his Negroes to help him into the church, where he took Communion. 'Dragging himself along the floor he made his last visit to Our Lady of the Miracle in front of whom he had said his first Mass, and confessed many thousands of souls.'

Several eye-witnesses reported his last hours. On the morning of the seventh he lost the power of speech and rumours ran through the city that Claver had received extreme unction. Father Juan de Arcos, in a letter to the Jesuits of Spain and America writes, 'straightway I was begged by many persons for permission to make portraits of him. Some of these persons were of such authority that they could not be denied entrance. His cell was soon crowded, and soon emptied of everything associated with him; only his bed-clothes were left . . .' As the news spread so more and more people forced their way in and the atmosphere in the cell became stifling. 'Priests, monks, people of high rank in the city, officers from the fleet, ladies, Negresses and nuns sent vast numbers of rosaries to be touched by the saint . . .' He died between one and two in the morning 'without the slightest movement or gesture, dying with the same peace and serenity with which he had lived'. Brother Nicolás describes his face: there was no physical change ' "and I only realized that he had died because suddenly his pale thin countenance shone with extraordinary brilliance . . ." '[1]

My last few days in Colombia I spent on the coast, around Cartagena. I visited La Boquilla, a typical fishing village straddling a narrow spit of sand. On one side it faces the sea and on the other a lagoon cushioned with mangrove swamps. Both looked equally muddy. There were log canoes and palm-thatched huts, coconut palms and papaws. The dry beaten earth around the huts was littered with shreddings of sugar cane, chickens and pigs. In the cemetery crosses of driftwood wreathed with white paper flowers lean at rakish angles in the sand. The wind tugs at the flowers and frets the flat, colourless sea. It is a familiar pattern and could be any of the many villages I had visited in the South Pacific, the

[1] Father Angel Valtierra, s.j., *Peter Claver, Saint of the Slaves*, translated from the Spanish by Janet Perry and L. J. Woodward, The Newman Press, Westminster, Maryland, 1960.

only difference being that the inhabitants are long-limbed Negroes instead of the more sturdy, flat-nosed Polynesians.

I stayed with friends at Periquito, the Island of the Little Parrots. To get there I sailed out through the Boca Chica, past the Castillo de San Fernando and the ruins of San José, a narrow opening that used to be defended at night by a chain stretched from fortress to fortress. Periquito rides the blue translucent sea like a great, green-backed whale; and life on the island is a Robinson Crusoe idyll. Pelicans, replacing gulls, stood lazily by the water's edge splashing their scissor beaks clumsily in a choppy sea teeming with bright-hued fish. A boat with much-patched sails and manned by Negroes hauled to for water. It was a trader bound for the mainland loaded to the gunwales with green plantains and rice. One morning we left on an expedition for the village of Baru, an old smuggling centre hidden away in the swamplands a little to the north of the island. Young Victor, the coloured boat boy, took charge and drove us spanking in a high-powered Criss Craft across the chalk-blue waters of a near lagoon. We hauled up for a brief stop at his aunt's hut to gather some mamei, a delicious hard round fruit with tobacco-brown skin and orange flesh that tastes something like apricot. The trees are twenty to thirty feet high with shiny dark leaves, and Victor, completely naked, shinned up into the branches to knock the fruit down with a stick. Under way again we cut the engine and nosed up a criss-crossing of canals banked each side with rushes. The village when we reached it, was not without certain pretensions. Some of the huts are faced with verandas, their columns cast in cement imitating iron, vestiges of the place's former affluence. For a moment, at the turn of the century the mulatto inhabitants carried on a highly remunerative trade with passing vessels, and it would surprise me if some bartering of a similar nature did not still exist.

15

Christmas in Quito

When planning my travels I had taken the precaution of arming myself with a whole battery of letters of introduction to people in every country I was to visit, with the exception of Ecuador. And it turned out that it was in Ecuador that I felt most in need of a helping hand. I was to arrive in Quito on Christmas Eve, and being something of a sentimentalist at heart I did not much relish the idea of spending Christmas alone in a completely strange city. But I took some comfort in Humboldt's assessment of the place. He certainly had found nothing to complain about, indeed quite the opposite. 'The town,' he wrote, 'breathes an atmosphere of luxury and voluptuousness . . . and nowhere is there a population so much given up to the pursuit of pleasure.'

Certain church dignitaries went so far as to complain of the sinful and dissolute life led by many of the religious communities. At least Quito did not sound provincial, nor was its history without event. During the second half of the fifteenth century the Ecuadorian highlands had been invaded by the Incas and only a few decades before the Conquest Quito had been declared the capital of this new extension. After Cuzco it was the second most important city in an empire that ran the entire length of the southern half of the continent, over more than 32° of latitude, approximately the distance from London to Baghdad. Wrested from the Incas by the Spanish, it continued to prosper and acquired a considerable reputation as a cultural centre. By the mid-eighteenth century its fame as an art centre had become widespread. Within a period of some ten years 250 chests of sculpture and painting were exported by way of Guayaquil. There is also proof enough of pronounced activity in the field of architecture – fifty-seven churches in the city alone. Among them, rising from the foundations of the Inca Huayna Capac's palace, is the great sixteenth-century church and monastery of San Francisco, the noblest building of that date in South America.

In reality the city was not quite all I had hoped for. It is a dour little place with no vestige left of luxury, but interesting, because it has a decided character of its own.

Again I was in a land where the women are coifed in trilbys. Those of Spanish descent are a small minority, something like fifteen per cent of the total population. How tawdry our western fashions are when worn inappropriately! Mestizo girls, denying their Indian blood, are clumsy and fat-legged in short skirts. High heels, usually so flattering, only make them totter absurdly as they stump their way over the cobbled streets. With what relief one sees full-blooded Indian women in skirts flaring to just above the ankles, no shoes, and a shawl wrapped tightly round their shapely shoulders! Their necks are encased in strands of glass beads and a trilby sits jauntily on their black heads. No matter what their age or their shape they stride out with aplomb and dignity. The men's *ruanas*, here known as *panchos*, are worn longer than in Colombia and are dyed different shades of red. The coarse homespun wool takes the colour well, each piece varying from scarlet to deep raspberry through rose. The country folk have yet another style of dress. In the cathedral I found two tribesmen praying. They wore loose cotton trousers and square-cut, dark blue *panchos*. Pigtails hung down their backs and they had pale, hairless faces. One had to look twice to see that they were not women.

I saw a quick-trotting Indian carrying a heavy load. A band round the forehead took all the weight as he bent slightly over. An old woman with a staff leading a donkey loaded with charcoal was no surprise in amongst the traffic, and outside the Jesuit church of La Compañía a blind man played an accordion, hidden under a length of dirty wool, presumably to protect it. The music was gay and at the same time mournful with a halting rhythm. The compelling tunes sent dancers spinning like tops. Round and round they turned, arms hanging out. More slowly, a halt, a bend of the knee and then round again. I stood there a good ten minutes listening.

Quito is a place of contrasts: a smart, white-helmeted guard presents arms at the entrance to the governor's palace, a handsome building faced with a long columned loggia, while around the corner a man urinates upon a pile of rubble outside the police station. No false modesty here, they just relieve themselves when they feel like it, outside the butcher's or against a wall. One young man chose the statue of Sucre, a brigadier-general at twenty-four and chief-of-staff of the liberating army, the great national hero who dominates the square named after him.

Few cities have a setting to match Quito. Although it is nearly two miles high, the mountains which circle it are still higher. Overhanging the city is the slumbering snow-capped volcano of Pichincha. I must confess that I never saw it because of low-lying banks of mist that trailed raggedly across the chequer-board pattern of fields above the rooftops. Official Quito rests on a plateau while the old streets dip steeply down the sides of a ravine. Kelemen also commented on their steepness, 'so hilly is the site that even in the pretentious eighteenth century practically everyone went on horseback or on foot – the gentry distinguished by large umbrellas borne by servants; only the president and the bishop rode in coaches, the navigation of which . . . was a special art'.[1] Skirting the town hurries the Machángara River, its brown waters cut deep into the soil. It remains invisible until one is right on top of it. Crowding the banks are the women scrubbing their washing in the old way, with a cactus leaf.

Christmas passed amidst the banging of petards. All night they exploded rockets and flung around squibs which crackled in wreaths of smoke at one's feet. On Boxing Night a special display was held in the great plaza sloping away below the Franciscan church. As the fireworks were home-made and their ingredients somewhat haphazard, anything could have happened. All were noisy and not a few a public danger. Some shot off as planned in a shower of silver rain, others, emitting not a single spark, exploded when ignited. The most alarming, though, were those that corkscrewed with devilish purpose in every direction: up, down, across, into the crowds, even splashing their rain against the dark, looming façade of the church itself. One penetrated the very portals, to burst above the high altar. A feat, one imagines, regarded by the firer as a most auspicious omen. One can only surmise the reaction of the devout at their prayers.

Old crones reduced to skin and bone, and beggars in tattered rags and strange misshapen hats, line the steps of the churches, their wailing supplications rewarded by a scanty sowing of largesse. The congregation, I noticed, come bearing platters of rose leaves which they scatter before entering to pray. Inside, kneeling figures gather in clusters, their heads and shoulders wrapped dark and tight as they sway with devotion. Bright patches of flickering flame illuminate the different madonnas: the tear-stained Dolorosa, or the Madonna described by John in an apocalyptic vision, winged and crowned, poised lightly on a silver crescent moon. There are Pietàs, Virgins of the Immaculate Conception, and an endless parade of saints. These effigies, carved out of wood, are entirely draped in gold leaf on which are painted brocade designs, a technique known as *estofado*. The finish on the faces and hands, ivory flushed with pink, is called the *encarnación*.

Two sculptors of note worked in Quito, and both during the eighteenth century: Bernardo Legarda, a mestizo, and an Indian called Caspicara.

[1] *Baroque and Rococo in Latin America.*

Caspicara's real name was Manuel Chili, or Chil, but he is better known by his nickname 'rough face' in reference to his pock-marked skin.

Quito, like Mexico City and Cuzco, was built on the foundations of a pre-Columbian capital, and as Kelemen points out there was a vast reservoir of native craftsmen at hand to help erect the new city, a fact which helps explain the remarkable quality and number of the buildings. With his invaluable book as a guide I spent my days exploring the churches and monasteries. There is little to recommend the cathedral; but the Jesuit church of La Compañía has a most remarkable brown stone façade designed by Leonhard Deubler, a German friar attached to the monastery. Work on it was begun in 1722; an earthquake intervened; and the project was finished forty-three years later by Leonard Gandolfi, an Italian from Mantua. This perhaps explains the fusion of styles as well as the twisted fluted columns reminiscent of Bernini's baldachino in St Peter's in Rome. John Stephens also remarked on the Corinthian columns entwined with wreaths of roses and lilies; it impressed him that he could slip a hand between the wreaths and the pillar and poke his fingers into Peter's and Paul's net represented in one of the panels.

A pleasant surprise after the deserted monasteries of Mexico was the number of religious institutions in Quito still inhabited by their original Orders, chief amongst them La Merced. I was shown around by a lay brother whose particular interest was the paintings. One portrays Santa María del Socorroco, the patron saint of sailors, cradling a full-rigged ship in her arms. Lining the walls of the upstairs gallery of the main cloister are a series of canvases depicting incidents in the life of St Francis Xavier by Antonio Astudillo, a follower of the mestizo painter Miguel de Santiago. The paintings, dating from about 1750, have a studied naïveté along with a vivid sense of storytelling. There is a complete absence of shadows and the colours are put on in flat washes. Mountains are delineated in a yellow-white, while the sea is pearly grey, and of an unnatural flatness. The colours look powdery, more like gouache than oil, because of having been painted on cotton cloth rather than canvas. The Spanish Crown held a monopoly of linen, and so imported canvas cost twice the price of the homespun cotton of many New World regions. As Kelemen explains, 'cotton cloth, no matter how tightly woven and firmly spanned, absorbs the pigments and dulls the colours'.[1] This, however, in Astudillo's work has a pleasing effect. The colours run from rose to lilac, muted vermilion and a dulled Prussian-blue. St Francis Xavier is always portrayed clad in black which on the cotton has faded to charcoal. He participates in a variety of saintly acts

[1] *Baroque and Rococo in Latin America.*

and is the victim, or hero, of numerous adventures. In one canvas he has narrowly escaped shipwreck and lies prone atop a bed of skins on a shell-strewn shore, surrounded by beplumed, golden-hued Indians. In other pictures he has been transplanted to far Cathay, or is seen in a hospital for plague victims. The patients are bedded in damask-curtained cubicles set in the thickness of the wall, and the saint, like Peter Claver, is kissing their suppurating sores. There are some twenty paintings in the series, and contemplating them I became lost in Astudillo's world. I turned my back on them with an effort. It had been raining earlier in the morning and now the weather was beginning to clear. Gossamer clouds scudded across the sky, thinly veiling the sun. Beyond the monastery, above its roof, rose undulating green hills patched with fields. Down below in the cloister the brothers in their white habits were gathering in the courtyard, drawn there by the warmth. At that moment the telephone rang and one of their number hurried to answer it, unhooking the ear-piece ingenuously hidden away in an old grandfather clock.

I have left San Francisco to the last for I was continually drawn back to it, and to its elliptical stairs theatrically flanked by obelisks. The steps spill outwards towards the cobbles of the square and then reverse, curving inwards as they mount to the austere, grey stone façade. Late Renaissance in design, with Baroque accents, the façade is almost totally lacking in sculpture. Paired columns frame the entrance, and bands of rustication run horizontally across further columns engaged in the wall. The composition is repeated in a second storey where dark stone contrasts sharply with whitewashed brick masonry. Monastery and church together form an elaborate complex covering several city blocks.

It is not known who designed the church, which was founded in 1535. Only the names of two of the master craftsmen, both Indians, have survived. On entering under the choir one is immediately struck by the grandeur of the proportions and the bold execution of the work. One feels that Michelangelo, or rather his buildings in Rome, must have inspired such details as the variety of stone work, the swags of gilded drapery, and the broken pediments. Large canvases darkened with age and elaborately framed blend well with the grey stone. Their gold frames make an effective foil for the elaborately coffered ceiling. The nave advances like a gilded tunnel leading to the dull splendour of the altar.

The main cloister, entered to the right of the church, is adorned with altars and hung with paintings. A fountain splashes in the middle of a garden planted with white geraniums and lemon trees. Wandering out beyond the kitchens I came to a walled garden in which an old

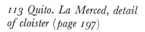

112 Quito. The cloister of La Merced dating from the first half of the seventeenth century. Severe earthquakes necessitated much rebuilding during the eighteenth century (page 197)

113 Quito. La Merced, detail of cloister (page 197)

114 *Quito. La Merced. Santa María del Socorroco, the patron saint of sailors (page 197)*

115 *Quito. La Merced. One of the panels depicting the life of St Francis Xavier by Antonio Astudillo (page 197)*

116 Quito. Steps leading up to the Renaissance-Baroque façade of San Francisco, 'the noblest building of that date in South America' (page 194)

117 Quito. Detail of San Francisco founded in 1535 upon the grounds of Huayna Capac's palace (page 198)

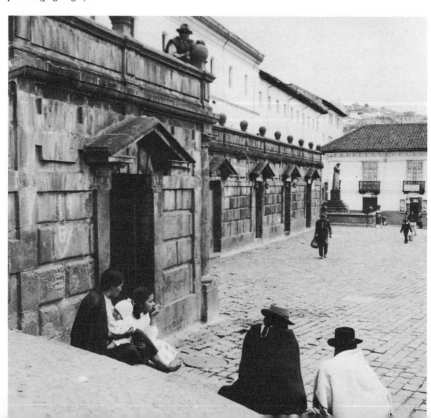

Franciscan was digging. Straightening up and unhitching his habit which had been tucked up in his belt, he offered me the time of day and we made the rounds of his garden together followed by his goat and a soft-eyed, playful dog. Fifteen miles from the Equator and at 9,375 feet there is practically no limit to the plants that can be cultivated: roses, hollyhocks, cabbages, double flowering poppies, antirrhinums and sifomandia. My guide referred to poinsettia as *Flora di Panama*, while some unknown shrub with green berries, he made me understand, was cultivated for its purgative qualities. A feeling of utter peace pervaded the place.

16

Lima

We flew south from Quito over thick jungle, rich land where the rivers sink deep into the soil. Climbing to avoid the bumps we levelled off among luminous clouds ranged in tight banks that dwindled into airy perspectives. Part of the way we flew blind, until eventually the visibility cleared to reveal a totally different landscape. The grass had withered leaving the mountains a naked ochre tinged with red and shaded with grey. I remembered reading somewhere that when no more trees were to be seen it was a sign that Peru had been reached. Peru's great coast is a rainless zone where nothing grows except under irrigation. Although a number of rivers flow from the mountains to the Pacific, their courses are short, none are navigable and few run the year round. This being the dry season, only nerve-like traceries were visible from the air, imprints that lay on the land like the skeleton of a leaf. Thin patches of green where man has scratched the soil relieved the splendid monotony, a waste across which threads the Pan American Highway, a black ribbon drawn across the desert towards Lima.

We flew in low to the approaches of the city, a city the colour of the soil. Spread out around us was nature in one of her grandest guises. The ocean, no longer very blue, beat gently on miles of sand, sand that piles up into blazing dunes backed by the far ranges of the Andes. Giant mountain peaks glazed with eternal snow gleam like white porcelain in the azure haze of distance.

From the Chilean border northward to Ecuador is a stretch of 1,400 miles and the coast of this entire area, a zone measuring anything from ten to a hundred miles in width, is bone-dry desert. Why? Obviously for want of rain, but why no rain next to an ocean? Humboldt also was mystified and set out to investigate the cause. Making elaborate barometric studies he found the water to be 13° cooler than the temperature on land. The relation between temperatures of the sea and land was reversed, and 'thus', as von Hagen so aptly explains, 'when the air from over the ocean rolled on to the land its temperature was raised instead of being lowered, and so its moisture-carrying capacity was increased. In place of condensation, absorption took place, and so long as these conditions prevailed, rain could not fall.'[1] Later investigation delved still further and found that the low temperature of the waters, an average 60°, was due to the offshore ocean currents. The entire length of the coast is bathed by an upwelling of cold water, a northerly branch of the Pacific Antarctic drift now known as the Humboldt Current. Only 12° south of the Equator and at an altitude of five hundred feet, Lima would have a tropical climate but for this current which holds the city temperature to an average 75° Fahrenheit. What little moisture the wind brings landward turns to fog with the result that the sun is obscured, or at best, reduced to a glowing orange ball, for weeks at a time during the winter season. The Peruvians, proud of their city, do their utmost to ignore this murky inconvenience. They shrug it off, referring to it as the *niebla perlada*, or 'pearly haze'. *Garúa*, its proper name, is far more appropriate and better suggests its clawing dampness that reduces the dust in the streets to a sticky paste.

Given the climate one wonders how Pizarro ever came to pick this particular spot as the site on which to found his city. According to Herrera, the Spanish historian, Alvarado's threatened inroad into Peru was responsible. Almagro, sent north by Pizarro to intercept the governor of Guatemala, had come to terms with him; but as Almagro did not have the money with him to pay the sum agreed upon, they set out together to meet Pizarro, then at Cuzco. Pizarro, informed of the result of these negotiations and not wishing Alvarado to see more of the riches of the country than could be helped, moved forward to meet them. The encounter took place in Pizarro's camp on the shores of Callao Bay, near the banks of the Rimac River. Looking around him Pizarro was impressed with the gentle plain mounting to the alps. There was no doubt that Cuzco, withdrawn among the mountains, was altogether too far from the sea for a people dependent on Europe for their trade. This site was not only adjacent to a possible port but also centrally situated. It never rained, but the dryness was counteracted by the *garúa*, which, as Prescott put it, 'hung like a curtain over the valley sheltering it from the rays of a tropical sun, a refreshing moisture'.[2] Prescott might have enthused over the climate, but not so the original inhabitants of Peru. The Incas believed the place to be the unhealthiest spot imaginable and were delighted when they heard that the conquistador was contemplating building there. They no doubt expected that the swirling mists would be the death of the hated Spaniards.

[1] *South America Called Them.*

[2] William H. Prescott, *History of the Conquest of Peru*, edited by John Foster Kirk, Bickers & Son Ltd., London, 1890.

The city was founded on 6 January 1535, the feast of the Epiphany, and was named *Ciudad de los Reyes*, City of the Kings, to commemorate the coming of the Magi. This grandiloquent title went out of use within the first generation, and was supplanted by the present name, a corruption of 'Rimac' which in Quechua means 'one who speaks', a reference to the murmuring of the river. Pizarro himself traced the outlines of the chief plaza, *Plaza de Armas*, and on the same day laid the corner stone of the cathedral where his big-boned skeleton reposes in a glass coffin.

Alas, the plaza is a bitter disappointment, for today little remains of the old luxurious capital of the viceroys. Lima has been shaken by a series of severe earthquakes roughly every fifty years, the most devastating having occurred in October 1746. Little in the present city antedates this catastrophe. Indeed a majority of the buildings around the *Plaza de Armas* dates no further back than the present century. Both the Archbishop's Palace and the City Hall have been entirely reassembled within the last forty-three years. Their great wooden *miradors*, based on the designs of those originally there, look all wrong, as does the Viceroy's Palace rebuilt in 1938 as the *Palacio de Gobierno*. Shaken and restored on various occasions it had already lost most of its allure by the time Basil Hall, an Englishman travelling in Peru in 1824, arrived. 'The Palace,' he wrote, 'had a good deal the air of a native court in India, the same admixture of meanness and magnificence which displays the wealth and labour and at the same time the want of taste.' To enter one passed by a dirty court 'like that of a stable yard, with the ragged soldiers of the guard lounging about smoking cigars'.[1] There is nothing shabby about the Palace these days, rather is it over-splendid. Guards, many of them coloured, are much in evidence in silvered and beplumed helmets goose-stepping smartly backwards and forwards before the blindingly white stone façade.

Hall described the audience chamber of the Viceroy's Palace as long and narrow:

an antique room with a dark wainscoting carved over with gilt ornaments. The floor was spread with rich Gobelin tapestry; and on each side was ranged a long line of sofas and high backed armchairs covered in purple velvet. The windows which were high and narrow looked on a large square court thickly planted with oranges and guavas, kept fresh and cool by fountains playing in the angles.

Hall did not mention that among the trees was the fig planted by Pizarro. It still bears, but no one dares pick the fruit: according to an obscure superstition, the figs bring unhappiness to anyone who eats them.

[1] Basil Hall, *Peru*, London, 1824.

In this same audience chamber used to hang full-length portraits of the forty-four viceroys who governed Peru. The Limenians will tell you of the curious coincidence that the hall was exactly filled when the Revolutionary forces entered the city, there being no place for another painting.

The north side of the Presidential Palace is the site of the original building inhabited by Pizarro, or the Marquis of Atavillos as he was usually known after the Conquest. It was here also that he was killed by members of the opposing side in the civil wars fought by the conquistadors. The Marquis was at dinner with his half-brother and a friend, when his Indian servant rushed in to warn him that a band of conspirators had gained the palace. Seizing a sword and wrapping his left arm in a cloak he jumped to the attack. 'Traitors!' he cried, 'have you come to kill me in my own house?' But the Marquis was about seventy at the time and hopelessly outnumbered. Eventually a wound in the throat brought him down. Lying on the floor he traced the sign of the cross in his own blood and kissing it drew his last breath.

The place where the Marquis fell is still pointed out. The position might be correct, but the original floor has long since disappeared, as have all other vestiges of any possible interest. On the other hand the Conqueror's remains in the cathedral have an air of authenticity. Unlocking a chapel door the sexton held up a candle to a dusty glass coffin reposing on a shelf some six feet from the ground. Within, looking like worm-eaten parchment, lay the naked corpse of a very tall man. It was hard to distinguish much in the gloom. The body was held together with wires and there were traces on the skin of the mortuary binding practised by the Incas. My guide wanted me to see the fatal gash in the neck and shoulders but the candle was guttering too much in the draught.

Not much is known about Pizarro, for unfortunately, unlike Cortés, he left no records – he could not write. The Museo de América in Madrid has a portrait of him which is 'generally considered' to be the most authentic, but the painting has no pedigree and is of little merit. Pizarro appears to have been of dark complexion with a well-shaped head, large eyes and a prominent, slightly beaked nose. Reading Gómara one gathers that he was temperate in his habits, ate and drank sparingly, 'usually rose an hour before dawn', was fond of gambling 'and cared little of the quality of those with whom he played'. He was 'punctual in attendance to business' and modest in his person, 'affecting on public occasions a black cloak with a white hat and shoes of the same colour'.[1]

It is remarkable what this man achieved when one considers his

[1] *Historia general de las Indias.*

humble beginnings. He was the son of an infantry colonel and a peasant woman of no education, 'so humble', writes Prescott, 'that gossip would have him suckled as a babe by a sow'.[1] The year of his birth is not known, and he never married. He did, however, have two children, a son and a daughter by an Indian princess of Inca blood, a daughter of Atahualpa, and granddaughter of the great Huayna Capac. Both children survived him. His son died in his teens and his daughter, Francisca, subsequently married her uncle Hernando Pizarro. No title descended to the Marquis's illegitimate offspring, but in the third generation, during the reign of Philip IV, the title was revived in favour of Don Juan Hernando Pizarro who was created *Marqués de la Conquista*, Marquis of the Conquest, and given a liberal pension by the government.

But more of Pizarro later; for the moment we return to the City of Kings and to Callao, its port. Hall described arriving at Callao and riding up to the city along a perfectly straight road, 'the rise so gradual as to be almost imperceptible'. On approaching:

everything speaks of past splendour . . . At the top of the road there is an approach a mile in length, between two double rows of fine trees – public walks and elegant stone benches all being now in ruins and choked up with weeds and shrubs. The principal entry is at the end of this grand approach, through a triumphal arch, tawdry and falling to decay, with the crown of Spain mouldering on the top.

The churches, according to Hall, made a fine effect from the distance, but turned out on close inspection 'to be very paltry structures'.[2] Indeed, owing to the frequent earthquakes, the old buildings were generally erected of brick and *adobe* with the upper storeys often of lighter construction. *Adobe*, clay and reeds are the building materials of the coast, and one has the impression that a deluge would immediately lay them in ruins. The cane-thatched, mud-walled huts and houses would crumble in heavy rains like a child's sand-pies before a rising sea.

I reversed Mr Hall's arrival and instead drove out through the city gates down to Callao. Within no time we caught sight of the mist. Behind lay dusty Lima bathed in sunshine while in front was the *garúa*, a white line hanging over the sea. Rutted grass tracks and mud walls border the road along one side of which runs a tramway. Behind the walls are fields of cotton, maize and sugar cane. I remember similar surroundings driving out of Cairo to Heliopolis. There is a definite oriental flavour about Lima, an impression given partly by the light and the dust and, of course, by the sand. The town taxis are definitely related to the transport found lurking around the picturesque ruins of

[1] *History of the Conquest of Peru.*
[2] *Peru.*

the Middle East, museum pieces with no mudguards and whole sides of the bonnet missing. Their engines, held together by wires, pump up intermittent jets of steam from capless radiators. It is a miracle that these cars work at all, particularly as they are always overloaded. The passengers, however, manage to ride in cramped quarters with a certain degree of dignity, an illusion enhanced by the unaccustomed height of the vehicles. It does not take much effort to imagine that they are carriages. The drivers have the habit of banging on the side of the door, for of course they have no horns. The banging, oddly enough, is far more effective than the most strident klaxon.

In writing about Lima I must be careful not to give the wrong impression. I spent a little over a month in the city and found myself becoming increasingly fond of it. The trouble, I think, is that one expects too much. It was, after all, the chief seat of government for the whole of Spanish South America for a period of 183 years: only comparatively late in its history was the viceroyalty split into two, and eventually into three. New Granada was carved out of north Peru in 1718. Chile was detached from the south in 1734, followed by Río de La Plata in 1770. Venezuela, adjacent to New Granada, became a Captain-Generalship. The elevation of subordinates to viceregal rank diminished the consequence of Lima, but it still retained its court. All the time one is conscious in Lima of the wish to impress. The grandiose is often achieved, but only too often quality has been sacrificed in the process. Certainly there are the exceptions, such as the famous Torre Tagle Palace or the beautiful seventeenth-century ante-sacristy of San Agustín.

The sacristy has a dado of glazed tiles and a magnificent coffered ceiling in natural wood picked out in deep turquoise, red and gold. The shell tympana over the doors and the windows are modifications introduced a hundred years later. In the embrasure of one of the windows facing the entrance stands a realistic, life-size figure of Death, the work of the mestizo sculptor Baltasar Gavilán. The Reaper is portrayed with shrivelled tendons and a frenziedly grimacing skeleton head. He draws his bow aiming the fatal arrow at the incoming visitor. So vividly rendered is this grisly spectre that it is said to have frightened its sculptor to death when one night he unexpectedly came upon his own finished work.

Another handsome room is the chapter-house of the Dominican monastery which once housed the first university established in the Americas. Here, within the chapter house's boldly rusticated walls, the earliest degrees granted in the New World were handed out in 1551.

There is no doubt that Lima, judging it by the extent of its viceregal remains, compares rather poorly to its rival, Mexico City. I am not sure, though, that what little remains is not of a stronger individual stamp and, in the long run, more subtle in its appeal. Patience and above all human contacts are vitally necessary, and given these elements the city then slowly unfolds, revealing itself like some exotic bloom, like the elusive night-flowering cereus.

I was staying in the old section of town next door to the Torre Tagle Palace. The palace was built by José de Tagle y Brancho, a Spanish knight who came to the New World as a captain of the lancers. One is immediately struck by its grandeur aud curious about the circumstances of its construction. After successful exploits in Chile against the Araucanian Indians, Tagle was given a marquisate and the highly lucrative position of Permanent Paymaster of the Royal Armada of the South Sea, in other words the Pacific silver fleet. With the title came a plot of land in the very heart of the capital. The house was completed in 1735 and one can see that no expense was spared in its building. Stone was brought from Panama and mahogany for the timbered ceilings from Costa Rica. Hard palm wood was also imported for its *miradores* and balustrades. These *miradores*, so much a feature of Lima, are of Islamic origin, brought to Spain by the Moors. A row of shutters upon horizontal bars opens outward to allow the ladies to peer down upon passers-by without being seen. They are replicas of the turned latticed *mushrabiyyahs* found throughout the East. 'They were in keeping,' as Kelemen writes, 'with the Lima custom that required ladies to go fully veiled in the streets.'[1] The entrance to the house is framed with splendid broken pediments, and although now the Ministry of Foreign Affairs it is of easy access.

The furnishing for the Torre Tagle Palace and other similar houses are in the Museum of Fine Arts and in the Pedro de Osma Collection: benches with spindled and gilded backs, gilded and lacquered cabinets and chairs set with sturdy legs and exaggeratedly turned arms. Much of the upholstery is brocade encrusted with gold and silver embroidery and further embellished with applications of rich coloured velvets. Some of the elaborately carved pieces made from dark tropical woods are obviously of Indonesian origin. On exhibit are two great gilded candelabra in the form of winged eagles, or are they perhaps condors? Their wings are outspread as in a lectern and in each feather is a sliver of mirror set to catch the light that would have been thrown by the candles branching out from the cruel beaked heads. The paintings I noticed were invariably set in heavy gilt frames, also inlaid with mirror. Mirrors imported from Spain were a great luxury in the colonies, and in order not to waste them when broken the gesso workers of Lima invented this method of using the pieces. They are decorative in a gaudy way, but splayed out like a peacock tail, they often swamp the paintings.

[1] *Baroque and Rococo in Latin America.*

118 Lima. San Francisco, main portal (page 209)

120 (opposite) Lima. Monastery of San Francisco (page 209)

119 Lima. San Francisco, roof (page 209)

121 Lima. Cloister of San Francisco monastery (page 209)

122 *Death by the eighteenth-century Limenian, mestizo sculptor Baltasar Gavilán* (page 205)

123 *A tapada painted by Pancho Fierro* (1803–79) (page 213)

124 *Manuel Amat y Junyent Planella Aymerich y Santa Pau, the viceroy from 1761–66* (page 211)

125 Lima. Quinta de
Presa (page 211)

126, 127 (right) Lima.
The Torre Tagle Palace
(below) Detail of the
ornately carved wooden
balconies, or miradores
(page 206)

128 *Santa Rosa of Lima by the Colombian painter Vazques Ceballos (1638–1711) (page 209)*

129 *Lady of the viceregal court at Lima. Painter unknown (page 207)*

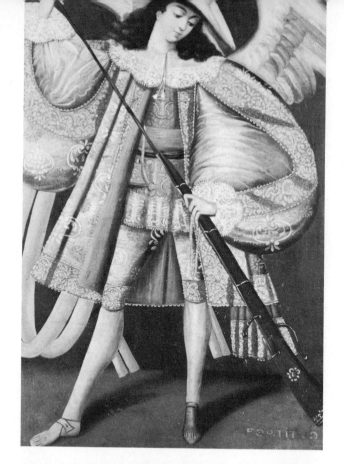

130 *Archangel,*
Bolivian School
(*page 207*)

131 *Virgin and*
Child, Cuzco School
(*page 207*)

Suffering already from surfeit, I found the Pedro de Osma Collection a veritable Aladdin's cave of prismatic reflections, of repoussé silver and gilded gesso. Señor de Osma lives in a large house in the fashionable residential district with a collection that overflows into several dependencies. He received us for drinks before dinner and my memory of the tour is completely unreal.

The paintings mentioned above are of a special style generally called the Cuzco school, a folk art (as Martin Soria points out) whose products are not unlike sixteenth-century icons, 'Byzantine icons where gold is sprinkled liberally over the garments'.[1] Already richly ornamented in themselves, the pictures would have looked better in simpler frames. The subjects are principally religious and the style is a flat one wherein the painters made no attempt to render drapery realistically. All garments are patterned in gold leaf, sprigged with flowers and bordered with yards of metallic lace. The gold leaf was applied like so many sequins to the canvas. Their dark colours have faded and cracked to even darker bituminous browns and olive-greens. In this state, brushed with gold, they resemble the tooled and embossed surfaces of Cordova leather screens. More formal representations of the Virgin show her garlanded in wreaths of tightly packed fritillaries, tulips and pinks; motifs obviously culled by the mestizo painters of Cuzco from canvases of the Flemish school. The Virgin herself has dyed plumes spraying out from her crown or bunched at the side of a stiffened headpiece clasped into position by a large drop jewel. Her dress stands out so stiffly all round her that were she to move her walk would be but a gentle swaying. Across the skirt are looped swags of pearls, twined into ropes caught up with satin bows. Her hands are beringed and lace cuffs turn back from her wrists on which are tied bracelets of pearls. Her ear-rings, small chandeliers, hang from under her cascading hair which is also starred with jewels. She is in fact dressed in the height of Lima fashion. We know from previous travellers of the important jewellery worn by the women at the viceroy's court. Edmond Temple wrote that 'the quantity of diamonds and pearls was immense'.[2] So ponderous were some of the ear-rings that they required a gold chain passed over the top of the head to relieve the weight on the ears.

Other popular Cuzco subjects were the archangels, portrayed life-size. Many such paintings exist, the earliest dating from about the middle of the seventeenth century. The Museum of Fine Arts has a delightful St Michael dressed, the catalogue maintains, in officer's uniform. Perhaps, but he is far too rouged and befrilled to inspire much confidence as a soldier, nor does one have much faith in the musket he

[1] *Art and Architecture in Spain and Portugal and their American Dominions, 1500 to 1800.*
[2] Edmond Temple, *Travels in Various Parts of Peru*, London, 1830.

is priming. With luck it might make a pop loud enough to scare away sparrows scavenging in a monastery garden.

On the rare occasions that the mestizo painters of the Cuzco school did not depict religious subjects they worked, with a certain nostalgia no doubt, on representations of the Inca race. One sees portraits of the different emperors and of the princesses married to Spaniards. Martín de Loyola, Viceroy of Chile and nephew of St Ignatius, is shown on his marriage day with his royal bride. She is represented in the untailored garments of her people. Behind her on a dais sit her family, sheltering from the sun under a striped parasol worked in flamingo and parrot feathers. Dwarfs are in attendance and strange diadems crown their heads. Portraits purporting to be of Huáscar Inca and Atahualpa, the half-brothers who were reigning at the time of the Conquest, give a somewhat garbled idea of the sacred *llautu*, or Inca crown. Garcilaso de la Vega, himself related through his mother to the royal family, writes that it was a form of braid 'the width of a finger, made of several colours, and rolled four or five times around the head'. Subjects of noble birth were allowed to wear similar headgear but 'on condition that it would not be of just any colour, only black'. Certain of the nobles:

wore their hair in the shape of a toque that came down over the lobes of their ears and left their foreheads and temples free; while others had the right to show half their ears – but only half – and no one had the right to crop his hair the way the king did. These traditions were faithfully held to during the entire history of Peru.[1]

In the paintings the *llautu* looks like a turban or hat, but from what one can gather this is a somewhat free interpretation. Many have tried to describe it, but Oviedo in his *Historia de las Indias* seems the most precise. He calls it a tassel of wool, 'as fine as any silk', and deep crimson in colour. This tassel was gathered in the middle, trimmed very evenly and made to stand up in the form of a sweeping aigrette, below which hung a deep fringe covering the forehead and eyebrows. So deep did it hang that in order to see properly the Inca was obliged to draw the fringe aside. Worn with the *llautu* were two *corequenque* feathers. One can see them in the paintings, sticking up at the sides. The *corequenque* was supposedly a mountain bird so rare anyone found hunting them was immediately killed. Actually the *corequenque* is thought to have been a mythical bird like the phoenix; according to experts the feathers came from a species of nightjar.

The first entry in my Lima diary records a visit to the church of San

---

[1] Garcilaso de la Vega (1539–1616), *The Royal Commentaries of the Inca*, translated by Maria Joles, Cassell, London, 1963.

Francisco, the most important example of seventeenth-century architecture in the city. The church's brick and plaster exterior simulates rusticated courses of stone and is painted light grey while the mouldings, architraves and cornices are picked out in white. The main portal is very impressive, like a *retablo* of gilded wood translated into stone. The great cloister faced with tiles from Seville gives an idea of the opulence and the scale of living once maintained in the city. I mounted the majestic stairway of brick leading to the upper gallery in a late afternoon sun that threw slanting pools of light, patterning the floor with lunettes alternating with arches. From the roof there is an excellent view of the city, stretching out flat and dusty, the colour of the pale, treeless hills which rise to the back of it.

I made a point of going to Santo Domingo to see the tomb of Santa Rosa of Lima. In the annals of the Church Santa Rosa is remembered as the sweetest and the most beautiful of saintly characters. Born in 1586, she died in 1617 at the age of thirty-one and was canonized in 1671, the only woman to be thus honoured in the New World. Much loved by the painters, she is seen crowned with roses in a halo of light in nearly every church throughout Latin America. A sanctuary now stands on the site of her parents' house where she was born and passed most of her short life. It is here, according to a legend, that there bloomed the first roses acclimatized to Latin American soil, and this no doubt influenced the Saint to relinquish her baptismal name, Isabel Flores de Oliva, and call herself Rosa de Santa María. It would seem that she had been conscious of her vocation from earliest youth. Admiring St Catherine of Siena, she modelled herself on this austere personage. She founded a hospital for the poor and herself led a life of absolute self-abnegation. '*On dit,*' writes François Cali, '*qu'elle se frottait le visage avec du poivre de Cayenne, plongeait ses mains, qu'elle avait belles, dans de la chaux vive, attirait les moustiques avec des onguents . . .*'[1] But all to no avail, for she died still beautiful. So she appears in the recumbent marble figure on her tomb commissioned by Pope Clement x from Melchor Caffa, a Maltese sculptor working in Rome at the time of her canonization. It is a sentimental work inspired by Bernini's well-known Death of Beata Lodovica Albertoni.

Diametrically opposed in character was Michaela or Miquita Villegas, better known as *La Perricholi*, the most popular woman, after Santa Rosa, in the history of Lima. Her tempestuous career inspired both writers and composers to choose her as heroine. Witness Prosper Mérimée's *Le Carrosse du Saint Sacrement* and Offenbach's operetta. She appears again in Thornton Wilder's *The Bridge of San Luis Rey*. Her beginnings were humble, of Indian and Spanish parentage, with

[1] *L'Art des Conquistadors*, text by François Cali, Barthaud, Paris, 1960.

perhaps a touch of Negro blood thrown in. The date of her birth is as obscure as the rest of her childhood, but it must have been about the 1730s. At the age of twelve she was already singing in cafés, and at twenty she was appearing on the stage of the Coliseo acting the great ladies in the plays of Lope de Vega. It was said of her that she was the best actress, not only of Lima, but of the entire Spanish speaking world. In my researches I found a reference to a marble bust of the young Michaela wherein the author talks of her 'meagre, boyish breasts', and of the roguishness of her eyes. There is also mention of a portrait 'that does not bear out the legend of her beauty'. I have made endless inquiries, but neither bust nor portrait has ever come to light. A print of her exists in the Museo de la Quinta de Presa, but this is certainly an apocryphal likeness because her long black hair is dressed in the fashion of the mid-1800s. In any case it is surely better, that we should be obliged to compose our own image of her. If not beautiful, she must have had the gift of making herself appear so, for the whole of Lima was at her feet, including its sexagenarian viceroy. For close on fourteen years she was Don Manuel Amat's mistress, and if the stories one reads about her are true, their relationship must have been a wearing one for the viceroy. Capricious, witty, proud, she scandalized the stuffy Castilian society, and often her whims seem to have been inspired by a spirit of revenge, as if she were paying back generations of slights meted out by the conquerors to the people of her caste. When in one of these moods she made Don Manuel pay highly for her favours. One night she sent her royal lover down to the fountain in the *Plaza de Armas* to fetch her a glass of water, the only water, she pretended, that could quench her thirst. Another time it was her mules; they were not being properly fed and the viceroy must needs interview the grooms. Ignoring the fetters that tradition imposed on the Spanish women, she flaunted herself in public. One afternoon returning from the smart Almeda de los Descalzos, her luxurious carriage passed a priest who was bearing the last communion to a dying person. Moved by the contrast between her own scandalous life and the humility of a minister of God, she made him climb into the chaise while she followed on foot. Later, it was said, she presented the carriage, mules, grooms and liveries to this same parish. Her unpredictable behaviour scandalized the court. Unable to snub her in public, the courtiers started referring to the Michaela as *la perra chola*, the half-caste bitch. But here again they were bested, for the enchantress knew very well how to cope with the intended slight. She immediately converted the harsh phrase into a term of endearment by simply adding a diminutive: *perrita*, little dog, which eventually became *perri choli*. It is as *La Perricholi* that we remember her.

There are various theories about *La Perricholi*'s end: one, that on

Don Manuel's recall to Spain, she forsook the stage and entered a convent; another that she married. But I think I prefer Thornton Wilder's version, that she just disappeared, her beauty consumed by smallpox. In his novel she sells her elegant little palace and moves to a farm in the hills. The farm is surely a literary invention, but not the little palace. I found it eventually, or what is left of it, in the northern outskirts of the city, almost on the desert's edge. A *mirador* overlooks the external wall, but the house itself has disappeared long ago, having been swept away in one of the many earthquakes. Something, however, remains of the garden and from its walls one looks out over the desolate slopes of the Cerro San Cristóbal, a cone-shaped hill on which are packed the mud-walled houses of the Lima poor.

La Perricholi can also be associated with another building not far from her own house: the attractive Quinta de Presa built for Count Fernando Carrillo y Albornoz from designs by Amat. In addition to his administrative talents Amat was a gifted architect. In Barcelona he was responsible for the Virreina Palace and several other buildings in Lima itself: the Rococo church of Santo Cristo de los Milagros, better known as Las Nazarenas, the tower of Santo Domingo and the already mentioned Quinta de Presa which was built within the city walls as a rustic retreat. No longer rustic, it now stands within the grounds of the *Guardia Republicana* barracks. Soldiers pass and repass across its paved yard but the building itself and the gardens beyond have been carefully restored. The house dates from 1766 and reminds one of country estates in Central Europe. The stone-trimmed windows with little carved balconies and the blue-washed walls could easily be Austrian, or perhaps Piedmontese. Amat, we know, had been much under the influence of the Bibienas, a family of North Italian stage designers, and in point of fact there is something charmingly theatrical about the Quinta. A small moat fed by a branch of the Rimac fronts the house and is crossed by a little balustraded bridge. The balustrades are built of chocolate-coloured stone capped with formalized tubs of geraniums. Further watercourses flash through the desert garden and these, tradition has it, were lined with silver in the viceroy's time.

In the entrance hall on the first floor hangs a portrait of Amat. He is small and immaculately turned out with a tightly prinked wig. The eyes are lively and the mouth small and pursed, the expression somewhat affected. From the portrait one could imagine him to have been a fussy, bustling little character. At any rate we know he was an ardent lover and a man of considerable taste with an original turn of mind, if one is to judge from the decoration of the Quinta. At the back of the Quinta a covered veranda almost as spacious as the interior looks out over the garden. Kelemen associates 'its tall, slim columns' with a pavilion in

Ispahan. Strangely evocative, too, are its dust-powdered arbours, its grape-shaded walks, its pale, wide open roses and the general tumbled air of jasmine-starred neglect.

I learned a great deal about Lima's old customs from the poetess, Chambuca Granda. She has a beautiful voice and chooses her words carefully in describing the habits of another era. 'Lima has changed so much in thirty years, and now to find any semblance of its former charm one has to know the life of its families. It is the unimportant details that I remember so well.' She tells how the gentlemen callers at her grandmother's house were always handed buttonholes as they stepped into the hall, while another maid scented their handkerchiefs with eau-de-Cologne. 'Flowers played an important role in the home and would be arranged in plates without water; they smell much stronger just before dying.' In her grandmother's day the women wore their hair carefully plaited and studded with jasmine, each flower carefully threaded with a ball of mimosa. In the evening the servants would carry in lighted braziers against the damp, and sweets would be handed around in little silver-wrapped packages, a secret confection of the nuns who had been making them for longer than anyone could tell. 'I remember also little green apples criss-crossed with incisions, into which had been packed sweet-smelling, aromatic arabesques, pointed here and there with a clove.' It was with a friend of Chambuca Granda that we visited the proud Aliaga house, the oldest inhabited house in the city. That same evening we dined at the Plaza de Acho bullring built by Amat. Distorted shadows thrown by flare torches leapt out at us from the uneven whitewashed walls. It is a splendid place, worthy of its viceroy architect.

Those who can remember the closing years of the nineteenth century will recount the niceties of Peruvian etiquette. A gentleman walking along the pavement was obliged to weave a sinuous course, winding in and out according to the social standing of the individuals he met. His equal or superior he passed on the outside; those less fortunate he passed on the inside. There must have been moments of hesitation. Families were at home every evening to their friends; people just walked in without ceremony and refreshments consisted of liquors, sweetmeats and a glass of water.

To learn about earlier times we must consult their writers, all of whom dwell at length on the charm of the Limenian women. Max Radiguet found them on the small side, svelte, well-proportioned and pale in complexion, *'mais qui n'a rien de maladif'*. Their great pride was their hands and feet, *'qui ont toute la perfection désirable. Les femmes dans leur intérieur ne portaient ni souliers ni bas; on se fardait le pied absolument comme le visage.'*[1]

[1] Max Radiguet, *Souvenirs de L'Amérique Espagnole*, Michel Lévy Frères, Paris, 1874.

Hall commented on their dress. 'The effect of the whole is exceedingly striking; but whether its gracefulness be sufficient to compensate for its indelicacy to an European eye will depend much upon the stranger's taste, and his habits of judging what he sees in foreign countries. Some travellers,' he concluded, 'insist upon forcing everything into comparison with what they have left at home, and condemn or approve according to this unreasonable standard.' Hall makes it quite clear that he personally had no complaints: the appearances of the women 'afforded much amusement and sometimes not a little vexation'. He is talking, of course, about the famous *tapadas*:

In the cool part of the day, for about an hour and a half before sunset, the ladies walk abroad, dressed in a manner as far as I know unique, and certainly highly characteristic of the spot. This dress consists of two parts, one called the *soya*, and the other the *manto*. The first is a petticoat made to fit so tightly that, being at the same time quite elastic, the form of the limbs is rendered distinctly visible. The *manto*, or cloak, is also a petticoat, but, instead of hanging about the heels as all honest petticoats ought to do, it is drawn over the head, breast and face; and is kept so close by the hands, which it also conceals, that no part of the body, except one eye and sometimes only a small portion of the eye, is perceptible.

Sacheverell Sitwell evokes a whole city of cyclopean women, 'cyclop heads with something of a sea-shape to them – they move and turn about rather like a sleek family of seals',[1] irresistible, swaying across one's vision and invested with the mysterious charm of women at a masked ball. With feminine guile the *tapadas* had turned a manner of dress designed originally to safeguard their chastity into a formidable weapon of seduction. There was also something very fascinating about the *tapadas'* little white satin slippers, and again I turn to Radiguet who refers to them as *'la pierre de touche de l'élégance, l'arme sans merci de la séduction. Nous nous inquiétions,'* he writes, *'de leur existence éphémère et plus encore de savoir comment un pied délicat pouvait, dans cette frêle enveloppe, braver sans être brûlé ou endolori le rude et ardent contact du pavé.'* Indeed, *'le pavé livre une telle guerre d'extermination aux souliers de satin, qu'il existe un marché spécialement affecté à cet article, où tous les samedis soir la plus charmante moitié de la population vient faire sa provision de la semaine – adorable population de sylphides.'*[2]

Tapadas, alas, are no longer to be seen in the Lima streets and I must admit that the few well-dressed women I saw walking about differed little from their counterparts in the other capitals of the world. This change, I am told, is of a comparatively recent date. Mr Enock, a

---

[1] Sacheverell Sitwell, *Golden Wall and Mirador*, Weidenfeld & Nicolson Ltd., London, 1964.
[2] *Souvenirs de L'Amérique Espagnole*.

mining expert travelling in Peru in 1907, still found the Limenians underdressed. He writes that they are often prepared to sacrifice their health to their vanity, 'and even on chilly and misty evenings these fair butterflies of fashion will be seen in their light costumes, without outer wraps; presenting a curious contrast to the husbands, brothers, or friends who accompany them – protected from the misty weather in overcoats, with the collars turned up!'[1]

[1] C. Reginald Enock, F.R.G.S., *The Andes and The Amazon. Life and Travel in Peru*, Charles Scribners & Sons, New York, 1907.

17

Of Guano and Mummies

Another world opens up to the explorer of Lima's beaches. To reach
the southern shoreline I drove out through the smart residential district,
a narrow belt of vegetation bounded on one side by the sea and on the
other divided from the desert by groves of untidy, dusty blue eucalyptus.
These bark-shedding giants give the impression of having always been
an integral part of the landscape. Actually the five hundred or more
species of the tree are, with very few exceptions, native to Australia. One
wonders when they were first brought to the New World. Were the
padres responsible for planting them, or were they introduced by the
railway builders? As the trees are very fast-growing and the timber
extremely durable, they would have been a convenient source for
ties.

The road reaches the sea at the largest, most important suburb of
Lima, Miraflores, a pleasant, sleepy place with a distinctly Edwardian
flavour. From Miraflores the road follows the coastline past Agua Dulce,
Punta Hermosa and Pacusaña, small resorts where one can lunch
overlooking the beach. Typical Peruvian dishes are *chupe de mariscos*,
a semi-tropical shellfish *bouillabaisse*, and *cebiche*, prepared with fresh
fish marinated in lime juice and highly seasoned with raw onion and hot
chili. The Peruvian yellow potato is very good and is usually served
mashed up with olive oil. The menus are normally prone to be over
starchy. A great favourite is *frijoles batidos con arroz*, boiled rice with a
purée of beans. Another popular dish is *olluo 'uito con charquí*, beef cut
into thin strips and lightly fried with vegetables and flavoured with
herbs, something like Japan's *sukiyaki* and said to be a recipe inherited
from the Incas. For puddings they have *mazamorra morada*, a dark wine-
coloured jelly made from a pink sweetcorn with fruit cut up in it. Beans
are beaten up with sugar to make a purée the consistency of *marron
glacé*, and there is a delicious ice-cream made from a fruit that only
grows around Lima. I was unable to find its correct name, but the
restaurants refer to it as *lancome* or *loucoumi*. I have seen the fruit growing:

it is about the size of a tangerine, ripening from green to orange on a tree some twenty feet high with dark, glossy leaves. Apparently one cannot eat the fruit raw. I had it as a concentrated syrup, chilled to the consistency of a water ice. It had a faintly scented flavour.

Peru also has its special drinks, like the pisco sour, to name only one, which is made from a very potent brandy distilled from wine produced in the Valley of the Ica, near Pisco. The ingredients are two parts pisco, one part *jarabe de goma*, a kind of sugar syrup, and one part lemon juice. These are shaken with crushed ice and the white of egg and topped with a dash of angostura bitters. The secret lies in shaking it well before adding the lemon. With pisco sours one often eats a delicacy known as *antcuchos*. These are squares of beef heart prepared with vinegar and chili sauce and skewered on bamboo sticks. I failed completely to guess the ingredients of what my Peruvian friends called an *allgarrobina*. From what I could gather it is made from the beans of the *espinoo*, which I imagine is a species of acacia. The drink, anyhow, tastes something like an Alexander and is considered by the Peruvians to be a powerful aphrodisiac. *Chicha morada*, another speciality of the country, is found mostly in small villages. It is a non-alcoholic, pink-coloured liquid made from purple corn, an Inca beverage popular with many other earlier pre-Columbian peoples.

Callao, the port of Pisco, was about 140 miles distant. I drove there with the idea of finding a boat in which I could sail to one of the principal roosts of the guano birds, the Chincha Islands due south of Pisco Bay. Unfortunately I discovered too late that a special pass was necessary to land on them. I did, however, manage to circle the islands which look like great, opaque icebergs, yellowed and glistening from the countless droppings with which they are lacquered. Though never very rough, there is always a heavy swell off the coast, and for someone who is not a good sailor, the gently heaving Pacific can prove quite an ordeal.

Garcilaso de la Vega in the sixteenth century first mentioned the guano deposits. He wrote of the Incas' agriculture, praising their ingenuity in terracing the mountainous land. 'The irrigation works carried out by them appear fantastic to us. The channels, some of them more than sixty-two miles long, are hollowed out of the rock, pass through tunnels and across valleys by means of aqueducts sometimes fifty to sixty-five feet long.' But before the terraces could be tilled, earth had to be brought in and fertilized. 'The fertilizers they used differed according to the region. In the Cuzco valley, and in its environs, the maizefields were fertilized with human manure...', which was carefully collected, dried and used in powdered form. 'In the high country, where it is too cold to grow corn, potato fields were enriched with animal manure. Along the entire coast . . . the only fertilizer used was that of seagulls.' Garcilaso tells how 'under Inca rule, the birds were protected by very severe laws; it was forbidden to kill a single one of them or even to approach their islands during the laying season, under penalty of death'.[1] He also records the quaint way in which even the beaches were fertilized: by digging holes with the end of a stick, then popping in a sardine head and two or three grains of corn.

With the arrival of the Spanish there was a disastrous decline in agriculture. The conquerors neglected everything in their newly gained land except the possible mineral wealth. The interest in guano fell off and the diggings were all but forgotten until Humboldt more or less rediscovered them. His observations encouraged further research which found that the bird droppings, extraordinarily rich in nitrogen, were exactly thirty-three times more effective as a fertilizer than ordinary farmyard manure. Guano was introduced to the foreign markets in about 1843 and was immediately in enormous demand. More than ten million tons were extracted between 1851 and 1872 from one small group of islands, representing an average annual export value of twenty or thirty million dollars.

It would seem that the guano itself is highly malodorous. Having only glimpsed the islands from a distance I cannot vouch for this. Others were voluble enough on the subject. Radiguet describes it as having an overpowering smell of ammonia, so acrid that it seizes you by the throat. Choking panic would seem to be the first reaction and then, after half an hour, you get used to it. Another traveller, George Peck, who sailed to Peru from Australia in 1853, writes that 'the guano when exposed to the air is of a reddish-brown, yellow colour'. Before being cut, 'it is like light dry earth and full of holes. It is difficult to walk upon, there being no certainty that every other footstep will not sink in nearly to the knee. If one hurries one is almost sure to fall', floundering in 'an unpleasant sticky sort of soil. A few feet below the surface it becomes compact, and from thence through its whole thickness is of nearly the consistency of Castile soap'.[2]

Dr Robert Murphy, one time curator of the department of natural science at the Brooklyn Museum, explains in his excellent book *The Bird Islands of Peru* that:

many species of birds have contributed to the accumulations of guano . . . It seems certain that in the past as well as at present first place has generally been occupied by three or more species of the single order known as the *Steganopodes*, the group which includes the cormorants, the pelicans and the gannets or boobies.

[1] *The Royal Commentaries of the Inca.*
[2] George Washington Peck, 'Melbourne and The Chincha Islands', *New York Times*, 1853.

The number of birds that flock together have to be seen to be believed. Dr Murphy conservatively estimating for just one of the Chincha Islands 'would place the total bird population, young and adult, at 5,600,000'. The guanayes, or white-breasted cormorants, move in such tremendous flocks that when resting on the water in between feedings whole areas of ocean become mottled brown. 'At other times,' writes Dr Murphy, 'when the guanayes are moving towards distant feeding grounds, they travel not in broad flocks but rather as a solid river of birds; an unbroken column' which 'takes from four to five hours to pass a given point'.[1]

Fish are in still greater abundance than birds. The cool, upwelling Humboldt Current, in marked contrast to the barrenness of the coast, teems with anchovies, young herrings, silversides and bonitos. 'Sometimes,' Mr Coker writes, 'great areas of the surface of the sea are reddened by numbers of small crustacea.'[2] The fish, especially the anchovies, travel in tremendous shoals so densely packed that they ruffle the surface of the sea. 'Their appearance from above is amazing, for the quivering, silvery creatures seem to be packed together like sardines in a tin, except that their heads point all in one direction.' These shoals are invariably followed by larger fish, bonitos and beakless porpoises and by sea lions.

Back in 1919–20, the period during which Dr Murphy embarked on his expedition, guano was still high on the list of Peru's exports. The annual output averaged about ninety thousand tons of which seventy thousand were used in Peru and the remainder exported. Within the last forty years, however, the country's economy has undergone radical change. Cotton, sugar and rice are now the big exports, and the guano supply is entirely absorbed by domestic needs. The Peruvian fisheries also have made enormous strides. In 1962, six million tons of anchovies were caught and processed. In 1964 the figures shot up a further two million. Dried and pulverized anchovies are converted into fishmeal and shipped the world over for poultry and pig food. One can't help worrying about the eventual fate of the guano birds. If the fishmeal industry continues to increase at the present rate, will there be food enough in the ocean to sustain a feathered population numbering, according to recent estimates, some forty million birds? Peru's crops can be maintained by synthetic fertilizers but not the gannets, cormorants and pelicans.

The occasional alteration of the Humboldt Current poses another threat to the birds. Suddenly, from unknown causes, the Current

[1] Robert Cushman Murphy, *The Bird Islands of Peru*, Putnam's Sons, New York, 1925.
[2] R. E. Coker, 'Peru's Wealth-Producing Birds', *National Geographic Magazine*, Vol. XXXVII, June 1920.

slackens off and fails to flow with its usual velocity. When this happens a warm current from the north pushes its way southward. This drives the anchovy, a lover of cold temperatures, to seek cooler waters at greater depths farther from the shore, which in its turn immediately affects the guano birds, especially the pelican who is unable to plunge much over two feet. A pronounced change in currents seems to take place only a few times in a generation, however; the last serious one was in 1925. Another one occurred shortly after my departure from Lima. An anonymous correspondent in the London *Times* reported that thousands of pelicans, desperate with hunger, hung round the fish markets like a crowd of famished beggars:

Some wait in resigned patience on a roof for the odd scrap or fish-head which with luck may come their way, but others, more daring – or more desperate – amble between the stands on the roads where, bewildered by the unaccustomed noise and fumes, they hold up the traffic and narrowly escape a quicker death than by starvation. A few are pursued by boys with stones, while others end their lives in a stewpot, helping to feed the Lima poor who otherwise rarely taste meat. Those who escape this fate and are unsuccessful in begging or stealing from the market return to the sea, where they await death silently and philosophically. The beaches close to Lima are littered with their sad remains.

As we chugged laboriously round the northernmost of the three islands that make up the Chincha group, the Captain pointed out the plateau where the Chinese coolies imported to work the guano diggings used to live. Some seven to eight hundred of them were housed in a shanty town of miserable cave huts. Peck, not mincing matters, referred to them in his book as slaves and exposed the monstrous way in which they were exploited. 'They are induced to make the voyage out by being made to believe they are going to labour in gold mines.' Digging guano in the conditions in which they lived was tantamount to a sentence of death. 'Most of them go nearly naked . . . they feed like dogs and there are no women among them, nothing to mitigate their hopeless toil.' No free days off, no protecting laws, no power to obtain even the pittance said to be paid them, no proper seasons of rest. Each one, strong and weak alike, was required to dig five tons of guano per day. They were kept at work by black drivers, hideous creatures who walked among them with heavy thongs. Peck watched them, their slender figures quivering under the weight of loads too heavy for them to wheel, shovelling and wheeling as if for dear life, their backs covered with great welts. 'It is easy to distinguish the newcomers from those who have been working already some time on the islands, they soon become emaciated, and their faces have a wild, despairing expression.' Men went blind if they dug too long on the islands and they were obliged to wear thick bandages over their mouths on account of the fumes. Through these gags issued 'strange cries'. It is a ghastly picture. Every week brought its toll of suicides. They would throw themselves from the cliffs in the belief that their spirits would waken in their native land. The Governor of the Islands told Peck that 'more than sixty had killed themselves in this way in the two years he had been there'.[1]

Dr Murphy on his visit to the north island found no trace of the settlement. 'It is blotted out like Nineveh. Neither wood, nor metal, nor stone remains – only the corpses of coolies, mummified by the guano, wrapped in their blankets, and with coins beneath their tongues.' In the glaring, dustiest, hottest and ugliest part of the island:

we came suddenly upon the place which the courteous Spanish tongue dignifies by the name of *panteon*. From the sides of dismal gulches human hands and feet were protruding; here and there, completely exhumed, lay heads partly covered with hair. Other corpses including some which, I fancied, looked like mongolians, lying with their mouths wide open as though they were yelling to the heavens.

Everywhere there were toes pointing skyward, but even these gloomy reminders the doctor predicted would soon be gone, 'for the present workmen pile up the old bodies when they uncover them, sprinkle them with kerosene and burn them to ashes'.[2]

On the drive back to Lima, we stopped at Pachacamac, in Pizarro's day the largest city on the coast and an important religious centre. Ruins now encircle the top of a low hill, the remains of a large brick pyramid. We know that this pyramid, built by the Incas, was superimposed on an earlier building of a pre-Inca civilization that was already a thousand years old when the Cuzco Empire occupied the territory. The original building was dedicated to an invisible deity, a Supreme Being, the Creator and Ruler of the Universe. Las Casas in his *Historia Apologética* called the god 'Con'. His myth has a familiar ring. 'By his word alone he created the world; but men fell into sin, and neglected their creator.' His retribution was an encroaching desert rather than an excess of water. 'The earth remained sterile and uninhabited until Pachacamac, the son of Con, renewed all the things that had been destroyed by his father, and re-created man.' The Incas, in true Roman fashion, adopted Pachacamac, identifying him with the sun. Both Pizarro and his brother Hernando visited the city named after him, 'a place of great buildings surrounded by ample courts and houses where they lodged the sacred virgins attached to the Temple of the Sun'.

[1] *Melbourne and The Chincha Islands.*
[2] *The Bird Islands of Peru.*

Floundering alone over the sand hills about the ruins, I met a large lizard which looked as if he had been steeped in a rainbow: blue head, black band across the throat, a green belly, tail and hind legs chestnut, and a red back sprinkled with white dots. Much has been restored recently at Pachacamac. One of the buildings would do credit to any contemporary architect.

Another place of interest connected with the coastal region is the famous Rafael Larco Herrera Museum in Lima, the largest private collection of pre-Columbian textiles and pottery in existence. The family owns a sugar *hacienda* in the Chicama Valley, north of Trujillo. The land incorporates much of the territory built over by the Chimu Indians, a powerful coastal tribe conquered by the Incas in about 1400. The collection was begun in 1926 with material unearthed at Chan-Chan, the capital of the Chimu Empire. By 1958 it had become so important that Rafael Larco Hoyle, Don Rafael's son, moved the collection from the Chiclin Plantation to its present site in the outskirts of Lima. It includes some sixty thousand pieces of pottery from the various pre-Inca cultures: Chavin, Mochica, Paracas, Ica-Nazca, and to the south east, in the Lake Titicaca area, the Tiahuanaco Empire dating from AD 1000 to 1300. The museum is a pleasant whitewashed house in the colonial style built round a central patio and expertly lighted. Rafael Larco Hoyle, an energetic, strongly built man, took us on a personal tour, his broad short-fingered hand flicking quickly from piece to piece as he explained its history: black Chavin ware dating from 1200 to 400 BC with geometric designs incised in bold relief; in another room row after row of Chimu, or Mochica effigy vessels depicting deities, men, birds, even fruit and vegetables. The daily life of this dry land is brilliantly portrayed. With wonderful economy of line the potter has shown a woman washing her hair; another gritting her teeth and sitting bolt upright is giving birth to a baby. Two very determined midwives assist in the undertaking: one squats behind and passes her hands under the labouring woman's arms to knead her tummy; the other sits below and pulls at the child's head.

In a separate room, kept under lock and key, are some four hundred couples in various positions of love making. Fellatio is much in evidence and more than half of the couples are practising sodomy. One young girl sleeping between her parents is thus being enjoyed by her suitor. Undoubtedly it was a form of birth control, but one knows from Garcilaso that it was a habit abhorred by the Incas. Tupac Yupanqui's brother, sent by the Inca to subdue one of the coastal tribes, was ordered back to Cuzco when he had done so. But first he was to burn all the people suspected of sodomy. Their houses were to be razed to the ground, 'their fields destroyed and their trees pulled up by the roots so that the very memory of their heinous practice should disappear from Peru for all time'.[1]

On my next visit to the museum I was taken around by a young assistant curator, a full-blooded Indian with an interesting, sensitive face. He was, in fact, the exact double of one of the Mochica portrait jars. I wondered if the resemblance had ever struck him. He had the hands to go with the head; and his long nervous fingers unlocked the cases, allowing me to run my fingers over some of the jewels, enormous drops of rock crystal the size of goose eggs and a beautiful plaque of obsidian inlaid with turquoise. There were bone and turquoise necklaces cut in different abstract forms and a pair of very handsome ear-disks edged with a beading of gold. The museum also boasts the regalia of a chieftain from Northern Peru, all in repoussé gold, the only complete set in existence. The crown sits like a tall hat with the brim flaring out well down over the eyes. Slightly waisted, it flares out again at the top. Four beaten gold feathers, fixed into slots, carry the crown to a height of two feet. There are ear-disks and a necklace of great hollow beads, each bead the size of a chestnut. These are attached to the neck like a choker and rest on a broad, golden collar fringed with gold pendants.

Perhaps the most interesting exhibits are the textiles. Peruvian weaving, developed by the coastal peoples and later adopted by the Incas, was a highly finished art. Silkworm and flax were unknown in Peru so that all the loomed material was either wool or cotton. For wool they had the llama, the soft alpaca and the still finer and rare wool of the vicuña, the smallest of the Latin American cameloids, now so scarce that they are protected. In general woollen materials came from the highlands, while the arid coastal plains produced cotton goods whose elaborate designs made up for what they lacked in texture. From the Paracas necropolis whole lengths of crocheted fabric survive, composed entirely of minutely knitted figures that must have required years of work. In the same place seated mummies have been found wrapped around with yards and yards of material. From these conical bundles quantities of belts, turbans, ponchos and shawls have been unwrapped. Incredible as it may seem, single fabrics have been found measuring as much as eighty feet in length by nearly twenty feet in breadth. Lothrop doubts 'that handlooms of such size have ever existed elsewhere in the world. Obviously they could have been manipulated only by a team of women, but it staggers the imagination to think of the task involved in setting up the warps and in controlling the wefts.'[2]

Exhibited at the Herrera Museum with the weaving is some very

[1] *The Royal Commentaries of the Inca.*
[2] *Treasures of Ancient America.*

accomplished feather work. One cloak is made up entirely of parrot feathers laid out in blue and yellow chequered oblongs of pure colour. The feathers overlap like shingles and are stitched to a net-like cloth, very similar to the Polynesian feather work of Hawaii. This particular cloak is over a thousand years old. As in Egypt the dryness of the climate has preserved these normally perishable materials.

The absence of rainfall combined with the alkaline soil has also had a remarkable effect on the dead. They are buried in sand, which, as Dr Murphy writes, flows about them like fluid; to dig them out 'one must begin with a wide trench at the top in order to have even a narrow one four feet below'. Dr Murphy had assisted at many digs and describes the bodies when unwrapped as being brown with the skin shrunken against their bones. 'They were so light from age-long desiccation that even the largest of the men could easily be held at arm's length in one hand. The hair on their heads was very long, but not always black, for in some instances it had bleached to a pale auburn.' The body of one little tot 'had a bushy crop of shiny black hair like that of a Japanese doll'.[1]

The museum possesses a fairly extensive collection of mummies. Some of them are stretched out flat, wrapped around in lengths of finely woven material; others are sewn into seal skins or shifts made from pelican hide. More common though is a seated position with knees flexed up to the chin and arms crossed over the chest. The wrappings were worked in a variety of shapes. Sometimes an attempt was made to mould it into human form with a mask and a wig of vegetable fibre on the head. Arms and legs were omitted but the sex was often indicated. Certain mummies were just lightly wrapped with the head exposed, coifed in a cowl. In one of the cases several mummies were gathered together in a circle as if lamenting their own demise.

The Incas believed in the resurrection of the body, and thus the dead were always carefully equipped for their journey. A touching example of the care lavished on the departed is the mummy of a Chimu priest recently excavated in the north of Peru. His tunic is entirely sewn with small gold sequins, thirty thousand of them, giving it the appearance of a coat of mail. Thus sheathed, he had been transformed into a golden fish and so was able to survive when plunged into the Sea of Eternity.

By far the most interesting of all the mummies were those of the Inca rulers preserved, until the arrival of the Spaniards, in the Temple of the Sun at Cuzco. Like the royal dead of Egypt they were elaborately embalmed. Little is known, however, about the method used. Bernabé Cobo, one of the early chroniclers, writes that it was a very long process but so expertly carried out that even after a lapse of two hundred years

[1] *The Bird Islands of Peru.*

the dead appeared as if they were living. Trepanning was practised and abdominal incisions made, but apart from these few details the information to be had is extremely vague. 'The bodies of queens,' writes Garcilaso, 'were laid away in the Temple of the Moon . . . Mame Ocllo, the wife of Manco Capac (the first Inca), occupied the place of honour, before the likeness of the moon.' Garcilaso saw some of these mummies. 'In the year 1560 I went to bid adieu to the scholar Polo de Ondegardo, Chief Justice of Cuzco, before leaving Peru for Spain. "Since you are going to Spain," he said to me, "come in this room, where you will see some of your relatives, whom I disinterred, and about whom you may want to speak over there." ' There were five bodies, three kings and two queens. One of the kings was thought to be Inca Viracocha (the eighth Inca). 'He had undoubtedly died when he was very old, because his head was as white as snow.' The second was the great Tupac Inca Yupanqui, great-grandson of Viracocha; and the third, Huayna Capac, the father of Huáscar and Atahualpa, between whom civil war was raging at the time of the Conquest. Garcilaso continues:

All these bodies were so well preserved that not a hair, not an eyebrow, not even a lash was missing. They were dressed in their royal garments and were seated Indian fashion, with their hands crossed on their breasts, the right hand reposing on the left, and their eyelids all but closed, as though they were looking at the ground.

Garcilaso also attempted to discover more about the embalming process, but:

I did not succeed in finding out how they went about it, nor with what ingredients: the Indians hid this from me, just as they did from the Spaniards, or may be they themselves had all of them already forgotten these things when I questioned them. I remember that I touched one of Huayna Capac's fingers, and found it as hard as wood. The bodies were so light that the Indians carried them in their arms with no difficulty, from one house to the other to show them to the gentleman who wanted to see them. In the street, they covered them with a white sheet; and all the Indians who saw them pass knelt down immediately and bowed, sobbing, their faces bathed in tears. Many Spaniards too, took off their hats in the presence of the bodies of these kings, which touched the Indians so much that they did not know how to express their feelings.[1]

In certain tribes of the Andes the mummies were part of the local fêtes and soldiers carried their embalmed chiefs to war. In Cuzco the deceased rulers took part in the coronation rites of the future sovereign. For instance, when Pizarro placed Inca Manco on the throne after the Conquest, 'he presented', writes Prescott, 'the young prince to the people

[1] *The Royal Commentaries of the Inca.*

as their future sovereign, the legitimate son of Huayna Capac'. Mass was publicly celebrated by Father Valverde, and the Inca Manco received the fringed diadem of Peru, not from the hand of the high-priest of his nation, but from his conqueror, Pizarro. 'The accession of the young monarch,' continues Prescott, 'was greeted by all the usual fêtes and rejoicings. The mummies of his royal ancestors, with such ornaments as were still left to them, were paraded in the great square.' The mummies were attended by a numerous retinue, and 'each ghostly form took its seat at the banquet table, now stripped alas of the magnificent service with which it was wont to blaze at these high festivals'.[1]

[1] *History of the Conquest of Peru.*

18

Drive to Cuzco

The agent in my hotel lifted his eyebrows in surprise when I told him I wanted to drive to Cuzco. Even the *South American Handbook* warned me against it, but I was interested in seeing the countryside. 'Well if you insist, sir, I will give you the name of a colleague.' The colleague produced a Land-Rover with an Indian driver. An ordinary car was out of the question for the thousand-mile journey, mostly over hard-surfaced roads, but so narrow in places that the traffic had to be one way, changing every few hours. Whether one waited or not depended on one's luck. Barring a landslide the trip should take four days. At one point the road winds over a pass at 15,885 feet and I had been warned that I might be affected by mountain sickness, called *soroche* in Peru. The curator of the Museum of Fine Arts had thought it alarmingly imprudent of me to set off without a doctor's certificate. The bank manager proved so equally pessimistic that I consulted a chemist who advised aminobutiric acid taken in pill form every four hours. I understand that mountain sickness can be very unpleasant, inducing nausea and terrible pains at the back of the head or dull headaches with intermittent flashes of pain. There have been fatal cases, ending in death from heart failure.

The road led off in fine style, crossing and recrossing the Rimac River. It is not until one reaches Chosica, thirty miles east of Lima, that the real climbing begins. Gradually the mountains change colour, turning a granite-red, shading from pale ochre to a blue-grey. The slopes are sparsely tufted with grasses, clumps of moss and here and there small cushions of some low-growing cacti covered with a silver-grey fur that gives them a deceptive appearance of softness. I had just been reading Harper Goodspeed's book on plant hunting in the Andes and remembered a shrub he mentioned that grows in the Rimac Valley, a species of *Jatropha* which is supposed to be a potent aphrodisiac. He writes:

A merchant in Chincheros was positive that a mere prick from a thorn induced the wildest impulses. In addition, he could vouch for the fact that when you inhale the smoke from burning brush in which stems of *huanarpo* (the vernacular name for the plant) are included a highly disturbing reaction is instantly obtained. He said that when a group of young people are picnicking it is considered a vulgar joke to bring in *huanarpo* and throw it on the camp fire.[1]

Jatropha belongs to the Euphorbiaceae or Spurge family and I thought I spied some of its blue-green leaves, but I could not stop, for it was on a corner with a steep drop on the far side.

Slowly we climbed, and with us climbed a train on the railway built by the nineteenth-century American engineer Henry Meiggs. It zigzagged upwards through endless tunnels, clattering over an impossible number of bridges, all paid for, one imagines, by guano droppings. Up and up it wound neck and neck with our Land-Rover, its shrill whistle echoing through the emptiness of the gorges. Galera, the next stop on the railway, lay at 15,693 feet – the highest station in the world. I felt for the passengers, many of whom were no doubt too poor or too simple to have recourse to my pills. To be taken from sea level to such an altitude, all within a few hours, is a severe experience. Small wonder that one hears of nose bleeds and whole cars full of people suffering the worst symptoms of sea sickness. I felt out of sorts myself, not exactly ill, but dizzy. When I stopped to eat my sandwiches, I walked slowly up a snow-covered bank hardly able to drag my feet over the ground and my heart pounded furiously. I remembered parting words of advice about keeping my head well covered and I had brought a muffler against the wind that now howled around my ears. High above, in the grey-white sky, wheeled a pair of condors with a wing span of about ten feet, the great *Vultur gryphus* of ethereal mountain peaks.

At one point, as we wound over the divide, we passed within five hundred yards of a glacier, blindingly white in its twisted descent. Snow lies on the mountains' cruel jagged peaks and lines the sunless crevices. For hundreds of miles running north and south along the central range of the Andes almost every crest tops twenty thousand feet. The Himalayas and the White Andes are the two highest mountain ranges in the world.

Late in the afternoon we started our descent towards Huancayo which lies at 10,690 feet. The road flattens out and threads through a green plateau planted with eucalyptus, agave and clumps of blooming genista. It had been market day at Huancayo and booths still lined its main street. The wares were disappointing, factory-made blankets and much enamel ware, most of it Japanese. The State Tourist Hotel was well run, though, and comfortable. A crackling fire of eucalyptus logs

[1] T. Harper Goodspeed, *Plant Hunters in the Andes*, Neville Spearman, London, 1961.

welcomed us in the lobby. I was not much affected by the height except that I found it hard to write, my pen tracing spidery scratches across the page.

The second day from Huancayo to Ayacucho is only 162 miles but the buses which run the route allow a good twelve hours for the trip. We therefore knew that the road must be bad, and it proved far worse than we expected. Rough, narrow and tortuous, it follows a river gorge for much of the way, winding along difficult and precipitous side-hills. The region is so crumpled, so broken up into ridges and valleys, that the traveller is forever rising and descending. There are moments when one wonders if it will ever end.

We made an early start. The air was fresh and exhilarating. A bright sun gleamed upon the wet herbage and silver streamlets, caught the rubbery-leafed eucalyptus and quickened the green of the pepper trees. The whitewashed earthen walls and thatched roofs of the villages blend in harmoniously with their surroundings. The churches, like the houses, are built of *adobe* with pitched cane roofs. Some even pretend to twin towers with occasional portals of stone or brick.

A flat valley of orange-brown soil quilted with fields leads away from Huancayo. Then almost imperceptibly the road begins to lift. Below, tiny figures made their way in groups to the fields : white-hatted women in kilted skirts with sheep, donkeys and little dogs with pointed ears. The crops in this calico landscape are broad beans and maize which had hardly sprouted. Almost immediately we joined the Mantaro River, sometimes bowling along its banks, but mostly running precariously along a shelf road which is a mere ledge along the face of a cliff some thousand feet up in the air. A rock placed in the middle of the road is a warning that the sides have fallen away. A couple of days ago, at this very spot a bus careered over the edge carrying with it all twenty-seven passengers. The Mantaro is so swift flowing that I doubt that they were able to recover many of the bodies. Only a few hours previously, a little further on, a car had tried to avoid a bus and had disappeared over the precipice. The echoes of these ghost transports were the only sign that traffic did actually circulate on this road.

In splendid isolation we twisted and turned. So alone were we that the driver stopped sounding the horn but this made me nervous on the corners and I insisted on his continuing to blast into the great Andean void. cliffs The that shut us in were daubed rose-madder and mauve. At one point the rock opposite curves, striated, like a dish cloth wrung out in some titanic upheaval at the beginning of time. We halted to stretch our legs, and the silence was oppressive. I threw a pebble over the cliff edge to break the stillness but its fall, echoing down a sheer drop of hundreds of feet, only accentuated the loneliness.

Constantly the landscape changed, the valley widened out suddenly, reducing us to a mere speck on a ledge-like road traced in a trail of dust against the vastness. As we dropped lower, the soil became calcined, dry and gashed with seams of erosion. Cactuses took over and we clattered over planks laid across log girders spanning the river. It was dark by the time we reached Ayacucho.

Ayacucho is an old place with cobbled streets and a quantity of dilapidated colonial buildings of coarse, robust plaster work. Again I lodged in a State Tourist Hotel.

The *South American Handbook* does not describe the road from Ayacucho to Abancay, yet I remember it as the most hauntingly beautiful drive I have ever taken. We spent most of the morning in cloud, a mysterious, half-revealed mountainous world, incredibly green. Slowly climbing we passed through the mists and found ourselves in rolling grasslands. I had forgotten to bring an altimeter with me, but as the limit of shrub vegetation is about twelve thousand feet, we must have been well above this. At last I was able to take my eyes off the road, which stretched out in front of us gently undulating for mile after mile. The colours were those of a grouse moor, soft and familiar. Allowing myself to be lulled into a sense of false security I was careless with the map. Until now there had been no possibility of making a mistake. Somewhere along the way we took a wrong turning and only discovered it after about an hour. Up here, in the solitude of yellow-green foregrounds and blue distances packed with clouds, there were no signs. It was a shepherd, appearing mysteriously from nowhere, who finally put us right. He talked to the driver in Quechua, the tongue of the Inca people and still the *lingua franca* of the highlands. Thinking back on it now, I am surprised that the shepherd knew enough to direct us, for the Indians in these parts are very primitive, and indeed they look the part. At these heights, with their extremely low night-time temperatures, the Indians swathe themselves in so many coverings that they are almost as shapeless as their mummies. Often one sees the men silhouetted against the skyline, bent over their rude ploughs harnessed to oxen. Only isolated patches are cultivated, small squares of potato in a sea of yellow alpine grass. Thousands of square miles are covered with its coarse tufts. They roll away into vast views dramatically lighted by a constantly changing sky, now grey, now blue riven with wind-blown clouds. At moments drifts of pale, spiked lupins vary the monochrome of the ground with mist-blue washes, as misty blue as the distant sky.

Against this sad, hauntingly beautiful landscape move the herds of shaggy, wool-flanked llamas. The supercilious animals prick their ears at you and flee on their spongy, padded hoofs if you try to approach too near.

All the colours in this mountain-top world are muted and dull, from the Indians' homespun clothes wetted from walking in the high, rain-damp grass to the alpine shepherd's humble, straw thatched hut. The huts are built of stone or of blocks of sod cut into flat squares like peat. This turf is also used for fuel. Its smoke seeps through the untidy thatching, giving the huts the appearance of smouldering haystacks.

We stopped for a late lunch at Ocros. These small interior towns are almost entirely cut off from communication with the outside world and rarely offer any form of public convenience. A recently inaugurated bus service must be responsible for the restaurant there, a clean little place where we ate off cedarwood tables overlooking a garden of flowers. The food was perfectly adequate: boiled potatoes covered with a hollandaise sauce and served with rings of raw onion, followed by a delicious soup flavoured with various herbs. The serving girl kept her money tied up in a handkerchief lodged between ample breasts. The women in these higher regions are far more robust than their pallid sisters down in the coastal cities. In their faces glows the healthy tint of wet winds and brisk, tonic temperatures. In the open air their copper skins often acquire a bluish cast from the cold.

The far side of Ocros we ran into a herd of llama grazing by the side of the road. More domesticated than most, they showed no fear at my approach other than nervously sniffing the air with their soft noses. They have no hump, but they still bear a strong resemblance to their cousins, the Arabian camels: the same full, overhung eye curtained with long sweeping lashes and the same wriggling upper lip split like a rabbit's. Some time in the dim past the Indians bred the llama from the native camelidae and domesticated it as a beast of burden, a giver of wool and a source of meat. In spite of continuous efforts to breed an improved stock, the llamas' slender legs and weak backs can only bear loads weighing no more than one hundred pounds. The Spaniards when they first arrived referred to them always as sheep. Agustín de Zarate, the Spanish treasurer-general sent to Peru about twelve years after the Conquest, tells of their being ridden, 'if the beast is tired, and urged to go on, he turns his head round, and discharges his saliva, which has an unpleasant odour, into the rider's face'. Their flesh he judged to be 'as good as that of a fat sheep of Castile'. One reads also of the beasts having been destroyed solely for the sake of their brains, a dainty morsel unfortunately much coveted by the Spaniards.

We dropped a thousand, two thousand, feet during the afternoon, leaving the grassy highlands. Immediately breathing became freer in honest-weight air. It was dark long before we reached Abancay.

From Abancay to Cuzco is a long morning's drive. Abancay is a charming little town built on a knoll nestled in a cup of green hills.

132 Second day out on the drive from Lima to Cuzco (page 228)

133 Herd of llama (page 230)

134 Farm in the highlands (page 230)

135 The Oropesa River flowing between a great red-walled canyon (page 231)

136 *Cuzco. View from roof of Cathedral*
(page 234)
137 *(opposite) Street in Cuzco showing*
houses built on Inca foundations
(page 233)
138, 139 *Cuzco. Casa de los Cuatro*
Bustos dating from the sixteenth
century, with the patio (below)
(page 234)

140 Cuzco. Cloister of the
Merced, one of the most
beautiful to be found in all
Latin America (page 235)

141 San Sebastián in the
suburbs of Cuzco. Detail
showing quality of carving
(page 236)

142 The coastal deserts when watered are very fertile (page 220)

143 *Pachacamac, the holy city* (*page 220*)
144 *A cache of mummies* (*page 223*)

145 *Dominating the Imperial City is the great fortress of Sacsahuamán* (*page 241*)

146 *Marcha del Inca by the nineteenth-century*   147 *Machu Picchu* (*page 248*)
Peruvian painter Teófilo Castillo (*page 240*)

I watched the dawn break from my window. With the coming of the sun the clouds began to lift and separate into straggling wisps that stuck to the wooded slopes beyond the tiled roofs like wet cotton wool.

For part of the way we followed the Oropesa River which snakes a course over a mile-wide bed of sand stretched between the red walls of a canyon. The majestic landscape gradually widens into a valley. Sugar cane, fenced round with pear-bearing cactuses, patches every available apron of earth, some of these aprons being vestiges of Inca terracing. From high up one can sometimes distinguish these old terraced fields. In places where they have been almost obliterated by the slow action of the elements, it is only when the sun is low and long shadows fall upon the hill-slopes that their blurred profiles are caught in relief.

The mountain road north and south of Ayacucho roughly follows the Inca imperial highway that ran between Quito and Cuzco. It was this route that we had been travelling. At one point I thought I detected a trace of the old paving, at a spot where below, on the banks of the Oropesa, were some stone supports between which might once have swung one of the famous suspension bridges, spun like a monstrous spider's web from thick cables of plaited agave fibre.

The Incas were remarkable road builders. Their most important highways were two parallel arteries that extended the entire length of the empire, one the mountain road, the other running through level country near the seashore. The Spaniards were greatly impressed. Cieza de León compared the mountain highway to the one Hannibal built to cross the Alps, 'and to tell the truth', he wrote, 'it seems to deserve even greater admiration'. It was about twenty feet wide and rested on an embankment of masonry. At many of the vantage points buildings had been constructed. Garcilaso wrote that 'the Inca's litter was carried up to these outlooks, to which one acceded by means of stone steps, to permit him to rest and, at the same time, to enjoy the imposing spectacle offered by the mountains'. Fruit trees bordered the coast road 'in which', continues Garcilaso, 'all sorts of birds flew about among the blossoms'. Both roads were lined with caravanserais and warehouses full of stores. Couriers were constantly on the watch, 'for the purpose of rapidly conveying the Inca's orders and delivering reports to him from his kingdoms and provinces'. These runners, called *chasquis*, 'lived in groups of four or six in thatched huts, located a quarter of a league apart'. They were all young and highly trained, 'and it was their duty to keep permanent watch on the road, in both directions, in order to catch sight of messengers from the other relays'. This human telegraph conveyed messages so rapidly that a dispatch could be sent about 150 miles in one day. A message from Lima reached

Cuzco three days later, four times as fast as the subsequent Spanish horse post.

These dispatches were either verbal or conveyed by means of a *quipu*, a mnemonic device composed of a cord knotted and tied with different coloured strings. The position of the knot and the colour of the string indicated certain abstract ideas. For instance, white signified peace, and red war. The knots served as ciphers.

These *chasquis* were not only messengers but also porters responsible for delivering to the Inca in his imperial palace at Cuzco such luxuries as fruits and game from the hot lands and fresh or even living fish from the waters of the Pacific.

The bridges were generally constructed of five thick plaits or cables. Two at the sides raised to about the height of a man served as handrails while the others were spaced out below and covered with planks or sticks about two feet wide. The cables were renewed every six months. One of these bridges remained in service until well into the nineteenth century. Another, Thornton Wilder's Bridge of San Luis Rey, collapsed one hot noon in the early part of the eighteenth century with a loud twanging noise, flinging its five gesticulating, ant-like passengers into eternity. In describing the bridge, Wilder said that the horses, coaches and chairs used to be sent down hundreds of feet below to pass over the narrow torrent on rafts. Perhaps, but not all of them. Garcilaso saw Spaniards gallop over bridges on horseback, a feat that needed considerable courage since these spans of thin slats were sometimes over two hundred feet long and dipped alarmingly in the middle, swaying from side to side as the traveller passed over.

After three days of twisting, winding, dipping, climbing and dipping again, I felt that the drive would never end. Then finally, at about midday the road levelled out at 11,400 feet. Flat and pebbly it spun out across the floor of an enchanted valley, smiling, green, and dotted here and there with little mud hamlets. Potatoes were in bloom as were the sweet smelling flowers of the bean. Eucalyptus, growing tall and thin, looked like poplars and ducks paddled around, quacking in willow-bordered streams. The women in their white straw hats smiled as we passed, unusual for the Indians who generally appear so morose. Breasting one last hummock we suddenly came upon Cuzco, a hollow of pinkish-brown tiled roofs pricked with the domes of its churches.

19

Cuzco

At the time of the Conquest Cuzco and Tenochtitlán were the two great cities on the American continent. Only a few fragments remain of the latter, and we have to depend on written sources to reconstruct what the city was like before its fall. With Cuzco it is just the opposite. There is little in the way of written material but a great deal that can be discovered from archaeological reconstruction. Almost every street in Cuzco is lined with beautifully worked Incaic walls. The important houses and various religious institutions are nearly all of them built on Inca foundations with solid Inca doorways on which the Spaniards proudly emblazoned their family shields. The church of Santo Domingo incorporates whole sections of the famous Temple of the Sun. The entire length of one street is faced on one side with the handsomely rusticated ground floor wall of Inca Roca's palace. In many sections the Spaniards come off rather poorly if one compares the architectural merits of these composite buildings. The rude *adobe* walls are very rustic in contrast to the carefully joined blocks from which they spring. Not so in the centre of the city. 'Here,' as Professor Wethey points out, 'the great tradition of the past did much to spur the haughty Spaniard to make his Cuzco still more magnificent than ever it had been under the mighty Incas.'[1] Competition put the Conquistadors on their mettle and led them to build a very fine square, the Plaza de Armas that slopes away from the hills, framed by columned arcades and four splendid churches. On the east is the beautiful seventeenth-century cathedral and to the south the almost equally impressive Compañía de Jesús. Two smaller churches flank the cathedral, to the north the Church of Jesus and Mary, badly damaged in the 1950 earthquake, and to the south the church of El Triunfo, built to celebrate the victory of Francisco Pizarro's brothers over Manco Inca in 1536, an engagement which finally convinced the Inca that further resistance was useless.

[1] Harold E. Wethey, *Colonial Architecture and Sculpture in Peru*, Harvard University Press, Cambridge, 1949.

A view of breathtaking beauty is to be had from the roof of the cathedral. From amongst the swelling tiles of the domes and the pawn-like terminals on the parapets one looks down over the city. The plaza can have changed but little since it was laid out in 1534. Beyond the convents and churches run cobbled streets curving out to a thin curtain of trees, beyond which, rimming the horizon, roll out velvet green hills. They echo the gentle rhythm of the domes and are dappled with cloud shadows, thrown by wind-driven cumuli that sail in a continual armada of blinding whiteness across the crystalline blue of the sky.

Acclimatization is a lengthy affair. It takes time to adjust to the rarefied air in which one must take double breaths to get enough oxygen. Climb a few steps in a hurry and one's heart pounds away at an alarmingly accentuated rate with a few extra fast quarter-beats thrown in now and then. Once you get used to the altitude, the atmosphere is bracing. 'The air', as Garcilaso writes:

could not be healthier; the climate is more cold than hot, without it being so cold that one must have a fire to keep warm, it suffices to shut out draughts to forget the cold out-of-doors; if a brazier is lighted, well and good, but if there is none, one does not miss it. The same can be said about clothing and beds: winter clothing is bearable, but one can well get along without it, and people who like to sleep with only one cover, sleep well, and those who like them do not suffocate, either. Another advantage of this climate is that there are no flies, especially in the houses, as well as no mosquitoes, or other disagreeable creatures.

The days passed all too quickly in this sunwashed city. It is one of the most rewarding places left to explore in a world where mystery and romance are rapidly disappearing. There was hardly a courtyard that I did not photograph. Little remains of the most publicized Cuzco site, the *Palacio del Ilmirante*. Badly shaken in the 1950 earthquake its caryatids, grotesques, capitals and fountains lie assembled on a square of pitted ground that once echoed with the bustling sounds of a signorial household. In pristine condition, though, is a house known as the *Casa de los Cuatro Bustos* on account of the four busts of men in sixteenth-century costume carved in deep relief on the lintel of its doorway. It is robust in character and splendidly weathered with the years. Water-worn pebbles from some mountain river line its patio which was splashed with a tender dappled shadow thrown by some willows.

In Professor Wethey's opinion Cuzco Cathedral, completed in 1654, is the finest church in the Western hemisphere. It is indeed splendid. The portal is full Baroque while inside the brick vaulting is Gothic. Gilded grilles close off a choir containing elaborate stalls of natural cedar remarkably finely carved. Corinthian columns netted over with

Renaissance arabesque frame each stall. Above is a whole host of martyrs, saints and popes. The pulpit, also of cedar, is even more extravagantly worked, but the sculptor's exuberance was masterfully controlled.

The cathedral is dedicated to the Assumption of the Virgin. High up on one of the piers to the left of the nave hangs a painting in which she appears dressed in the height of fashion with a gold and white dress of stamped velvet. Lace and pearls trim her pale shoulders, and pretty lace cuffs tied with green bows turn up off her delicate wrists. Large pendant ear-rings and jewelled stars in her hair complete the toilet. The eyes are downcast and the hands, heavily ringed, are joined in prayer. But no halo is visible and only a crown, signifying Mary, Queen of Heaven, identifies her. Many eyes must have been turned to her in adoration but I would not like to vouch for the exact nature of the homage, more a matter of accelerated heart beats, one feels, than of pious thoughts about heaven.

There were other paintings but the only one I remember in any detail was a large canvas of the Last Supper by a Cuzqueno artist. The figures remain a blur in my memory but not the spread on the table which featured bananas and, on a platter set before Christ, a trussed-up guinea pig, a great Indian delicacy, I am told, tasting something like rabbit.

Another memorable experience was my visit to the main cloister of the convent church of La Merced. Built in the middle of the seventeenth century, it is the most beautiful enclosure in the city, testifying to its architect's highly developed feeling for textures and contrasting materials. The stone is a warm golden-brown and all the wood is natural cedar weathered to silver-grey. The arcades are carried on rusticated piers in front of sharply carved, free-standing columns. In both galleries the columns have Corinthian capitals and cut in changing patterns have their separations marked by crowns of acanthus leaves. The ceilings are as opulent as the columns. Their rich, arching brackets remind one of the elaborate woodwork found in the temples of southern India. Two immense staircases with great heavy rusticated ramps connect the lower and upper storeys. In the upper storey hangs a series of paintings depicting episodes in the life of St Peter of Nolar, who founded the Order of La Merced. He was born in Ireland in 1218, but the mestizo painter of the panels, a stranger to the bogs, lichens and grey skies of the Celts, has wisely transported his saint to familiar surroundings. The scenes are mostly set in Cuzco and the characters have the dusky skin and slanted eyes of the Incas. A touch of fantasy is given by the pied birds that strut around the streets, incorrect renderings of peacocks inspired, one supposes, by some half-remembered print.

Another building I recall is the church of San Sebastián situated in an Indian village on the outskirts of Cuzco. The quality of the carving on the façade is extraordinary. Don Manuel de Mollinedo, at one time bishop of Cuzco, mentioned it as being 'of such beauty that it might have been worked in wax'. Kelemen believes it was made by the sculptors of the cathedral choir stalls, to which it is superior, I think, in quality, striking one all the more forcibly because of its humble surroundings.

Among the interesting sights is the house in which Garcilaso de la Vega spent his youth. A plaque commemorates his dates and noble ancestry. He was born in Cuzco in 1539 and died in Cordova in 1616, a respected old man and the most widely known writer on ancient Peruvian history. The de la Vegas were of an old Spanish house and Garcilaso's mother was a princess of the Peruvian blood royal, niece of Huayna Capac and granddaughter of the renowned Tupac Yupanqui.

The entrance is through a dank hall and up a dark interior staircase. A general air of decay prevails, and the house has suffered many changes since Garcilaso's day. But what fascinates one is that within these walls young Garcilaso once sat listening to the tales told him by his uncle. 'My mother,' he writes, 'residing in Cuzco, which was her own country, those few kindred and relations of hers which escaped from the cruelties and tyrannies of Atahualpa, came almost every week to make her a visit.' The conversation naturally turned to the past, to 'the majesty and greatness' of the Inca empire. 'From their past happiness they descended to their present condition,' and 'their visits were always concluded with tears.' During these discourses:

I, that was a boy, often ran in and out, pleasing myself with some pieces of the story, as children do with the tales of nurses. In this manner days and months, and years passed, till I was come to sixteen or seventeen years of age. Being one day present with my kindred, who were discoursing of their kings and ancestors, it came to my mind to ask the most elderly person amongst them, 'Inca,' said I, 'and my uncle, how is it possible, since you have no writings, that you have been able to conserve the memory of things past?'

More questions followed and 'the Inca was much pleased to hear me make these enquiries and turning to me, "cousin," said he, "I most willingly comply with your request; for it concerns you to hear them, and keep them in your heart." ' And how vividly, when the time came, did Garcilaso recall all that he had heard!

Garcilaso was twenty-one when he left America for Spain. He held a captain's commission in the army but when unable to recover the large inheritance of landed property belonging to his mother because it had escheated to the crown, he indignantly sent in his resignation. 'I left the army so poor,' he writes, 'and so much in debt that I did not care to show myself again at court, but was obliged to withdraw into an obscure solitude . . .' The solitude was not quite as deep, however, as he would have us believe, for Cordova, the place of his retirement, had the reputation of a gay town. It was here that he set about his literary labours and as he admitted in the preface to one of his works, 'I have no reason to regret that Fortune has not smiled on me, since this circumstance has opened a literary career which, I trust, will secure to me a wider and more enduring fame than could flow from any worldly prosperity.' How right he proved!

The first part of Garcilaso's *Commentarios Reales*, devoted to the history of the country under the Incas, appeared in 1609. In 1616, a few months before his death, he finished the second part, dealing with the story of the Conquest, which was published in Cordova the following year.

Parts of the *Commentarios* read like a fairy tale, 'yet', writes Prescott, 'there is truth at the bottom of his wildest conceptions'. One can reproach Garcilaso for exaggerating the importance of the role played by his mother's people. To him the pre-Inca civilizations (which were indeed seven hundred years older than the Cuzco Empire) seemed little better than savage, 'nations that must be weaned from their barbarity and vain superstitions'. But he was just repeating the myths of his ancestors, and apart from this understandable fault no man in that age was better qualified to write the history of the Incas.

His illustrious origin was described to him by his uncle. 'I am unable to say exactly at what date the Sun sent his first children down to earth . . . let us say that it was at least four hundred years ago. Our first Inca's name was Manco Capac.' He married his sister 'and they were the children of the Sun and the Moon'. 'My uncle,' writes Garcilaso, 'had told all this in his own language which is my mother tongue, and I have tried to translate it faithfully, without, however, being able to convey all the majesty and significance of his words.' Again the uncle speaks:

our father the Sun placed his two children in the Lake Titicaca, which is about eighty leagues from hence, giving the liberty to go, and travel which way they pleased, and that in what place soever they stayed to eat, or sleep, they should strike a little wedge of gold into the ground, being about half a yard long, and two fingers thick, and where with one stroke this wedge should sink into the earth, there should be the place of their habitation, and the court unto which all people should resort.

Cuzco, of course, was the chosen place, a name that 'signifies navel . . . meaning the navel of the world . . . This name was well chosen, since Peru is long and narrow like the human body, and Cuzco is situated in the middle of its belly.'

The gradual ascendancy of the Incas is similar to that of the Aztecs.

They were petty chiefs who after years of struggle rose to a position of power by military domination. 'The Incas,' writes Professor Lothrop, 'had one great military advantage over the highly developed coastal valleys because they could attack from the rear and divert the vital irrigation waters.'[1] Once in power their rule seems to have been a benevolent despotism. There were thirteen emperors, called the Incas, in the dynasty. The crown, or *ayllu*, passed in direct line from father to son. Peru was the estate, in fact, of the sovereign, and his court was the centre of the system. The emperors were astute statesmen as well as warriors. Garcilaso tells us:

The first gesture of the Inca after he had conquered a province was to take its principal idol as a hostage and have it transported to Cuzco until such time as the cacique and his Indians had understood the vanity of their false gods and surrendered to the cult of the Sun. The head cacique and his elder sons were also brought to Cuzco so that they could become familiar with court life and learn not only about the laws and customs that governed the Empire, but also the new rites, ceremonies, and superstitions that they would have to observe. The cacique was then reintegrated into his former dignity and governed his people like a king.

Under Inca law the family rather than the individual was important. Loss of personal liberty was the price paid by the masses for economic security. 'Each man,' writes Garcilaso, 'should stay in his own home, and never move from it, since vagrancy makes ne'er-do-wells and disturbs the peace.' Tribute was paid in wool, cotton, sandals and weapons for the Inca's troops:

We shall add to these the special tribute that, every year, the poor and disinherited paid to the governors of the territory they lived in; which consisted of a tube filled with lice. This token tribute was intended to show that everyone, no matter what his station, owed something to the state, in exchange for the benefits he received from it.

The edict 'owed its existence to the vigilance of their kings and to their love for the poor: because in this way, these wretched people were obliged to get rid of their vermin which, in their indigence, they might otherwise have died of'.

And what of Cuzco itself? The city was walled and the streets were long and narrow, arranged with perfect regularity, crossing one another at right angles. 'From the great square diverged four principal streets connecting with the high-roads of the empire.' It appears to have been a strange combination of sophistication and crudity; of buildings thatched with straw, windowless and barely lighted, yet inside, glowing with tapestries of silver and gold. The buildings must have been rather

[1] *Treasures of Ancient America.*

squat, yet 'were assembled with the greatest nicety', admirably suited to the climate, and resistant to the terrible convulsions which completely shattered the modern constructions of the conquerors. Garcilaso fortunately describes in detail the great Sun Temple surrounded by convents, dormitories and spacious gardens laid out with broad parterres that sparkled with gold flowers.

Wishing to present his mother's race in the best possible light, Garcilaso glosses over the human sacrifices, which indubitably were offered, though only on rare occasions. Nor was the Temple of the Sun tainted, like the step pyramids at Tenochtitlan, with deluges of gore. The victims, generally young children, were dispatched by strangulation. The Temple contained a series of dark halls thatched with straw interwoven with thin strands of gold. The walls:

were hung with plaques of gold . . . and a likeness of the Sun topped the high altar. This likeness was made of a gold plaque twice as thick as those that panelled the walls, and was composed of a round face, prolonged by rays and flames; the whole thing was so immense that it occupied the entire block of the temple, from one wall to the other.

The soldier and historian Cieza de León, a contemporary of Pizarro, tells us that the great plaque hung directly in front of the eastern portal and so caught the full light of the rising sun 'which shining on it flooded the whole apartment with an unearthly effulgence'.[1] There were other rooms giving on to a cloister. 'The first of these,' Garcilaso writes, 'was dedicated to the Moon, the bride of the Sun. It was entirely panelled with silver, and a likeness of the Moon, with the face of a woman, shone out from the wall. The room nearest that of the Moon was devoted to Venus. Venus was honoured as the Sun's page.' The other stars were considered servants of the Moon. 'The constellation of the Pleiads was particularly revered. The next room was dedicated to lightning and to thunder and this room was entirely covered with gold.' Water from the temple gushed from pipes of solid gold and the garden 'in which today the convent brothers cultivate their vegetables' was adorned with trees and shrubs:

all very faithfully reproduced in gold and silver. There were similar gardens about all the royal mansions. Here one could see all sorts of plants, flowers, trees, animals, both small and large, wild and tame, tiny, crawling creatures such as snakes, lizards and snails, as well as butterflies and birds.

Garcilaso further describes the chamber of the Sun. On either side of the great disk:

[1] *The Incas of Pedro Cieza de León*, translated by Harriet de Onis and edited by Victor W. von Hagen, University of Oklahoma Press, 1959.

were kept the numerous mummies of former Inca kings, which were so well preserved that they seemed to be alive. They were seated on their golden thrones resting on plaques of this same metal, and they looked directly at the visitor. Alone among them, Manco Capac's body had assumed a peculiar pose, facing the Sun, as though from childhood, he had been its favourite son who deserved to be adored for his unusual virtues.

Manco Capac, it will be remembered, was the founder of the dynasty. In another part of his narrative Garcilaso tells us that 'the Indians hid their bodies along with other treasures that have not yet come to light'. We know from a previous chapter, however, that five of the mummies were eventually discovered. As to the Sun disk, 'it fell into the hands of one of the early conquistadors, who was a man of noble birth by the name of Mancio Serra de Leguisamo, whom I knew very well before I came to Spain. He was a great gambler and he had no sooner acquired this treasure than he gambled and lost it in one night.'

Helping the priests in their religious duties were the Wives of the Sun. They numbered about 1,500 and were lodged in a convent adjoining the temple. Qualifications for service were based on beauty and lineage. 'They had all to be of royal blood, free of all taint.' Apart from their occupations in the temple they spun, wove and sewed garments for the Inca and his queen. Though Virgins of the Sun, they were also brides of the Inca. At a marriageable age the most beautiful among them were selected for his bed, and transferred to the royal seraglio. Woe betide the unfortunate nun – 'should she fail to keep her vow of chastity; she was buried alive and her accomplice hanged'. His family, if he had one, were all put to death, his cattle killed and his house razed to the ground.

The Peruvians would appear to have been a virtuous people, or is it perhaps Garcilaso's Spanish upbringing? 'I have yet to speak of the prostitutes,' he writes, 'whose activities were authorized by the Incas in order to avoid worse catastrophes. They lived in the country in wretched thatched huts, each one separated, and they were forbidden to enter the towns and villages in order that no virtuous woman should ever encounter them.'

From Garcilaso we also have a fleeting glimpse of the Inca, a god-like figure, even more inaccessible than the emperors of the Aztecs. He sat on a solid gold throne resting on a dais of the same metal. Zarate, who went to Peru with the first viceroy, recounts that even the proudest of the Inca nobles, claiming a descent from the same divine origin as himself, could not venture into the royal presence unless barefoot and bearing a light burden on his shoulder in token of homage. The Inca lived in a prodigious state. Garcilaso writes:

All the tableware in the palace, whether for the kitchen or for the dining hall, was of solid gold, and all the royal mansions in the empire were abundantly furnished in tableware, so that the king need take nothing with him when he travelled, or went to war. These mansions and the warehouses along the royal roads were also well stocked with robes and other garments which were always new, since the Inca only wore a costume once, after which he gave it to someone in his entourage.

Goblets that had been touched by the royal lips were also discarded 'and from that moment on were considered sacred. Their fortunate possessors never used them again but kept them as idols.' Prescott pictures the Inca dressed in gold with a cloak of bat's wings thrown over his shoulders. We know also that his blankets, woven from vicuña wool, were so fine that they looked like silk. The admiring Spaniards sent some to Madrid for the use of Philip II in his bedchamber.

There must have been moments in Cordova when Garcilaso felt pangs of home sickness. He never complains, but one senses his sadness. Nostalgically he refers to Peru's great past and her beautiful monuments, all destroyed by the Spaniards. 'In their own interest,' he writes, 'they ought to have preserved all those marvellous things . . . they would have borne witness to the grandeur of the empire that they had succeeded in conquering.' He singles out the ruined fortress of Sacsahuamán a mile out of Cuzco, built on the brow of a hill. Not only should they have maintained it:

but also repaired it at their own expense, because quite alone, it gave proof of the grandeur of their victory and would have served as a witness to it for all eternity. And yet, not only did they not keep it up but they hastened its ruin, demolishing its hewn stones in order to construct their own Cuzco homes at less cost. They made their portals and thresholds with the big flat stones that formed the ceilings, and to make their stairways they did not hesitate to tear down entire walls.

Enough remains, however, of Sacsahuamán to impress the visitor. Three giant, parallel, zigzag walls mount in platforms to the top of the hill. A great tower once capped the hill but of this only the foundations remain. The walls are amazing, especially the outer wall which averages some twenty-seven feet in height and is built of massive granite blocks, the largest of them thirty-seven feet long, eighteen feet high and six feet thick. These huge boulders weigh many tons and no two are alike. They bulge and curve, their coursings as irregular as a weather graph, yet there is something eminently satisfactory about the general composition. The gigantic blocks have a wonderful tactile quality. Smooth and faintly pitted, they are irresistible to the touch. Garcilaso, with his observant eye, remarked that in the joining, 'only the edges of the stone blocks were finely hewn, along a band about four fingers wide'. Indeed so incredibly accurate and close are the fittings that it is virtually impossible to slip a knife between the joins.

Garcilaso in Cordova met a monk recently returned from Peru who 'told me that he would never have believed what people tell about this fortress if he had not seen it with his own eyes. In reality, it seemed hardly possible that such a project could have been successfully carried out without the help of the Evil One. These were his very words.' And how does one explain the fact 'that these Indians were able to split, carve, lift, carry, hoist, and lower such enormous blocks of stone, which are more like pieces of a mountain than building stones, and that they accomplished this without the help of a single machine or instrument'?

Each encircling wall had a gate which closed by means of a single big stone that worked like a drawbridge. An underground network of passages connected the different towers:

This was composed of a quantity of streets and alleyways which ran in every direction, and so many doors, all of them identical that the most experienced men dared not venture into this labyrinth without a guide, consisting of a long thread tied to the first door, which unwound as they advanced. I often went up to the fortress with boys of my own age, when I was a child, and we did not dare to go further than the sunlight itself, we were so afraid of getting lost.

Archaeologists studying the ruins have been able to distinguish three distinct types of stone. Two of them, including the gigantic blocks for the outer wall, were found close to the site. The third kind, the black andesite used for the towers, came from other quarries over the mountains. But even the giant blocks hewn within a hundred yards of where they now stand still had to be hauled to the brow of the hill and hoisted into position. Really an amazing feat.

Below Sacsahuamán's great walls lies the Inca's parade ground on the far side of which rises a granite bluff. A path going up this leads to a sort of throne hewn from the living rock. Here, on stepped seats cut with diamond-like precision, the Inca reviewed his troops. Standing there today one looks down on the huge, man-hewn boulders; above ride billowing clouds; and between, in the great Andean stillness, wheel taut-winged buzzards. It is a grandiose spectacle but haunted and sad. On this very spot the Indians made their last desperate effort to rid themselves of the invader. The story is sickening. We must admire the tenacity and courage of the Spaniards but the original inhabitants win our sympathy.

In Peru, as in Mexico, a powerful nation ridiculously preponderant in numbers was vanquished by a small group of invaders despite the immensely favourable advantage the country gave to the defence.

Garcilaso questioned his uncle on the subject. How was it possible?
' "Inca," I said, "how could it happen . . .?" ' It is the Indian in
Garcilaso that is speaking and he is driven almost frantic with the idea.
' "Inca," ' he wails, ' "how could you let yourself be conquered and
depossessed by a handful of Spaniards?" ' Again the reason lay in
superstitious and crippling predictions. What was the point of struggling
against the inevitable? Garcilaso's uncle showed a certain irritation 'as
though my questions implied that the Incas had lacked courage'.
' "You must know," he said, "that the words spoken by our king were
more powerful than all the weapons carried by your father and his
companions . . ." '

Long before Pizarro's arrival, Huayna Capac had been brought
news 'of strange people cruising along the coast of his empire'. The ship
was none other than that of Vasco Núñez de Balboa who had just
discovered the Southern Sea. Huayna Capac was much disturbed and
made inquiries. His priests did nothing to reassure him. Bad omens
gave weight to their gloomy forebodings. 'A royal eagle pursued by a
flock of buzzards was wounded and fell dying at the Inca's feet. On
another occasion three haloes or rings were observed to encircle the
moon: the first one was the colour of blood, the second a greenish
black, and the third seemed to be made of smoke.' The royal soothsayer
croaked his warning 'in a voice that was almost unintelligible, it was so
choked with tears'. The rings betokened terrible wars and the total
obliteration of the Inca people.

Several years were to elapse, however, before the Spaniards landed.
In the meantime civil war broke out in the country between two of
Huayna Capac's sons. Huáscar, Huayna Capac's son by his lawful wife
and sister, and thus the legitimate heir to the throne, was challenged by
Atahualpa, Huayna Capac's child by the Scyri of Quito's daughter,
a princess in her own right, but a foreigner and therefore considered by
legitimists as a concubine. The princess had been very beautiful; and
the son she bore Huayna Capac had grown up, according to Garcilaso,
to be 'a pleasant gentleman, well built and with an attractive face'. The
ageing Inca, deeply in love with the Scyri's daughter, doted on her
child. We are told he 'would gladly have left Atahualpa the empire'
had not the laws of succession forbidden it; and he did decide to make
him heir to the kingdom of Quito. Huáscar was accordingly summoned
hence by his father. Garcilaso reports the interview. ' "It is well known,
Prince," ' the father says to his son, ' "that according to the desires of
our ancestors this kingdom shall fall to you. It has always been thus,
and all the land that we have conquered has been annexed to the
empire and subjected to the jurisdiction and power of our imperial city
of Cuzco." ' With great cunning the old Inca argued the case. ' "You

know, moreover, that the kingdom (Quito) comes from Atahualpa's maternal ancestors and that, today, it should belong to his mother." ' There was little that Prince Huáscar could do but acquiesce.

But the end predicted by the court soothsayer approached. The rings were gathering tighter around the moon. Pizarro, in Panama, heard rumours of gold and of a rich and powerful country lying to the southward. The tales multiplied till action was taken. In March 1526 a contract was drawn up between Diego de Almagro, a companion at arms of Pizarro, and Hernando de Luque, the vicar of Panama. In 1527, the year of Huayna Capac's death, Pizarro landed at Tumbes on the northernmost confines of present-day Peru. The rest of the story is well known. In brief, Pizarro returned to Panama with glowing tales of what he had seen; and to substantiate his story he brought back lengths of beautifully woven material, some solid gold vases, three llamas and several Indians. With these as proof of his discoveries he sailed for Spain and an audience with his sovereign. Already habituated by Cortés to the fabulous, the Emperor listened willingly to the outpourings of this gaunt soldier of fortune, and on the spot assigned him the government of a yet unconquered country. Armed with this proclamation and accompanied by four brothers, Pizarro returned to Panama and immediately re-embarked for Tumbes. In the meantime the civil war between Huáscar and Atahualpa had been fought out and the victorious Atahualpa was at Cajamarca, whither Pizarro with his 183 men made their way.

Atahualpa advanced to meet Pizarro:

on a golden litter carried on the shoulders of his men, accompanied by his entire household, displaying no less military power than pomp and majesty. The escort was composed of four squadrons, each one comprising eight thousand men. The first preceded the king, two more surrounded him, and the fourth closed the ranks, in the role of a rear guard.

Atahualpa's camp was about three miles from Cajamarca's main square, where the Spaniards were waiting. So impressive was the royal procession that it took four hours to cover this distance. The meeting passed off with comparative calm and another was arranged the following day. Quite obviously Pizarro's only chance against such odds was a bold stroke of subterfuge. It was decided to ambush Atahualpa and seize him in the ensuing skirmish. Cavalry was therefore concealed in the buildings giving on the square and ordered to charge the Inca's guard at a given signal. Pizarro with a few picked men was to make straight for the Royal litter. All went as arranged, except that Pizarro was slightly wounded in the hand. This was the only casualty sustained by the Spaniards, whereas some two thousand Indians were killed. The contemporary sources quoted by Garcilaso must have been correct in saying that Atahualpa forbade his troops to fight. No other explanation is possible. One wonders what persuaded this ambitious man to give such an order. Like his father he must have been paralysed by the predictions.

There then followed the well-known story of the ransom. In return for his freedom Atahualpa offered the Spaniards a vast fortune. Garcilaso writes that:

he touched the wall of his room as high as he could raise his arms, and, at this height, drew a red line that ran around the entire room. 'The gold and silver of my ransom will make a pile that high,' he said, 'on condition that you will neither break nor smelt any of the objects that I shall have brought.'

Pizarro agreed on a date for payment and the treasure began to flow into Cajamarca. Other sources give the measurements of the room as being 22 by 27 feet by some seven feet high. According to Reginald Enock, a mining expert, the value of the cubical contents of the apartment, taking the price of gold in 1907 when he made his calculations, amounted to £100,000,000. 'This,' he writes, 'would be about the equivalent to four years' production of the Transvaal Mines, taking their present output at £25,000,000.'[1]

The story of the Inca's capture does not make pretty reading, his death still less so. Having fulfilled his part of the bargain the unfortunate man expected the Spaniards to do likewise. Instead he found himself standing trial for the murder of his half-brother. He had, it must be admitted, behaved with abominable cruelty when his troops attacked Cuzco in the spring of 1532, a few months before the Spaniards landed. All with the royal blood in their veins had been put to death. Only a few children managed to escape: two *ñustas*, or infantas, one of them Garcilaso's mother, and one of Huayna Capac's young sons by a third wife, the future Manco Inca. But whatever Atahualpa's crimes it was hardly Pizarro's concern to judge the Inca on the affairs of his own state.

He was condemned to be burned, but then told that if he consented to being baptized his sentence would be commuted: he would be garrotted, a mode of punishment by strangulation used for criminals in Spain.

Xérez, Pizarro's secretary who was at the trial, described Atahualpa as being about thirty years of age, a man of fine presence, tending to corpulence with a large, handsome, cruel-looking face and bloodshot eyes. 'His disposition was gay – not that his gaiety was manifested with his own people for dignity forbade that, but in his conversation with the Spaniards.'[2] Garcilaso adds that he was always carefully groomed, and

[1] *The Andes and the Amazon.*
[2] *Conquest of Peru.*

extremely clean. 'He never spat on the ground but always in the hand of a woman of quality, out of dignity.'

Atahualpa was murdered on 29 August 1533. In November Pizarro entered Cuzco. There was no opposition for, as Garcilaso points out, 'once the two kings, Huáscar and Atahualpa, were dead the Spaniards remained supreme masters. All the Indians', whether of the Cuzco or Quito region, 'had remained, after their kings were gone, like sheep without a shepherd'.

With the two main capitals occupied, Pizarro, his brothers and companions were now faced with the problem of reorganizing the empire that had fallen into their hands. This was no easy matter since the area concerned was vast, including, in modern terms, northern Chile, parts of Argentina, all of Bolivia, the whole of Peru, most of Ecuador and a small part of Colombia. Almagro set off southward to deal with Chile. Pizarro, realizing that a mountain capital was useless to the seagoing Spaniards, decided to reconnoitre the coast. Before leaving Cuzco he allowed Manco, the last legitimate son of Huayna Capac, to be solemnly crowned, a mere gesture, for although Inca in name he was not allowed any real power.

The next few years were a difficult period for the Spaniards. The rapacities and rivalries of their leaders made their situation even more alarming. Disillusioned with Chile, Almagro returned to Cuzco where he at once quarrelled with the Pizarro brothers about the limits of their respective jurisdictions. The long resulting strife was as fierce and bloodthirsty as the Thirty Years War in Europe. The great captains of the Conquest, all without exception, died tragically either assassinated, or on the gibbet. The Indians had recovered from the shock of the Conquest and were no longer in awe of the Spaniards. The young Inca and his nobles seized the occasion to stage an uprising. Slipping quietly away to the hills, he recruited a sizeable army and came back to lay siege to his own city. There may have been one or two thousand Indian auxiliaries attached to the Spanish, but the attacking forces under the command of Villaoma, the Inca's high priest, outnumbered them at least fifty to one. Things looked pretty black for the Spaniards, especially as Sacsahuamán had been reoccupied. Using the fortress as a base Villaoma made repeated sorties. One night armed with burning arrows his troops set fire to the outlying houses. A high wind whipped up the fire and in no time the whole city was in flames. As the houses burned the Indians mounted the blackened walls and pressed the attack.

The battle started on 6 May 1536, and seesawed backwards and forwards until the end of the month. Almost incomprehensibly the Spaniards emerged victorious, thanks to Fernando Pizarro's extraordinary courage. Vicente Valverde, chaplain to the expedition and

150 *Lake Titicaca, the highest navigable lake in the world (page 253)*

151 *Lake Titicaca from the heights above Pomata (page 256)*

152 San Pedro Mártir at Juli (page 255)

153 (opposite) Church at Chihuata. Good example of Andean Baroque (page 257)

154 *Arequipa, La Compañía,*
cloister (page 257)

155 *Church of Santiago at Pomata.*
Detail of carving (page 256)

later bishop of Cuzco, lauds his capable leadership, 'he knew that not only the existence of all the Spaniards who were there, but that the security of the Spanish empire in that part of the world was at stake'. A desperate man, he stopped at nothing. Some of his actions do not make pretty reading. On one of his expeditions all the Indians captured had their right hands hacked off and thus maimed were sent back to the Inca.

The eventual fall of Sacsahuamán to the Spanish is an equally sad story. Villaoma fled, but the fortress was not altogether lost. 'In it,' writes Helps, 'there remained an Indian chief of great estimation amongst his people.' Helps quite rightly compares the chief to the staunchest heroes of antiquity, 'there is not written of any Roman such a deed as he did'. Patrolling the walls with club in hand, 'whenever he saw one of his warriors who was giving way, he struck him down, and hurled his body upon the besiegers. He himself had two arrows in him, of which he took no more account than if they were not there.' At the end realizing the situation to be hopeless, 'he hurled himself from the heights down upon the invaders, that they might not triumph over him'.[1]

With the fall of Sacsahuamán Manco Inca's last hope had gone. He fled into the Urubamba Valley and with him, it is believed, went much of the Inca treasure. It was not until 1911 that the mystery of his disappearance was cleared up by the discovery of Machu Picchu, a fortress town in the clouds, whose existence was not even suspected by the Spaniards.

Machu Picchu is now reached by a narrow-gauged autorail from Cuzco. There is a daily service at seven in the morning. A series of switchbacks scaling the heights north of the city; a last glimpse of its tiled roofs through the eucalyptus trees; a pause for the points to be switched; then a long ride down to the floor of the Anta Canyon – it is a remarkable journey. On one side runs a steep mountain wall and on the other are the Indians' farmed terraces, parallel steps that sweep around the hills accentuating their contours. Above us, through the glass-topped roof, jogs a view of snow-capped peaks, a vast landscape that rocks with the train and echoes to the hollow clatter of wheels.

From the Anta Canyon we turned at a sharp angle into the Urubamba Valley, the Sacred Valley of the Incas. Look-out towers dot the hills and below us eddied the swirling waters of a swift-flowing river. There are orchids, tree ferns and a feathery bamboo that seems to be almost a climbing variety. Steaming in the early sun, the vegetation fell in a lush tangle, trailing its ends in brown whirlpools. This frantic eddying

[1] *The Spanish Conquest of America.*

eventually merges with and is stilled by the gargantuan flow of the Amazon.

Not far from our destination a landslide obliged us to change carriages, which entailed a short walk down the tracks by the roaring waters to another waiting autorail. At Puente Ruinas the train was met by the Machu Picchu Hotel bus. More zigzagging, two thousand feet of precipitous climbing, and we were there. The whole trip had taken exactly four hours.

Do these prosaic details seem incongruous? This is not the effect intended, for the train ride in no way diminished the sense of mystery that envelops the place. Rather, its very improbability enhances the sense of adventure. The narrow gauge snaking its way in between tortuous gorges, the vegetation, the landslide and the rushing river were all ingredients of an adventure story. The hotel, a temporary structure, fits the general atmosphere. It is built of unpainted wood and roughly hewn stones and has long wooden corridors that should be echoing, and do indeed echo, to the clopping of heavy boots – which one certainly needs. On the hall porter's desk are jars of snakes preserved in alcohol, among them the deadly bushmaster known to the Spaniards as *verdugo*, the executioner. It seems that the ruins abound in snakes, and the management finds this as good a way as any of drawing their clients' attention to the fact. Above the bottles hangs a faded photograph of Hiram Bingham, at one time Professor of Latin American history at Yale, who discovered the ruins. He is shown as a serious, tight-lipped man in his thirties, dressed in an explorer's conventional shapeless felt hat, khaki jacket, breeches, boots and puttees. Behind him stands a field tent.

Bingham made his wonderful find in July 1911 on a morning of cold drizzle, weather that predominates in this lost city perched between mountain and cloud. The lie of the land completely hides it from anyone passing through the valley two thousand feet below. To reach it from the hotel one takes a narrow path that winds round a corner and through an Inca house with a steep thatched roof restored to show how all the houses must once have coped with the rain.

The setting is extraordinary. The lost city lies on a saddle between the fog-bound peaks of Machu Picchu and Huayna Picchu. A complex of roofless gables, it hangs in a series of precipitous terraces on the slopes of a canyon of solid granite. The masonry is some of the most beautiful in the world. Walls lie flush with the sides of green-clad peaks, stupendous drops of hundreds of feet, certain death for the masons if they had slipped. The heights above are equally steep, cone-shaped and gathered in pleats, the kind of mountain one would find in a Chinese drawing.

Not much is known of Machu Picchu's past, and its origin is a matter of conjecture, though archaeologists have pieced together a mosaic of facts. The finest of the constructions would seem to date from the fifteenth century. The Inca Pachacuti, the great empire builder, is thought to have founded the city as a bulwark against the warlike tribes from the forests of the upper Amazon, but it became also an important religious centre. Above an oblong clearing known as the Field of the Sun the terraces build up to a culminating point on which stands an open temple crowned with a sundial, 'The Stone of the Sun'. Known to the Incas as the *intihuatana*, the hitching post, it was the column to which the high priest was supposed to anchor the fiery orb. This important ceremony took place in June at the winter solstice when the sun in Peru reaches its greatest declination northward, its path traced in lengthening shadows. 'It was natural,' writes Bingham, 'to fear that the sun would continue its flight and might leave them eventually to freeze and starve.' The ceremony was designed to prevent this disaster.

Bingham and members of his expedition made interesting finds in the various cemeteries surrounding Machu Picchu. Of the 173 skeletons unearthed, 150 proved to be those of women, 'an extraordinary percentage unless this was a sanctuary whose inhabitants were the Chosen Women of the Sun'.

One day while exploring some caves Bingham located the burial place of the High Priestess of the Sun. Close to her delicate bones lay her toilet set and the skeleton of her dog, a form of collie bred by the Incas. Another object was a concave bronze mirror that had been used on certain ceremonial occasions to ignite tufts of cotton with the reflected rays of the sun. Examined by pathologists, the remains of this noble devotee, Bingham tells us, 'show that unfortunately she suffered from syphilis'.

How fascinating also is Bingham's account of the morning he made his discovery of the city itself! The expedition had pitched their tents down by the Urubamba River on a sandy beach not far from the grass-thatched hut of a Quichua Indian called Melchor Arteaga. Arteaga claimed to know of some ruins on top of the opposite mountain and it was arranged that he should guide the expedition to them the following morning. When morning dawned Arteaga 'shivered and seemed inclined to stay in his hut. I offered to pay him well . . .', but 'he demurred and said it was too hard a climb for such a wet day'. The offer of half a dollar, however, did the trick:

When asked just where the ruins were, he pointed straight up to the top of the mountain. No one supposed that they would be particularly interesting and no one cared to go with me. The naturalist said there were 'more butterflies near the river!' and he was reasonably certain he could collect some new varieties. The surgeon said he had to wash his clothes and mend them. Anyhow it was my job to investigate all reports of ruins and try to find the Inca capital.

They left camp at 10 a.m. and plunging through jungle, started immediately to climb. 'Here and there, a primitive ladder made from the roughly notched trunk of a small tree was placed in such a way as to help one over what might otherwise have proved to be an impassable cliff.' In another place the slopes were covered with slippery grass. 'Arteaga groaned and said there were lots of snakes.' Shortly after noon, 'just as we were completely exhausted, we reached a little grass-covered hut two thousand feet above the river where several good-natured Indians, pleasantly surprised at our unexpected arrival, welcomed us with dripping gourds full of cool, delicious water.' Arteaga stayed to gossip with the Indians and Bingham finished the climb with a small boy sent with him as a guide. Hardly had they left the hut and rounded a promontory when they were confronted with a flight of beautifully constructed stone-faced terraces, 'perhaps a hundred of them, each hundreds of feet long and ten feet high. They had been recently rescued from the jungle by the Indians.' Beyond lay the city. It was hard to see, for the buildings were partly covered by moss and trees, 'the growth of centuries, but in the dense shadow, hiding in bamboo thickets and tangled vines' appeared carefully cut and exquisitely fitted white granite boulders, the finest examples of masonry Bingham had ever seen.

It is impossible to convey in words the extraordinary beauty of Machu Picchu's stones, the symmetry with which they are arranged and the carefully selected graining. One wonders how such textures were achieved with nothing but stone hammers and bronze axes. Their surfaces were apparently smoothed with abrasives, in all probability sand. I spent one whole morning photographing details of the facings, trying to capture the sensuous quality of the gently bulging curves. There is no stonework to equal it, even in the splendid moat walls of the medieval castles in Japan. Eusebio Zapata, an eighteenth-century dilettante writing about the Inca masonry in Cuzco, found it so admirable that he supposed the Indians understood the art of softening and moulding the stones. One sees why he thought up this pleasing explanation.

Completely smothered when Bingham first found the site, the ruins now present the romantic aspect of a park. Different lichens cover the walls and splendid red *maxillaria* orchids grow on the terraces, also clumps of dwarf bamboo. Harper Goodspeed identified a handsome species of *Oxolis* and a succulent that looks like *sedium*.[1] I picked different

[1] *Plant Hunters in the Andes.*

species of fern and a giant 'slipperwort', the *Calceolaria tomentosa* which Goodspeed suggests the Incas might have grown as ornamentation. Climbing Huayna Picchu, which rises in an abrupt cone directly north of the city, I waded waist high through bracken. Below me, on a perpendicular cliff-facing, grew a colony of one of the numerous *Tillandsias*. I have a vague recollection of a small mauve flowering orchid, but what remains burnt into my memory is not the flora but the climb.

Having been advised by an archaeologist friend to watch the sun rise over Machu Picchu from the neighbouring mountain, the left hand horn, as it were, of the saddle, I persuaded one of the waiters to act as my guide. Leaving the hotel in the small hours we set off resolutely into the mist. The path dips down from Machu Picchu, clinging to the side of a razor-like ridge flanked on both sides by precipitous plunges of two thousand feet. One of them ends in the foaming rapids of the Urubamba River. Mercifully the other and worse of the two drops was wadded in cloud, otherwise I should have been floored before the climb had even begun. Up and up the path winds, a tortuous zigzag intended for sure-footed Indians. At moments the way leads across slippery slabs of grey rock with nothing but toe-holds cut into the surface. Some thoughtful soul has had iron spikes drilled into the granite with lengths of twisted wire between them. Such aids, however, occur only at the very worst spots.

To reach the top one has to wriggle through a narrow funnel of stone bored through the rock. If one is not already prostrate from the climb, this last ordeal is the *coup de grâce*, or so I found it. A watch tower, or possibly a signal station, rises from the uppermost pinnacle and the view of the ruins is breathtaking. Looking down on Machu Picchu from this eyrie one realizes the extent of ground the place covers, the many stairways that were necessary to join its different levels and the number of fountains, shrines, temples and ruined palaces. It is difficult to understand why the Spaniards, who maintained contact with the Inca through messengers, failed to discover his remote and secret fortress. Armed patrols came and went up and down the Urubamba valley, but never suspected the existence of the Inca's refuge in the mountains above their heads.

The end is a sad story. Manco Inca died in 1545 to be succeeded by his oldest son Sayri Tupac who reigned for ten years. A half-brother, Titu Cusi, followed to the throne, and after him Manco's third son, Tupac Amaru in 1571. His reign was short. He made the mistake of leaving his mountain fortress and was eventually tracked down by the Spaniards in the Amazon jungle. With his wife and children he was carried in triumph to Cuzco where he was condemned with his whole family. The captured Inca chiefs were brutally tortured while Tupac

Amaru's wife 'was mangled before his eyes'. The Inca himself was beheaded and his children died shortly afterwards. One wonders when Machu Picchu was finally abandoned. The city without the Inca had perhaps become pointless.

20

The Altiplano

The scene now changes and Machu Picchu, hidden by whirling mists, recedes from view. In its place appear the tundra-like reaches of the *Altiplano* and the blue reaches of Titicaca, the highest navigable lake in the world. Titicaca's farthest shores are already Bolivia, once known as Upper Peru and a part of the viceroyalty until 1776, when it was transferred to the Río de la Plata.

The drive from Cuzco to Puno, the principal port on Titicaca, is just under four hundred miles, and a hard day's drive in a Land-Rover. As it was Sunday we made a slight detour to the market at Pisac, a typical Indian town on the banks of the Vilcanota River. Indian *Alcaldes*, mayors of the local villages, turn out for Mass in their colourful costumes of black woollen jackets embroidered with buttons and strange circular hats that flare upwards from the tops of their heads, like large saucers. Their station is proclaimed by silver-studded canes and attendant youths blowing on conches. Less spectacular than the *Alcaldes*, but highly picturesque, are the women in their many skirts. They too are specially coifed in flat disks of moss-green or mole-brown velvet. The disks are set straight on the head and are gathered round the rim with flounces that fall all around, shading the eyes. On the flat tops are arranged poufs of fresh white and yellow roses, or large white poppies.

The market wares displayed on blankets included decorated gourd boxes with designs cut or burnt into the surface. But trade was concentrated mainly on victuals: legs of guinea pig, strips of dried llama meat and an impressive array of potatoes. The highland Indians grow some fifty different varieties, all rather small, and in every conceivable vegetable colouring: brown, yellow, russet and scarlet. Some are sweet while others have an agreeable nutty flavour. Potatoes are the Indians' most valuable crop and they have a particular way of treating them. After harvesting they are immersed for several days in cold river water, after which they are dried until they look like desiccated dahlia roots and are as hard as stones. They are then pounded into a coarse flour called *chuño*. *Chuño* keeps indefinitely, so long that some found in an Inca tomb is said to have produced an edible meal.

Most of the market people were speaking Quechua. Spanish is the language of the well-to-do minority and understood by comparatively few Indians. I noticed also that many Indians were chewing coca. Coca leaves are laurel-like in form and come from the *Erythroxylon coca*, a shrub native in its wild state to the Peruvian jungle. The dried leaves supply the world markets with cocaine. Here, in Pisac, they were being sold by the handful, together with little balls of charcoal ash and lime. The active narcotic principle is not readily released from the leaves, even when they are chewed, unless an alkaline substance is added.

Before the coming of the Spaniards, coca was the prerogative of the Inca and his nobles; now it can be had by anyone who can afford to buy it. The highlanders chew the leaves against hunger, cold and thirst, and, I suppose, eventually from habit, as betel is chewed in the East. I understand that the chewers are capable of almost unbelievable feats of endurance, but like most narcotics it has a marked effect on the health. Those who chew it to excess take on a greenish cast of skin and are said to age rapidly.

From Pisac we turned southwards and followed the Vilcanota River. The first miles run through rich agricultural land settled with small *haciendas* and picturesque *adobe*-walled villages. At Checacupe, sixty miles from Cuzco, we found a sixteenth-century church with a detached bell tower. Its simple mud walls leave one unprepared for the rich interior aglow with ornately framed tempera murals and dimly gleaming, beautifully carved altars. A ceiling prettily painted in blue, white and pink foliations completes the décor. The sumptuousness reflects the village's former prosperity. In colonial times a gold mine was worked nearby.

At Sicuani we left the river and climbed gradually to the *Altiplano*, an all but treeless land, a vast melancholy isolated region of flat horizons across which cold, inhospitable winds blow continually.

Founded in 1668 by Viceroy Count de Lemos, Puno is a disappointing, austere little town, but as soon as one leaves it the landscape, dominated by its lake, takes on a strange haunting beauty. Titicaca has an area of 3,427 square miles and spreads out, blue and transparent, in a bareness of low-lying hills. The colours are the pale buff of the reed-grown shores and the faintest of blues. Over it all lies a great stillness. A rough trail follows the lake side, sometimes running next to the water, then planing three to four hundred feet above it. Close to the shores one meets an all but extinct race of Indians, the Urus, who live off the produce of this watery world. They fish for small, indigenous white-fleshed *bogas* and rainbow trout, imported originally from North

America. They trawl a net between reed-bound boats with square cut sails. Tapering and lifting up out of the water at each end, the boats resemble the Nile craft depicted in Egyptian tombs. The reeds, too, are Nilotic in character, similar to papyrus with pithy, three-sided stems. *Totoras*, the Indian name for these grasses, are also a source of food. The pith is cut into slices and eaten as a salad. It tastes of seaweed.

Various missions were established along the lake shore, the most important of them at Llave, Juli and Pomata. Earthquakes are frequent throughout this area and nothing much remains of Santa Barbara at Llave. Of the three churches at Juli only San Juan, founded at the end of the sixteenth century, remains more or less intact, although even here one of the *adobe* towers has crumbled.

San Juan is an exotic local rendering of the Baroque and an excellent example of the Peruvian mestizo style (or 'provincial highland' style as it is sometimes called) – a cross between European and indigenous elements depending for its effects upon rich surface decorations. Crisply-cut foliated garlands of calligraphic, curving rhythms run in broad bands around arches and over the flat sides of piers, door jambs and pilasters. The patterns are highly stylized: starlike flowers worked in deep relief, rosettes of acanthus leaves, monkeys, bananas, papayas and tropical birds. The cherub heads have a decided Indian cast of feature. So rich is the carving that it has the character of textile design: arches and door jambs appear to have been embroidered rather than carved. Cut deep into the pinkish-brown stone of the district, the foliation looks like the incrustations found on church vestments or on bullfighters' clothes.

The San Juan mission is now run by American nuns of the Maryknoll Order. A young sister from St Louis made the rounds of the church with us. As in most Peruvian provincial churches, the walls of the nave are covered with large canvases, in this particular case depicting scenes from the life of the patron saint, John the Baptist. Their gilded surrounds are so wide that they look like wall surfaces rather than frames. Gilded wood panelling lines also the deeply recessed windows which are glazed with thin sheets of alabaster through which the sun poured in honeyed pools of light.

While on our rounds I asked our Sister about other missions in Juli – San Pedro Mártir with its disintegrating façade and roofless interior, and the late-Renaissance church of the Asunción with its great square belfry tower almost totally destroyed. I wondered if the earthquakes were entirely responsible. The nun thought not and claimed that general neglect was one of the principal causes, except that the Asunción had been struck by a thunderbolt. I wanted to know also about the general effect of the altitude. The nun admitted that none of her Order had ever become properly acclimatized.

Away from the shores of the lake the land becomes painfully bleak. It is hard to believe that this particular district once enjoyed great prosperity: its riches, though, had been in the minerals hidden under the earth. Once these were exhausted, nothing much remained but loose stones and tufts of yellow grass and streaks of dirty snow lying in the seams of the rocks. Drifting across this waste, in dreamlike isolation, are occasional herds of llama tended by lone shepherds. Villages are few and, alas, can no longer be counted on to adorn the landscape. Gone is any trace of the picturesque, gone with the thatching now replaced by tin sheeting that was inevitable with the Bolivian mines just across the lake. Corrugated roofing, which in the Pacific has become almost traditional and pleasing, here on the shores of Titicaca is a disaster. One quality alone it has in its favour. For the brief months before rust sets in its mirror-like surfaces act as reflectors to the sun. The roofs become points of effulgence which might possibly comfort the Indian, if comfort is to be had in remembering his old beliefs – the god and the greatness that had once been.

Pomata lies some eighteen miles south of Juli and is situated on a promontory at an altitude of nearly thirteen thousand feet. Its eighteenth-century church, built of a lovely deep-rose-coloured stone and almost complete, is considered a masterpiece of the mestizo style, a tantalizing thought for us, because its doors were firmly locked and no one could be found to produce a key. Thus frustrated, we mounted a slight rise behind the village and picnicked in an open *adobe* chapel looking down on the impregnable church. From above we had a fine view of Santiago's main portal placed within a great arched recess between two tower bases, only one of which now has a belfry. In the forecourt stands an alabaster cross, mutilated but still very beautiful, turned by the sun to a translucent yellow. The sites of the churches bordering Titicaca were all beautifully chosen. They lie on high ground while below the land slopes gently away towards the stillness of pale blue waters.

Arequipa is another great centre of Andean Baroque. The drive there from Puno is even bleaker than along the eastern shores of Titicaca. Like a ship at sea the Land-Rover pitched over vast stretches of utter wilderness. Even the sandalled Indians with their flocks of llama and herds of alpaca shun these bleak plateaux. At one point we passed a soda lake inhabited surprisingly to me by flamingoes, the Peruvian *Phœnicopterus chilensis*. Only their under-pinnings are definitely pink so that, wedged together on their stilt-like legs, their colour barely showed from a distance. Merely the acrid smell of their droppings came to us over the burnt grasses, reminding me of Africa. The hours ticked by in solid silence as the cloud shadows played over the heathlands. Reaching fourteen thousand feet we were suddenly confronted with a lunar desolation. Nothing grows except cushions of phosphorescent moss. Over this terrible emptiness a cold wind moans and whips the pale earth till it appears to pour forth smoke.

The approaches to Arequipa are dominated by El Misti, a snow-capped volcano rising to 19,200 feet, its perfect cone faintly delineated against the faintest of skies. The colours are all muted but Arequipa itself is a place of abundant sunshine, a blinding white city built almost entirely of *sillar*, a pearly, volcanic material so soft that one can gouge it out with one's nail. Taking advantage of this, the sculptors have covered the whole city, or rather what is left of it, with a tracery of entwined initials, and deeply cut foliations. The second largest city in Peru, it has suffered a series of disastrous earthquakes, particularly in 1784 and again in 1868. 'Ten minutes,' wrote the local newspaper of the time, 'were sufficient to bring to the ground the work of three centuries. Beautiful Arequipa exists no more!' It was shaken again recently in January 1958. A second even more violent shock occurred two years later, oddly enough on the same day in the same month. The only building to have survived intact from these repeated disasters is the Jesuit church of La Compañía. There are also various little chapels in the surrounding villages. Among them is the church of Chihuata, remarkable for its dome, where between segments of stylized garlands twelve carved angels in flounced skirts and with arms upraised appear to float in mid air, having flown up from the corbels beneath their feet in the ecstasy of some 'Gloria'.

21

Bolivia

La Paz, the highest capital in the world, lies at an altitude of 12,400 feet. It is built in a natural canyon 1,200 feet below the level of the surrounding country, a strange place for a city, but chosen no doubt by the Spaniards to avoid the searing winds that whip across the *Altiplano*. A good half of the population today is Indian. They live on the terraced sides of the canyon. The rest live below. The lower the people drop, in fact, the higher they mount in the social scale. One descends from square to square, first through the business section, to arrive finally in the smart residential district. From a bronze Bolívar on his horse in a Plaza Venezuela to a white marble Isabel la Católica in another square of the same name, one travels some three miles and descends a welcome number of feet. The altitude is extremely tiring. The natives have adapted to the scarcity of oxygen by an amazing lung development, but the unfortunate stranger must continually pause for breath. Indeed so rarified is the air that for years the city did without a fire brigade. It is virtually impossible for anything to burn, and one supposes that it was merely civic pride that eventually persuaded the municipality to embark on such an extravagance.

La Ciudad de Nuestra Señora de la Paz, to give the city its full name, was founded in 1548 as a rest station for mule trains journeying between Lima and the all important mining centre at Potosí. The title was grandiloquent, one might think, for what amounted to little better than a caravanserai. But no, for La Paz rapidly grew in importance. Not much, however, remains of its prosperous colonial era. The two major buildings of the period are the highly decorated mid-eighteenth-century house of the Marquis of Villaverde and a large Franciscan monastery in the Indian quarter of the city. The original church collapsed shortly after its completion, and the present edifice dates from the Baroque period. The ornamentation on the façade, like that on the Villaverde house, is typical of the area, exhibiting all the exuberance usual in the mestizo style: tropical plants, birds, puma masks and monstrous faces. Inside, the church is splendidly austere and has a great barrel-vaulted ceiling with heavy cornices. The carving is confined to the pendentives under the dome, triangular panels carrying elaborate flower-filled vases. The broad undecorated surfaces of warm, yellow-brown stone give an impression of sturdy, rustic simplicity, a refreshing change from the proliferations so much loved by the Indians.

Mass was being said at the time of my first visit. Petticoated women in bowlers with pigtails and shawls sidled through the half-open door, bent their knees to the altar and then, before advancing any farther, doffed their hats like men. On my second visit a pure-blooded Indian, cowled in the habit of his Order, climbed the belfry with me. Small columned lanterns cap the skylights of the church and I had the fleeting impression of being among the weather-beaten chimney stacks of some Jacobean mansion on the isolated shores of north-west Scotland.

Sucre and Potosí were the principal reasons for my coming to Bolivia. Sucre was the ancient capital of the country, and Potosí, the great 'imperial city', was at one time the largest city in the New World. My itinerary appeared simple enough and indeed rather pleasurable: fly to Santa Cruz in the Bolivian tropics, change planes there for Sucre, spend a day in Sucre and then catch a train for Potosí. I would return to La Paz by bus. But nothing in this country works out quite as arranged, certainly not when flying is involved, which often is the only possible way of transport. The first hitch came when my flight to Santa Cruz was cancelled owing to weather conditions. Then in Santa Cruz I was obliged to wait the whole day for the weather to clear over Sucre – more precious time wasted. But this was only the beginning.

The morning we left La Paz the clouds had lifted to reveal the snow-capped peaks above the rim of the airfield, the highest landing strip in the world and the one, I understand, with the highest casualty rate. So sudden and deep is the ravine in which La Paz is situated that after the take-off the city becomes invisible. No sooner airborne, than the woman next to me asked for her oxygen tube. The plane was old and not properly pressurized. Mercifully, Cochabamba, our next touch down, was only an hour from La Paz. Shortly after this the *Altiplano* begins to break up. The flat, infertile plains fall away into a series of crinkled valleys. Beyond, washing around the hills, laps endless jungle that runs eastwards to merge with the vastness of the Brazilian hinterland. Landing at Santa Cruz we were in the tropics at an altitude of just over a thousand feet. Our scheduled stop was timed to give us lunch, but when the weather reports came through it was decided that those of us who wished should adjourn to the local hotel and there wait for the airline to give us the all clear.

The guide lists Santa Cruz among the eight foremost cities of the country, which comes as something of a surprise when one sees its frontier-like character. But Bolivia, the size of France and Spain combined, has a meagre population of four million and is the poorest country on earth. Santa Cruz owes its backwardness to its extreme isolation. Even now that it can be reached by aeroplane, the streets are still unpaved, and the only way of getting about in the shifting sand is by jeep. The telephone wires are festooned with orchids, and the one-storeyed houses have a certain picturesque charm with their tiled roofs extending out over the sidewalks.

Towards evening the all clear came and climbing aboard we bumped south-west to Sucre under a huge spreading sky of golden mackerel scales.

Sucre, known as Charchs until it was renamed in honour of Bolívar's brave lieutenant, remained but a tantalizing vision. Everything was shut, but rumbling over the cobbled streets in a taxi I managed to snatch fleeting impressions. Lying at ten thousand feet the climate is comparatively mild. I remember squares with palms, and in the main plaza there was a form of giant privet with yellowish spikes of pungent flowers. An impression remains of carved cedar wood doors, of finials and balustrades, shallow tiled roofs, arched cloisters and thick, uneven, whitewashed walls. The hotel had the lively atmosphere of a coaching inn. The front hall was the bus terminal and the passengers the clientele.

I was advised to travel from Sucre to Potosí by train, just under a hundred miles. It looks nothing on the map, the matter of a few pleats in the cartographer's shading, but in fact one is dealing with the giant Andes which at this particular point heave themselves upward into an enormous conglomerate mass. What by rights should be a matter of two or three hours is a whole day's journey.

Slowly, painfully, the train chugged up to fifteen thousand feet. I seemed to have adjusted myself as far as mountain sickness was concerned, but breathing remained difficult, always that sensation of struggling for air. We stopped at various small stations along the way, where our passing was obviously quite an event. Women squatted along the side of the tracks with enamel basins of food and rickety tables on which were ranged glasses of amber-coloured *fresco*, a drink concocted from heaven knows what ingredients. I tried it anyhow, and bought some hard biscuits to eat with the cream cheese an old crone in a high-crowned hat sold me. To the amusement of my neighbour, the only other European on the train, I also sampled a simmering stew of llama. The flesh is white and resembles pork. My neighbour told me that he preferred vicuña which he described as somewhat like venison, dark with a gamey flavour.

The seats were cramped and the afternoon seemed endless. The

UNITED STATES

ATLANTIC OCEAN

Mississippi

MEXICO

CUBA

DOMINICAN REPUBLIC

JAMAICA

HAITI

PUERTO RICO

Guanajuato
Querétaro
San Miguel de Allende
Actopán
Perote
Jalapa
Mexico City
Puebla
Cuernavaca
Vera Cruz
Taxco
Oaxaca
Tehuantepec
San Cristóbal de las Casas

Mérida

Caribbean Sea

Cartagena

CENTRAL AMERICA

VENEZUELA

GUYANA

SURINAM

FR. GUIANA

Tunja
Bogotá
COLOMBIA

0   200
MILES

Quito
ECUADOR

PERU

BRAZIL

Lima
Huancayo
Cuzco
Abancay
Puno
Juli
L. Titicaca
Arequipa
La Paz
Pomata
BOLIVIA

Potosi

PARAGUAY

CHILE

ARGENTINA

URU-GUAY

ATLANTIC OCEAN

PACIFIC OCEAN

Mérida

YUCATAN

MEXICO

CARIBBEAN SEA

BRITISH HONDURAS

GUATEMALA

Antigua
Guatemala City

HONDURAS

SALVADOR

NICARAGUA

Léon

Managua
Granada

COSTA RICA

CANAL ZONE
Puerto Belo
Nombre Dios
Colón
PANAMA
Panamá City

PACIFIC OCEAN

Latin America Today

sunshine helped, however, as did the speckled, blue and white dwarf lupins growing in drifts over the countryside.

The *South American Handbook* does not even list a hotel at Potosí and after having spent three days in the place I can understand why. The best hotel was full and with sinking heart I made my way to the *Londres*. One wonders about the name, for I doubt whether the proprietor even suspected that such a place existed: he had never left Potosí. Certainly the news that I had lived in London had absolutely no effect on him. I did, however, procure accommodation in the basement, a horribly damp little room with an iron bedstead and a tin wash basin. Water came from an outside tap across a stone-paved yard, which for the first twenty-four hours was permanently awash with rain. Till late at night and long before dawn heavily booted steps sloshed by my shuttered skylight, and this, I might point out, was the height of Potosí's summer.

But what of the place itself? Remarkable though many of the buildings are, it is the setting that one is first conscious of. Behind the town, dominating it, rises the gaunt Cerro Rico, the Rich Mountain, discovered by the Spaniards in 1545. It is impossible to get away from it. It rises through arches and above walls and over the tops of houses. The Cerro Rico is, in fact, Potosí, for from its mutilated flanks flowed fabulous hoards of silver, bars enough, it was said, to fashion a bridge from Potosí to Spain.

Along with certain parts of Tibet, Potosí is the highest inhabited district in the world, over two and a half miles above sea-level. It is too high for any crops, so high in fact that the Spaniards were at first unable to reproduce in the highlands and waited fifty years for the birth of the first live offspring at Potosí. It appears that humans suffer varying degrees of infertility on exposure to altitude and it can take many years for a population from the lowlands to become successfully established.

The landscape is appropriately bleak. All round spread bare, treeless mountains. Grey clouds press down on the mountains and spread in a mist of drizzle over a silhouette of towers and domes.

Hypnotized by the Cerro Rico I spent the first day exploring its slopes, wandering in and out of the ruins that lie in a crumble of boulders around the old diggings. The mountain rears up in a great shallow cone, raw, indecent, peeled of its skin, the colours of rusted iron, streaked here and there with different greys, indicating changes in the composition of the rock. Streams, like exposed veins, net its flanks. Amongst the desolation, among the litter of boulders, broken walls and bridges the poorer inhabitants of the city have moved in to live. Empty lots are tenanted by squatting groups of women. Youths stand aimlessly around with their hands in their pockets, staring. But not everyone was

157 Potosí. The Cerro Rico rising behind the town (page 262)

*158 Potosí. Courtyard
of town house (page 263)*

160 *Potosí. Entrance to La Casa Real de Moneda* (*page 263*)

161 *Potosí. La Casa Real de Moneda* (*page 263*)

162 Potosí. La Casa Real de Moneda (page 264)

164 (opposite) La Paz. Church of San Francisco. Detail of carving (page 258)

163 Hostel at Copacabana (page 265)

165, 166 Potosí. House
of the Corregidor
(page 263)
(below) Courtyard of
same house (page 263)

idle. Overhead, scurrying backwards and forwards, were buckets slung to steel wires that march in irregular lines up over the denuded flanks. All day long they fetch and carry. Men are still busy at their plunder, exploiting wolfram and tin, the base metals ignored by the Spaniards. But all this is a mere shadow of what must have been. Just fifty years after its founding the population of Potosí was estimated at 120,000 and by the middle of the seventeenth century it had grown to almost half as many again. Its very name became synonymous with unlimited wealth. Here, suddenly, in this colourless table-land flowered a fantastic city. One on which Charles v conferred his royal arms; the 'great imperial city', an oasis counting some thirty churches, monasteries and nunneries. Everything had to be imported: food, clothing, wood, furniture, all the household commodities. It was an extraordinary achievement. Then gradually the silver lode began to be depleted. Competition came from the newer silver mines of Mexico and by the beginning of the nineteenth century Potosí had shrunk to little more than a ghost town numbering a scant eight thousand people kept alive by the more recent demand for tin.

It is a cold uninviting town but not without moments of melancholy beauty. There are far too many churches for present needs and more than half of them have been closed. One or two serve as cinemas, and you can imagine what demoded fashions flicker across their screens. I remember one of the churches on the outskirts, in the mining district. The approach is through an overgrown garden of red poppies, sweet-williams and stunted cedar. A twisted, carved wooden column, once part of the altar, serves to jack up the door. Inside, the dome is lined with a splendid coffered ceiling and torn canvases droop from the walls. Two Indian women were busy sweeping the floor. The dust swirled up in thick, rust-coloured clouds, the rust from the Cerro Rico, with which everything is impregnated, even the limp oft-folded *peso* notes handed to one in the shops.

I took photographs of the house of the *Corregidor*, or mayor's house, with a three-gabled façade and peculiar undulating pilasters. It has become an ironmonger's premises and the elaborately stuccoed courtyard is stacked high with iron rods, lengths of corrugated iron and old empty cans. The windows are broken but the iron grilles are still in place, and the finely carved shutters. I hope that the government will rescue the house, unique of its kind, which otherwise will collapse within a few years.

The two most important monuments in the city are the famous Casa Real de Moneda and the small church of San Lorenzo, the masterpiece of the Andean mestizo style. The one is austerely functional and the other as frivolous as the lace paper in a chocolate box. The mint occupies several city blocks and consists of a series of barrel-vaulted halls joined by great flying arches. Boulders, bricks and finely cut stone were used in its construction and the architect has handled this variety of material with great imagination. Walls are made chiefly of natural rounded forms, while cut stone and thin layers of brick frame the doors and window openings. Wherever the wall surfaces threaten to become tedious they are broken up by irregular coursings of brick, laid in arbitrary patterns, like the hatchings in an engraving. The portal of San Lorenzo is a complete contrast. It stands within an arched recess, the work, one would say, of a wood carver rather than that of a mason. Deeply cut surfaces accentuate the shadows giving a lacy pattern to the entire composition. Twisted columns frame the heavy brass-studded door, columns that half way up blossom out into exotically costumed figures with arms akimbo. Above them, carved directly into the wall, mermaids are playing a form of guitar. Above these again is a galaxy of stars with the moon on one side and a sun-face on the other. Further pre-Columbian echoes are found in the masks that peer out from among clusters of grapes. St Michael dominates the composition and on an inscription at the very top is the date, 1728–44.

My drive back to La Paz by bus remains a nightmare memory. We left Potosí in a gentle drizzle at seven in the morning and arrived at 3 a.m. the following day in a deluge of rain. Twenty hours and mile after mile of slithery, mud-churned roads! The driver, an Indian, appeared absolutely nerveless, an inert automaton. So also were my fellow passengers, swaying bundles in their seats who seemed blithely unconscious of the dangers we were running. Nor were they all properly seated, for the bus was outrageously overcrowded. Further fares were squeezed in at the different stops and with them came a variety of livestock, nothing larger, fortunately, than a kid. I had mistakenly reserved a single seat, right up in front over the right mudguard. The bus was of an old vintage and the seat was over the axle so that when we swung round the corners on these narrow roads the side of the bus, from where I sat, seemed to be suspended over a void, a drop, usually of over a thousand feet. Three times we skidded during the first hour. At the third skid I felt certain that we should never reach La Paz, but there was nothing I could do but to stop the bus and get out. It was a question either of almost certain death or of being marooned for twenty-four hours until the next bus came along, which would certainly repeat my present predicament, for there was little likelihood of the roads drying. Towards noon the drops diminished to some thirty feet and a halt was called. One of the Indians, I noticed, relieved himself through a section of bamboo, which he kept in his pocket.

With my return to La Paz came the sad realization that my travels, so far as they concern this book, were nearly over. Chile, once abounding in colonial architecture, has been continually scourged by earthquakes. Little remains in Paraguay either of the ruined forest missions founded by the Jesuits in the region of Asunción. In Argentina I was to visit the old town of Cordoba situated well inland from Buenos Aires in a rich agricultural area of rolling hills. Its cathedral, designed by two Jesuits, is a somewhat stolid building, strongly simplified Baroque dating from the latter part of the eighteenth century. In the vicinity is to be found the former Jesuit mission of Santa Catalina, now the country estate of an old and distinguished Argentinian family. But apart from these isolated examples little remains of Argentina's past. Buenos Aires has the appearance of a city conceived by Hausmann, with the scale of the buildings magnified, but otherwise strongly reminiscent of nineteenth-century Paris. As for Uruguay, its capital Montevideo is to all intents and purposes a modern city. Brazil, a fascinating country with enough material to furnish a whole library of books is, alas, out of our jurisdiction, excluded by the Borgia Pope, Alexander vi, who to preserve the peace divided the world about to be discovered between the Portuguese and Castilian monarchs. The frontier he fixed was an imaginary line drawn from Pole to Pole about three hundred miles to the west of the Azores and the Cape Verde Islands.

On my last day in Bolivia I made an excursion to the seventeenth-century Augustinian pilgrim church of Copacabana, a peaceful place of green tiles and weed-grown cloisters set on the slope of a rocky promontory overlooking Lake Titicaca. The next morning, back in La Paz, I boarded the plane for Buenos Aires.

Index